YALE JUDAICA SERIES

Volume I

SAADIA GAON

THE BOOK OF BELIEFS AND OPINIONS

PUBLISHED FOR

JUDAICA RESEARCH AT YALE UNIVERSITY

on the

LOUIS M. RABINOWITZ FOUNDATION

SAADIA GAON
THE BOOK OF BELIEFS
AND OPINIONS

TRANSLATED FROM THE ARABIC AND THE HEBREW BY

SAMUEL ROSENBLATT

THE JOHNS HOPKINS UNIVERSITY

YALE UNIVERSITY PRESS
NEW HAVEN AND LONDON

Printed in the United States of America by
Thomson-Shore, Inc., Dexter, Michigan.

Library of Congress catalog card number: 49-9495
International standard book number: 0-300-00865-1 (cloth)
0-300-04490-9 (pbk.)

The paper in this book meets the guidelines for permanence
and durability of the Committee on Production Guidelines
for Book Longevity of the Council on Library Resources.

14 13 12 11 10 9 8

PREFATORY NOTE

In the autumn of 1944 a project for the promotion of research "in Hebrew lore and literature" was inaugurated at Yale University. The project has since been known as *Judaica Research at Yale University on the Rabinowitz Foundation*. The present Series is its direct outgrowth.

The Foundation came into being through the farsightedness and generosity of Mr. Louis M. Rabinowitz of New York City. It was conceived from the outset as a project dedicated entirely to cultural and scholarly ideals, thus continuing the great tradition in the field of Hebrew and cognate studies established and maintained at Yale by Dwight, Salisbury, Harper, and Torrey. The work of the Foundation has been administered by a committee made up of members of the Yale Faculty appointed by President Charles Seymour, who have been assisted by a group of advisers from other institutions. A Board of Editors was designated to supervise the Series as a whole and the preparation of its individual volumes.

The Yale Judaica Series will consist mainly of translations of ancient and medieval Jewish classics, whether the original be Hebrew, Aramaic, Greek, Ethiopic, or, as in the case of the present volume, Arabic. The Editors recognize that in certain instances it may prove desirable also to prepare studies either prerequisite or supplementary to translations, such as critical editions of texts to be translated or critical monographs on works already translated. At the moment a number of individual translations are in an advanced stage of preparation and several volumes of the Series should appear soon.

The Editors have felt that each contributor to the Series should as far as possible have freedom and responsibility in his own work. This, it need hardly be said, has not in any way affected the readiness of the Editors to offer freely such advice and assistance as a contributor might request. It is their hope that the stamp of individual scholarly initiative and literary responsibility will heighten interest in the publications.

It is gratifying that the Series should be inaugurated by the magnum opus of a sage to whom homage has recently been paid by scholars the world over. The present publication appears soon

enough after 1942 to claim admission to the impressive line of me-
morials and tributes that have commemorated the one-thousandth
anniversary of Saadia's death in 942. May, then, *The Book of Beliefs and Opinions* help to spread among modern readers the fame of
the great Gaon, and to keep alive the memory of his philosophical
achievements.

J. O.

New Haven, Connecticut
February, 1948

PREFACE OF THE TRANSLATOR

It was in the fall of the year 1944 that Professor Julian J. Obermann of Yale University first invited me, on behalf of the Judaica Research on the Rabinowitz Foundation, to prepare a translation into English of the complete text of Saadia Gaon's Jewish philosophical classic, the *Kitab al-'Amanat wal-I'tikadat* or *Book of Beliefs and Opinions*. The basis of the translation was to be Landauer's edition of the Arabic original. The rendering was to adhere faithfully to the wording of the original, and yet to be of such a character that the contents would be comprehensible to the general reader. Technical terminology was to be avoided and only such footnotes were to be introduced as were essential for the understanding of the text.

This was by no means a simple assignment. The first problem was presented by the nature of the subject itself. Metaphysical treatises rarely make easy reading and Saadia's profound work was not conceived in the most popular style. A second handicap was the defective state of preservation of the manuscripts on which Landauer's edition was based, as well as of the Hebrew version of Ibn Tibbon, which was constantly consulted for comparison. A third difficulty that had to be contended with was the author's brevity of expression, leaving a great deal to the imagination of the reader. A fourth was the long involved sentences that were apt to make one lose the trend of thought.

All these peculiarities of the *Book of Beliefs and Opinions* had to be borne in mind by the translator in the fulfillment of his task. While endeavoring to refrain, as much as possible, from doing any violence to the sense of the original, it was necessary for him, as the occasion demanded, to deviate from a strictly literal rendering. Long sentences were cut up, and the syntax adjusted accordingly. Emendations were made only when warranted by the context or supported by outside sources. Frequently it was found helpful in the interests of clarity to add words for which there is no basis in the text but which make it easier to follow the argument. These additions by the translator were usually indicated by means of brackets.

Further to facilitate the mastery of the contents of the *Book of Beliefs and Opinions*, the treatises have been divided into chapters, following the example of the Josefow edition of Ibn Tibbon's Hebrew version. As an additional guide an analytical table of contents has been provided modeled after that of Israel ha-Levi, the author of the commentary *Šěbhil ha-'Ĕmunah,* that is published in the aforementioned edition. All Hebrew words used in the Arabic text have been italicized in this translation.

The most important aids used by the translator, especially in the interpretation of obscure passages, were the thorough exposition of Saadia's magnum opus by Jakob Guttmann (Göttingen, 1882) in his *Religionsphilosophie des Saadia,* which is still the best monograph on the subject, and by Moise Ventura (Paris, 1934) in his *La Philosophie de Saadia Gaon.* Both of these works follow the text used by Ibn Tibbon rather than the Oxford manuscript on which Landauer's edition is based. For the introduction and the first treatise the German translation of Philipp Bloch (Munich, 1879) was consulted. In the translation of the passage on music in the last treatise the conclusions of H. G. Farmer's *Sa'adyah Gaon on the Influence of Music* (London, 1943) were utilized. The summaries of Saadia's philosophical system given by H. Malter in his *Life and Works of Saadia Gaon* (Philadelphia, 1921, pp. 193–261) and Isaac Husik's *History of Medieval Jewish Philosophy* (New York, 1930, pp. 23–47) were also found to be very helpful.

The text of this translation was already set up in type when an abridged rendering into English, that was published by Alexander Altmann in Oxford, 1946, under the imprint of the East and West Library, was brought to this translator's attention. While it seemed to be a careful piece of scholarship, it did not render superfluous or serve the purposes of the publication of the present volume, which is the only unabridged translation into a modern language of not only the entire text of Saadia's masterpiece but the variant of the seventh treatise as well.

S. R.

Baltimore, Maryland
   November, 1947.

As this book is going to press I take pleasure in acknowledging my indebtedness to all those who have been of assistance to me with their advice and counsel and in the reading of the proof.

In the first place I wish to express my gratitude to Professor Julian J. Obermann of Yale University, who not only presented the project to me but supervised it from its beginning to its completion, making valuable suggestions of stylistic as well as technical character. I owe thanks to Professor Harry A. Wolfson of Harvard University for the conception and improvement of the analytical table of contents as well as his fine observations and revision of the introductory material. I am indebted to Professor Louis Ginzberg of the Jewish Theological Seminary of America for his share in the general plan which was worked out in conjunction with the aforementioned members of the editorial committee; and to Professor Alexander Marx of the same institution for suggesting the translation of the variant of the seventh treatise and the literature used by me. Finally I wish to thank Professor W. F. Albright of the Johns Hopkins University for his constant encouragement, the Yale University Press for its splendid cooperation, and the Rabinowitz Foundation for sponsoring the undertaking and making possible the disclosure of the magnum opus of the Gaon of Sura to the English-reading world.

S. R.

Baltimore, Maryland
February, 1948

SYSTEM OF TRANSLITERATION

For technical reasons the following system of transliteration for Hebrew and Arabic has been adopted in this volume:

Hebrew consonant	symbol used
'aleph	'
beth	b, (spirant) bh
gimel	g, (spirant) gh
daleth	d, (spirant) dh
he	h
waw	w
zayin	z
ḥeth	ḥ
ṭeth	ṭ
yodh	y
kaph	k, (spirant) kh
lamedh	l
mem	m
nun	n
samekh	s
'ayin	'
pe	p, (spirant) ph
ṣadhe	ṣ
ḳoph	ḳ
reš	r
šin	š
sin	s
taw	t, (spirant) th

No differentiation has been made between long and short vowels a, e, i, o, u, except that šĕwa has been indicated by the symbol ĕ, and the ḥatephs by the symbols ă, ĕ, and ŏ, respectively. Dagheš forte has been indicated by duplicating the consonant. The He-

brew letter *he* occurring at the end of a word has been repro-
duced only in feminine singular endings.

The same scheme was followed in the transliteration of Arabic
consonants, except that vocalic *ya* at end of a word was not re-
produced in the transliteration. Arabic consonants that have no
equivalents in Hebrew were rendered as follows:

Arabic consonant	*symbol used*
jim	j
pointed cha	ch
pointed ṣad	ḍ
pointed ʿayin	g
fa	f

CONTENTS

CONTENTS

INTRODUCTION

Saadia Ben Joseph

SAADIA BEN JOSEPH, the greatest of the Geonim, as the heads of the celebrated Babylonian Talmudical academies of Sura and Pumbeditha during the post-Saburaic period were called, was born in the spring of the year 882 C.E. in the village of Dilaẓ located in the Fayyum district of Upper Egypt. Next to nothing is now known about his immediate forebears, his youth, or his education. All that can be stated with certainty is that the Egypt in which the future leader of Jewry grew up was by no means a spiritual desert, lying midway, as it did, between the two cultural centers of Babylonia and Kairuan; and that by the time he left his native land at the age of twenty-three he already had to his credit the composition of a Hebrew dictionary and a refutation of the views of the founder of the Karaite sect, Anan.

From the time of his departure from Egypt until the fall of 921 C.E. the young scholar moved between Palestine, Aleppo, and Bagdad, separated from his wife and children and his pupils. The outbreak in the autumn of the latter year of a violent controversy between the Jewish religious authorities of Palestine and Babylonia over the right to fix the calendar, upon which depended the dates of the holidays, gave Saadia an opportunity to display both his erudition and his ability as a polemist. Espousing the cause of the Babylonians, he succeeded in completely refuting the rival claims of the Palestinian leader Ben Meir. In recognition of his services he was made an official member of the academy of Sura with the title of Alluf.

The next time Saadia is heard from is in the year 928, when he was appointed to the Gaonate of Sura, being the first foreigner to be invited to occupy this most important and influential position of leadership in the Judaism of his day. He had been in office only two years when a fierce quarrel ensued between him and the man who had been chiefly responsible for his elevation, the Exilarch

David ben Zakkai, the hereditary secular head of the semi-autonomous Jewish community of Babylonia, who traced his descent from the royal house of David. The cause of the conflict was a decision rendered by the Exilarch concerning an inheritance dispute, to which Saadia refused to give his endorsement because he considered the decree illegal. This action on the part of Saadia, especially since his colleague, the Gaon of Pumbeditha, had unhesitantly affixed his signature, so enraged the Exilarch that he pronounced a ban on Saadia and appointed another Gaon in his place. Saadia retaliated by outlawing the existing Exilarch and naming one of his own choice instead.

For two years two Exilarchs and two Geonim of Sura were functioning side by side until, owing to a change of government, David ben Zakkai contrived to have Saadia officially removed from the Gaonate. The five years during which he lived in retirement were devoted by Saadia to intensive literary activity. Then, through the mediation of mutual friends, a reconciliation was effected between the Exilarch and the Gaon. However, the period of renewed friendship was not destined to last very long, for three years later David ben Zakkai died, and after the lapse of another two years—that is, in the year 942—the man, whom he had appointed to the stewardship of the academy of Sura and who had, by means of his great learning and his fearless championship of the cause of Rabbanite Judaism invested the position of Gaon with new luster and prestige, himself passed away.

The Book of Beliefs and Opinions

SAADIA's magnum opus, the *Book of Beliefs and Opinions,* constitutes the first systematic presentation of Judaism as a rational body of beliefs. It was begun apparently as a series of independent treatises, which were later combined into an organic whole, except for the concluding treatise which gives the impression of having been added as a sort of appendix.

In conformity with the procedure in all his writings Saadia prefaces the body of his *Book of Beliefs and Opinions* with a comprehensive introduction in which he states the reasons that prompted him to undertake its composition and outlines the method he intends to pursue in his argument. What induced him to write this book was the confusion of his contemporaries who were wavering between blind faith on the one hand and arrogant unbelief on the other. It was his aim to lead them on to the road of truth. In order to attain his objective he was going to make use of the various natural sources of human knowledge to confirm the truths already divulged by means of the divine revelations recorded in Israel's Holy Scriptures. Far from being proscribed, speculation about the basic dogmas of religion was regarded by Saadia as not only permissible but a positive duty. This to him, however, did not do away with the need for revelation with which even the profoundest thinker could not entirely dispense.

The ten main treatises into which the *Book of Beliefs and Opinions* is divided deal respectively with

1) the creation of the world;
2) God's unity and other divine attributes;
3) the commandments of God and the means of their revelation;
4) man's freedom to either obey or disobey God;
5) virtue and vice;
6) man's soul and its immortality;
7) the doctrine of resurrection;
8) the age of the Messiah and of Israel's redemption;
9) reward and punishment in the hereafter; and
10) the golden mean.

In all of these treatises the author presents besides his own view a summary of the most important divergent opinions. These latter are refuted by him, while what he considers the right teaching is supported from Scripture and tradition as well as by means of rational proofs. Thus, for example, in the first treatise he establishes the doctrine of *creatio ex nihilo* as the correct theory of how the world came into being, disproving the tenability of twelve dissenting views which he lists. In the second treatise he upholds the Jewish conception of the unity of God over against the Christian dogma of the trinity and Zoroastrian dualism. In the third, after demonstrating the necessity of revelation, he polemizes against the Christian and Mohammedan claims of the abrogation of the Mosaic Law. In the fourth he argues against the allegation that man is hampered in his freedom of choice by God's foreknowledge of things. The sixth treatise contains a rejection of six unacceptable views of the nature of the human soul as well as a refutation of the theory of metempsychosis. The seventh takes up various arguments propounded against the doctrine of resurrection and tries to show that they are all null and void. In the eighth the Christian teaching concerning the Messiah is refuted. In the ninth, again, in addition to proving the necessity of reward and punishment in the hereafter, the objections against this theory are reviewed and answered.

In discussing the various subjects Saadia makes use of illustrations derived from nearly all the sciences cultivated in his time and surroundings, from medicine, anatomy, mathematics, astronomy, and even music. He drives home his points by means of apt quotations from the Bible, which is cited by him no less than 1,300 times. Even though as a Gaon he was the authority in his day on the Talmud, he makes comparatively sparing use of this source of Jewish tradition, apparently because it was his desire to defeat with their own weapons the Karaites who accepted only the Written Law as binding. The views of these sectarians, which Saadia combatted throughout his life, are, indeed, mentioned several times directly in the *Book of Beliefs and Opinions* but more often by implication.

In his philosophical ideas Saadia might best be characterized as an eclectic although he followed in the arrangement of his book the pattern of the works of the Mohammedan theologians of his time known as the Mutakallimun, particularly those of the school of the Mu'tazilites, whose philosophical treatises usually revolved about the two subjects of *unity* and *justice,* that is, the nature of the Creator and man's freedom of will.

The original Arabic text of the *Book of Beliefs and Opinions,* was published by S. Landauer (Leyden, 1880) on the basis of a

Bodleian manuscript and with the use of the variants presented by the manuscript of the Leningrad library. A second version of the seventh treatise, which was the one used by Ibn Tibbon and which is contained in the Leningrad recension, was edited by W. Bacher in the Steinschneider Festschrift (Leipzig, 1896, Hebrew section, pp. 98–112).

Although paraphrases in Hebrew of Saadia's *Book of Beliefs and Opinions* were made much earlier, the first literal translation into Hebrew of the entire work, which according to the author's own dating had been completed in the year 933, was that of Judah ibn Tibbon, finished in the year 1186 in Lunel, Southern France. Of the seven individual editions of this Hebrew translation that have appeared since the *editio princeps* of Constantinople (1562), that of Josefow (1885) with the commentary *Šěbhil ha-'Ěmunah* by Israel ha-Levi is undoubtedly the best.

The only complete rendering into a modern language of the book to have made its appearance hitherto is that of Julius Fürst (Leipzig, 1845), who translated all but the last treatise into German. In reality, however, Fürst's work is a paraphrase rather than a translation of the original, and a very inadequate one at that, for the reason that he was able to utilize only Ibn Tibbon's Hebrew version, which on account of its terminology and its slavish adherence to the syntax of the Arabic text is very difficult to understand without the use of the original.

Other Writings of Saadia Gaon

If Saadia had produced nothing else than the *Book of Beliefs and Opinions,* his claim to live in the memory of posterity would have been established. The fact is, however, that he was a most prolific writer, whose literary works extended over many branches of knowledge, in a number of which he was not only a pioneer but an unexcelled master. The fields of learning covered in his writings have been described by H. Malter in his *Life and Works of Saadia Gaon* as follows:

A) Hebrew philology (comprising grammar, lexicography, and exegesis);
B) Liturgy (including poetics in general);
C) Halakhah in its manifold ramifications (covering the various branches of the Jewish religious and civil law);
D) Calendar and chronology (largely polemical);
E) Philosophy (especially the philosophy of religion and embracing the author's systems of ethics and psychology);
F) Polemics against the Karaites and other opponents of traditional Judaism (of diversified content and written at various periods of the author's life).

Listing Saadia's works in accordance with this scheme we may say that we have in his *'Agron,* in the first part of which Hebrew words were arranged in alphabetical order according to their initial letters and in the second part of which the final letters were arranged alphabetically to facilitate versification, the first Hebrew dictionary. In his *Books on Language,* again, a grammatical work in twelve parts written in Arabic, we have the oldest known grammar of the Hebrew language. Besides these he also wrote an explanation of ninety so-called *hapax legomena* and other very rare Hebrew and Aramaic words of the Bible.

Saadia was the first to translate the Hebrew Scriptures into Arabic, and this version is still used by Jews in Arabic-speaking countries. The translation is on the whole literal, paraphrase being resorted to only when found to be absolutely necessary. Just as in the Targum of Onkelos anthropomorphisms are avoided and unfamiliar names are rendered by appellatives known to the Arabic-speaking reader.

According to a catalogue of Saadia's works discovered among the Genizah fragments (see J. Mann in *Jewish Quarterly Review,* n.s., XI, and S. Poznanski, *idem,* Vol. XIII) Saadia wrote commentaries in Arabic on about one half of the Pentateuch, as well as on Isaiah, the twelve minor prophets, Psalms, Proverbs, Job, Lamentations, Esther, and Daniel. These were usually provided, as was his custom, with full introductions, and they discussed many of the subjects from the philosophical as well as the philological standpoint. The above-named list speaks also of sermons, not mentioned elsewhere, that he is said to have composed.

In the field of liturgy, too, Saadia's works were epoch-making. His *Siddur* or "Order of Prayers," which has recently been published in Palestine with a Hebrew translation of the Arabic text, besides being the first scientific investigation of the ritual of the synagogue, is valuable also as the record of many liturgical compositions—other than the basic prayers—emanating from authors who would otherwise have remained unknown. However besides being a systematizer and classifier of the works of others Saadia was also a religious poet in his own right, who tried his hand at almost every type of liturgical poetry in vogue in his day. Most of his verses that have been transmitted to us seem extremely artificial. Some of his prose compositions, however, such as two of his *Baḳḳašoth* that have been preserved, reveal deep religious fervor and real grace and purity of style.

In his capacity of Gaon, the head of the Talmudical academy of Sura and the chief Jewish legal authority in the world, Saadia's prime concern was with Jewish law. In this field, too, as Louis Ginzberg notes in his Geonica, "Rabbi Saadia was the most important author of the Geonic time," distinguishing himself not only by the number but also by the originality of his contributions to Halakic literature. He is quoted as having written an *Introduction to the Talmud,* which was still extant in the sixteenth century. He composed an *Interpretation of the Thirteen (Hermeneutical) Rules (of Rabbi Ishmael).* Both of these were written originally in Arabic. There are also attributed to him commentaries on various tractates of the Talmud, likewise in the Arabic tongue.

Of particular interest in the Halakic field, however, are his monographs on various legal subjects, which he treated with his characteristic thoroughness. The following titles are quoted: 1. On *Inheritance;* 2. On *Pledges;* 3. On *Testimony and Contracts;* 4. On *Incest;* 5. On *Meat Disqualified for Food (tĕrephah);* 6. On *Usury;* 7. On *Defilement and Purity;* 8. On (legal) *Gifts;* 9. On the *Gifts Due to the Priests;* 10. On the *Laws Concerning Menstruation.* The only one of these works preserved in its entirety is the first.

It reveals in its style as well as its method the influence of Mohammedan jurisprudence. It, too, was written in Arabic.

Finally mention must be made of numerous *responsa* to questions directed to him as Gaon that Saadia wrote from time to time either in Arabic or in Aramaic, the official language of the Geonim.

The leading role that Saadia played in the Ben Meir controversy reveals him as an expert on the Jewish calendar, the regulation of which demanded a considerable knowledge of mathematics and astronomy. At the request of the Exilarch David ben Zakkai he drew up *A Record-Book and Memorial Scroll for Generations,* dealing with the differences between the four principal rules of the calendar as accepted by the Babylonians and those advocated by their opponents. Copies of this book, which was written in the summer of the year 922, were sent not only to the communities of Eastern countries but to those of Egypt and elsewhere too.

In addition he is quoted as having composed the *Four Gates* on the four principles of the traditional calendar; the *Book of the Festivals* on the appointment of the Jewish festivals in accordance with the accepted calculations; three *Letters,* two in Hebrew and one in Arabic, soliciting the assistance of his pupils in Egypt in suppressing Ben Meir's changes; and *The Order* (or *Mysteries*) *of the Calendar.*

In the realm of chronology, the importance of which lay in the support that it lent to the belief in the uninterrupted continuity of Jewish tradition, Saadia is credited with the composition in Arabic of a *Book of Chronology* in seven parts covering the history of the world from the creation down to the author's time. He is believed also to have written, in Hebrew, a *Chronology of the Teachers of the Mishnah and the Talmud,* a *Genealogy of Rabbi Judah the Patriarch,* and an Arabic translation of the original Aramaic text of *The Scroll of the Hasmoneans,* which gives a detailed and partly legendary account of the victories of the Maccabees over Antiochus and his generals.

As far as philosophy is concerned, Saadia wrote, in addition to his masterpiece, the *Book of Beliefs and Opinions,* which is the subject of our translation, a philosophical commentary, the first on record, on the mystical *Book of Creation,* the authorship of which he ascribed to the patriarch Abraham. In a lengthy introduction, with which he prefaces his book, he takes up seven Greek theories of the creation of the world which he refutes and rejects in favor of the doctrine of *creatio ex nihilo.* In the body of the commentary itself he discusses such matters as the variations between the Tiberian and the Babylonian pronunciations of the consonants and vowels of the Hebrew alphabet, the significance of numbers and letters, the process of creation according to the author of the book, the meaning of such terms as *šĕkhinah,* "the Holy Spirit," "The Word (of God)," and the "Echo" (that is the resonance of God's voice), as well as the measurements of various planets and other astral bodies. There is included also a discussion of the functions of the internal organs of the human body.

But Saadia's philosophical remarks are not confined to this commentary and the *Book of Beliefs and Opinions* alone. They are to be found in his Bible exegesis and in other writings as well. Everywhere is there evidence of the rational, scientific bent of his mind.

We come now to the last classification of Saadia's works, the polemical literature that he left behind. As a matter of fact most of his writings were more or less of a polemical character, even his translation of the Bible which served him as an instrument for upholding traditional Judaism and combatting the Karaite schism. However whereas in his exegetical books and in his philosophical masterpiece the polemic was only incidental, there were others of which the controversial purpose was direct and deliberate. The earliest of his polemical writings was one entitled a *Refutation of Anan,* aimed against the founder of Karaism. It was composed by him when he was still in Egypt. His most important polemic, written in 926–927, when he was already officially connected with the academy of Sura, was his *Book of Distinction,* in which such matters of controversy between Karaites and Rabbanites as the kindling of lights on the Sabbath eve, the date of the Feast of Weeks, and the validity of the Oral Law are discussed. Whether the *Book of Proofs for Burning Candles on the Sabbath,* which is mentioned in the list of Saadia's writings published by Mann, was a part of this work or not has not yet been decided.

Another anti-Karaite work of Saadia's was his *Book of Refutation of Ibn Sakawaihi,* a Karaite who in a brochure entitled *Book of Shameful Things* had attacked the essential parts of rabbinic law. It was possibly against the same author that Saadia's *Book of Refutation of an Overbearing Antagonist,* in which the question of the proper appointment of the festivals of Passover and Tabernacles is dealt with, was directed. His *Refutation of Ḥiwwi al-Balchi,* again, was aimed at a Jewish radical, who denied not only the validity of the Talmud but of the Bible as well.

One of Saadia's latest polemics, in which he justified his position in his struggle with the Exilarch and which was composed during his period of seclusion was *The Open Book.* In contradistinction to his previous polemical works it was written in Hebrew instead of Arabic. Later on he issued a sequel in Arabic entitled *The Book That Refutes.*

Saadia Literature in the English Language

The standard work in any language on the career and the writings of the Gaon Saadia is Henry Malter's *Life and Works of Saadia Gaon* (Philadelphia, 1921). Besides giving a full-length biography of the greatest of the Geonim, Malter has also compiled in this book an exhaustive bibliography of all the works by and about Saadia either extant or quoted at the date of its completion.

Articles dealing with various phases of the life, works, and teachings of Saadia, as well as additional bibliographical lists, are to be found in the following volumes:

Saadia Anniversary Volume, American Academy for Jewish Research, New York, 1943.

Saadia Studies, edited by Abraham A. Neuman and Solomon Zeitlin, Philadelphia, 1943. Special edition of *Jewish Quarterly Review,* n.s., XXXII (1943), 109–401.

Saadya Studies, edited by Erwin I. J. Rosenthal, Manchester University Press, 1943.

Rab Saadia Gaon, edited by Louis Finkelstein, Jewish Theological Seminary of America, New York, 1944.

THE BOOK OF
BELIEFS AND OPINIONS

COMPOSED BY

SA'ID 'IBN YUSUF

[OTHERWISE] KNOWN AS SA'ADYA THE FAYYUMITE

INTRODUCTORY TREATISE

I

THE author opened his remarks with the words:
"Blessed be God, the God of Israel, Who is alone deserving of being regarded as the Evident Truth, Who verifies with certainty unto rational beings the existence of their souls, by means of which they assess accurately what they perceive with their senses and apprehend correctly the objects of their knowledge. Uncertainties are thereby removed from them and doubts disappear, so that demonstrations become lucid for them and proofs become clear. May He be lauded, then, above the highest commendation and praise."

II

Now after these preliminaries in praise of our Lord and our brief expression of tribute to Him, I shall preface this book, which it has been my intention to compose, with an account of the causes by which uncertainties may beset the minds of men in their search for the truth, as well as of the method by which they may resolve these uncertainties, and thus reach the goal of their search. I shall show, furthermore, how some of these uncertainties so intrigue [1] some men that in their fancy and belief they become established [2] truths. As for myself, I invoke God's help in lifting such uncertainties from my mind so that I may fully attain the means of serving Him, just as His pious one besought Him when he said: *Uncover mine eyes that I may behold the marvels of Thy Law* (Ps. 119:18).

This [introductory essay], as well as the subject matter of the

Note. The English translation of the title of the book follows the Hebrew rendering of Ibn Tibbon.

1. "intrigue"—literally "dominate." Cf. Bloch's translation.
2. "become established"—literally "establish them as."

book proper,[3] I propose to formulate in simple rather than recondite terms, in easy rather than difficult language, making use of only the principal proofs and arguments and not of their subdivisions. Thus the contents will be plain to follow and simple enough to grasp and easy to master; and he who diligently studies the book may thereby arrive at equity $<2>$ [4] and truth—as the saint said of wisdom when it is made accessible: *Then wilt thou understand righteousness and justice and equity, yea every good path* (Prov. 2:9).

I shall, then, first make note of the cause by which uncertainties arise in the minds of men. I maintain that the concepts of the intellect are based on the perceptions of the senses. However, the things perceived by sense are subject to confusion for one of two reasons: either (*a*) because the seeker is not sufficiently acquainted with the object of his search, or (*b*) because he takes his task lightly and falls short in the thoroughness and persistency of his quest. For example, if a person were to seek one Reuben, the son of Jacob, he could be in doubt about him for only one of two reasons: either (*a*) because he does not know him well, so that the latter might be standing [5] before him without being recognized by him, or he might see someone else and think he is Reuben; of (*b*) because [6] he takes the easiest course, abandoning thoroughness. The result [in the latter case] is that his love of ease inclines him to seek his object with the least effort and the slightest concern, wherefore, indeed, he does not discern it.

Similarly in regard to things of the intellect, confusion may arise from one of these two causes: either (*a*) because the seeker of intellectual knowledge is unacquainted with the methods [7] of evidence, so that he declares a valid proof to be no proof and, conversely, he declares what is no proof to be a valid proof, or (*b*) because, even though he is conversant with the processes of reason-

3. "book proper"—literally "entire book."
4. Beginning of page 2 of Landauer's edition of the Arabic text. Subsequent pages will be similarly indicated.
5. "the latter might be standing"—so according to Ibn Tibbon's Hebrew version.
6. "because"—Ibn Tibbon.
7. "methods"—Ibn Tibbon.

ing, he takes the quickest and easiest course so that he jumps at the conclusion before having completed the task of reasoning about it.

How [much more would this apply] in the case in which both these conditions are combined in the same person! I mean that he be unacquainted with the art of reasoning and, together with that [deficiency], lack the patience to explore fully such correct knowledge as he has. Such a one would be far removed from his goal or in despair of ever reaching it. Now of the first class of individuals mentioned by us the saint has said: *Every one that had knowledge and understanding* (Neh. 10:29), and of the last-named: *They know not neither do they understand* (Ps. 82:5).

Still more would this be true where to these two factors is added <3> a third; namely, that the seeker does not know what he is seeking. Such a one would be even further removed and more distant from his goal, so much so that he would fail to recognize the truth even if it should by chance occur to him or [8] he should happen to come upon it. He is thus like a creditor [9] who does not know the art of weighing, or even the nature of a balance and weights, nor yet how much money is due him from his debtor. Even if his debtor were to pay him his debt in full, he would be uncertain whether he had paid it. Or if he were to receive from his debtor less than what was owing to him, he might fancy that it was he who had defrauded his debtor.

Just like this case of the ignorant creditor who sues his debtor [10] is also that of the individual who seeks to weigh something for himself but is totally ignorant of the nature of weighing instruments and the quantity to be weighed. He might furthermore be compared to a person who receives money for himself or somebody else and relies on his own sorting although he is unacquainted with the art of sorting. As a consequence he would often accept defective coins and refuse the good. Something like that would

8. "or"—Ibn Tibbon.
9. "creditor"—literally "an individual."
10. "the ignorant creditor who sues his debtor"—literally "the two litigants one of whom sues the other."

also happen where he is acquainted with the art but fails to observe carefully.

Scripture does indeed liken the sorting of just statements to the sorting of money when it says, *Like tested silver is the speech of the righteous whilst the heart of the wicked is of little worth* (Prov. 10:20).[11] Those whose knowledge of the art of sorting is limited or who have but little patience are presented as wrongdoers, because they wrong the truth; Scripture says, namely, *The heart of the wicked is of little worth.* On the other hand, those expert in sorting are presented as righteous men on account of their knowledge as well as their patience, as it is stated first, *Like tested silver is the speech of the righteous.* Thus praise is bestowed on the learned, and doubts are removed from them, only on account of their patient penetration into all the phases of their art after acquainting themselves thoroughly with it, as the saint said, *Behold, I waited for your words, I listened for your reasons whilst ye searched out what to say* (Job 32:11). In like manner did the other saint say, *And take not the word of truth utterly out of my mouth* (Ps. 119:43).

What has prompted me to speak explicitly about this matter is my observation of the state of many people in regard to their beliefs and convictions. There is among them, for instance, the type of person who has attained the truth <4> and is cognizant of it and rejoices in it.[12] Of him does the prophet say, *Thy words were found, and I did eat them; and Thy words were unto me a joy and the rejoicing of my heart* (Jer. 15:16).

Again there is among them he who has attained the truth but who is nevertheless in doubt about it, being neither wholly convinced nor holding it firmly in his grasp. In reference to him the prophet says, *Though I write for him ever so many things of My Law, they are accounted as a stranger's* (Hos. 8:12).

There is further among them he who holds to be true what in reality is false, thinking that it is the truth; he thus clings to false-

---

11. The usual translation is *The tongue of the righteous is as choice silver; the heart of the wicked is little worth.*

12. "in it"—Ibn Tibbon. These words are omitted in the Arabic text.

hood and abandons what is right. Of him Scripture says, *Let him not trust in vanity, deceiving himself; for vanity shall be his recompense* (Job. 15: 31).

There is, lastly, among them the type of person who for a while follows one system of thought and then abandons it on account of some flaw that he has noticed in it. So he transfers to another system from which he also withdraws on account of some point in it which he rejects. Then he passes on to still another for a while but gives it up again on account of something in it which has made it reprehensible to him, and so he remains unsettled all his life. Such a one might be compared to a person who wishes to go to a certain city but does not know the road leading to it. Consequently he walks a parasang along one highway and hesitates. Then he turns back and walks a parasang along another highway and hesitates and so turns once more and repeats this procedure on a third and a fourth highway. Of him does Scripture say, *The labor of fools wearieth every one of them, for he knoweth not how to go to the city* (Eccles. 10: 15), that is *since he knoweth not.*

When, now, I considered these fundamentals and the evil resulting therefrom, my heart was grieved for my species, the species of rational beings, and my soul was stirred on account of our people, the children of Israel. For I saw in this age of mine many believers whose belief was not pure and whose convictions were not sound, whilst many of the deniers of the faith boasted of their corruption and looked down upon the devotees of the truth although they were themselves in error. I saw, furthermore, men who were sunk, as it were, in seas of doubt and overwhelmed by waves of confusion and there was no diver to bring them up from the depths nor a swimmer who might take hold of their hands and carry them ashore.

But inasmuch as my Lord had granted me some knowledge by which <5> I might come to their assistance and had endowed me with some ability that I could put at their disposal for their benefit, I thought that it was my duty to help them therewith and my obligation to direct them to the truth. Something of this order was also expressed by the saint: *The Lord God hath given me the tongue of them that are taught, that I should know how to sustain with words him that is weary; He wakeneth morning by morning, He wakeneth my ear to hear as they that are taught* (Isa. 50: 4).

Although I do acknowledge that my learning is far from perfect and admit that my scientific attainments are lacking in excellence, and I am not wiser than my contemporaries, yet according to my capacity and to the extent of my understanding—and as the saint expressed it, *But as for me, this secret is not revealed to me for any wisdom that I have more than any living, but to the intent that the interpretation may be made known to the king, and that thou mayest know the thoughts of thy heart* (Dan. 2: 30)—I beseech God, exalted be He, to help me and grant me what He knows to be the aim and object of my quest, not according to my attainments and my powers, as His other saint said, *I know also, my God, that Thou triest the heart, and hast pleasure in uprightness* (I Chron. 29: 17).

I also adjure by God, the Creator of the universe, any scholar who, upon studying this book, sees in it a mistake, that he correct it, or, should he note an abstruse phrase, that he substitute for it a more felicitous one. Let him not feel restrained therefrom by the fact that the book is not his work, or that I had anticipated him in explaining what had not been clear to him. For the wise have a tender solicitude for wisdom, entertaining for it a sympathy similar to that entertained for one another by members of the same family, as Scripture says: *Say unto wisdom: "Thou art my sister"* (Prov. 7: 4)—although the fools, too, are devoted to their folly, and are loath to forsake it, as Scripture says: *Though he spare it, and will not let it go, but keep it still within* <6> *his mouth* (Job 20: 13).

Furthermore I implore in the name of God, exalted be He, every seeker of knowledge who studies this book to read it without bias and have in mind the same objective as I, and to desist from narrow-mindedness and conjecture and confutation, until he will have obtained benefit and have acquired profit by the power and the might of Him, who teaches us what profits us, as the saint has said: *I am the Lord thy God, that teaches thee for thy profit, that leadeth thee by the way that thou shouldest go* (Isa. 48: 17).

If, now, the scholar and the student will pursue such a course in the perusal of this book, then he that strives for certainty will gain in certitude, and doubt will be lifted from the doubter, and he that believes by sheer authority will come to believe out of insight and understanding. By the same token the gratuitous opponent will come to a halt, and the conceited adversary will feel ashamed, whilst the righteous and upright will rejoice, as Scripture says: *The upright see it, and are glad, and all iniquity stoppeth her mouth. Whoso is wise, let him observe these things, and let them consider the mercies of the Lord* (Ps. 107: 42, 43).

Thus will men improve in their inner being as well as in their outer conduct. Their prayers, too, will become pure, since they will have acquired in their hearts a deterrent from error, an impulse to do what is right, as the saint has said: *Thy word have I laid up in my heart, that I might not sin against Thee* (Ps. 119: 11).

Thus, also, will their beliefs prevail in their affairs, their mutual jealousy over things of this world will diminish. They will all tend toward the realm of wisdom and feel no inclination for anything else. Theirs will be salvation and mercy and grace as He, may He be praised and sanctified, has said: *Look unto Me, and be ye saved, all the ends of the earth; for I am God, and there is none else* (Isa. 45: 22).

All this will become possible when doubts are dispelled and uncertainties removed. For then the knowledge of God and acquaintance with His lore will spread even as water spreads at the shores [13] of the sea—as Scripture says: *For the earth shall be full of the knowledge of the Lord, as the waters cover the sea* (Isa. 11:9).

III

<7> Now someone might perhaps ask: [14] What was the purpose of [15] the Creator, exalted and magnified be He, in permitting these uncertainties and doubts to prevail among His creatures? To

---

13. "shores"—literally "parts."
14. "ask"—Ibn Tibbon.
15. "What was the purpose of"—Ibn Tibbon.

this question we here offer an answer. We maintain that the very fact of their being created entities necessitates their entertaining uncertainties and illusions. That is to say: by the plan of creation, they require for every act they perform a span of time within which to complete that act step by step. Cognition, therefore, which is one of these activities, obviously depends upon a like condition. Now the process of knowing on the part of men begins with things that are at first jumbled, obscure and ambiguous. However by the power of the intellect, which they possess they do, in the course of time, continually refine and purify these [complexities] until the uncertainties depart from them and the pure essence is extracted dissociated from any doubt.

Now, since all human arts consist of phases, if men were to stop in their endeavors before these phases were completed, the operation in question, such as sowing or building or weaving or other tasks, that can be brought to completion only by the perseverance of the worker to the last phase, would never be completed. In like manner does the art of cognition require that one start in it at the beginning and proceed step by step until its end. At the initial stage, for example, there may be ten problems, which at the second are reduced to nine, and at the third to eight. Thus each time that man's reasoning and reflection are applied to them these problems decrease, until at the last of these stages, the sole object of his quest is extracted and left isolated, [free] from all ambiguity or doubt.

For the sake of elucidation let it be assumed that a person is looking for proof by means of which he might arrive at the truth. Now such a proof is a statement, and a statement is a kind of sound, and sounds are of many types. When, then, the seeker sets out to distill the object of his quest—and the sounds confronting him, which he has begun to classify, are ambiguous and unintelligible—he first eliminates <8> from the complex of noises those produced by 1) the concussion of bodies, such as the falling of stone on stone, and 2) the cleaving of certain bodies, and 3) sounds like that of thunder and crashing and similar noises, for he knows that from these types of sound he could not derive any proof. So he arrives, in the second stage, at sounds produced by animated beings only, seeing that it is among these [alone] that he may expect to find the [desired] demonstration. Next, however, he will eliminate from these the sounds made by all animated things not endowed with speech, such as neighing and braying and lowing and the like, since these are no less unintelligible.[16] Thus he arrives, in the third stage, at the sounds produced by human beings in particular, since it is by this species of sounds [only] that all knowledge [is expressed]. From these, again, he eliminates such natural sounds as "Ah" and the like, since these would be of no use to him, so that, in the fourth stage, he comes upon the articulate [17] sounds produced by man, which consist of the twenty-two letters of the alphabet. From these, again, he eliminates unconnected consonants, since none of them, when pronounced separately, would serve any purpose, as if thou wert to say: A, B, C, D, E, each by itself.

He now arrives, in the fifth stage, at consonants combined with one another so as to form nouns, consisting each of two or three or more consonants. From these, however, he eliminates every instance of a noun that is detached, spoken alone, as when one says: "heaven," "star," "man," since it is not inherent [18] in any of these nouns, when spoken in isolation, to indicate any more than what is designated by them. Thus he arrives, in the sixth stage, at [sounds of] connected speech, as when one says: "A star shining"; "A man writing"; and other such combinations of two words, or of a word and a noun or more, for he expects by means of these combinations to attain his object. From these he now eliminates instances of the [mere] coupling of two or more words or of any [utterance] that does not constitute a statement, and he thus comes, <9> in the seventh stage, upon statements such as those made by the person who says: "The sun has risen," or "The rain has fallen," and the like.

He knows, however, that statements are [divided] into three

---

16. "these are no less unintelligible"—literally "there is no wisdom in them."
17. "articulate"—or "technical."
18. "inherent"—so Ibn Tibbon, literally "in the nature."

different categories: (*a*) necessary, such as the statement: "The fire is hot"; (*b*) impossible, such as the statement: "The fire is cold"; (*c*) possible, such as the statement: "Reuben is in Bagdad." He thereupon puts aside the necessary and the impossible categories, and arrives, in the eighth stage, at the possible [type of] statement, and investigates whether what is contained in it [19] is correct or not.

Then, in the ninth stage, he begins to subject the matter in question to rational analysis, either [starting] from a necessary [premise] and demonstrating—by means of certain methods which we shall elucidate hereafter—that by that premise the matter under discussion, too, must be affirmed as necessary; [20] or starting from an impossible premise and showing that by it any such statement must be declared impossible. When, then, all the alternatives have been excluded and there remains only the one he has reached in the tenth stage, which is now lucid and clear to him, he drops from his mind all previous divisions that had rendered his objectives both ambiguous and obscure before his inquiry had eliminated these divisions one by one.

It is clear, then, that the person who speculates begins with a great many things that are all mixed up, from which he continually sifts nine out of ten, and then eight out of nine, and then seven out of eight, until all confusions and ambiguities are removed and only the pure extract remains. If, therefore, he were to stop in his investigation upon reaching the fifth or the fourth stage or whatever station it be, the number of uncertainties resolved by him would be in proportion to the stations he has put behind himself, and he would still be left with a number proportionate to the stations before him. Should he hold on to what he has accomplished, there is hope that he may come back to it and complete the process. If, however, he does not retain it, then he would be compelled to repeat the entire process of reasoning from the beginning.

19. "is contained in it"—literally "the informant stated concerning it."
20. "that by that . . . necessary"—literally "the necessary conclusions that it leads to."

It is on this account that many people remain in error, spurning wisdom. Some do it because they do not know the road leading to it. Certain others [take this attitude] because, although they had begun to travel on this road, they did not <10> traverse it completely, and were, therefore, among those who perished, as Scripture has said: *The man that strayeth out of the way of understanding shall rest in the congregation of the shades* (Prov. 21:16). The sages of the children of Israel have also said with reference to him who has not fully studied the subject matter of wisdom: *Ever since the number of disciples of Hillel and Shammai increased who did not wait upon scholars sufficiently there has been an increase of the number of disagreements* (Sanh. 88b). This utterance of theirs indicates to us that when pupils do complete their course of study, no controversy or discord arises among them.

Let, therefore, the worried fool refrain from ascribing his failings to the Creator, exalted and magnified be He. Let him not say that it was He who had implanted the doubts in him. Rather it was his own folly or his worry that had hurled him into these doubts, as we have explained. In fact it is untenable that a single act on his part should instantaneously remove all uncertainties. That would constitute a deviation from the law governing all creatures, and he is, after all, a created being. Furthermore, if a person does refrain from assigning this failing of his to his Master, yet desires that God endow him with a knowledge free from all uncertainty, such a one asks that his Master make him His equal. For, as we shall explain in what follows, he who is capable of knowledge without depending upon a cause is none other than the Creator of the universe, blessed and hallowed be He.

But, as far as all created beings are concerned, they cannot acquire knowledge except by the mediation of a cause; that is, by the process of research and analysis, the performance of which requires certain measures of time, as we have demonstrated. Accordingly, from the first to the last moment of these intervals, they will of necessity find themselves in a state of uncertainty, as we have shown. Those, then, are worthy of commendation who wait patiently until they have purified the silver of the dross, in accordance with the statement of Scripture: *Take away the dross from the silver, and there cometh forth a vessel for the refiner* (Prov. 25:4); or, until they have distilled the clear milk of the art [of research] and extracted its cream, according to another utterance of Scripture: *For the churning of milk bringeth forth curd, and the wringing of the nose bringeth forth blood* (Prov. 30:33); or, until their seed is fully grown and they can harvest it, as Scripture says: *Sow* <11> *to yourselves according to righteousness, reap according to mercy* (Hos. 10:12); or, again, until the fruit of their trees has ripened and become nourishment, as Scripture says: *A tree of life is she to them that hold on to her* (Prov. 3:18).

IV

And now that we have finished expounding, as much as we felt it desirable, the matter of resolving uncertainties and doubts, it behooves us to explain what is meant by belief. We say that it is a notion that arises in the soul in regard to the actual character of anything that is apprehended. When the cream of investigation emerges, [and] is embraced and enfolded by the minds and, through them acquired and digested by the souls, then the person becomes convinced of the truth of the notion he has thus acquired. He then deposits it in his soul for a future occasion or for future occasions, in accordance with the statement of Scripture: *Wise men lay up knowledge; but the mouth of the foolish is an imminent ruin* (Prov. 10:14); and it says also: *Receive, I pray thee, instruction from His mouth* (Job 22:22).

Now beliefs fall into two categories: true and false. A true belief consists in believing a thing to be as it really is; namely, that much is much, and little is little, and black is black, and white is white, and that what exists exists, and what is nonexistent is nonexistent. A false belief, on the other hand, consists in believing a thing to be the opposite of what it actually is, such as that much is little, and little is much, and white is black, and black is white, and that what exists is nonexistent, and what is nonexistent exists.

The praiseworthy wise man is he who makes reality his guiding principle and bases his belief thereon. Notwithstanding his wisdom, he relies only on what is deserving of trust and is wary wherever caution is in order. The reprehensible fool, on the other hand, is he who sets up his personal conviction as his guiding principle, assuming that reality is patterned after [21] his belief. Notwithstanding his ignorance, he trusts in what should be shunned and shuns what is deserving of trust. All this is borne out by Scripture, which says: [22] *A wise man feareth, and departeth from evil; but the fool behaveth overbearingly, and is confident* (Prov. 14:16).

To this [last] observation I must append the expression of my amazement at [the view of] certain people who, being <12> slaves, yet believe that they have no master, and who are confident that any object the existence of which they deny must be non-existent and whatever they declare to be in existence is so. These individuals are so sunken in folly as to have reached the very nadir of mental deterioration.[23] For if they be right, then let him among them who has no money take it into his head that his coffers and chests are filled with money, and see what it would profit him. Or let him believe he is seventy years old, when he is only forty years of age, and see what good it would do him. Or let him assume that he is sated when he is hungry, or that his thirst is quenched when he is thirsty, or that he is covered up when he is naked, and see what would happen to him. Or let him among them who has a vicious enemy believe that his enemy has died, aye perished, with the result that he no longer takes precautions against the latter. But, oh, how quickly will he [in such a case] be overcome by the misfortune [24] of which he was not [sufficiently] apprehensive.

Now it is sheer folly on the part of people to imagine that their [mere] refusal to acknowledge the sovereignty of the Lord exempts them from [heeding] His commandments and prohibitions and from [being subject to] His promise of reward and threat of punishment and other such things. It is such individuals that

21. "is patterned after"—literally "follows."
22. "All . . . says"—literally "and as it says."
23. "mental deterioration"—literally "perdition."
24. "misfortune"—Ibn Tibbon.

Scripture quotes [as saying]: *Let us break their bands asunder* (Ps. 2:3).

Thus there are certain Hindus who have hardened themselves against fire, although it burns them whenever they come in contact with it. Again there are individuals who, affecting youthfulness, have hardened themselves to endure the blows of the cane and the scourge, although they smart from them whenever they are struck by them. How much more should this apply in the case of those who in this wise embolden themselves against the Creator of the universe! Their [mere] ignorance [of it] will not cause them to escape the lot that His wisdom has decreed for them, as Scripture has indeed said: *He is wise in heart, and mighty in strength; who has hardened himself against Him, and prospered?* (Job 9:4).

V

Having concluded now what we thought fit [25] to append to our first statement, it behooves us to give an account of the bases of truth and the vouchers of certainty which are the source of all knowledge and the mainspring of all cognition. Discoursing about them in keeping with the aim [26] of this book, we declare that there are three [such] bases. The first consists of the knowledge gained by <13> [direct] observation. The second is composed of the intuition of the intellect. The third comprises that knowledge which is inferred by logical necessity.

Following up [this] enumeration with an explanation of each of these roots of knowledge, we say that we understand by the knowledge of observation whatever a person perceives by means of one of the five senses; that is, by means of sight or hearing or smell or taste or touch. By the intuition of the intellect, we mean such notions as spring up solely in the mind of a human being, such as approbation of truthfulness and disapproval of mendacity. By the knowledge derived from logical necessity, again, is meant conclusions, which, unless they are accepted by the individual as

25. "thought fit"—Ibn Tibbon and codex M quoted by Landauer.
26. "aim"—so M.

true, would compel his denial of the validity of his rational intuitions or the perception of his senses. Since, however, he cannot very well negate either of these two, he must regard the said inference as being correct. Thus we are forced to affirm, although we have never seen it, that man possesses a soul, in order not to deny its manifest activity. [We must] also [agree], although we have never seen it, that every soul is endowed with reason, [merely] in order not to deny the latter's manifest activity.

Now we find that there are many people who deny [the reliability of] these three sources [of knowledge]. A small minority of them reject the first source. Of these we shall give an account in the first treatise of this book, together with a refutation of their view. By rejecting the first source, they have automatically rejected the second and the third, since the latter two are based upon the first. More numerous than this group are those that acknowledge the validity of the first but reject the second and the third [sources]. Of their thesis, too, we shall make mention in the first treatise and refute it. Most numerous of all, however, are those who acknowledge the validity of the first two sources [of knowledge] and reject the third. The reason for the difference in their rating of these [various sources of knowledge] lies in the fact that the second [type of] knowledge is more recondite than the first, and likewise the third more so than the second, and that whatever is invisible can more readily be denied than what is visible.

Again there are people who reject the validity of this [last type of] knowledge in certain instances [27] and recognize [28] it in others, each group among them affirming what its opponent negates. Their argument [in each case] is that logical necessity led them to the particular conclusion. Thus there is he who affirms that all things are at rest. <14> He consequently denies the reality of motion. Another, again, affirms that all things move, and by virtue thereof denies the reality of rest. Each one declares the evidence adduced by his opponent dubious and unconvincing.

27. "instances"---so M.
28. "recognize"—literally "hold on to," so Ibn Tibbon. Cf. also Abraham Heschel, *The Quest for Certainty in Saadia's Philosophy* in *The Jewish Quarterly Review*, XXXIII, 290, and n. 139.

As for ourselves, the community of monotheists, we hold these three sources of knowledge to be genuine. To them, however, we add a fourth source, which we have derived by means of the [other] three, and which has thus become for us a further principle. That is [to say, we believe in] the validity of authentic tradition, by reason of the fact that it is based upon the knowledge of the senses as well as that of reason, as we shall explain in the third treatise of this book.

At this point, however, we remark that this type of knowledge (I mean that which is furnished by authentic tradition and the books of prophetic revelation), corroborates for us the validity of the first three sources of knowledge. Thus it enumerates the senses in connection with the denial of their functioning in the case of the idols, making them a total of five with two more added to them. It says, namely: *They have mouths but they speak not; eyes have they but they see not . . . neither speak they with their throat* (Ps. 115:5-7).

The first five [organs] mentioned refer to the senses themselves, whilst of the two [functions] that are added to them, one is motion. This is implied in the statement: *Feet have they but walk not* (Ps. 115:7). By means of this faculty [incidentally] there is also obtained consciousness of heaviness and lightness. Thus a person may be prevented from moving about [freely] by reason of his weight, whereas he would not thus be hindered if he were light. On this account, indeed, certain people were minded to add to the number of the senses, for they asked [themselves]: "How [else] can the sensation of lightness and heaviness be experienced?" Our answer is: "By means of the sense [29] of motion, according to whether the latter is found to be easy or difficult."

The other one [of the added faculties] is [that of] speech. It is implied in the statement: *Neither speak they with their throat.* [By] that [of course] is [meant] speech in general, [whether it consists] of individual nouns or combinations [of words], or premises, or proofs, as we have previously explained.

Furthermore [authentic tradition] verifies for us the validity

29. "sense"—M and Ibn Tibbon.

of the intuition of reason. It enjoins us, namely, to speak the truth and not to lie. Thus it says: *For my mouth shall utter truth, and wickedness is an abomination to my lips. All the words of my mouth are in righteousness, there is nothing* <15> *perverse or crooked in them* (Prov. 8: 7, 8).

Besides that it confirms for us the validity of knowledge inferred by logical necessity, [that is to say] that whatever leads to the rejection of the perception of the senses or rational intuition is false. The untenability of any [theory] that rejects the perception of the senses is affirmed by such Scripture statements as: *Thou that tearest thyself in thine anger, shall the earth be forsaken for thee, or shall the rock be removed out of its place?* (Job 18: 4). Again, apropos of the untenability of any theory that rejects rational intuitions concerning the falseness or truth [of propositions], it remarks: *And if it be not so now, who will prove me a liar, and make my speech nothing worth?* (Job 24: 25).

Next [tradition] informs us that all sciences are [ultimately] based on what we grasp with our aforementioned senses, from which they are deduced and derived. Thus it says: *Hear my words, ye wise men; and give ear unto me, ye that have knowledge. For the ear trieth words, as the palate tasteth food* (Job 34: 2, 3). Moreover this last source of knowledge also confirms for us the validity of trustworthy reports. That is the import of its statement: *I will tell thee, hear thou me; and that which I have seen will I declare— which wise men have told from their fathers, and have not hid it; unto whom alone the land was given, and no stranger passed among them* (Job 15: 17–19). The [reliability of the] types [of knowledge] referred to depends, of course, on conditions which we have explained in the interpretation of these verses in their [respective] places.

Having given an account of these four sources of knowledge, it behooves us [now] to explain how they are to be used for purposes of evidence. We say, then, that as far as the knowledge [derived] from sensation is concerned, whatever is correctly perceived with our senses, by virtue of the connection existing between us and the object in question, must be acknowledged by us to be in truth as it has been perceived by us, without [the admission of] a doubt. [This is, of course] posited on the assumption that we are [sufficiently] experienced in detecting illusions so as not to be led astray by them. [We should not, for example, act] like those people who believe that the image which they see in the mirror is an image that has really been created there, when in fact it is only a property of polished bodies to reflect the outline of objects facing them. Nor [should we be deceived] like those people who regard the figure, which appears reversed in the water, as possessing a reality which was created at that [particular] time, not knowing that <16> the cause of that [illusion] resides in the fact that the water is deeper in measurement than the length of the figure. So long, then, as we beware of such illusions and the like, our cognition of what is perceived with the senses will be correct, and we will not be led astray by such fancies as the one referred to by Scripture in its statement: *And the Moabites saw the water way off as red as blood* (II Kings 3: 22).

Now as for the intuitions of the intellect, anything that is conceived in our mind in complete freedom from accidents [of any sort] is to be regarded as true knowledge about which no doubt [is to be entertained]. [This, too, is] posited on the assumption that we know how to reason and carry the reasoning process to its conclusion, being wary [at the same time] of fancy and dreams. There are, namely, people who definitely consider these dreams to be realities created in the forms seen by a person. They feel compelled to abide by this view, so they maintain, in order not to reject what they have seen with their eyes, not realizing that [what they believe they have seen] may be due partly to the previous day's affairs that flitted through the mind, of which Scripture says: *For a dream cometh through a multitude of business* (Eccles. 5: 2).

Some [of these musings] again may be the result of the victuals consumed, according to whether they were hot or cold, or great or small in quantity. Hereof Scripture says: *And it shall be as when a hungry man dreameth and, behold, he eateth* (Isa. 29: 8). Others may be brought on by the fact that the humor has exceeded its proportion in the mixture [of the elements of which the body is

composed], with the consequence that the resulting heat and moisture produce the generation of [uncalled-for] mirth and gaiety.
On the other hand, excessive dryness would cause the generation
of [unwarranted] sadness and sorrow. In regard to this matter the
pain-racked invalid said: *When I say: "My bed shall comfort me,
my couch shall ease my complaint"; then thou scarest me with
dreams, and terrifiest me through visions* (Job 7: 13, 14). Of course
there is also apt to be mingled with these dreams a glimmer of
heavenly light in the form of a hint or a parable, as Job intimates
in his statement: *In a dream, in a vision of the night, when deep
sleep falleth upon men, in slumberings upon the bed; then He
openeth the ears of men* (Job 33: 15, 16).

As for the knowledge which is inferred by logical necessity,
whenever our senses perceive anything the existence of which has
been verified, and [the belief in the reality of] that thing can be
upheld in our minds only by virtue of the simultaneous acknowledgment [of the reality] <17> of other things, then we must
acknowledge [the existence of] all of them, be they few or
many in number, since the validity of the sense percept in question is maintained only by them. Now these [necessary postulates]
may be one, or they may be two or three or four or more than tha:.
But whatever [figure] they may reach [really makes no difference,
for], since there is no negating of the sense percept in question,
there is no negating any of them either.

As an illustration of a single [concomitant] let it be supposed
that we see smoke, but do not see the fire from which that smoke
originates. We must [in that case] assume the existence of the fire
because of the existence of the smoke since the one can be effected
only by means of the other. Likewise if we hear the voice of a
human being from behind a wall, we must assume the existence
of that human being, since a human voice can emanate only from
an existing human being.

As an example, again, of more than one [concomitant phenomenon that must be postulated, the following might be cited.] When,
for instance, we see food go down in bulk in the belly of an animate
being, and its refuse come out from it, then, unless we assume

[that] four operations [were involved in the process], what has been perceived by our senses could not possibly have been carried out. That is [to say] that there must be in the belly of that being a force that draws the food into the interior, and a force that holds it until it has been digested, and a force that furthers its digestion and disintegration, and a force that expels the refuse that is in it as it goes out. Now inasmuch as what has been perceived by the senses could be effected only by means of these four [operations], we must assume that these four [forces] are a reality.

Sometimes, too, our acknowledgment of the reality of what we observe becomes possible only by the invention of a science that verifies it for us. We may even be compelled to resort to many such sciences. Once, however, it is realized that the sense percept in question is dependent [for its corroboration] on the said [sciences], it follows of necessity that we must acknowledge all of the latter as valid so that the reality of the sense percept in question may be upheld.

Thus, for example, we see the moon rise upon the earth and set again at different moments of the night and the day. It does this by following either a long or a short route, according to whether it consumes less time than is required for reaching one of the twenty-eight stations that we have distinguished and designated by name or it consumes more time and so passes the latter. <18> We note, furthermore, that at one time it travels to the south [of the sphere of the constellations] [30] and at another to the north. From this we infer that, if it had only one motion, there could have been no variation in either the speed [31] of its course or its extent. The fact, therefore, that we see these two [factors] vary leads to the inevitable conclusion that the moon has many motions and that these multiple motions can be due only to a multiple number of bodies, since one body cannot be endowed with two different motions at one and the same time, let alone three or four motions.

30. So according to the exposition by Abraham ben Hiyy.. quoted by Moise Ventura, *La Philosophie de Saadia Gaon*, p. 85, n. 26.
31. Cf. *ibid.*

Furthermore [we know] that, when a multiple number of bodies equal in form intercept each other, they thereby diminish or increase the speeds of their respective motions.

[All] this is demonstrable only by means of the science of geometry, which shows us synthetically how one figure enters into the other. [That is to say] we must first master the science of plane geometry. Having acquainted ourselves with [the properties of] points and lines, we begin with the study [of the properties] of plane figures, such as the triangle, the square, the circle, the concentric, the tangent, and the secant, until we get to know the properties of the intercepting [spherical] figure,[32] and which of its segments is impossible and which is tenable. This finally enables us to recognize that the figures of the heavenly bodies are spherical or circular, and that some are concentric with others.

Once these sciences have been thoroughly mastered, it becomes clear to us that the moon's course is a composite of five distinct motions. We must, therefore, acknowledge [the theorems of] all these sciences as being correct, since it is only by means of them that our hypothesis of the variation of the moon's course by natural law can be upheld.

And now that we have explained the character of knowledge obtained by logical inference, we must note how it may be preserved against defect, for most of the controversies of men and the variation of their evidence center about it or are due to it. We say, then, that when someone declares: "I believe such and such a thing to be true in order not to negate a percept of the senses," we must inquire whether that percept might not be sustained by some other hypothesis than the one he puts forth. For in the latter event his assumption would fall to the ground.

<19> Thus, for example, there are those who believe, because of its whiteness which they observe, that the Milky Way had formerly been circled by the sphere of the sun. However, when we test their hypothesis, we find that another [explanation] is equally possible. This whiteness might, for instance, be an ascending mist,

32. "until . . . figure"—added by Ibn Tibbon and M.

or a permanent particle of fire, or a conglomerate of little stars, or some other such thing. Their allegation, therefore, falls to the ground.

Again, if someone were to say: "I believe such and such a thing to be true in order not to negate a rational concept," we must make inquiry [into the matter]. [For] if that concept could be upheld by a hypothesis other than the one propounded by him, that assumption of his becomes null and void. Thus, for example, there are those who maintain that there exists another earth aside from this one in which we live. Their argument [in support of this view] is that thereby the fire would be located in the center [of the world], it being acknowledged that whatever is highly prized is kept in the center. However, such [a position of distinction] is already accorded by us to man, who dwells on the earth, which is the center of the universe. Their conclusion, therefore, falls to the ground so far as we are concerned.

Suppose, again, that someone were to say: "I believe such and such a thing to be true by way of analogy with what is perceived with the senses." It so happens, however, that that assumption on his part would invalidate another sense percept. In that case one must decide in favor of the more important of the two percepts, and of the arguments that support it. Thus, for example, there are those who maintain that all things were created from water, because animals originate from the humid element. They fail to consider, however, the water's visible tendency to percolate and flow over. It is, therefore, impossible that it should be the origin of all things, since it does not stand up by itself. When, then, in the search for explanatory hypotheses, two such [contradictory phenomena] are encountered, the more important of the two is the more deserving of being accepted as such.

Again, if someone were to say: "I believe such and such a thing to be true by way of analogy with a certain sense percept," but one part of his theory contradicts another, then his theory is null and void. Thus there are those who maintain that the good is that which gives us pleasure, because that is how they feel it to be. They do not recall, however, that the killing of them would please their enemies just as much as the killing of their enemies would please them. The act would consequently be good and evil at one and the same time, [which is, of course,] a contradiction.

Suppose, furthermore, that someone were to say: "I believe such and such a thing to be true for such and such a reason," but upon a thorough investigation of that reason, we find that it leads to a conclusion other than that which he believes to be true. <20> That reason would then be voided. Thus, for example, there is the theory of the proponents of the eternity of the world who declare: "We believe that all things have existed since eternity because we do not regard as real anything except what our senses perceive." However, the fact that they do not regard anything as real except what their senses perceive would prevent them from believing that all things exist since eternity, because it is impossible that they should have perceived in its prime what exists since eternity.

Again someone may say: "I reject such and such a thesis for such and such a reason." Yet thou findest that he ventured into [a theory] more difficult [of entertainment] than the one he had sought to avoid. Thus, for example, certain monotheists shunned the view that God was unable to bring back yesterday in order not to ascribe to Him impotence. They thereby, however, let themselves into something worse by ascribing to God an absurdity, as we shall note in part of the second treatise of this book, if God, exalted be He, is willing.

So, then, if we seek to establish the truth in the domain of knowledge obtained by logical inference, we must guard it against the above-mentioned five types of vitiating factors. [We must,] namely, [make certain] (a) that there is no other [means than the theory in question] of sustaining the truth of what is perceived [with the senses], nor (b) any other [method] of upholding what is [intuitively] apprehended [by reason]. Furthermore (c) it must not invalidate any other [accepted] fact, nor (d) must one part of it contradict another, let alone (e) that a theory be adopted that is worse than the one that has been rejected.

[All] these [precautions are to be taken] in addition to exercising, in the determination of the sense percepts and the rational concepts, such expert care as we have outlined before. Add to these the quality of perseverance until the process of reasoning has been completed, and we have a total of seven points that must be observed to make possible for us the accurate emergence of the truth. Should, therefore, someone come to us with an allegation in the realm of inferential knowledge, we would test his thesis by means of these seven [criteria]. If, upon being rubbed by their touchstone and weighed by their balance, it turns out to be correct as well as acceptable, we shall make use of it. Similarly also must we proceed with the subject matters of authentic tradition—I mean the books of prophecy. However, this is not the place for explaining the properties of these books, something that I have already done for an extensive portion of this subject in the introduction to my commentary on the Torah.

VI

Now someone might, of course, ask: "But how can we take it upon ourselves to indulge in speculation about the objects of knowledge and their investigation to the point where these would be established as convictions according to the laws of geometry and become firmly fixed in the mind, when there are people who disapprove of such an occupation, being of the opinion that speculation leads to unbelief and is conducive to heresy?" Our reply thereto, however, is that such an opinion is held only <21> by the uneducated among them. Thus thou seest the masses of this country labor under the impression that whoever goes to India becomes rich. It has likewise been reported about certain uneducated people of our own nation that they labor under the illusion that something resembling a whale swallows the moon as a result of which it becomes eclipsed. [It is] also [related] about certain uneducated Arabs that they are under the impression that whoever does not have a she-camel slaughtered on his grave is brought to the last judgment on foot. And many other such ridiculous [stories are circulated].

Should one say, however: "But did not the foremost of the sages of the children of Israel forbid this sort of occupation, and especially speculation about the beginning of time and place, saying: *Whoever speculates about the following four matters would have been better off had he not been born; namely, 'What is below and what is above, what was before and what will be behind?'* " (Ḥăgh. 11b), we would reply—and we ask the Merciful One to stand by us—that it is inconceivable that they should have prohibited us from [engaging in genuine speculation]. For did not our Creator Himself enjoin us to do this very thing apropos of authentic tradition, as it is evident from the declaration [of the prophet]: *Know ye not? Hear ye not? Hath it not been told you from the beginning? Have ye not understood the foundations of the earth?* (Isa. 40: 21). Furthermore there is the remark made by the saints to each other: *Let us choose for us that which is right; let us know among ourselves what is good* (Job 34: 4). Extensive statements of a similar nature on this subject were moreover made by the five persons figuring in the Book of Job—I mean, Job, Eliphaz, Bildad, Zophar, and Elihu.

What the sages forbade was only to lay the books of the prophets aside and accept any private notion that might occur to an individual about the beginning of place and time. For whoever speculates in this wise may either hit the mark or miss it. Until he hits it, however, he would be without religious faith, and even when he has hit upon the teaching of religion and has it firmly in hand, he is not secure against being deprived of it again by some uncertainty that might arise in his mind and corrupt his belief. We are agreed, then, on charging one who behaves in this fashion with sin, even though he be a professional thinker. As for ourselves, the congregation of the children of Israel, we engage in research and speculation in a way other than this. It is this method of ours that I wish to describe and clarify with the help of the Merciful One.

<22> Know, then, and may God direct thee aright, Oh thou that studiest this book, that we inquire into and speculate about the matters of our religion with two objectives in mind. One of these is to have verified in fact what we have learned from the

prophets of God theoretically. The second is to refute him who argues against us in regard to anything pertaining to our religion.

Our Master, blessed and exalted be He, has namely given us complete instructions in regard to our religious requirements through the medium of His prophets. [He did this] after [first] confirming for us their possession of the gifts of prophecy by means of [sundry] miracles and marvels. Thus He has enjoined us to accept these matters as binding and observe them. He has furthermore informed us, however, that, if we would engage in speculation and diligent research, inquiry would produce for us in each instance the complete truth, tallying with His announcement to us by the speech of His prophets. Besides that He has given us the assurance that the godless will never be in a position to offer a proof against our religion, nor the skeptics [33] [to produce] an argument against our creed.

These facts are borne out by the statement in which God informs us that all things had a beginning, that He was the Creator who originated them, and that furthermore He was one, having no associate with Him. *Thus saith the Lord, the King of Israel, and his Redeemer, the Lord of hosts: "I am the first, and I am the last, and beside Me there is no God"* (Isa. 44:6).

He tells us also immediately thereafter that, whatever He has commanded or forbidden us to do or informed us about, has been and will be: *And who, as I, can proclaim—let him declare it and set it in order for Me—since I appointed the ancient people? And the things that are coming, and that shall come to pass, let them declare* (Isa. 44:7).

Next He allays our fear of those who disagree with us, stating that they will not be able to prevail against us in argument, nor be successful in producing convincing proof against us. That is the import of His subsequent remark: *Be not afraid, neither fear ye; have I not announced unto thee of old and declared it? And ye are my witnesses. Is there a God beside Me? Yea, there is no Rock; I know not any* (Isa. 44:8).

33. "skeptics"—Ibn Tibbon.

When He says: *Be not afraid,* He means: [Be not afraid] of the character of your opponents, of their numerical strength, their [physical] power and other traits, as He says elsewhere: *And thou fearest continually all the day because of the fury of the oppressor* (Isa. 51:13). The expression *wĕ'al* <23> *tirhu,* again, is equivalent to *wĕ'al tirĕ'u* (neither fear ye), for by the process of substituion the *he* may stand in place of the *'aleph.* He means thereby that ∟we must not stand in fear] of the allegation [of our opponents] or their arguments in themselves. This is borne out by what He says elsewhere: *And thou, son of man, be not afraid of them, neither be afraid of their words* (Ezek. 2:6). In a similar vein it is said: *He that feared the word of the Lord* (Exod. 9:20).

God's statement, moreover, *Have I not announced unto thee of old?* (Isa. 44:8) refers to the prophetic revelations concerning the future. His remark again, *And I declared (ibid.)* has reference to the prophetic revelations concerning the past. Thus, too, does He say elsewhere: *The former things, what are they? Declare ye, that we may consider, and know the end of them; or announce to us the things to come* (Isa. 41:22).

When, furthermore, He says: *And ye are My witnesses* (Isa. 44:8), He alludes to the marvelous signs and the manifest proofs witnessed by the [Jewish] people. These [were revealed] in many forms,[34] such as the visitation of the ten plagues and the cleaving of the [Red] Sea and the assemblage at Sinai. Personally, however, I consider the case of the miracle of the manna as the most amazing of all miracles, because a phenomenon of an enduring nature excites greater wonderment than one of a passing [35] character. Aye it is hard for the mind to conceive of a scheme whereby a people numbering something like two million souls could be nourished for forty years with nothing else than food produced for them in the air by the Creator. For had there been any possibility of thinking up a scheme for achieving something of this nature, the philosophers of old would have been the first to resort to it.

34. "forms"—Ibn Tibbon and M.
35. "passing"—Ibn Tibbon and M.

They would have maintained their disciples therewith, taught them wisdom, and enabled them to dispense with working for a livelihood or asking for help.

Now it is not likely [36] that the forbears of the children of Israel should have been in agreement upon this matter if they had considered it a lie. Such [proof] suffices, then, as the requisite of every authentic tradition. Besides, if they had told their children: "We lived in the wilderness for forty years eating naught except manna," and there had been no basis <24> for that in fact, their children would have answered them: "Now you are telling us a lie. Thou, so and so, is not this thy field, and thou, so and so, is not this thy garden from which you have always derived your sustenance?" This is, then, something that the children would not have accepted by any manner of means.

His statement, again, *Is there a God beside Me?* (*ibid.*) means: "If, now, perchance you be afraid that some of the things, about which I have told you that they had come to pass or some of those concerning which I have told you that they would come to pass, are not true, [that fear on your part might be justified] if a creation had been effected by someone else than Me. In that event I might perhaps not have been posted on what he was making. But inasmuch as I am One, My knowledge embraces everything that I have made and that I will make."

Finally under His statement, *And there is no rock (ṣur) that I do not know* [37] (*ibid.*) are subsumed the distinguished men of the human race and its sages. For the expression *ṣur* may be applied to great men. Scripture says, namely: *Look unto the rock (ṣur) whence ye were hewn and to the hole of the pit whence ye were digged. Look unto Abraham your father, and unto Sarah that bore you* (Isa. 51:1, 2). It says also: *Yea, thou makest the rock (ṣur) turn back his sword, and hast not made him to stand in the battle* [38] (Ps. 89:44). What is meant by the verse under discussion is therefore: "There is no wise or distinguished man that I do not

36. "not likely"—Ibn Tibbon and M.
37. The usual translation is: *Yea, there is no Rock; I know not any.*
38. These quotations are given as in Ibn Tibbon.

know. Hence it is impossible that he should be able to produce an argument against you in the matter of your religion or do injury to your creed, because My knowledge is all-embracing and I have imparted it to you."

In this way, then—may God be merciful unto thee—do we conduct our speculation and inquiry, to the end that we may expound concretely by means of rational intuition and logical inference what our Master has imparted unto us. With this thesis, however, there is intimately bound up a point that we cannot avoid [bringing up]. It consists of the question: "Inasmuch as all matters of religious belief, as imparted to us by our Master, can be attained by means of research and correct speculation, what was the reason that prompted [divine] wisdom to transmit them to us by way of prophecy and support them by means of visible proofs and [39] miracles rather than intellectual demonstrations?"

To this question we should like to give, with the help of God, exalted be He, an adequate answer. We say, then, [that] the All-Wise knew that the conclusions reached by means of the art of speculation could be attained only in the course of a certain measure of <25> time. If, therefore, He had referred us for our acquaintance with His religion to that art alone, we would have remained without religious guidance whatever for a while, until the process of reasoning was completed by us so that we could make use of its conclusions. But many a one of us might never complete the process because of some flaw in his reasoning. Again he might not succeed in making use of its conclusions because he is overcome by worry or overwhelmed by uncertainties that confuse and befuddle him. That is why God, exalted and magnified be He, afforded us a quick relief from all these burdens by sending us His messengers through whom He transmitted messages to us, and by letting us see with our own eyes the signs and the proofs supporting them about which no doubt could prevail and which we could not possibly reject. Thus He said: *Ye yourselves have seen that I have talked with you from heaven* (Exod. 20:19). Furthermore He addressed His messenger in our presence, and made it an ob-

39. "and"—Ibn Tibbon.

ligation to believe him forever, as He said: *That the people may hear when I speak with thee, and may also believe thee forever* (Exod. 19:9).

Thus it became incumbent upon us immediately to accept the religion, together with all that was embraced in it, because its authenticity had been proven by the testimony of the senses. Its acceptance is also incumbent upon anybody to whom it has been transmitted because of the attestation of authentic tradition, as we shall explain. Now God commanded us to take our time with our speculation until we would arrive thereby at these selfsame conclusions. We must, therefore, persevere in this standpoint [40] until the arguments in favor of it have become convincing for us, and we feel compelled to acknowledge God's Torah [that has already been authenticated] by what our eyes have seen and our ears have heard.

So, then, even if it should take a long time for one of us who indulges in speculation to complete his speculation, he is without worry. He who is held back from engaging in such an activity by some impediment will, then, not remain without religious guidance. Furthermore women and young people and those who have no aptitude for speculation can thus also have a perfect and accessible faith, for the knowledge of the senses is common to all men. Praised, then, be the All-Wise, who ordered things thus. Therefore, too, dost thou often see Him include in the Torah <26> the children and the women together with the fathers whenever miracles and marvels are mentioned.

Next I say, in further elucidation of this matter, that one might compare the situation to that of a person who out of a total of 1,000 drachmas weighs out 20 [41] to each of five men, and 16⅔ to each of six, and 14²⁄₇ to each of seven, and 12½ to each of eight, and 11⅑ to each of nine, and who wishes to check with them quickly on how much money is left. So he tells them that the remainder amounts to 500 drachmas, supporting his statement by the weight of the

---

40. "standpoint," i.e., that of the acceptance of the teachings of the Jewish religion.

41. "20"—so according to Landauer's emendation.

money. Once, then, it has been weighed by them [42] quickly and found to be 500 drachmas, they are compelled to credit his statement. Then they can take their time until they find out [that] it [is really so] by way of calculation, each one according to his understanding, and the effort he can put into it and the obstacles he might encounter.

One might further compare this case to that of a person who, upon being informed about an illness accompanied by certain pathological conditions, designates it by a natural symptom [whereby it may be] immediately [recognized], until the diagnostician is able by means of [his] investigations to check the matter.[43]

It behooves us also to believe that even before the era of the children of Israel God never left His creatures without a religion fortified by prophecy and miraculous signs and manifest proofs. Whoever witnessed the latter in person was convinced of their authenticity by what he had perceived with his sense of vision. He, again, to whom it was transmitted, was convinced by what he had grasped by means of his sense of hearing. Thus the Torah says about one of these [who lived before the rise of a Jewish nation]: *For I have known him, to the end that he may command his children* (Gen. 18:19).

VII

To this statement I should like to append what occur to me to be the principal causes responsible for keeping infidels and heretics from believing [in the authenticity of] miracles and marvels, and from engaging in speculation about religious doctrines. <27> Of these I consider eight as being particularly prevalent. The first of these is that human beings find the effort to be naturally burdensome. When, namely, they perceive instinctively a certain matter that ought to be confirmed and corroborated by means of logical proof and be applied practically in religious life, they take flight and run away from it. That is the reason why thou seest many people say: "The truth is burdensome. The truth is bitter." For they

42. "them"—m. Cf. Landauer p. 26, n. 6.
43. "matter"—literally "his quest."

desire freedom [from such burdens] and so they flee from them.[44] Of such persons does Scripture say: *Get you far from the Lord! Unto us is this land given for an inheritance* (Ezek. 11:15). They do not realize, these thoughtless individuals, that if they were [consistently] to obey their natural instinct in its tendency to avoid exertion and effort, they would starve to death by virtue of failing to cultivate [the soil] or to build [homes].

The second is ignorance which predominates among many men. [There are, namely, people] who express themselves foolishly, are lazy in their thinking, and say unreflectingly: "There is nothing at all." And this is what they meditate inwardly also. Of such does Scripture say: *Surely now shall they say: "We have no king; for we feared not the Lord; and the king; what can he do for us?"* (Hos. 10:3). Nor do they consider the fact that if they were to make such inane statements and wild utterances about human rulers, they would court death and destruction.

The third [cause of heresy] is the inclination of the average man toward the gratification of his appetites, such as greediness for every [type of] food and sexual intercourse and acquisition. [On account of this tendency] he hurls himself into such activities hastily [and] without deliberation. It is of individuals of this character that Scripture says: *The fool hath said in his heart: "There is no God."* (Ps. 53:2). A person of this type does not bear in mind the fact that if he were to act in such a manner in the event of illness—nay even when he is well—eating whatever he lusted for and cohabiting with whomever he found, he would perish therefrom and die.

The fourth [cause of heresy] is an aversion to speculation and an incapacity for listening attentively and engaging in sustained thinking. [All this causes the individual] to be easily contented and say: "I have already looked into the matter and this is all I got out of it." Of such a one does Scripture say: *The slothful man (rĕmiyyah) shall not hunt <28> his prey; but the precious substance of men is to be diligent* (Prov. 12:27). The meaning of [this word] *rĕmiyyah* is "one who is without ambition." Such a one does not attain what he needs. Those belonging to this class do not realize

44. "from them"—Ibn Tibbon.

that, if they were to employ such tactics in their worldly affairs, they would never be successful in them.

The fifth [cause] is arrogance and conceit, by which a person is so dominated as not to concede the existence of any wisdom that might be hidden from him or of any science that still has to be mastered by him. Of such a one does Scripture say: *The wicked in the pride of his countenance saith: "He will not require." All his thoughts are: There is no God.* (Ps. 10:4). This type of individual does not perceive that such an argument would do him but little good in the fashioning of a signet ring or in the writing of a letter of the alphabet.

The sixth [cause of heresy] may be a word that a person hears from the mouth of the godless that touches his heart and unnerves it, so that he remains for the rest of his life in this state of nervous prostration, occasioned by this word. It is of such persons that Scripture says: *The words of a whisperer are as dainty morsels and they go down into the innermost parts of the belly* (Prov. 18:8). But why doesn't this [sort of individual] likewise consider the fact that, if he were not to shield himself against heat and cold so that they do not react against him, they [too] would destroy and kill him?

The seventh [cause of heresy] may be some weak, ridiculous argument [in favor of the true belief] that one has heard propounded by a certain monotheist, and that one believes to be typical of all [arguments of this order]. Of persons thus [misled] does Scripture say: *But they laughed them to scorn, and mocked them* (II Chron. 30:10). Now it does not enter the mind of this sort of individual that the fact that a dealer in fine linens does not know how to describe the costly [45] cloths he offers for sale does not diminish their worth.

The eighth, finally, is the animosity existing between a man and certain monotheists. The unfortunate situation causes him to hate, together with his enemies, also their Master whom the latter wor-

45. "costly"—Ibn Tibbon. The Arabic text uses the adjective *dabiḳiyyah*, i.e., a fabric manufactured in Dabiḳ, a town in Egypt (cf. *Jacuts Geographisches Woerterbuch*, ed. F. Wuestenfeld, II, 548), which was world-renowned during the Abbasid period. (See Hitti, *History of the Arabs*. [London 1937], p. 346.)

ship. It is of persons [who permit themselves to be] thus [carried away by their feelings] that Scripture declares: *My zeal hath undone me, because mine adversaries have forgotten Thy words* (Ps. 119:139). Such a fool does not realize that his enemy is incapable of bringing upon him [so great] an evil as he has brought upon himself, since it is not within his enemy's power to subject him in perpetuity to painful torment.

There may, however, exist a person the error of whose way is due to the fact that in the course of his interpretation of the verses of the Bible <29> he noted something that he regarded as objectionable, or that he had prayed to his Master and received no answer from Him or that he had made a request of Him which was not granted. Or [there may be one] who sees evildoers who are not punished, or who takes exception to the continued existence of the rule of the infidels, or who notes how death indiscriminately gathers in all creatures, or who is unable to grasp with his mind the meaning of God's unity or that of the soul or of reward and punishment. [For the benefit of such let me state that] all these and related subjects will be taken up individually by me in the respective treatises to which they belong and in the appropriate chapter. I shall discourse about them according to my ability, and I hope, if God, exalted be He, is willing, to contribute thereby to the welfare of those that venture into this discussion.

VIII

And now that our discussion has reached this point, I deem it proper to make mention of the aim of this book and the number of its treatises. This is to be followed by an elaboration upon each subject, it being noted first what the books of prophecy have to say in each case, after which will be presented the rational proofs, as I have stated previously.

I say, then, that the total number of treatises of which this book consists is ten.

The first treatise [aims to prove] that the world, together with all that is in it, was created in time.

The second treatise [aims to prove] that the Creator, may His greatness be magnified, is one.

The third treatise [is concerned with proving] that He, exalted be He, has issued to mankind commandments as well as prohibitions.

The fourth treatise [deals] with [the subjects of] obedience and disobedience [to God].

The fifth treatise [deals] with good and evil deeds.

The sixth treatise [deals] with the soul and the state of death and the hereafter.

The seventh treatise [deals] with the resurrection of the dead.

The eighth treatise [deals] with the redemption of the children of Israel.

The ninth treatise [deals] with reward and punishment.

The tenth treatise [discusses] the question of the best possible behavior for man in [this] nether abode.

<30> In each treatise I shall begin with [an exposition of] what has been imparted to us by our Lord and of whatever corroboration is furnished by reason. This is to be followed by [a citation of] such diverging views as have been reported to me. In each instance there will be given a statement of the thesis as well as of the arguments against it. I shall conclude with the proofs furnished by prophecy bearing on the subject of the treatise in question. On behalf of myself, as well as of anyone who studies this book, I beseech God to make even our path and to enable me to realize my aspirations on behalf of His people and His saints, for He is attentive and near at hand.

TREATISE I

CONCERNING [THE BELIEF] THAT ALL EXISTING THINGS HAVE BEEN CREATED

EXORDIUM

THE author of the book said: "This treatise starts out with the preliminary observation that whoever ventures into it is seeking [light on] something that has never been beheld with human eyes nor been perceived by the senses, but which he is nevertheless anxious to ascertain by means of rational deduction. [The problem I have reference to] is: 'How did all things come into being before our time?' Now the principal object of his investigation is something so subtle and fine that the senses are unable to grasp it. He therefore endeavors to attain it intellectually. Since, then, it has all along been the intention of the investigator to achieve the object of his investigation in just this manner, therefore once he has found it in the form in which he has sought to find it, it would be improper for him to reject it or to desire to attain it in any other form."

Now as far as the knowledge of how things came into existence before our time is concerned, that is a phenomenon that no rational being has ever personally witnessed. Yet we all strive to attain with our minds things distant and remote from our senses, as the saint has remarked thereon: *That which is far off, and exceeding deep, who can find it out?* (Eccles. 7: 24). When, then, we reach the conclusion that all things were created out of nothing, although our senses have never experienced anything like it, it is not meet for us to reject that conclusion or <31> to say frivolously: "How can we acquiesce in anything the like of which we have never seen?" For our investigation was from the very start of such a nature as to yield for us something the like of which we have not seen. We should rather welcome it and rejoice in it, since we shall thereby have attained what we have sought.

I felt it necessary to make this prefatory observation lest the reader of this book demand that I present to him a visible instance [of the creation] of something out of nothing. I have, therefore, told him by way of anticipation that, if there had been any such possibility, there would have been no need for proof or speculation or deduction. Furthermore we, as well as the rest of humanity, would have been in agreement about its reality and we would not have differed with respect to any of its aspects. The fact is, however, that we are obliged to have recourse to an inquiry that would reveal it to us and to proof that would clarify it for us because this matter is neither visible nor subject to the observation of the senses.

But we are not the only ones to have persuaded themselves to put forward the allegation [about the existence] at the beginning [of creation] of something the like of which we have not seen. All those who venture [into speculation] and logical deduction do likewise. Thus the proponents of the eternity [of the world], too, endeavor [1] to assert the existence of something that has neither beginning nor end, although their senses have never experienced anything that they could have perceived or understood as having neither beginning nor end. Nevertheless they try to establish this rationally. Similarly do the Dualists bestir themselves to affirm the existence of two mutually exclusive and distinct principles, through the union of which the world came into being, although they have never seen two such mutually exclusive and distinct elements nor how they could become united and commingled with each other. Still they try to prove this rationally.

In the same way do the advocates of the doctrine of original matter strive to present it as a sort of formless mass, a thing possessing neither heat nor cold nor wetness or dryness, which, transformed by some force, acquired these four attributes, although their senses had never perceived anything that did not possess one of these four attributes nor how it could be transformed and how [these] four [attributes could] originate in it. Their aim is, then, to apprehend this matter solely by means of logical analogy and reason.

1. "endeavor"—Ibn Tibbon and M.

The same applies to all <32> systems [of thought], as I shall explain. Since, then, the matter stands thus, all those who speculate about the origins of things must have persuaded themselves to acknowledge the existence at the beginning [of creation] of something that has never been beheld by human eyes.

Therefore, O thou that seekest the truth, may God be gracious unto thee, if our discussion yield to thee any conclusion of such a nature as [for example] the doctrine of *creatio ex nihilo,* do not hasten to reject it, since it was precisely something like this that thou didst look for from the beginning of thy quest, and [since] whoever else goes out in search of the truth does likewise. Hear, rather, and realize that thy proofs are stronger than those of the others and that thou art in possession of arguments by means of which thou canst refute any faction of them. Furthermore thou hast over them the advantage of being in possession of miracles and marvels that have been established for thee [as trustworthy]. Therefore hold on to the following three points in every chapter of this book: namely, (*a*) that thy proofs are stronger than those of the others, (*b*) that thou art able to refute anyone that disagrees with thee, and (*c*) that the miracles of thy prophets are a part of thy advantage.

CHAPTER I

And now that I have made this preliminary observation perfectly clear, I say that our Lord, exalted be He, made it known to us that all things were created and that He had created them out of nothing. Thus Scripture says: *In the beginning God created the heaven and the earth* (Gen. 1:1). It says also: *I am the Lord, that maketh all things; that stretched forth the heavens alone; that spread abroad the earth by Myself* (Isa. 44:24). Besides that, all this was verified for us by Him by means of miracles and marvels, so that we accepted it as true.

I next inquired into this matter to see whether it could be supported by reason as it had been verified by prophecy, and I found that it could be thus supported in many ways. Out of the sum of these I shall excerpt [the following] four proofs.

The first is the one from finitude. That is to say: it is certain that heaven and earth are both finite, because the earth is in the center of the universe and the heaven revolves around it. It therefore follows, of necessity, that the force inhering in them be finite, since it is impossible for an infinite force to reside in a finite body, for such a possibility is rejected by all that is known. Now, since the force that maintains these two is finite, it follows necessarily that they must have a beginning and an end.

After this proof had occurred to me, <33> I checked it at leisure, being in no hurry to formulate it until I had verified it. I asked myself: "Perhaps the earth is unlimited in its length, breadth, and depth?" But then I said: "If it were so, the sun could not have encompassed it so as to complete its revolution around it once every day and night, rising repeatedly at its place of rising and setting where it sets, and the same thing holds for the moon and the rest of the stars."

After that I asked [myself]: "Perhaps, then, it is the heavenly bodies that have no finitude?" [On second thought,] however, I reflected: "But how is that possible, seeing that all of them in their entirety move and revolve perpetually around the earth?" For it is inconceivable that it is the section of them that is adjacent to us alone that revolves and that the remainder of them is too large to revolve, for what we understand by the term *heaven* is only this thing that revolves. We have no conception of anything beyond it, let alone that we believe it to be a heaven and maintain that it does not revolve.

Then I went further in my investigation, saying [to myself]: "But perhaps there are many earths and many heavens, each of which heavens encompasses its own earth, so that there would be an infinite number of worlds?" However, I realized that that was impossible from the standpoint of nature, for it is not admissible according to nature that the [element] earth be above that of fire nor that the [element of] air be by nature below that of water, for both fire and air are light, whereas earth and water are both of them heavy. In fact, I knew that if there were in existence a clod [2] of dirt outside of this earth of ours, it would have penetrated through the entire layers of air and fire until it had reached the dirt of this earth. Likewise if there had been a gathering of water aside from these seas of ours, it would have cut through the air and the fire until it had reached these bodies of water.

Thus I arrived at the unshakable conclusion that there was no heaven other than this heaven of ours, nor any earth besides this earth. Also this heaven was finite and so was this earth finite. Now, since <34> their bodies were limited, the force inhering in them too had to be limited, reaching a boundary at which it stopped. Nor could they continue to exist after the cessation of that force, or have been in existence before it came into being.

[Then] I found that Scripture, too, testified to the fact that they were both finite. It says, namely: *From one end of the earth even unto the other end of the earth* (Deut. 13:8); and again: *And from one end of heaven unto the other end of heaven* (Deut. 4:32). It also testifies to the sun's revolving around the earth and to its repetition of this revolution every day, declaring: *The sun also ariseth, and the sun goeth down, and hasteth to his place where he ariseth* (Eccles. 1:5).

The second proof is [derived] from the combination of parts and the composition of divisions. That is to say, I noted that bodies consisted of a combination of parts and a composition of connecting links. Therein were clearly revealed to me signs of the handiwork of the Maker, as well as of creation.

Thereupon I said [to myself]: "But perhaps these links and joints are to be found only in the small bodies—I mean the bodies of animals and plants?" So I extended my thought toward the earth and, behold, it was like that also, for it is made up of an aggregation of dust and stones and sand and the like. I then lifted up my thought to heaven and I found that it consisted of many layers of spheres, one within the other, in which were set individual

2. "clod"—Ibn Tibbon. The corresponding term in the Arabic original has not been identified.

luminaries called "stars," of varying sizes, large and small, and of varying degrees of luminosity, great and little, all of them fitted into these spheres.

When, then, there became evident to me this aggregation and combination and composition—which [could be construed only as] things created—in the body of heaven and outside of it, I was convinced because of this proof also that the heaven and all that it contained was created.

I furthermore found Scripture saying that the division of the parts of the animals and their combination points to their having been created. That is [the implication of] its statement with reference to man: *Thy hands have made me and fashioned me* (Ps. 119:73). [It is implied] also [in] its statement about the earth: <35> *That formed the earth and made it, He established it* (Isa. 45:18); and its statement about the heaven: *When I behold Thy heavens, the work of Thy fingers, the moon and the stars, which Thou hast established* (Ps. 8:4).

The third proof is [taken] from the accidents. That is to say, I found that no bodies were free from accidents, either such as arise in each of these bodies themselves or from external sources. Thus animals grow and increase in size until they have reached maturity. Then they diminish again and their parts disintegrate.

Thereupon I said [to myself]: "But perhaps the earth is immune from these accidents?" So I studied the earth carefully, and I found that it was never without plants and animals, both of which are, so far as their bodies are concerned, created, and it is well known that whatever is inseparable from what is created is like the latter in its nature.

Next I said [to myself]: "But perhaps the heavenly bodies are immune from such accidents?" So I observed them clearly, and behold they could not be ridded of these accidents, for the first and principal one of these accidents was that of continuous, unceasing motion. In fact [they are subject to] many motions, varying to such an extent that by comparing them with one another thou discoverest their slowness or their speed. Among these [accidents] must also be included the light shed by some upon others, resulting in the illumination of the latter, as happens in the case of the moon. Another accident is the assumption by certain stars of a whitish, reddish, yellowish, or greenish coloration.

When, then, I found that these accidents extended to these [heavenly bodies also], and that the latter did not precede their accidents in time, I was fully convinced that whatever did not precede its accident in coming into being must be like this accident in nature, since the latter is included in the definition of the former. Furthermore there is the statement of Scripture to the effect that the accidents of earth and heaven prove that both of them had a beginning. It says, namely: *I have made the earth, and created man upon it; I, even My hands, have stretched out the heavens, and all their hosts have I commanded* (Isa. 45:12).

<36> The fourth proof is [based] on [the conception of] time. That is to say, I know that there are three [distinct] periods of time: past, present, and future. Now even though the present is shorter than any moment of time, I assumed, [for the sake of argument,] that this present moment is a point, and said [to myself]: "Let it be supposed that a person should desire mentally to advance in time above this point. He would be unable to do it for the reason that time is infinite, and what is infinite cannot be completely traversed mentally in a fashion ascending [backward to the beginning]."

Now this same reason makes it impossible for existence to have traversed infinity in descending fashion so as to reach us. But if existence had not reached us, we would not have come into being. The necessary conclusion from this premise would, then, have been that we, the company of those that are, are not, and that those that exist do not exist. Since, however, I find that I do exist, I know that existence has traversed the whole length of time until it reached me and that, if it were not for the fact that time is finite, existence could not have traversed it.

I also applied this conviction of mine to future time as unhesitatingly as I had done it to the past. Moreover I found Scripture making a similar remark about distant time: *All men have looked thereon; man beholdeth it afar off* (Job 36:25). Furthermore the saint said: *I will fetch my knowledge from afar, and will ascribe righteousness to my Maker* (Job 36: 3).

Now it has come to my attention that a certain heretic, who happened to meet a monotheist other than myself, argued against this proof, saying: "Is it possible that a human being should be able to traverse by walking something that consists of an infinite number of parts?" For any mile or ell that a person might travel would be found by us, if we pondered it in our mind, to be divisible into an infinite number of parts.

Certain thinkers, therefore, had recourse to the theory of atoms, whilst others advanced the hypothesis of the leap from particle to particle. Still others proposed [as a solution of the problem] the theory of the coincidence of an infinite number of [3] particles of time with an infinite number of particles of space.

Now I studied this argument [that was presented by the heretic], and I found it to be deceiving, because the infinite divisibility of a thing can occur so far as we are concerned, only virtually. It cannot possibly occur <37> in fact, because it is too subtle to be realized in actuality or for division to take place in it. Now if [it had been asserted that] the past time was traversed by existence only virtually and not in reality, then, as sure as I live, this would have been practically identical with the argument [presented by the heretic]. But since [it is maintained that] existence traversed the time in question in fact until it reached us, this theory constitutes no argument against our proof, since it [alleges an act that] is only virtual.

In addition to these four proofs I have also others, some of which I have noted down in my commentary on the Book of Genesis, while others have been recorded by me in "the Laws of Creation" [4] and in my book of refutation against *Hiwwi, the Balchite*, aside from further incidental remarks to be found in the rest of my works. Nevertheless the arguments that I cite in this treatise in refutation of the opponents of this thesis of mine are all of them basic for this thesis, serving to corroborate and confirm it.

3. "an infinite number of"—literally "many."
4. i.e., the mystical *Sepher Yĕṣirah*.

They should, therefore, be investigated, and whatever in them is germane to this view be adduced [as proof].

CHAPTER II

Once, then, it had become perfectly clear to us that all things were created, I inquired further as to whether they could possibly have made themselves, or if it be allowable only that someone external to them had made them. It seemed impossible to me, however, that they should have created themselves for sundry reasons, of which I shall mention three.

The first reason is that we know that any body among the things that exist, that we might point to or assume as having made itself, would be in a stronger position and better able to reproduce its like after having come into being than before. If, then, it had made itself when it was weak, why should it not also produce its like when it is strong? Since, however, it is incapable of producing its like when it is strong, it is incredible that it should have done that when it was weak.

The second reason is that, if we were to suppose that a thing could make itself, we would find such a hypothesis to be untenable for <38> either of the two [main] divisions of time. For, if we were willing to grant that it made itself *before* it had come into being, we know that it was then nonexistent and what does not exist does not effect anything. If, on the other hand, we were to grant that it had made itself after it had come into being, then since its existence preceded its reproduction of itself, it would have no further need, because of its preëxistence, for reproducing itself. And there is no third division of time to be considered except for the present moment, which does not lend itself to any action.

The third reason is that, if we are to assume that a body is capable of making itself, such an assumption is admissible only provided we assume that it is capable of desisting from making itself also. But if we were to make such an assumption, we would obtain as a result something that exists and that does not exist at one and the same time. For, when we affirm about something that it is capable, we have reference to what is in existence, whereas, when we associate with it the allegation that it does not produce itself, that is equivalent to the affirmation that it does not exist. Now any hypothesis that is conducive to the identification at any given moment of the existent and the nonexistent is absolutely absurd.

I also found that Scripture had long ago remarked about the absurdity of the theory that a thing could produce itself. [That is] the import of its statement: *It is He that hath made us and not we* [5] (Ps. 100: 3). It is, furthermore, [implicit] in God's displeasure with him who had said: *My river is my own and I had made myself* (Ezek. 29: 3), and the latter's punishment by Him on account of that remark.

After these considerations, which proved to me the untenability of the hypothesis that a thing could create itself and which led to the necessary conclusion that someone outside of itself must have created it, I inquired by means of the art of speculation whether its Maker had created it out of something else, or [whether He had done it] out of nothing as it has been transmitted in the Holy Scriptures. I found, however, that to entertain the thought that it was created out of something else would be a mistake, because it would constitute a contradiction. For our statement "created it" necessarily implies that its essence has been produced for the first time and originated just then. Again, when we ponder the meaning of the expression "out of something," we are compelled to regard its essence as being eternal, not having been produced for the first time or originated at a particular moment. When, therefore, we entertain the notion of a thing's having been created out of nothing, we find it to be a tenable hypothesis.

Now, of course, someone might say: "Thou hast <39> made it evident that things must have a Maker only because thou dost not behold in the sensual world anything made that is not the product of a maker, nor any effect that is not the handiwork of an author. But thou hast likewise never seen in the sensual world anything being generated except it be from something else. How,

5. Saadia follows the kĕthibh rather than the kĕri, according to which the translation would be: *It is He that hath made us, and we are His.*

then, didst thou base thy proof on the premise that there can be no act without an agent rather than the premise that a thing can be produced only out of another, seeing that these two assertions are of equal force?"

My reply to him is: The reason for my preferring the one to the other is that the question of whether all things are generated from others or are created *ex nihilo* is the point I am seeking to prove by means of logical demonstration. Also it is not seemly that the thing that one desires to demonstrate testify concerning itself by serving as one of the two premises on which the proof is based. It must rather be demonstrated by means of a proposition other than itself. Since, then, the proposition, "there is no act that does not stem from an agent," is extraneous to the matter the truth of which we are seeking to establish, I have selected it for the purpose of demonstrating the latter. Thus did I arrive at the conclusion that things have been created out of nothing. I have chosen this method of using outside proof only, even though I have found that in certain cases the employment of the conclusion as one of the premises is admissible. However, the discussion of this point is too subtle and goes beyond the scheme of this book. I have therefore refrained from dwelling on it, making use only of such [arguments as are] perfectly evident.

Now it also became clear to me that whatever we might assume to have been the source from which existing things have been created it must necessarily be eternal, and if it is eternal, it is equal in its eternity with the Creator. Now the necessary implication of this thesis would be that the Creator is unable to create any part of it, and that it does not accept His command to be made in accordance with His wish and to be fashioned according to His desire, unless, by way of supposition, we associate with these two a third cause which differentiates between them so that one of them thereby becomes the maker and the other the product. To propound such a hypothesis, however, is to speak of [a creature] that does not exist, since all things present themselves to us only [in the form of] either maker or product.

I recalled also that the chief object of our quest was to determine who had created the essence of things, it being understood by us that the maker must precede <40> his handiwork, so that by his preceding the essence of the thing the thing itself would come to be created. If, however, we assume the essence of things to have existed since eternity, then the maker cannot have preceded his handiwork, and neither would be more deserving of being the cause of the creation of the other—which is, of course, sheer nonsense.

I recalled, furthermore, that if a person followed [to its logical conclusion] the assertion that God had created things out of something, it would lead him to believe that God did not create anything at all. That is to say that the cause of the prevailing impression that things are generated from others is that we find that the sensual world is thus constituted. But we might just as well say that whatever is perceived with the senses is also found to be located in space and time and to possess form and dimension and position and relationship and other such attributes. For in this respect of being characteristic of things sensual these attributes are all of the same order as the creation of one thing from another. If, then, we were to enumerate the actual characteristics of things exhaustively to the point of asserting that a certain thing was created from another, which existed at a certain place and time and in a certain form and dimension and position and relationship and the like, all these categories would be eternal and there would in that case be nothing left for the Creator to create, and creation would be voided altogether.

I determined also that, unless we conceded the existence of a thing that was preceded by nothing, it would be impossible for anything to exist at all. That is to say: if we were to consider, for the sake of argument, one thing that was derived from another thing, then the second thing that was mentioned would have to be of the same character as the first. That is [its existence] would be conditioned upon its origination only from a third thing. This third thing again would have to be of the same character as the second. That is [its existence] too would be conditioned on its coming into being only from a fourth thing. Thus the process would continue *ad infinitum,* and since the infinite cannot be completely traversed, so that we might come to be, the necessary conclusion would be that we do not exist. The fact is, however, that we do exist. Yet if the things that were prior to our existence had not been finite, they could not have been completed so as to make possible our existence.

<41> This conclusion that we have reached by means of our reasoning is precisely what is written down in the books of the prophets; namely, that all bodies trace their origin to the Creator. That is the tenor of the statement of Scripture: *Before the mountains were brought forth, or ever thou hadst formed the earth and the world, even from everlasting to everlasting Thou art God* (Ps. 90:2).

CHAPTER III

I have now succeeded in verifying by the speculative method, just as they have been borne out by the account of the prophets and the miracles, the three above-mentioned principles: namely, (*a*) that all things were created in time, (*b*) that their Creator was someone else than they, and (*c*) that He had created them out of nothing. This constitutes the first theory [to be listed] in this treatise, the aim of which was to inquire into the beginning of the world. It behooves me, therefore, to append thereto twelve theories of those who disagree with me in regard to this doctrine, making a total of thirteen. My procedure will be to expatiate on the arguments advanced by each faction as well as their refutation, and if there be in the Scriptures any statements seemingly lending color to their views,[6] I shall elucidate them, too, with the help of God.

I say, then, that the second theory is that of him who asserts that the bodies had a Creator, who had at His disposal eternal spiritual beings out of whom He created the above-mentioned composite bodies. This view is supported by its proponents by the thesis that a thing can come into being only from another thing. Soaring upward in their flight of thought and attempting to picture to them-

6. "statements . . . views"—literally "resemblances."

selves how the Creator created composite things out of spiritual
beings, they declare: "We picture to ourselves that He collected
little points of these spiritual beings; namely indivisible atoms—
which they conceive to be as fine as the finest particles of dust—
and made of them a straight line. Then He cut that line into two
halves. Next He superimposed one upon the other crosswise so
as to form the figure of the Greek letter X, which resembles that of
the *Lam 'Alif* in Arabic without the base. Then he fastened them
together at the point of their juncture. After that, He cut them at
the place where they were fastened together and made out of one of
the pieces the large uppermost sphere, whilst out of the other He
made the little spheres. Next He fashioned from these spiritual
particles a cone-shaped figure and created out of it the sphere of
fire. <42> Then He fashioned out of them an octahedron and
created therefrom the sphere of earth. Then He fashioned out of
them a dodecahedron and made with it the sphere of the air. Then
He fashioned out of them an icosahedron and created from it all
the water."

Now they decided upon this hypothesis and adopted it as their
unshakable belief. What led them to propound it was the fact that
they did not acknowledge the existence of anything that was contrary to the observation of their senses. As for these figures, which
they took such great pains [to invent], the reason [for adopting
them] was their resemblance to the figures found in nature.

Let me now make an exposition of the objections against the
theory advanced by these individuals in this connection. I say that
there are twelve refutations that may be cited against their assertions. These include the first four that have demonstrated to us
previously that all things were created in time. They embrace also
the last four that have demonstrated to us that the Creator of things
had created them out of nothing. In addition to being subject to
these eight refutations, I find that there are four others which they
must face.

The first of these objections is that they profess the belief in something that has no parallel among things visible; namely, the spiritual beings, which they picture as being like the dust, and strands

of hair, and like the very finest of the fine, and like an indivisible atom—which is something that cannot be conceived.

Secondly, as I see it, these things, which they maintain exist, cannot possibly be hot or cold or moist or dry, since these four natural characteristics [7] were created from these beings themselves. As I see it also, they cannot possess color or taste or smell or limit or dimension. Nor can they be [described] as many or few in number, or be [said to have been created] in space or time, because all these categories are attributes applying to material bodies, whereas these beings preceded, in their opinion, the bodily state. This is, then, still more inconceivable. The proponents of this theory did, therefore, avoid the hypothesis of *creatio ex nihilo* on account of its improbability, only to let themselves in for something that is even more improbable and remote.

Thirdly, I consider <43> as remote—nay, as utterly untenable—the notion that a thing that is formless can be changed so as to assume the form of fire and water and air and earth; and that what is neither long nor wide nor deep can be so modeled that there would be produced in it length and width and depth; and that what possesses none of the categories can so be altered as to acquire all those characteristics that are at present visible [in things]. If, however, they hold that these transformations and changes are possible, it is because the All-Wise Creator is able to effect them. His wisdom and power must, therefore, have been capable of *creatio ex nihilo,* and we may drop the hypothesis of these non-existent spiritual beings.

Fourthly, the trouble to which they went in assuming a scission and a union and a superimposition and a fixation and a second scission, and whatever else was connected with these operations, was fruitless, since there was no proof to uphold anything thereof. These assumptions are, therefore, pure conjecture and fancy. Nay I see in this process of reasoning an inherent contradiction. For if, as they would have it, the Maker has the power to transform spiritual into corporeal beings, then He should be able to do it at one blow. That would render the detailing of the operation into sections un-

7. "natural characteristics"—added by Ibn Tibbon.

necessary. If, on the other hand, He could, in their opinion, carry them out only piecemeal just as His creatures produce one thing after another, He would all the less be able to transform them from the spiritual to the corporeal state. Whilst, then, they tolerated all these absurdities, they rejected those marvelous miracles mentioned in Scripture. Yet [with all that] they did not desist from conceding the reality of what is not subject to the perception of the senses.

It has also been reported to me that certain persons of our own people were under the impression that the subject referred to by Scripture in its statement: *The Lord has made me as the beginning of His way, the first of His works of old* (Prov. 8:22), as well as in the rest of that passage, was these spiritual beings. Now I considered the matter carefully and I found that they had erred in the interpretation of this passage on fifteen counts. Twelve of these are the twelve refutations from the standpoint of reason upon which I have previously elaborated. As for the other three, they are due to [a misunderstanding of] the character <44> of the Hebrew language and the style of the Bible.

The first of these is that the expression *ḳanani* refers to the creation of a thing. Thus Scripture says elsewhere: *The Most High Creator (ḳone) of heaven and earth* (Gen. 14:22). It says, furthermore: *The earth is full of Thy creatures (ḳinyanekha)* (Ps. 104:24). Should they, however, insist that this expression affirms eternity, then they would be maintaining that heaven and earth and whatever is between them are eternal, having existed always, and they would be denying that they had been created out of spiritual beings, which was what they had intended to prove. If, on the other hand, in their opinion the expression *ḳinyan*, as employed with regard to heaven and earth, affirmed their creation, it would automatically affirm the creation of the spiritual beings.

The second [count on which they are wrong] is that the expression *rešith darko* (the beginning of His way) points to the connotation of "an original creation," because a similar term is used with regard to the largest of the beasts; namely, *He is the beginning (rešith) of the ways of God* (Job 40:19). Now just as the connotation of the expression there is that that particular creature was the first beast to be created, so must also its connotation here [i.e. in Prov. 8: 22] be that what is mentioned here is the first thing to have been created. Should they, therefore, reject this interpretation, they would be affirming that that particular beast [of Job 40: 1] was also eternal, having always been in existence.

The third [count on which they are mistaken] is that the subject mentioned [in the passage of Scripture under discussion] loves the truth and spurns falsehood, as it says: *All the words of my mouth are in righteousness, there is nothing perverse or crooked in them* (Prov. 8:8). Whoever loves it, [furthermore], has chosen life, and whoever spurns it loves death, as it says: *For whoso findeth me, findeth life, . . . but he that misseth me, wrongeth his own soul; all they that hate me love death* (Prov. 8: 35, 36).[8] Finally there is the injunction to seek it out and hold on to it carefully, as it says: *Now, therefore, ye children, hearken unto me,* etc.[8] (Prov. 8: 32.)

Now, if the subject [of the aforementioned passage] were identical with the [supposedly uncreated] spiritual beings, the attributes listed would have to appertain to them either in their [original] simple state or after they had attained their composite status. But if we were to assume that these attributes appertained to them in their simple state, [that would be an absurdity since] there would not be within their competence at that time [such concepts as] truthfulness or mendacity, nor [such conditions as] life or death, nor would there be in existence any creature <45> to seek them out and reach them. If, again, we assumed that these attributes appertained to them after they had attained the composite status, then that part of these beings which is with us would necessarily be within our reach. The remaining portion, however, that has not reached the composite stage, would be inaccessible to us, since, according to their theory, the composite things constitute a partition between us and it.

It has, furthermore, been reported to me that others thought that the scriptural passage: *But wisdom, where shall it be found? And*

8. Our translation follows the version of Ibn Tibbon.

where is the place of understanding? (Job 28:12), as well as the rest of that passage, was a description of the spiritual beings because the end of it states: *God understandeth the way thereof, and He knoweth the place thereof* (Job 28:23). But I found that these also were guilty of an error of interpretation, even more clearly than those previously mentioned. True, in the first passage quoted by us there is no explicit statement [to the effect] that [its subject] is *Wisdom,* although there is really no doubt that it was spoken about *Wisdom.* As for this second passage, however, the mention of *Wisdom* in it is explicit. How, then, could they have deluded themselves into interpreting it figuratively?

I see, also, that Scripture explains that this *Wisdom* in question came into existence only contemporaneously with the creation of the four elements, not prior thereto. For after declaring, *God understandeth the way thereof, and He knoweth the place thereof,* it says: *For He looketh to the ends of the earth, and seeth under the whole heaven* (Job 28:24). The mention of earth and heaven is followed [immediately] by [the statement:] *When He maketh a weight for the wind, and meteth out the waters by measure* (Job 28:25). The mention [again] of the air and the water is followed by [the remark:] *He established it, yea, and searched it out* (Job 28:27).

The untenability of the interpretation of these two passages as referring to [uncreated] spiritual beings has thus been clearly demonstrated. They are concerned, rather, with *Wisdom.* What they mean to indicate is not that this *Wisdom* served the Creator as the instrument whereby He created all things,[9] but that He revealed this *Wisdom* at the time when He created the elements and their derivatives, His wisdom becoming manifest when He so wisely created all that.

The third theory is that of him who asserts that <46> the Creator of the bodies had created them out of His own substance. I have found the proponents of this view to be people who are unable to deny the existence of a maker. Yet their reason would not,

9. The interpretation adopted by Saadia here rejects that given to this passage at the beginning of Genesis Rabba.

so they maintain, [allow them to] accept the doctrine of *creatio ex nihilo*. Since, then, originally nothing existed except the Creator, they believe that He created all things out of Himself.

These are, however, may God have mercy on thee, more senseless than the proponents of the theory mentioned previously, and I shall expose their shallowness [10] in thirteen ways. Of these, eight [11] are identical with the arguments cited against the advocates of the doctrine of the spiritual beings; namely, the four proofs [in favor of] creation in time and the four [in favor] of *creatio ex nihilo*. As for the four types of refutation [of the doctrine] of the eternity of the spiritual beings, they do not apply to them. They are, however, subject instead to five others, each of which [attacks a notion that] is rejected by reason.

The first [objection] is [directed against the belief] that an eternal being, that is subject to neither form nor quality nor dimension nor limit nor place nor time, can so be changed that a part of it becomes a body possessing form and dimension and qualities and place and time and other attributes belonging to corporeal beings. This is only most remotely conceivable.

The second is [the assumption] that the All-Wise, who is immune against all pain and unaffected by action and not subject to accidents, should choose to turn a portion of Himself into a body so that He would become exposed to accidents and be affected by action, and suffer loss of knowledge after having been endowed with wisdom, and be in pain after enjoying complete repose, and experience hunger and thirst and sadness and fatigue and become subject to other such evils, when He has always been immune from all these things. Besides, He has no need for securing advantages by such means, especially since it is not at all likely that He would secure any advantage thereby. Such an idea partakes, then, of the characteristics of the absurd.

The third [difficulty presented by this theory] is how the righteous God, who does no injustice, could have decided to hurl a certain portion of Himself into such misfortunes. Indeed, when I

10. "shallowness"—literally "folly."
11. The original, as well as Ibn Tibbon, mistakenly reads "four."

try to fathom [12] this matter, I find one of the following two alternatives to be inescapable: either this misfortune had been incurred
by the part in question <47> deservedly—and it could have
merited such punishment only because of some crime it had committed or certain reprehensible acts that it had perpetrated—or
else it had come about undeservedly, which would be a wrong and
an injustice against it. From whichever one of the two directions
one would approach the notion, one would find it to be unsound
and false.

The fourth [difficulty presented by this theory] is how the portion of God in question accepted the command of the remaining
parts so as to receive impression and shape and form and expose
itself to pain. Was this due to some fear that it entertained, or to
some expectation that it cherished? To whichever of these two
causes this self-subordination may have been due, it must be the
characteristic of either the whole to entertain fear and hope, or of
the part only. But if it be the characteristic of the whole, what,
pray, should it be afraid of or hope for, seeing that there is no being
outside of it? If, on the other hand, it be the characteristic of the
part, what could have caused the part to entertain such hope and
fear when the rest is given to neither hope nor fear? If, again,
the acceptance by the part of the command of the greater portion
was due not to expectation or fear, that would be a poor [solution
of the problem], since its action would then remain without a
cause known to us. All this is, therefore, false and wrong.

The fifth [objection to this theory] is that it is inconceivable
that one endowed with intelligence, who is capable of averting pain
from portions of himself, would not avert it. But if we were to
entertain the supposition that he would do that, that would spell
the end of all creation.

Again, if [the coming into being of the created things] after
[the deliverance from pain of the part of God in question] is as
unavoidable as [their coming into being] prior [to that event],
then these portions would successively [13] become transformed into

12. "fathom"—Ibn Tibbon.
13. "successively"—or "alternately."

bodies. Each part of them would thereupon receive material shape and form for a certain length of time, and then be delivered and removed, while another part would take its place and become the recipient of the action. With all that, however, it is impossible that this series of periodic successions [14] should ever come to an end, since the totality from which the parts are derived is infinite. This is, therefore, a hypothesis that is rejected by reason and negated by sound reflection.

Now I account these senseless individuals, who have eschewed <48> the doctrine of *creatio ex nihilo* only to accept these nonsensical ideas, as behaving exactly like those who run away from the heat to a glowing hot stone, or from the rain to the gutters, to say nothing of their rejection [15] of the miracles and marvels [mentioned in Scripture].

The fourth theory is that of him who combines the two previously described hypotheses. It maintains that the Creator had created all existing things from His own substance as well as from things coeternal with him. According to it, the spirits are derived from the Creator and the bodies from the things coeternal with Him.

This theory is subject to the following seventeen refutations: namely, the twelve first-mentioned applying to the proponents of the doctrine of the spiritual beings, and the five appertaining to him who maintains that the Creator created everything from Himself. The advocate of this theory is, however, more senseless than the two preceding factions. If all these absurdities were entertained by them, it was due solely to [their false conception of] the omnipotence of the Creator, whom they regarded capable of every absurdity, such as changing Himself and whatever is connected therewith. It seems to me, however, that to regard Him as capable of creating something out of nothing is more easily comprehensible for the soul and rationally more plausible, besides being in keeping with the miracles and marvels [of God].

The fifth theory is that of him who asserts the existence of two

14. "successions"—or "alternations."
15. "their rejection"—Ibn Tibbon.

eternal creators. Those that profess it are, may God guide thee aright, more senseless than all those previously mentioned. They, namely, deny the possibility that two opposing acts could originate from one author, [merely] for the reason that, [as] they maintain, they had never seen anything like it.

Starting out with this conclusion of theirs, they declare: "We see that all things contain elements of good and evil, and harm and benefit. The good that is in them is, therefore, necessarily derived from a principle that is entirely good, whilst the evil that is in them is derived from a principle that is entirely evil." This, then, leads them to affirm that the source of the good is limitless in five directions: namely, the upward [direction], the east, the west, the south, and the north, while it has a limit downward where it touches the source of evil. Likewise <49> the source of evil is limitless in five directions: namely, the downward [direction], the east, the west, the south, and the north, while it has a limit upward where it touches the source of the good.

They maintain also that these two principles were originally always separated. Then they became commingled, and as a result of their mixture, the bodily substances came into being. However, they differ in regard to the cause of this mixture, some of them maintaining that it was due to the fact that the good was anxious to soften the edge of the evil that was contiguous with it, whereas others maintain that it was due to the evil's desire to enjoy whatever was pleasant in the good. Yet they agree herein: namely, that this mixture is destined to last only for a while, and that once this term is ended, victory will belong unto the good, while the evil will be subordinated and its activity cease.[16]

Let me now note down my objections to each individual assertion of these people. In the first place, I cite against them the four arguments whereby we demonstrated that all bodies have been created. Next [I invoke] the four arguments whereby we demonstrated that they came into being out of nothing. Then [come] the five arguments advanced against the assertion of him who maintains that the Creator created them out of Himself. This

16. Cf. Guttmann pp. 55 ff. for the sources.

makes a total of thirteen. In addition, there may be [urged] against them in this treatise fifteen special types of refutation, aside from those contained in the second treatise of this book. In other words, I took the axles of their thesis and wound around them the spiral of reason so that they were dislodged thereby and naught remained of them.

Now I first turned my attention to their assertion that there is no visible instance of two opposite acts emanating from the same author, and I found that the possibility of the emanation of two acts from one author could be demonstrated by [many] examples. One of these is that we [often] see a person become enraged and angry, and then become consoled and reconciled again, saying: "I am satisfied and have forgiven." Now if it is the good in him that forgives, then that is also the thing which was enraged. If, on the other hand, it is the evil that forgives, then that person performs a good deed when he forgives. In either case <50> the two opposite acts emanated from one and the same person.

Again we see a person commit murder or theft. Then, when forced to confess, he avows his crime and his misdeed. Now if it is the evil in him that confesses, then it is also that principle in him which has spoken the truth—and veracity is a good. If, on the other hand, it is the good in him that confesses, it is also that principle in him which committed murder or theft. In either case, then, the two opposite acts have been clearly established as going back to one author. And even if [it be granted that] the faculty of anger is not identical with that of conciliation, and similarly that the impulse to steal is not identical with that which makes one confess, it would be necessary for him who becomes reconciled in his conciliatory state not to remember what happened to him at the moment of his anger, and for him who confesses not to remember, while he makes confession, what happened to him when he committed his crime. Yet we find all this to be contradicted by the observation of our senses.

Next I considered the allegation by the proponents of this theory apropos of the possibility of the emanation of one and the same act from two authors. This, however, is untenable for two reasons.

One is that if we were to assume that two persons were making one and the same object and we were to suppose that one of them was making all of it and the other was also making all of it, that would be an absurdity, because once the first individual has made all of the object, there is nothing left for the second to make. If, again, we were to suppose that one of them was making a part of the object and the other another part, then every product would have had one distinct maker who had nobody associated with him in its production.

The second reason for the untenability of the above-mentioned hypothesis is that if it be conceivable that two things could perform one and the same act, it must also inevitably be held that just as each of them is capable of doing the thing in question, it is also capable of desisting from the act. Now suppose we were to assume the existence of two opposing choices with regard to the same act, one of the would-be authors choosing to perform that act whilst the other chooses to desist therefrom, that would mean hypothesizing something that is at once produced and not produced, which is a clear contradiction.

Thou seest, then, how they deny what is affirmed by visible testimony and avow what is disproven by such evidence. Thus <51> we have a total of five refutations, three of them refuting their denial of the possibility of the derivation of two opposite acts from one author and two invalidating their affirmation that one act can emanate from two authors.

Furthermore let me state that they eschewed the doctrine of *creatio ex nihilo* on the ground that they had never seen anything like it, only to throw themselves into the morass of something the like of which they had never seen either. They avowed, namely, in the first instance, that each of the two above-named principles was limitless in five directions, when in reality what they noted with their senses was only the limit on the sixth side. They refused, then, to conclude that the five sides that they had not seen were limited on the analogy of the sixth which they had seen, but concluded the contrary instead.

Moreover, according to their hypothesis, the greater portion of each of the two principles is found in isolation and in the unmixed state. Yet whatever they have been able to perceive thereof they have perceived only in mixture. They refused, then, to acknowledge that the whole might be mixed on the analogy of the part perceived by them, but adopted the contrary view.

Also if they maintain that the mixture was something created, not an eternal state, and that it was not preceded by any other mixture, whence did they obtain this notion? Is it not possible that the two above-named principles had perpetually been mingling with each other and separated from one another again innumerable times? Finally, what is the basis of their allegation that after a while these two opposing principles, that had become commingled, would separate once more? Is it not possible that, in keeping with present observation, they will never separate, or if they will separate, they may mingle again indefinitely in the future?

Mark, then, how they eschewed the doctrine of *creatio ex nihilo* on the ground that they had never seen anything like it, and yet accepted that of the existence of unmixed parts that were without limit besides, and the theory of a mixture that was not preceded by any other mixture, and of a separation that would not be followed by any further mixture. [They did this] notwithstanding the fact that they had never seen any of these things, but, on the contrary, noted that reality contradicted all that. These constitute, then, four further refutations.

Next I inquired into the two causes <52> that they present for the mixture [which they allege to have taken place] and I found that they were both unsound. For if, as some of them declare, the act of mingling was due to the tendency of the good [principle], that [principle] has become evil by virtue of intending to mingle with the [principle of] evil. If, again, it was due to the tendency of the evil [principle], that [principle] has been transformed into goodness by its striving for the good. Whichever of these two hypotheses happens to be true, a transformation will have taken place in the subject. But this the proponents of this theory refuse to admit.

Also if the mixture [of the two principles] was due to the activity of the good, it has not attained its object of mellowing the side [of the principle of evil] which is supposedly contiguous with it. On the contrary, we note that its pain resulting from its entrance into the [principle of] evil is greater than it would have been as a result of mere contact. On the other hand, if the act of mingling was due to the [principle of] evil, it did attain the object of its desire. In fact we note the pleasure it derives from its mingling with the good, by eating and drinking thereof and inhaling its fragrance and embracing it. In either case, however, we must give up all hope in the triumph of the good over the evil.

After this I considered the question of how [two originally separate principles] could mingle, and I noted that such a possibility was contradicted by the observation of the senses. For we see that fire has a disinclination for uniting with water, and that the air eschews mingling with the [element of] earth. If, then, this incompatibility applies to these few portions of the two principles, how much more would it be true of their many other parts! Hence the mixture could never be realized. This, now, is clear and evident.

If, therefore, these advocates [of dualism] base their position on logical proof, we present against their view the last three refutations. On the other hand, if they make their assertion from the standpoint of revelation, then let them be mindful of the fact that authentic revelation can come about only by means of prophecy. However, no prophet could have come into being until after the above-mentioned mixture had taken place. Hence their theory is here subject to three invalidating arguments.

The first is that since the prophet makes his appearance in the world after separating from his source, which is the pure good, he cannot know anything about the destiny of that source. The second is that, by virtue of his mingling with the evil, the prophet's veracity would become impaired, with the result that the souls of men would not repose confidence in him any more. The third is that the authenticity of a prophet's prophecy is established only by <53> means of extraordinary miracles. But these extraordinary miracles can come about only through the creation of what does not correspond to nature or to the habitual course of things.

The advocates of this theory, however, reject whatever contradicts the natural and habitual, for they always draw their arguments in support of their opinions exclusively from nature and law. This attitude prevents them from supporting their argument from prophecy, since they have no means of substantiating the latter.

This completes my account of the fifteen reasons [for my opposition to the theory of the dualists]. If God will give me the help and power, I shall also mention other reasons later on in the second treatise of this book; namely, the treatise on the unity of God. Yet I cannot be content at this point with all that I have mentioned until I have made it clear that this thing to which these proponents of dualism adhere so firmly—I mean [what they call the principle of] *darkness*—is not a principle opposed to that of light, but merely the absence of light. And if they will say: [17] "On what ground dost thou assert that darkness is not a principle opposed to light?" my answer will be: [18] "On that of [the following] three proofs."

One of them is that although a human being is admittedly unable to produce any principle whatever, yet we note that when he stands facing the sun and forms an arch by means of his hands, the space between them becomes darkened. Now that human being did not really create the principle of darkness [in that particular case]. He merely screened the light from the air between his palms so that it became dark on account of the absence of the light.

The second proof is that I note that when a human being stands in front of one lamp, he casts a shadow. But if we were to surround him with many lamps, he would cast no shadow at all. Now it is certainly not within the power of a human being to annihilate a principle. [What has happened in this case, then, is] merely that he has permitted the light which was absent in the part of the air that had surrounded him to reappear.

The third proof is that I have never seen two substances of opposite nature to be transformed completely into one another. Water, for example, is never transformed into fire, nor fire into water.

17. "and if they will say"—added by Ibn Tibbon.
18. "my answer will be"—added by Ibn Tibbon.

When, then, I saw the dark air become bright, I knew that darkness was not the opposite of light but merely the absence thereof.

Furthermore I found that the same thing applied also to other sense experiences. <54> I discovered, namely, that the air receives the sound of a speaker and transmits it to us. When it is not struck by a sound, however, we hear nothing. Yet we do not on that account say that the air, which does not transmit any sound, is the opposite of sound, but merely that it betokens the absence of sound. A similar assertion may be made with reference to smell; namely, that the air picks it up wherever it happens to be and transmits it to us. When it does not exist, however, we smell nothing. That does not indicate that that air is the opposite of smell. It merely betokens the absence of smell. In this same manner, then, does the air receive the light and transmit it to our eyes. When, therefore, there is no light, we do not see anything. Yet that is not [due to the presence of] the opposite of light. It represents only the absence of light.

Moreover, when I noted that opaque bodies formed a sort of screen keeping out the light so that it seemed to men as though the darkness were generated by these objects, I said [to myself:] "Perhaps it will now be claimed by them that the darkness arises from the [element of] earth." However, I ascertained that if we were to take a clod [19] of earth and stand in front of the sun and scatter its dust in the air, we would see absolutely no trace of this darkness. But I said to myself again: "Might it not be claimed by them in the case of a person who had been surrounded by lamps which were later removed, that his shadow had returned to his body?" I realized, however, that if that were so, then the exterior of his body would have to be black. These are, then, perfectly obvious matters, evident to our senses, and therefore refute the erroneous theory that the darkness is a principle like the light.

Now I know, of course, that God has described Himself as being *the former of light and creator of darkness* (Isa. 45:7). I say, therefore, in keeping with what may be observed by our senses, that the meaning of this verse is that God created the air which is the

19. "clod"—so Ibn Tibbon. See n. 2, above.

vehicle of *light and darkness,* according to whether [the former] is present or absent [respectively]. This parallels the statement immediately after it to the effect that He is *the maker of peace and the creator of evil.* Now we are, of course, all agreed on this that the All-Wise did not create evil. He merely created those things that are capable of becoming, through man's choice, sources of *peace or evil.* Thus, for example, if he eats food or drinks water in accordance with his need, <55> that sort of behavior redounds to his *well-being.* If, on the other hand, he takes thereof what is beyond his capacity, that becomes an *evil* for him, as we shall explain further in the fourth treatise in the chapter on justice.

As for the ascription of the creation of light and darkness to God, that was due only to the desire to offset the reprehensible theory of the Dualists. That is why Scripture asserts that God is *the former of light and creator of darkness.* It also informs us that light and darkness have a limit and a boundary, in refutation of the allegations of these people, by saying: *He hath described a boundary upon the face of the waters, unto the confines of light and darkness* (Job 26: 10).

The sixth theory is that of him who professes as the origin of all things the four natural qualities.[20] The proponents of this doctrine maintain that all bodies are composed of four elements,[21] namely, heat and cold, and humidity and dryness; that each of these four qualities existed originally in isolation, that they then united, and that as a result there originated from them the presently existing bodies. In proof hereof they cite their observation of the fact that the bodies receive from without the heat and cold of the air. Now, inasmuch as a thing accepts only what resembles it, it is deduced herefrom that these four qualities exist in the interior of their bodies.

But the advocates of this theory are really more senseless than all those previously mentioned. [They must be regarded as such] for considerations, that I shall describe and explain, wherein they forsook the method of logical demonstration and strayed from the

20. "natural qualities"—literally "natures."
21. "elements"—literally "natures."

path of truth. I say, then, first of all, that they rejected the doctrine of *creatio ex nihilo* in order not to admit the existence of something for which there is no visible analogy. Yet they ventured into the assumption of the existence of what cannot be seen at all and adhere firmly to that belief. No one has, namely, ever seen isolated heat or absolute humidity or pure cold or dryness by itself. The senses perceive these qualities only in combination, in conjunction with a body. The proponents of the theory in question, however, claim that originally each of these four qualities existed in isolation, although they have never seen anything thereof.

Furthermore, their hypothesis that these elements united after having existed in isolation is also <56> contrary to the observation of the senses, because neither we nor they have ever seen water combine with fire or fire combine with water. Aye, even water and earth, which are able to unite without destroying each other, would, if we were to combine them and then leave them alone for a while, begin to separate again, the earth sinking to the bottom while the water would float on top. Now a thing that separates even when it is forced to unite cannot be expected to unite voluntarily with its opposite.

Next I examined their affirmation in regard to this union, and I found that this union must have taken place either because of these qualities themselves or as the result of the action of something external to them. Now, if the union was due to these qualities themselves, then the claim of the proponents of this theory that these qualities had in their primitive state existed in isolation falls to the ground. For these qualities would necessarily have to appear, from the time of their coming into being, in composition. On the other hand, if their union was due to the action of something external to them, that was exactly the thought we had in mind when we said that they had a Creator who created them [in this] united [form].

After this I inquired into this matter of isolation which they posited as the primitive state [of these qualities]. If this isolation was due to their essence, then as long as their essence is in existence, they cannot be anything but separate, in which case the hypothesis of a union falls to the ground. If, on the other hand, it was due to the activity of another thing, that would bring into play a fifth causal factor which they should be asked clearly to define, but that is what they are not too anxious to do.

As for the proofs that they cite apropos of the presence of these four [qualities] in the bodies, they do not constitute a refutation of our view, because we, too, declare that they exist, but we add that they had a Creator who brought them into being.

These are, then, the four refutations [that we can offer] in opposition to their view. In each one of the instances enumerated they made assertions that are contrary to observation. [They stated], namely, that each of these four [qualities] was found in isolation, that they tended voluntarily toward composition, and that their existence in each respective state was due either to themselves or to something external to their essence. [We raise] these [objections] against their view, in addition to the twelve previously mentioned refutations: I mean the four arguments [in favor] of creation, the four proofs of [the hypothesis of] *creatio* <57> *ex nihilo,* and the four proofs [demonstrating] that nothing is created by itself. That makes a total of sixteen arguments, outside of the conclusions forced upon us by the miracles and marvels [recorded by Scripture].

As for those of our own people whom I have known as entertaining the belief in the eternity of certain elements of nature, I have found only such as believe in the eternity of water and air, because of the explicit reference by the Torah to the spheres of fire and earth as the objects of creation. Thus it says: *In the beginning God created the heaven and the earth* (Gen. 1:1).

Now the only reason why they assumed that the water and the air had existed since eternity was that they were under the false impression that the meaning of *And the earth was void and without form upon the face of the deep and the wind* [22] *of God hovered upon the face of the water* (Gen. 1:2) was that these elements were in such a state before creation. But such an interpretation is sheer nonsense, because the Torah says: *And the earth was* only after

22. "wind"—the usual translation is "spirit."

having first stated: *In the beginning God created*. It was, therefore [only] subsequent to [23] its creation that the earth consisted [of the elements] of earth and water and air. Furthermore, Scripture explicitly refers to the creation of the wind in its statement: *For, lo, He that formeth the mountains, and createth the wind* (Amos 4:13). It does the same for the lower water in its statement: *The sea is His and He made it* (Ps. 95:5), and for the upper water in its statement: *And the waters that are above the heavens . . . for He commanded and they were created* (Ps. 148:4, 5).

The seventh theory is that of him who professes as the origin of things the four elements of nature and matter (*hylē*). The proponents of this theory are more senseless than all those previously mentioned, because they take the product for the maker and affirm the existence of things that are neither substance nor accident. These are subject to the sixteen inescapable objections that were raised against the proponents of the doctrine of the natural qualities, in addition to the five applying to the advocates of the theory of [uncreated] spiritual beings, making a total of twenty-one.

When we ask these two factions: "Since you have never seen the maker of these bodies, why do you assert that the natural elements have made them rather than that they had no maker?" we find them saying in reply: "Even though no maker is manifestly visible to us, we must believe that they have a maker hidden from our view, since there can be no <58> act that does not spring from an agent." But this very argument of theirs refutes the view that a lifeless object should be able to make anything, for we do not see any maker of things who does not possess freedom of choice.

We also find them saying: "We see that, when water is withheld from trees, the trees do not produce fruit. This proves that the act of fructification is performed by the water." Our reply thereunto is that He who has created the body without any intermediary cause is able also to create it by means of such a cause. For it is inconceivable that He should be capable of performing the bigger task and incapable of the smaller. Since, then, an act can emanate

23. "subsequent to"—so M, literally "since."

only from an agent who is free to choose, it must be one who exercises such choice that produced the fruit by means of the intermediary cause which is the water.

Finally we find them saying: "We are all agreed that fire burns. Why, then, do you ascribe the act to someone else?" Our reply hereunto is that just as we agree that the knife cuts although the act of cutting is really due to the person that moves the knife, who in turn may be moved by another mover, thus do we say that fire burns, although the fire has a mover, namely the air, which is in turn moved by the Creator. The act ought, therefore, to be credited to the Creator, who is the prime mover.

Scripture does, indeed, say that all acts are to be traced back to the prime mover when it declares, by way of parable: *Should the axe boast itself against him that heweth therewith? Should the saw magnify itself against him that moveth it? As if a rod should move them that lift it up, or as if a staff should lift up him that is not wood* (Isa. 10: 15). I have appended [the statement of] these erroneous ideas to the end of these theories in order that certain students who might encounter them might not be confused by them.

The eighth theory is that of him who asserts that the heavens are the makers of the bodies, and who consequently regards them as eternal and as not being composed of the aforementioned four natural qualities but of another—that is, a fifth—thing. And when one cites, in refutation of this view, the heat of the sun, they declare that the substance of the sun itself is not hot but that it heats the air by means of the rapidity of its rotation and that is how its warmth reaches us. He who makes this assertion adduces as proof for the heaven's being composed of a fifth natural element the fact that its motion appears to him circular, as opposed to that of the fire and the air, both of which tend upward, as well as <59> that of the water and the earth, both of which tend downward.[24] However, he is clearly mistaken in the arguments he employs, as well as in what he intends to prove.

Now I shall explain all this and say that the cause of his mistake

24. For the references to the sources cf. Guttmann p. 61 notes 1–5.

lies in his argument that, if the heaven had been [composed of the element of] fire, its motion would have been upward like that of fire. We declare, however, that the natural motion of fire itself is circular. The proof hereof is the motion of the heaven, which is pure fire, as is clearly proved to us by the perceptible heat of the sun. As for this apparently upward motion of the fire, *that* is entirely accidental, its purpose being to enable the fire to emerge from the sphere of the air. Once, however, it has emerged from the sphere of the air and reached its own source, it resumes its circular motion.

Our case is analogous to that of the stone which is essentially motionless and yet has a tendency to sink. When it is thrown from on high, it moves downward until it leaves the sphere of the air. Once it has done this, however, its [true] nature appears; namely, that of immobility. If, then, we see that the stone, which has no motion of its own, moves under compulsion until it has reached its center, it becomes easier for us to understand how fire, which has a circular motion, could move by means of a motion other than its own until it reaches its source.

Dost thou not see [now] how, on account of this weak doubt, this person has forced himself to affirm the existence of a fifth element, which is rationally unsubstantiated, and tries to explain the perceptible heat of the sun by ascribing it to the air rather than to the sun's own substance? Isn't it an amazing bit of logic on his part that he should make of certainty something doubtful, requiring explanation, whereas he makes of what is doubtful a fixed certainty? [Isn't it also extraordinary] that he should eschew the doctrine of *creatio ex nihilo* because he has never seen anything like it whilst he adheres to the belief in a fifth element of nature, although he has never seen anything like that either, and that he should furthermore be compelled by this erroneous belief to assume that, even though the substance of the heaven is finite, the power inhering in it is infinite, wherefore in his opinion <60> it is indestructible?

This constitutes, then, our initial effort to refute him, besides the twelve other observations made previously. In addition to that, however, I shall now rebut his allegation that the heaven is eternal on four other grounds. The first of these is [the fact of] the gradation of the heavenly spheres. It is, namely, impossible for one part of a thing that is eternal to be higher in degree than another. Whether, therefore, the innermost sphere be the more distinguished or the outermost, his hypothesis has been refuted. The same conclusion is to be drawn from [a consideration of] the gradation of the stars, some of which are located in the inner spheres whilst most of them are situated in the outermost sphere.

The second argument is [derived] from what we are able to perceive of heaven with our eyes. It is well known to us that our eyes can perceive only what is composed of the four elements spoken of previously, because the natures of these elements unite with the natures of our eyes. If, therefore, such a thing as a fifth element had been in existence, there would be nothing corresponding to it in our eyes with which it might unite so that we might see it, unless it be assumed that there is also contained within us something of this fifth natural element. But that is [precisely] what the proponent of this theory does not believe.

The third argument is [based on the nature] of increase and diminution. Every day, namely, that elapses of the time of the revolution of the sphere constitutes an increase in past time and a diminution of the time to come. Now what is susceptible of increase and diminution must be finite in power, and finitude necessarily implies creation. And if anyone were to be bold enough to maintain that the passage of a day did not add to the past nor diminish the future, he would be flying in the face of reality and the testimony of our eyes.

The fourth argument is [taken] from the variation of the movements of the heavenly spheres. That is to say, an infinite force does not vary in and by itself. When, therefore, we see that the movements of the heavenly bodies vary to such an extent that they are related to each other by a ratio of 1 to 30 or to 365 or more, we know that each of them is finite.

The explanation hereof is as follows: Thou seest that the cycle of the eastern movement of the uppermost sphere is carried out once every <61> day and night, whereas the western movement of the fixed stars traverses every hundred years a distance of one degree. On the basis of this ratio the latter would first complete its revolution in 36,000 years, which equal 13,140,000 days. These are the multiples of the eastern movement alone, not to speak of the intermediary movements. How, then, canst thou say that a force, the movement of which varies so widely, is not finite?

These are, then, the seventeen different types of refutation that may be cited against him who holds this theory, aside from the arguments presented by the miracles and marvels. Furthermore the Scriptures state that the heavens produce nothing, but that all their acts are to be attributed to our Creator, exalted and magnified be He. That is [the tenor of] the Scriptural statement: *Are there any among the vanities of the nations that can cause rain? Or can the heavens give us showers? Art not Thou He, O Lord our God, and do we not wait for Thee?* (Jer. 14:22). Scripture also says: *I, even My hands, have stretched out the heavens, and all their host have I commanded* (Isa. 45:12).

The ninth theory is that of "chance." Its proponents are people who maintain that their reason has shown them that the heavens and the earth came into being by chance without premeditation on the part of a planning [mind], nor as the act of an agent, whether acting from choice or inanimate. And when they are confronted with the question of how they conceive this to have taken place, they reply that certain bodies of unknown nature converged toward the space occupied by our world and crowded and pressed together. The light portions of this conglomeration thereupon escaped and separated, going upward to become the heaven and the stars, whilst the heavy parts sank to the bottom with the moisture floating on them. Midway between these two the rare part, namely the air, settled, enveloping them, establishing their equilibrium and upholding them.

Now there can be no doubt but that the advocates of such a view are more senseless than all those previously mentioned. They are subject first of all to the twelve types of refutation that we have listed before. <62> Besides these, there apply to them also the three types that I shall presently describe.

The first of these is that [the concept of] something having come to pass by chance is of a relative character [presupposing] the presence with it of something natural, so that the one would be [said to exist] by nature, whereas the other [came to be] by chance. But if everything happened by chance, what, pray, is there that took place by nature?

The second [objection to this theory] is that the things that are supposed to have come about by chance are relatively few. But if all bodies be included in this minority, what, tell me, would the majority consist of?

The third [objection] is that the thing that happens by chance lacks constancy because it has no principle that it might follow nor any basis that would contribute to its survival. Now if everything were inconstant, what would one understand by the term "constant"? These are, then, may God have mercy on thee, unsound, defective arguments that do not stand up when they are tested and weighed.

Now just as I have exposed the flaw in [their hypothesis] that things happened by chance, so shall I expose [the error] in the rest of their assumptions and suppositions. I say, then, that as far as their allegation that things came forward and were crowded together is concerned, let them define for us whence they came, and whether, so far as they know, there is any place in which they might have been located other than this world in which some things constitute the place for others. Furthermore, what was it that these things fled from and what thing was the cause of their leaving their first location and going to the second? Then let them tell us in what state things were before the supposed union, whether in the same state as at present or otherwise. Again, if their condition then was different from what it is now, how do they conceive the former situation to have been?

A further instance of their shallowness [25] is their allegation that

25. "shallowness"—literally "folly."

everything shining and smooth tends to go upward. This statement of theirs indicates that they are under the impression that the stars are of the dimension of pebble stones or pearls that are found in the earth, not knowing that one of the stars is many times as large as the entire earth. The truth of the matter is that they are far removed from this star, and it is its great distance from them that is the cause of the illusion.[26]

Furthermore I say that if they are <63> right, so far as their doctrine of chance is concerned, let them show us or state that it is possible for the parts of a house, namely the stones and the wood, to unite by themselves and fall into order and combine so as to constitute a house. Or [let them demonstrate] that the constituent parts of a ship, namely the wood and the iron, could fit together and hold fast to each other of their own accord and travel on the sea. Of this, however, they will never discover any visible evidence, and therefore they will not admit it vocally in order not to be considered as fools. Now if thou wilt add these seven refutations to those previously listed, they will make up a total of nineteen, aside from what has been proven by the miracles and marvels.

The tenth theory is that which is known as the doctrine of "eternity." It is a theory that appears in various forms. At times it is associated with the idea of the *hylē,* and at times with that of the four elements of nature, and at times it occurs alone by itself. Its proponents assert that all things as we see them, namely, the heaven and the earth and the plants and animals and the other phenomena, have always been in existence, having neither beginning nor end. Their foremost argument in support of this theory is that they believe only in what is subject to the perception of their senses, although in reality their senses have never perceived a beginning and will never perceive an end of these bodies.

Now these, may God have mercy on thee, are a group of people, so it strikes me, who think that they could wear out anyone who would dispute with them and that there is no argument that could prevail against them. Let me, then, make it clear that these in-

---

26. "and it is . . . illusion"—this is the interpretation proposed by Guttmann (p. 68) of the incomprehensible reading of the Arabic original.

dividuals are more senseless than all those previously mentioned, and I ask God's assistance in smiting them with the cane of reason until I shall have reduced them to admitting what is a matter of common knowledge.

I say, then, first of all that the first mistake made by these individuals is that after having asserted: "We profess only what is subject to the observation of our senses," they expressed a belief in what they had never perceived. For they do not say: "We have never seen the beginning and the end of bodies," in which case they would have told the truth concerning [the perception of] their senses. They declare rather: "We regard it as a certainty that these bodies have neither beginning nor end." But this is something that they could not possibly have seen with their sense [of vision]. Should they, again, venture to affirm that they arrived at this conclusion by means of analogical reasoning based on sense perception, then they would have abandoned the very principle of their system by acknowledging an idea <64> derived from a source other than the observation of the senses.

Indeed I find that they contradict their thesis whenever any one of them recognizes the reality of the countries he has traversed and the deeds he has performed and the people he has seen and the calculations he has executed, notwithstanding the fact that these are currently absent from him or are dead. Now he does not see these things with his senses, because they have disappeared from him. He knows of them only by means of his intellectual faculty, which received their form and imprint so that they became impressed upon him and were completely appropriated by him.

In fact, I note that they contradict their thesis whenever they see or hear something. This is due to the fact that the sense of sight has no control over that of hearing, nor the sense of taste over that of touch. When, then, the senses of a human being confront a thing that possesses color and sound and taste and touch, if there were no mental faculty whereby the soul could combine these sensations, it would never attain them.

Furthermore, I find that when one of them, after having seen a certain person, is asked whether he has seen him, he answers, "Yes." Now if this answer is attributable to the sense of sight, that sense does not speak. If, again, the reply springs from the faculty of speech, it did not see anything. This proves, therefore, that there must be a certain kind of cognition that was first served by the sense of sight and then expressed by the faculty of speech.

Also by their very statement that there is no knowledge except sensation they abandon this principle of theirs, for, if they must not affirm anything except what they can perceive with their senses, they should likewise not deny anything unless it be with their senses. Now would that I knew by means of what sense they could reject all knowledge outside of that of sensation! Is it by the sense of sight or that of hearing or something else?

Furthermore, the fact that we find them apprehensive of things inspiring fear, such as that a dilapidated house might fall on them, and expectant of things hoped for, such as the results of sowing and childbirth, indicates that they conduct themselves in accordance with the teachings of science and not according to the indications of the senses alone, since the senses have nothing to do with hope and fear.

Again, when we see that <65> in the event of sickness they give each other medical treatment, and especially when they make use of repugnant medicaments, the unpleasantness of which is felt by them, merely because they believe that these remedies are naturally effective, we have therein a proof that they do not rely on sensation but on science.

Moreover, if we were to ask them whether the snow that we see coming down from the air is a part of the air, their actual position would become clear. For if they declare it to be a part of the air, they would show themselves up as ignorant, and if, on the other hand, they declare it to consist of particles of water merely solidified by the air, they would be acknowledging the sciences and thereby have abandoned mere sense perception. All the more would they be doing this if they were to admit that it was vapor before it became water, and that there was a cause that made it rise from the earth', and that that cause had another cause. Then they would certainly be acknowledging the reality of things that are beyond sensation.

We shall, therefore, not relax our whip from them until we have driven them from the belief in sensation alone to the belief in what follows upon it, and, if there be a third link in the chain, in what follows upon what follows it, and, if there be a fourth, in what follows upon what follows what comes next to it, and so forth until the process of cognition has been completed, and we prove to them thereby that all things were created.

These are, then, the eight types of refutation to which they are subject, besides the first twelve—I mean the four proofs of creation, and the four proofs of the existence of a Creator, and the four proofs of the doctrine of *creatio ex nihilo*—making a total of twenty. He, again, among the followers of this system of thought, who includes the *hylē* in his theory, is subject to whatever objection is raised against that theory, while whoever includes in his thesis the doctrine of the four elements of nature is subject to whatever objections exist against them. The Scriptures, too, connect the knowledge obtained by reasoning with natural sensation when they declare: *Doth not the ear try words, even as the palate tasteth its food? Is wisdom with aged men, and understanding in length of days?* (Job 12:11).

The eleventh theory is that of the Sophists.[27] These regard all creatures as both eternal and created, because, according to them, the reality of things depends solely on [men's] opinions concerning them. These are, however, <66> more senseless than all those previously mentioned.

The first [remark I must make] in order to point out their folly is that things do not proceed from opinions but rather opinions from things, so that the opinions formed of the latter might correspond to their reality. But these fools reversed the process of reasoning by making the thing follow the belief. This matter has already been briefly discussed by us in the introduction to this

27. Cf. Guttmann p. 71 for this translation. Ventura translates the term employed "the obstinates."

book.[28] However, I have held over another remark pertaining to it which I shall make here; namely, that the proponents of the theory we are now dealing with maintain that things have no fixed reality. That is to say that according to them, if two persons entertain different opinions about the reality of a thing, one conceiving it in one form and the other in another, then that thing must possess two realities at one and the same time. This hypothesis of theirs leads them to many kinds of absurdities, of which I shall mention seven.

I say, then, that just as two opinions about a thing would, according to them, require that that thing have two realities, so ten opinions about that same thing would necessitate its having ten realities. From that it would follow by logical necessity that a thing that has ten realities by virtue of the entertainment of opinions about it by ten individuals, should have its realities increased by one as soon as another person entertains an eleventh opinion about it. Also if one of the ten opinions about a thing be given up by the person entertaining it, one of its realities would thereby be forfeited. Nor could one ever determine how many realities one and the same thing may have, because it is impossible to meet all men in order to find out from them how many types of opinion they entertain with regard to it.

Aye, according to this process of reasoning it would follow that, if people happen to be too busy to investigate the character of a given thing and consequently form no opinion concerning it at all, that thing would become null and void <67> and be completely deprived of all reality. Again if two opinions, supported by proof, would necessarily cause one thing to acquire two realities, similarly would two opinions, one of which is based on proof while the other is arbitrary—I mean an untruth is arbitrarily intended thereby—necessarily cause that thing to acquire two realities.

The consequence would be that the false statement made by him who mendaciously asserts about a certain individual who is alive, that he is dead, would cause the latter to acquire the reality

28. Cf. above, p. 15.

of death, just as the true report made by him who speaks the truth about him grants him life. And if this applies in the case of two statements, one of which is true while the other is false, it should apply also in the case of two statements both of which are false. [If this be so,] then if two persons see the color "red" and one of them believes it is white while the other believes it is black, that color would have to become white and black at one and the same time and forfeit its own reality of redness.

All these objections, then, may be raised against this theory,[29] aside from the [statement about the] truths of things which we have set down in the introduction to this book, that its proponents must accept, as well as the previously mentioned proofs of creation. Scripture, too, says in regard to him who is under the impression that a thing is dependent upon [man's] belief concerning it, and that it is removed again, together with his mistaken notion of it: *Thou that tearest thyself in thine anger, shall the earth be forsaken for thee? Or shall the rock be moved out of its place?* (Job 18:4).

The twelfth theory is that of skepticism.[30] The proponents of this theory are people who maintain that it is proper for man to refrain from believing anything, because they claim that human reasoning is full of uncertainties. We see the truth like a flash of lightning that cannot be held or reached. It behooves us, therefore, to refrain from forming any opinion.

These are more senseless, however, than even the Sophists, for the latter make the mistake of admitting lies into the company of real truths, whereas the former refrain from both truth and falsehood. Now I see fit to explain the objections against their views in this matter in order that I may thereby cause them to return to the truth, provided, of course, they are qualified for engaging in controversy and are not already so submerged in ignorance as to make one despair of doing anything with them, <68> as is the case with the faction that I shall mention later.

29. "All . . . theory"—added by the older translation, cited by Bloch p. 94 and n. 2.
30. "skepticism"—literally "abstention."

I say, then, that if, as they would have it, the truth in everything consisted in refraining from thinking about it, then they would have to abstain from abstention itself and not decide that it is the correct procedure. Nor did I apply this judgment to them before applying it to myself, for when I acknowledged that science constituted the truth, I recognized also that it was by means of this science that I came to know that it was the truth.

Furthermore, I say that their very entering into controversy with their adversaries in order to compel the latter to abstain from reasoning also constitutes an abandonment on their part of their thesis and a tendency toward the recognition of the truth of the sciences. For unless they did that, they could not establish the doctrine of abstention.

I say also that the fact that they resort, as we do, to their reason whenever they have need for regulating their affairs, just as they resort to their vision when they have need to see or to their hearing when they need to hear, refutes their theory of abstention and corroborates the affirmations of the sciences as well as it does those of the senses.

I say, moreover, that the fact that they engage expert craftsmen and experienced physicians and outstanding engineers proves that they are not sincere in their profession of abstention. For if they had been so, they would have employed whomever they could find.

I say, furthermore, that the fact that they remember the acts performed by them and the experiences they have had, especially if they present accurate testimony concerning them, refutes the doctrine of abstention and corroborates the truths.

I say also that the fact that in every matter that is fraught with consequences they take measures to obtain a commendable rather than a reprehensible result constitutes a renunciation of abstention and a submission to the truth.

And thus, too, do I say that the fact that they praise those who do what is good and disapprove of those who do what is evil, as well as the credence they give to those that speak the truth and their charging with mendacity those that lie, refutes the theory of abstention and corroborates the belief in the truth.

These seven points, then, in addition to what was stated in the introduction to this book, should rouse them to acknowledge the validity of the truth, so that we might thereby prove to them that [all] things were created, as divine Wisdom bids [us do] when it says: <69> *O ye thoughtless, understand prudence, and, ye fools, be ye of an understanding heart* (Prov. 8:5).

The thirteenth theory is that of those who feign complete ignorance. Its proponents are people who, in addition to rejecting the teachings of science, reject also the observation of the senses, asserting that nothing possesses any reality whatever, be it scientific knowledge or sensation.

These, however, are more senseless than all those previously mentioned. For just as, upon being asked whether it is possible for a thing to be eternal and uncreated, or created and not eternal, or created and eternal, at one and the same time, or neither created nor eternal, they would reply, "Yes," so also would they, if one of them were asked whether it is possible for a certain person to be a human being and not a donkey, or a donkey and not a human being, or a donkey and a human being at one and the same time, or neither a donkey nor a human being, also reply, "Yes."

Now when one's pretended ignorance has advanced so far, or his obstinacy has been carried to such a point, there is no means of speaking to him nor any sense in engaging in further controversy with him. For whatever argument one might produce against him would be denied by him and combated with conceit and beaten back with the attempt to confuse the opponent. About individuals like them Scripture says: *He snarleth against all sound wisdom* (Prov. 18:1). It says also: *Speak not in the ears of a fool; for he will despise the wisdom of thy words* (Prov. 23:9).

Furthermore, whoever enters into controversy with them by asking them, "Is it by virtue of scientific knowledge that you assert that there is no knowledge or by virtue of ignorance?" is wasting his time, because, according to them, reasoning does not lead to the knowledge of the truth. The only means of procedure in such a case is, may God have mercy on thee, to wait for them to get so hungry as to complain of hunger, and so thirsty as to be overcome by thirst, or to be struck so painful a blow that they would weep and cry out. When they finally acknowledge *viva voce* the experiencing of hunger or thirst or the smart of a blow, they will have admitted the reality of sensation. When, again, they ask for food and drink and relaxation, they will have admitted the reality of the first thing following upon sensation.

Thus shall we unremittingly make them <70> advance step by step, until we shall have forced them to acknowledge the adequacy of thorough knowledge and we shall thereby have proven to them that all things are created. Should they, however, refuse to admit all the things enumerated, then they would be beyond any hope of being set right. It is of such that Scripture says: *Though thou shouldst bray a fool in a mortar with a pestle among groats, yet will not his foolishness depart from him* (Prov. 27:22).

It behooves me now to explain that there exist theories other than the twelve just enumerated. However, these do not constitute primary categories, some of them being derivatives of one and the same principal division, while others represent a combination of the derivatives of two or three principles. It is, therefore, not necessary to list them individually nor to refute them, for by my mention of the twelve principal categories and my exposition of their refutation, their derivatives have automatically become nullified and their offshoots cut off, and the first principle has been established that all things were created and that their Creator created them out of nothing, as I have explained and made clear.

CHAPTER IV

And now that I have fully explained these theories, as well as the proofs upon which the advocates of each based themselves and the arguments that could be urged against them, let me append to these remarks certain questions that people might raise in regard to the subject matter of this chapter. They might, for instance, ask: "If all things were created, how could the sage say: *One generation passeth away, and another generation cometh; and the earth abideth forever?"* (Eccles. 1:4.) Let me explain, then, and say that the sage did not mean by this statement to affirm that the existence of the earth was unlimited. On the contrary, he made this statement as a proof of the fact that it was created. This is evident from the circumstance that we see that created things are inseparable from it. For [31] *one generation passeth away and another generation cometh*—that is, the generations of men and animals and plants—and *it* persists in this state until the end of the period of time allotted to it. Hereby, then, it becomes certain to us that the earth must have been created, since whatever cannot be divorced from things created must itself have been created, inasmuch as the former include the latter.

Or perhaps some thoughtful person will think to himself and ask: <71> "How can something be derived from nothing?" Our answer is that if mortal creatures had been in a position to conceive of how such a thing could come about, it would not have been necessary for our reason to attribute it exclusively to the eternal Creator, since each one of us would have been able to comprehend something of this nature. However, our reason has decided to ascribe this act exclusively to the Creator, precisely because there is no way whereby a mere creature could conceive of how such an event could have taken place. Whoever, therefore, could compel us to demonstrate this process, would be forcing us to make creators of ourselves as well as of him. Hence we must be content to contemplate this process with our reason without picturing it concretely or representing it in imagination.

Or perhaps someone, thinking about the space presently occupied by the earth, will ask: "What was there originally in this its space?" Now this question on his part is prompted entirely by his ignorance of the definition of "space" and his notion that what is meant by "space" is the substratum of things. The consequence hereof would be to make him look for a substratum of the substratum and, seeing that there is no end to this process, to become confused. I must, therefore, make it clear that the true significance of the term "space" is not what he thinks it is, but simply the meeting of two contiguous

31. "For"—literally "but."

bodies the place of whose contact is called "space." In fact, each one of them becomes the locale of the other. Thus one part of the earth, as it revolves, serves as the locale for the other. If, therefore, there were no earth nor any bodies, it would be idle to speak of space in any shape or form.

Perhaps, also, thinking about the concept of "time," someone might ask: "But before these bodies came into being, how was it possible for this phenomenon of 'time' to be bare of all existing things?" However, such an assertion, too, is made only by one who is ignorant of the definition of "time" and who thinks it is something transcending the sphere of the universe and that the entire world is comprehended in it. As a matter of fact, the true significance of "time" is nothing like this. It constitutes, in reality, only the duration of existing beings, the successive stages in the history of the sphere [of the universe] and what is beneath it. Consequently, so long as these beings do not exist, <72> it is idle to speak of "time" in any shape or form.

But perhaps also the bodies presently in existence seem too few in number, so that one would ask: "Do these represent all the power and wisdom of God?" Our answer is that God created as many bodies as He knew we would be capable of taking cognizance of and holding in our minds and as would suffice to serve us as proof of His sovereignty. Should someone, therefore, ask, "Is there, then, anything that He has failed to create?" our reply would be: "Is He not the Creator of everything?"

Now perhaps someone will say, "How can it be acceptable to reason that the world has been in existence only 4693 years?" [32] We reply thereunto that since we acknowledge that the world has been created, it must have had a beginning. Dost thou not see, even if we [mortal] creatures had been living in the hundredth year of creation, would we have been astonished at that fact or denied it? All the less can we deny it at this age in which we live.

Perhaps, furthermore, someone will say to himself: "Since in our opinion he who desists from doing something is regarded as

32. This reveals to us the date of the composition of this work as having been the year 933 C. E.

performing an act when he desists therefrom, and since the Creator had, before creating all things, desisted from doing that, could not that abstention on His part be called 'action,' so that it could be said that He had really been inactive during the whole course of time preceding the creation of the world?" To this we reply that only the abstention of human beings constitutes action, because their acts pertain to accidents. Thus when they are not favorably disposed, they become angry, and when they do not hate, they love. The Creator's activity, however, has to do with the creation of substances, and substances have no opposites, so that the failure of the creation of some would automatically have brought about the creation of the others. Therefore, when God desists from creating any of these substances, no others come into being.

Perhaps again someone will wonder: "For what reason did the Creator create all these beings?" To this question there are three answers. The first would be to say that He had created them without any motive, and yet it could not be considered a wanton act, because only man acts wantonly when he does anything without a motive, inasmuch as he would thereby be neglecting his own benefit. But such a thing is far removed from the Creator. The second answer is that God intended thereby to reveal and make manifest His wisdom, as Scripture says: *To make known to the sons of man His mighty acts and the glory of the majesty of His kingdom* (Ps. 145: 12). <73> The third is that His intention therein was to benefit His creatures by their use of all these things so that they might obey Him, as He says: *I am the Lord thy God, who teacheth thee for thy profit, who leadeth thee by the way that thou shouldest go* (Isa. 48: 17).

If, again, that individual were to ask, "Then why did He not create them before this time?" our reply would be: "There was no time in existence as yet that one could ask about, and furthermore it is of the very nature of him that acts by free choice to do what he wants when he wants."

The first treatise is hereby completed.

TREATISE II

CONCERNING [THE BELIEF] THAT THE CREATOR OF ALL THINGS, BLESSED AND EXALTED BE HE, IS ONE

EXORDIUM

As a preliminary to the central theme of this treatise, let me state (*a*) that the data with which the sciences start out are concrete,[1] whereas the objectives that they strive for are abstract.[2] Also (*b*) there is reached in the field of scientific research a last terminal beyond which no further knowledge is possible. Now (*c*) man's progress in his intellectual attainments is gradual, proceeding from point to point. (*d*) Every station reached by him in his advance in knowledge consists of necessity of ideas more abstract and subtle than the preceding, (*e*) the last constituting the most abstract and subtle of all. When, therefore, in the course of his reasoning a person arrives at conclusions of so abstract a nature, that is in itself a guarantee that he has achieved the object of his quest. He can certainly not demand that (*f*) they be of a concrete character, for to make such demands is to seek to return to the first datum of knowledge from which he started out or to the second which served as the second step in the process of his reasoning. Aye he would be doing violence to and distorting the methods of science. Every attempt on his part, therefore, to make concrete the ultimate goal of cognition would be tantamount only to rendering his speculation null and void, bringing about nullification of whatever knowledge he may have acquired and thereby a return to ignorance.

It behooves me now to explain the basis of the six observations

1. "concrete"—literally "big" or "coarse."
2. "abstract"—literally "fine" or "subtle."

that I have just made. That explanation will then be followed by an exposition of the motive that impelled me to introduce them at the beginning of this treatise.

Let me, therefore, first of all make clear the meaning of the remark that the data with which the sciences start out are concrete, by saying that the reason for this assertion is that these basic data are derived from the perception of the senses. Now whatever is subject to sense perception <74> is a matter of common knowledge in which men enjoy no advantage over one another so that one would be superior to another in respect to it. Aye, they are not even distinguished in this regard above the beasts, for we find that the latter exercise the senses of sight and hearing as well as the former. There cannot, then, be anything more crass than that in which beasts and men are equal.

Now when a person regards the object which is perceptible to the senses and recognizes it as a body, he infers by means of the subtlety of his intellect that it is endowed with accidents. He arrives at this conclusion by virtue of the fact that he notes that this body is black at one time and white at another, and that it grows now hot and now cold. Increasing the refinement of his investigation, he next notes that this body possesses an attribute which brings to mind the category of quantity. This comes about as a result of his considering the matter of its length and width and depth. At a still more subtle stage, he notes that the object in question is invested with an attribute accompanying its position—one that produces the idea of space; namely, contact with it.

Continuing with the refinement of his speculation, he then arrives at the point of discerning an attribute appertaining to the object in question which intimates to him the idea of time; namely, its duration. In this way does he, without interruption, proceed zealously, spurred on by his thinking and his understanding, until he has reached the utmost that he is able to grasp. Now this ultimate is the subtlest attained by him, just as the first datum of his knowledge is the crassest attained by him. This is, then, the basis of my conclusion that the ultimate objectives of science are the most abstract of scientific ideas.

I have furthermore stated that man advances from one idea to another until he arrives at a point beyond which no further knowledge is possible. There are three reasons for this. One of these is that since man's body is limited, finite, whatever powers reside in it—and the faculty of knowledge is one of them—must necessarily be finite. This corresponds to my remark in regard to the heavens that the period of their duration is necessarily finite.[3] The second reason is that science is capable of being grasped by man only because it is finite, for, if <75> it were thought to be infinite, it could not be grasped in its totality, and, once that becomes impossible, it is no longer subject to the cognition of anyone. The third reason is that the source whence all the sciences are derived—I mean sensation—is unquestionably finite. It is, therefore, impossible that what is derived therefrom should be infinite, so that the offshoot would differ from the stock.

I have stated, furthermore, that man's progress in his intellectual attainments is gradual, proceeding from point to point, because the sciences have, all of them, a source from which they spring. Ignorance, on the other hand, has no such source from which it is derived, being merely the absence of knowledge, as we explained in the matter of darkness that it constitutes the absence of light and not its opposite.[4] Just as we pointed out there that, if the darkness had been the opposite of light, the dark air could not have been transformed into brightness, so do we say here that, if ignorance had been something positive like knowledge, it would have been impossible for an ignorant person to be transformed into one possessing knowledge. [What would have happened is] simply [that] knowledge and ignorance would have been combined in one particle and excluded each other.

This is, then, the basis of my remark that man's progress in knowledge is gradual, because he starts from the root and branches out. Such progress from one point to the next is impossible in the case of ignorance, since there are in it no stations that have to be traversed, constituting as it does merely the abandonment of the

3. Cf. above, p. 71.
4. Cf. above, p. 64.

knowledge of one thing after another and the absence of that knowledge.

I have said, moreover, that the last rung in the ladder of knowledge is the most abstract and subtle of all. This may be illustrated by our observations in the case of the snow. When it falls from its source in the air, it appears to us in the form of stones. Upon examining it more closely, however, we realize that it is derived from water. By means of still subtler reflection we learn that this water could not have risen upward except by way of vaporization and the ascent of the vapors. Thus we arrive at the belief that the snow starts out as vapor. Then we probe still more deeply and say that it is impossible for this vapor to be without <76> a cause that makes it rise. This cause, then, so it becomes clear, which is the final result of our investigation, is finer than the vapor, which, in turn, is finer than the water which is finer than the snow. Hence it is this cause that contributes the aim and goal of man's quest.

I have stated also that whoever demands that the final results of his scientific research be as concrete as its starting point does violence to the rules and method of this research that I have explained elsewhere. Aye I say that he forfeits whatever knowledge he has acquired and recedes from his very objective, like the person who insists that what makes the vapor rise from the earth is snow, like the snow the examination of which he took up at first.

But in that case he has set at naught his quest, for if it is merely snow that he is looking for, he can get it without going in search of it. And even if he does not say expressly that his objective is something like snow or water but merely declares, "I want to see it, else I do not accept it," his remark is [really] equivalent to [saying]: "I am looking for snow or water or vapor." He merely looks for it under a different term from the one used at the beginning [of his investigation]. [That is what his statement amounts to], since in this instance only these things are visible. But if he thus goes back on the [real] cause of the vapor by declaring it null and void because his research has not yielded anything visible and he, therefore, concludes that there is no cause, then he forfeits even what he has already achieved on account of a futile hope and an idle belief [in the attainment of what does not exist].

Since now I have fully explained these matters, it behooves me to make clear the motive that impelled me to introduce them here. I say, then, that when I approached the subject of the idea of the Creator, I noted that some people rejected it on the ground that they had never seen Him.[5] Others did it on account of the profundity of the matter and its extreme subtlety. Still others think that beyond the idea of God there is another idea. Others, again, believe that they can picture God in their imagination as a body. Others, finally, without expressly attributing to Him corporeality, yet arrogate for God quantity or quality <77> or place or time or other such categories. However, when they make these arrogations, they really insist upon His being corporeal, for such characteristics appertain only to the body.

My purpose, then, in making these preliminary remarks was to forestall the illusory notions of these individuals and relieve the minds of men of their burden. [I aimed] also to prove that the extreme abstractness of the idea of the Creator was its true character, and that, when we have found by means of our reason that it is the subtlest of all things knowable, we have discovered its real nature.

As for those who assert, "We believe only what our eyes can see," and who thus reject the sciences, they have been refuted by me sufficiently in my exposition of the theory of the advocates of eternity, as well as that of the Sophists and the Skeptics,[5] so that if the student finds it necessary to consider these matters again, he might review what I have said there.

Those, again, who repudiate the idea on account of its subtlety and its profundity, abandon their second objective after having established the first. Thou knowest, namely, that I explained in the chapter on the creation of the world [6] that we had in mind, when we propounded that theory, something recondite, abstract,

---

5. Saadia is here referring back to the proponents of the 10th, 11th, and 12th theories of creation discussed by him in the first treatise. Cf. above, pp. 75–82.

6. Cf. the beginning of that treatise, p. 38.

subtle, and profound, the like of which had not been seen. I stated, furthermore, that it was with reference to it that Scripture said: *That which is, is far off, and exceeding deep; who can find it out?* (Eccles. 7: 24). Thou hast, moreover, seen how others conceived of this matter [from which the world supposedly originated] as resembling dust and strands of hair and indivisible atoms [7] and how we ourselves arrived at the doctrine of *creatio ex nihilo*.

If such, then, be the nature of the object of our knowledge at this lower rung of the ladder, the character of the concept on the rung after it—I mean the idea of the Creator, exalted and magnified be He—must of necessity be subtler than the subtlest and more recondite than the most recondite and more abstract than the most abstract and profounder than the most profound and stronger than the strongest and more exalted than the most exalted, so that it would be impossible to fathom its character at all. It is in regard to it that Scripture says: *Canst thou find out the deep things of God? Canst thou attain unto the purpose of the Almighty? It is high as heaven; what canst thou do? Deeper than the nether world; what canst thou know? The measure thereof is longer than the earth, and broader than the sea* (Job 11: 7–9).

Those, again, <78> who demand that we present God to them as a body should awaken from their lethargy. Was not the body the first step in our process of cognition, and was it not by means of its earmarks that we conducted our investigation and our research until we attained the knowledge of its Maker? How, then, can they, to put it figuratively, return to the ABC and endeavor to treat the Creator as a physical being? Is the body whose Maker we are seeking a specific individual so that it might be assumed that its Maker was another person? Is it not rather the Maker of every body that we can see and think of that we are looking for, One of Whom it could be said that every body that comes to our mind has been made by Him, whilst He Himself transcends this [physical universe]?

As for those who seek something beyond the idea of God, we

7. Cf. above, p. 52. Saadia refers here to the second theory of creation discussed by him.

have already demonstrated the futility of their quest from the standpoint of the character of the person engaged in the acquisition of knowledge and the necessary limitation of his knowledge by the limited nature of his faculties. [We have proved it] also from the standpoint of the character of the object of knowledge, [showing] that what is infinite and endless cannot be embraced by the [human] mind. [Finally we pointed it out] from the standpoint of the [material] basis upon which all the sciences are founded.

Let me now explain this [matter] further at this point and say: "But perhaps there is someone who thinks that beyond this ultimate object of knowledge there is something else that is knowable which, however, has not been attained by the mind of a certain individual or by the minds of all men." My reply hereto is that that is an unsound assumption, because all objects of knowledge are comprehended through the mediation of the body, as we have stated before in the introduction to this book.[8] When, therefore, what is comprehended is of an extracorporeal character and not contained within a bodily frame,[9] the possibility of any further knowledge beyond it is absolutely excluded.

As for those who do not seek to affirm that God is a body but yet insist on arrogating for Him motion or rest or anger or good will or the like, they really arrogate for Him a corporeal character by way of implication, even if they do not do it expressly. They act like the individual who says, "I do not demand of Reuben one hundred drachmas, but I demand of him the square root of 10,000." That one has indeed in [his claims against] Reuben eliminated the expression "one hundred." The implication has, however, been retained. Once, then, the demand that the Creator be a physical being has been proved to be absurd, <79> the arrogation to Him of bodily accidents in general must likewise be excluded.

Now the reason for my verbosity and my dwelling at such length on this preliminary observation in contrast to my customary brevity

8. Cf. above, pp. 16 ff.
9. "within a bodily frame"—Ibn Tibbon.

is that it constitutes the foundation and the axle of the entire book. I shall, therefore, pause a little at this point in order to spare myself great exertion later on. And if someone were to ask, "How does this matter come to require such great exertion and such extensive explanations?" our answer would be that that is due to two causes. One of them is that whatever is valuable demands greater and more extensive effort to attain than what is worthless. Thus it is well known that it is easier to find glass than it is to discover a precious stone. The second is that there prevail so many different opinions among those who occupy themselves with this science. The cause of this divergence may be either lack of insight or deliberate contentiousness or laxity and lassitude or an inclination for the [gratification of the] appetites, as we have stated previously in the introduction to this book.[10] It was therefore necessary to expose their error when the truth had to be elucidated.

CHAPTER I

Now, then, that I have done with these false notions,[11] let me begin with the main subject of this treatise and say that we have been informed by our Lord, magnified and exalted be He, through the pronouncements of His prophets that He is one, living, omnipotent, and omniscient, that there is nothing that resembles Him, and that He does not resemble any of His works. This thesis [the prophets] supported by means of miracles and marvels, so that we accepted it immediately while waiting for its verification for us by speculation.

As for the fact that God is one, that is expressed in the statement of Scripture, *Hear, O Israel, the Lord our God, that Lord is one* (Deut. 6:4), as well as in its statement, *See now that I, even I, am He, and there is no god with Me* (Deut. 32:39), and its statement, *The Lord alone did lead him, and there was no strange god with Him* (Deut. 32:12).

10. Cf. above, pp. 4 ff.
11. "false notions"—Ibn Tibbon and M.

As for God's vitality, that is borne out by the statement of Scripture, *For who is there of all flesh, that hath heard the word of the living God speaking out of the midst of the fire?* (Deut. 5:23) and its statement, *But the Lord God is the true God, He is the living God,* <80> *and the everlasting King* (Jer. 10:10).

As for God's omnipotence, that is made explicit by the statement of Scripture, *I know that Thou canst do every thing, and that no purpose can be withholden from Thee* (Job 42:2), and its statement, *Thine, O Lord, is the greatness, and the power, and the glory, and the victory, and the majesty, etc.*[12] (I Chron. 29:11).

As for God's omniscience, that is made explicit by the statement of Scripture, *He is wise in heart, and mighty in strength* (Job 9:4), and its statement, *His discernment is past searching* out (Isa. 40:28).

Finally, the view that nothing resembles either God or His works is supported by the statement of Scripture, *There is none like unto Thee among the gods, O Lord; and there are no works like Thine* (Ps. 86:8).

Having learned about these five [13] facts from the books of the prophets, we proceeded to confirm them by means of logical reasoning and found them to be correct. We were thereby also successful in refuting whatever argument might be presented against any of them by our opponents. These latter do indeed endeavor to do that for two reasons, there being no third. One of these is that they think of God after the analogy of His creatures. The other is that they take every expression we employ in describing Him and every expression written down in His Scriptures in its corporeal rather than its figurative sense. Once, however, we have mastered this science, we shall make all that clear with the power of the Merciful One and His might.

I say, then, first of all, that I find a proof of God's uniqueness— in addition to the proofs mentioned previously [14]—to be contained

---

12. This quotation follows Ibn Tibbon.
13. "five"—Ibn Tibbon. The Arabic original erroneously reads "six."
14. Cf. above, pp. 59 ff.

in the following thesis; namely that, since the Creator of all bodies cannot be of the same species as His creatures,[15] and since the bodies are many in number, it follows of necessity that He be one. For if He were more than one, there would apply to Him the category of number and He would fall under the laws governing bodies.

Furthermore, the idea of a Creator as indispensable [to the explanation of existence] is dictated by reason. However, what is indispensable is one [God].[16] More than that would be neither indispensable nor necessary.

Again, the existence of one Creator is established by means of the first proof; namely, that of the creation of the world. To demonstrate the existence of more than that number would require a second proof, outside <81> of that first proof. There is, however, no means of proving the existence of a Creator other than that of creation.

CHAPTER II

After [listing] these three proofs, now, [in favor] of God's oneness, I say that every argument refuting the existence of two gods constitutes an argument in favor of the one. Our previously mentioned reply to the proponents of this theory [of dualism] has already been noted by thee. I shall, therefore, add here the fact that I have found that when these [Dualists] are asked, "Why do you relate all existing things to two sources only and why don't you maintain that each species of them has a separate source?" they reply: "According to our observation, even though they fall into many classifications, they may all be subsumed under the two divisions of the useful and the harmful, there being no third possibility other than these. That is why we related all existing things to two sources."

Now I examined this assertion, and I found that it could be

15. This argument was, according to Maimonides (*Guid*·, I, 76), also presented by the Mutakallimun in order to demonstrate God's incorporeality.

16. This argument was also attributed by Maimonides (*idem*, I, 75) to the Mutakallimun.

countered with the remark that we find that whatever is useful and harmful might also be subsumed under the classification of the five senses, for some of these things are perceived by means of the sense of sight and some by means of that of hearing, and the same applies to the three other senses. "It is, therefore, with no more propriety that you subsume them under two categories than others do it under five."

One might also counter them with the rejoinder that whatever is useful and harmful might be subsumed under the classification of color, and the principal natural colors are seven in number, to wit: white, black, green, yellow, red, and the color of the sky, and the color of earth.[17] It is, therefore, with no more propriety that they comprise all things in two categories than when others do it in seven.

One might furthermore counter that these two things may be subsumed under the classification of taste and the principal divisions of taste are nine in number; namely, the sweet and the fat—both of which are hot and moist; the bitter and the salty and the sharp—which are hot and dry; the sour and the acid and the astringent—which are cold and dry; and the tasteless, which is the taste of water and cucumbers—which is cold and moist. It is, therefore, with no more propriety that they subsume these things under two categories than if they had done it under nine.

Thus, too, might their division into two be countered by the derivation of all things from four natural elements, <82> or the ten categories pertaining to substance, or the six types of motion, or the seven kinds of quantity, or the three tenses, or the three types of propositions, or the three forms [of logical syllogisms].[18] However, I shall not dwell any longer on this subject, but shall go on to prove, from the standpoint of judgment also, the unsoundness of their method in arbitrarily picking out one number from among the rest and accepting it as final.

And now let me explain this matter further and say that if neither of the two [principles by whom the world was supposedly

17. "earth"—M.
18. "of logical syllogisms"—so Ventura, p. 197, n. 27.

created] could, if he wished to create something, carry out this impulse except with the help of the other, they would both be impotent. If, again, the will of the one could compel the other to help him, then both would be acting under compulsion. Should it be assumed, on the other hand, that both exercise complete freedom of choice, then if one of them were to desire to keep a body alive whilst the other wanted to put it to death, that body would necessarily have to be alive and dead at one and the same time.[19]

I say furthermore that if each one of them could hide something from his peer, they would both be ignorant. If, however, he could not do that, then both would to that extent be lacking in omnipotence. I say also that, if these two [principles] are [to be conceived as being] connected with one another, they are really one. If, on the other hand, they are to be considered as distinct from each other, that would have to be due to a third [principle] separating them.

Nor would I concede to the proponents of [this theory of] two [principles] the right to compare the latter to darkness and light which are contiguous to one another, no third factor coming between them. For these two are only accidents, whereas the former constitute, according to the proponents of the theory of dualism, substances.

These arguments do, then, turn out to be in agreement with the assertion of the Scriptures to the effect that there is no Creator other than the one and only God, as they state: *Unto thee it was shown, that thou mightest know that the Lord, He is God; there is none else beside Him* (Deut. 4: 35). They declare also: *Know this day, and lay it to thy heart, that the Lord, He is God in heaven above and upon the earth beneath; there is none else* (Deut. 4: 39). They say furthermore: *Look unto Me, and be ye saved, all the ends of the earth; for I am God, and there is none else* (Isa. 45: 22). They state, moreover: *That they may know from the rising of the sun, and from the west, that there is none <83> beside Me; I am the Lord, and there is none else* (Isa. 45: 6). They say also: *I am*

19. This argument combines two arguments of the Mutakallimun quoted by Maimonides, *loc. cit.*

the Lord, and there is none else, beside Me there is no God (Isa. 45: 21), and other things of this tenor.

CHAPTER III

Now if someone were to ask: "But in that case what is the meaning of these two names *'Ădhonay* and *'Ĕlohim* that are constantly employed in the Bible with reference to God?" our answer would be that Scripture makes it quite clear that they both have one connotation. This is borne out by its statement: *For thus saith the Lord that created the heavens, He is God* (Isa. 45: 18), as well as its statement: *Know ye that the Lord He is God* (Ps. 100: 3).

After this definition, then, no attention is to be paid to the fact that one of these two appellatives is used in the description of one action whilst the other is used in describing another,[20] for there is many a parallel to this usage in the language of Scripture. Thus it states: *And Jerubbaal the son of Joash went and dwelt in his own house* (Judg. 8: 29), and after that: *And Gideon had threescore and ten sons of his body begotten* (Judg. 8: 30). One name is here used in the description of one act and another in connection with another without any scruple, because it has already been definitely stated that Jerubbaal was identical with Gideon.

Should someone, again, ask: "Then what, pray, is the meaning of the declaration of Scripture: *Even unto my cause, my God and my Lord* (Ps. 35: 23), and similarly of the statement: *The Lord thundered from heaven, and the Most High gave forth His voice?"* (II Sam. 22: 14) our reply to him would be that this [redundant appellative] constitutes merely a second motivation. *He thundered* because He is *the Lord* and also because He is *the Most High*. *Rouse Thee* because Thou art *my God* and also because Thou art *the Lord*.

A parallel to this usage in the language of Scripture is to be found in the verse, *Hear this, all ye peoples; give ear, all ye inhabitants of*

20. Saadia undoubtedly has in mind such statements as the one quoted in Genesis Rabba (chap. xxxiii) on Genesis 8: 1 to the effect that the name *'Ădhonay* stands for God's quality of mercy, whereas that of *'Ĕlohim* betokens His quality of justice.

the world, both the children of Adam and the sons of man,[21] *rich and poor together* (Ps. 49:2, 3). The meaning thereof is: because you are the *peoples,* and because you are *inhabitants of the world,* and because you are *children of Adam (Bĕne 'Adham)* and because you are *sons of man (Bĕne 'Iš).* This usage is also similar to that found in the statement of Scripture, *Fear not, O Jacob My servant, and thou, Jeshurun, whom I have chosen* (Isa. 44:2). That is to say: because thou are both *Jacob* and *Jeshurun.*

I would, therefore, say in general that, whenever there is encountered in either the assertions of Scripture or in the speech of any one of us monotheists an expression pertaining to the description of our Creator or to His handiwork, which stands in contradiction to the requirement <84> of sound reason, there can be no doubt about it that that expression was meant to be taken in a figurative sense, which the diligent students will find if they seek it. Now there is no need for me to expatiate on the exposition of this subject in this book nor to explain the ways of metaphors and other rhetorical usages as well as the extension of meaning in language, for I have already explained an ample proportion of this subject in the introduction to my interpretation of the Torah. I shall, therefore, be brief here and dispense with repeating it, restricting myself solely to the explanation of any doubtful passage that may present itself to me.

If, again, someone were to ask: "But what is the meaning of the statement of Scripture, *And now the Lord God hath sent me, and His spirit?"* [22] (Isa. 48:16), our reply would be that that could very well be rendered as having the meaning of *with His spirit.* This usage of the conjunction would be similar to that prevalent in the statement of Scripture: *Seek ye the Lord and His strength* (Ps. 105:4), the connotation of which is *in His strength.* It is also analogous to that contained in its statement: *But upon thee the Lord will arise, and His glory shall be seen upon thee* (Isa. 60:2),

21. "both the children of Adam and the sons of man"—the usual translation is "both low and high."

22. Saadia is here polemicizing against the Christian exegetes of the Old Testament who endeavored to support their doctrine of the trinity by means of such passages. Cf. Guttmann, pp. 101 ff. and p. 106.

which is explained by the verse: *When the Lord hath built up Zion, when He hath appeared in His glory* (Ps. 102:17).

It resembles also the usage employed in the Scriptural phrase: *Even the Lord, and the weapons of His indignation* (Isa. 13:5), which is explained by the verse: *Thou marchest through the earth in indignation* (Hab. 3:12). Thus, too, the expression of *the spirit of God* here is to be interpreted according to its meaning in the verse: *And Thou didst forewarn them by Thy spirit through Thy prophets* (Neh. 9:30). Whenever, therefore, any such expression presents itself to us and we find it possible to interpret it in a metaphorical or figurative sense, we need not go any further.

CHAPTER IV

Next let me say that I have found by means of logical speculation proofs of God's vitality and His omnipotence and omniscience. All this is evident from the fact that He created all things, for, according to what our reason discloses to us, it is clear that only he that possesses the power can create, and that only one who is alive has the power, and that whatever is created and well made can emanate only from one who knew, before he made it, how the thing to be created was to come into being.

These three attributes were, then, discovered by our reason as appertaining to our Maker suddenly, at one blow. That [is to say] by virtue of what He has created, it is established that He is living, omnipotent, and omniscient, as I have explained. Nor is it possible for reason to arrive at any one of these three attributes before the other. It can only attain them at once. For, according to reason, it is inconceivable that anyone that is not <85> living should create, or that one that does not possess power should create, or that any perfect, well-made handiwork could emanate from one who does not know how the act is to be carried out. For when an individual does not know how the act is to be carried out, his handiwork will be neither well nor wisely executed.

Yet although these three attributes are grasped by our minds at one blow, our tongues are unable to convey them with one word, since we do not find in language an expression that would embrace these three connotations. We are, therefore, compelled to employ in designating them three expressions, after remarking, by way of explanation, that the mind has recognized them simultaneously. For it is not to be imagined that the Eternal, blessed and exalted be He, possesses several distinct attributes. All these attributes are rather implied in His being a Creator. It was only our need to transmit it that impelled us to formulate this concept in three expressions, since we did not find in existing speech an expression that would embrace all of the ideas. Nor was it seemly to coin a special expression for them, because, being unknown, that expression would require a commentary and we would have to have recourse to much verbiage on account of that one word.

In the event, again, that someone thinks that the possession of these attributes by God implies mutability [in His essence]—I mean [the possibility of] the existence of one without the other—let me explain how unsound such a view would appear upon correct scrutiny. For change and mutation [23] appertain only to material substances and accidents. The Creator of such bodies and accidents, however, is above all change and mutation.

But I shall not be content until I have explained this fully. I say, then, that just as our calling God "Creator" does not produce an increase in His essence but merely the thought of the presence of something created by Him, so our application to Him of the epithets "living," "omnipotent," and "omniscient," which are explanations of the term "Creator"—only one who possesses these attributes at one and the same time can be a Creator—does not produce any increase in His essence but merely the thought of the presence of something created by Him.

After making this observation and establishing it firmly, I went back again to the Holy Scriptures and I found in them, in negation of the existence of any distinction in the essence of God, such statements as *There is none else beside Him* (Deut. 4:35), and *And how small a whisper is heard of Him!* (Job 26:14), as well as <86> *The Lord shall be one and His name one* (Zech. 14:9).

23. "change and mutation"—Ibn Tibbon and M.

CHAPTER V

Furthermore, let me say that in this matter the Christians erred when they assumed the existence of distinction in God's personality which led them to make of Him a trinity and to deviate from the orthodox belief.[24] I shall, therefore, take occasion here to make note of what refutation of their doctrine is offered by reason, invoking the aid of the truly One and His uniqueness.

Now I do not have in mind when I present this refutation the uneducated among them who profess only a crass materialistic trinity. For I would not have my book occupy itself with answering people like that, since what that answer must be is quite clear and the task simple. It is rather my intention to reply to their elite, who maintain that they adopted their belief in the trinity as a result of rational speculation and subtle understanding, and that it was thus that they arrived at these three attributes and adhered to them. Declaring that only a thing that is living and omniscient is capable of creating, they recognized God's vitality and omniscience as two things distinct from His essence, with the result that these became for them a trinity.

Now the first point that their rebuttal reveals is that they have only the following two alternatives: either they believe (a) that God is a physical being or (b) that He is not a physical being. But if they believe that He is a physical being, then they are on a par with the common herd of their people and are accordingly subject to whatever refutation has been presented of the view of those who anthropomorphize God. If, on the other hand, they do not believe God to be a physical being, their allegation of the existence within His essence of distinction, with the result that one attribute is not identical with the other, is equivalent to an allegation on their part that He is really a physical being. They merely used another term to express the same thought. For anything that harbors distinction within itself is unquestionably a physical being.

We have, then, established the fact that these three matters constitute one attribute. It is only impossible for a human being to

24. "deviate from the orthodox belief"—literally "go forth to heresy."

combine them in speech as the mind does by means of its cognition. One might cite as an analogy to the above the case of him who says that he does not worship the fire but the thing that burns and gives light and rises upward, which is in reality nothing else than fire.

Next we demand of the proponents [of the doctrine of the triune nature of God] that they declare explicitly that He is a physical being. For if they refuse to do that, asserting, "We cannot say that He is a physical being because every physical being is created," they would by the same token be compelled <87> to deny that God's vitality and omniscience are things distinct from His essence, since any being whose vitality and knowledge are distinct from its essence is created. Those who hold this view are, therefore, may God have mercy on thee, ignorant of the methods of logical proof.

What I mean is that the reason why we, the community of monotheists, believe that the life of a human being is distinct from his essence is because we sometimes see him alive and sometimes dead. Therefrom we infer that there is something in him by virtue of which he lives and which, if it is removed from him, causes him to die. Likewise do we believe that man's knowledge is distinct from his essence because we note that he sometimes knows and he sometimes does not, whence we infer that there is something in him by virtue of which he possesses knowledge and which, if removed from him, causes him to be ignorant. Were it not for our personal observation apropos of these two traits in man, we would have assumed that man is essentially endowed with life and knowledge. Since, however, it is really out of the question that there be found a time in which the Creator of the universe is not living nor endowed with knowledge, as is true in the case of man, it follows of necessity, without any doubt, that He is intrinsically alive and possessed of knowledge. The course that these people followed [in theology], therefore, becomes nullified from its very root.

Moreover, the advocates of the doctrine [of the trinity] did not really pursue their theory to its logical conclusion. They namely mentioned only God's essence and His vitality and omniscience, but failed to speak of His omnipotence, as well as of the fact that

He is the one that hears and sees. On the other hand, if their allegation that God is alive makes it unnecessary for them to assert that He possesses power and their allegation that He is omniscient renders it unnecessary to state that He sees and hears, then their allegation that He is omniscient should also make it unnecessary for them to assert that He is alive, since only one that is alive can know anything. Dost thou not see that they are not consistent with their own system and that they do not even follow their own logic? They merely make up this artificial thesis in order to uphold what they have been told [by their teachers].

Furthermore I say that if even a single change were to be allowed in the case of God, every change in the world would have to be granted as possible in Him. For scientific inquiry appertains to the generality of things and their species, not to the individuals and the particulars thereof. Hence, if these people base their proof on rational considerations, the unsoundness of their view has been clearly demonstrated by us.

If, again, <88> they derive their proof from Scripture, as, for example, someone of them might assert: "I see that Scripture says that God is possessed of a spirit and a word, as it is borne out by its statement: *The spirit of the Lord spoke by me and His word was upon my tongue*" (II Sam. 23:2), our answer thereto is that this *spirit* and *word* are things specially created by God, constituting the detailed [25] speech revealed by God to His prophet. We know, in fact, that the Scriptures call the name of God "soul" (*nepheš*), as Scripture says: *Who hath not taken My soul in vain* (Ps. 24:4) instead of *My name*. Now inasmuch as in the case of the creatures "soul" (*nepheš*) and "spirit" (*ruah*) have one connotation and the Creator also has a "soul" (*nepheš*), by which is meant His name, the "spirit" (*ruah*) which is attributed to Him means "revelation" and "prophecy." The misinterpretation of these terms on the part of these individuals who cite them as proof of their theory is, then, due to unfamiliarity with the Hebrew language.

Similarly I find some of these [trinitarians] cite as proof [of their doctrine] the fact that the Scriptures declare that the spirit of God

25. "detailed"—Ibn Tibbon. Cf. also Ventura, p. 183, n. 38.

engages in creation. They say [for example]: *The spirit of God hath made me, and the breath of the Almighty giveth me life* (Job 33:4). Also they assert that the word of God engages in creation. That is the import of their statement, *By the word of the Lord were the heavens made, and by the breath of His mouth . . .* (Ps. 33:6).

I note, however, that this, too, is due to [the trinitarians'] unfamiliarity with the language of Scripture. For the Scriptures wish to say by means of these assertions only that the Creator created all things by means of His word, His command, His will or His wish, that He created them with intent,—not wantonly, unintentionally,[26] or from necessity. This is borne out by the Scriptural remark: *But He is at one with Himself, and who can turn Him? And what His soul desireth, even that He doeth* (Job 23:13)

The Scriptures also mean by their assertion that God had created these things by means of His word and *the breath of His mouth* and His speech and His call, that He had created them at one blow, not within a certain interval of time or piecemeal. This is expressed in the statement: *When I call unto them, they stand up together* (Isa. 48:13). Such action on the part of God might be compared to our saying to a thing: "Come here!" or our blowing upon it with the breath of our mouth. Thus, [for example, does Scripture express it in the phrase] *And all the host of them by the breath of His mouth* (Ps. 33:6), [as well as in] *At the blast of the breath of Thy nostrils* (Ps. 18:16).

Besides <89> that, I find that, by basing their proof on Scripture, they abandon their system because the Scriptures assert that God's hand, too, engages in creation, saying: *That the hand of the Lord hath wrought this* (Job 12:9). They declare, furthermore, that His eye watches: *The eyes of the Lord watch* [27] *knowledge* (Prov. 22:12); and that His glory gathers in: *The glory of the Lord shall gather thee in* (Isa. 58:8); and that His anger goes up: *And the anger of the Lord went up against them* (Ps. 78:31); and that His mercy approaches: *Let Thy mercies come unto me*

26. "unintentionally"—Ibn Tibbon.
27. "watch"—the usual translation is "preserve him that hath."

that I may live (Ps. 119:77). Each one of these things and whatever is found resembling them would, accordingly, become other properties of God in addition to the *spirit* and *word*, since each of the former has a special function just like the latter.

All these expressions that have been enumerated and those resembling them are, may God guide thee aright, in our opinion only figures of speech and extensions of meaning employed by language. They can also all be made accessible and comprehensible, as will be explained in the sequel, with the help of the Merciful One.

CHAPTER VI

Now I also encountered one of them who interpreted the passage: *The Lord made me as the beginning of His way* (Prov. 8:22), to indicate that God possesses an eternal word that has always been in existence together with Him.[28] This point has, however, already been refuted by me once before in connection with those who applied this passage to the spiritual beings.[29] I explained [there] that the expression *ḳanani* had the meaning of creation, and I made it clear that it was [divine] wisdom that was characterized there. What is meant by it is not that God created all things by means of wisdom as an instrument, but merely that He created them wisely so that whoever saw them would testify that a wise being had made them.

Again I have seen others who, basing themselves on the declaration of God: *Let us make a man in Our image* (Gen. 1:26), assert that that expression points to a plurality of creators. These latter are, however, more ignorant even than those previously mentioned, because they do not know that the language of the children of Israel gives a distinguished person license to say: "Let us do," and "Let us make," although he is singular in number. Thus Balak said: *Peradventure I shall prevail, that we may smite*

28. It is the idea of the *Logos* that is referred to here. Cf. Guttmann, pp. 106 ff. and Ventura, p. 183.
29. Cf. above, p. 53.

them (Num. 22: 6). Similarly Daniel said: *This is the dream; and we will tell the interpretation thereof before the king* (Dan. 2: 36). Manoah, too, said: <90> *I pray thee, let us detain thee, that we may make ready a kid for thee* (Judg. 13: 15), and there are [many] similar [expressions to be found in Scripture].

Others, [finally] conjecturing about the implication of the passage: *And the Lord appeared unto him by the terebinths of Mamre* (Gen. 18: 1), declare that the thing that appeared to Abraham and was designated by this name was a trinity, because Scripture later on explicitly states: *And, lo, three men stood over against him* (Gen. 18: 2). Let me explain, then, that these are more ignorant than all those that have been mentioned, because they did not wait until they reached the end of the passage. For had they had patience until they heard the verse: *And the men turned from thence, and went toward Sodom; but Abraham stood yet before the Lord* (Gen. 18: 22), they would have realized that the *men* had departed while the light of God remained stationary with Abraham, who was in its presence. The thought, therefore, that God was identical with these men is completely refuted.

The truth of the matter is that the light of God appeared to Abraham first in order that he might infer therefrom that his visitors were good and saintly men. That is why Abraham said to them: *My lord, if now I have found favor in thy sight* (Gen. 18: 3). What was actually meant was *angels of the Lord* or *messengers of the Lord,* by way of ellipsis, which is of frequent occurrence in the language of the children of Israel, as well as in other languages. Thus, for example, they said: *For the Lord and for Gideon* (Judg. 7: 18), when they meant: *The sword for the Lord and for Gideon.*[30] They also used the expression: *Unto the Gazites saying* (Judg. 16: 2), suppressing the phrase: *And it was told.*[31] Furthermore they said: *And Absalom sent for Ahithophel the Gilonite* (II Sam. 15: 12), imaginatively supplying after that statement the words: *And he took Ahithophel,* and [one might cite] other such [instances].

30. As in verse 20 of the same chapter.
31. Cf. Judg. 9: 47.

CHAPTER VII

Now these advocates of the doctrine of the trinity, may God have mercy on thee, are divided into four sects, three of which are the older while the fourth appeared only recently. The first of these is of the opinion that the body, as well as the spirit of their Messiah, is derived from the Creator, exalted be He. The second holds the view that his body was created, his spirit alone having emanated from the Creator. The third, again, believes that both his body and his spirit were created, but that he also possessed another spirit that was derived from the Creator. As for the fourth group, it assigns to him the position of the prophets only, interpreting the sonship of which they make mention when they speak <91> of him just as we interpret the Biblical expression: *Israel is My first-born son* (Exod. 4:22), which is merely an expression of esteem and high regard, or, as others interpret the meaning of the phrase: "Abraham, the friend of God." [32]

As far as this last group is concerned, it is subject, in the matter of refutation, to all that I shall mention in the third treatise of this book in the chapter on the abrogation of the Law,[33] as well as to all that I shall mention in the eighth treatise apropos of the coming of the Messiah.[34] As for the first sect, which asserts that a portion of God became the body and spirit of Christ, it is subject, in addition to these two refutations, to whatever applies to those who assert that the things created are derived from the Creator.[35] The third sect, again, which asserts that the body and the spirit of their Messiah were created, is compelled to assume that a created physical being could become God through the association with it of a divine element. They cite as an analogy the descent of the glory of God on Mount Sinai and its appearance in the Burning Bush and the Tent of Meeting. Such a comparison would, however, compel them to acknowledge the Tabernacle and the

32. He has in mind the Mohammedans. Cf. Koran 4:124.
33. Cf. below, pp. 157 ff.
34. Cf. below, pp. 312 ff.
35. i.e., such as the proponents of the third theory of creation mentioned above, pp. 55 ff.

Bush and the mountain also as deities, which would be going from bad to worse so far as they are concerned. Besides this, they are also subject to whatever I shall mention by way of refutation in the chapter on the abrogation of the Law [36] and the one on the coming of the Messiah.[37]

As for the intermediary sect, it is subject to all the refutations applying to the other two. It is subject to the refutations applying to the first on account of its assertion that the spirit of the Messiah is divine, celestial, as well as to those applying to the last because of its assertion that the body of the Messiah was created. In addition, it cannot extricate itself from the arguments presented in the two chapters on the abrogation of the Law [36] and the coming of the Messiah.[37] This constitutes, then, in brief the exposé of my reply to whoever affirms the belief in the existence of two or three or more persons of God. God is rather an indivisible unity.

CHAPTER VIII

Hereunto let me append a question that might be asked by someone; namely, how it is possible for what is actually the subtlest of all that is subtle to be conceived of as the strongest of all that is strong. In reply thereto let me state that the All-Wise has given us many illustrations of such a phenomenon in the realm of existence. Thus the soul is subtler than the body and yet stronger than the latter, for it is upon the soul that the conduct of the body is dependent. That is why our forefathers used in their oaths the formula of *As the Lord liveth, that made us this soul* (Jer. 38: 16). Similarly is reason subtler than <92> the [other faculties of the] soul [38] and yet stronger than they, because the latter are subject to its management. That is why thou findest it to be especially ascribed to the Creator, as Scripture says, *The Lord by wisdom*

36. Cf. above, n. 33.
37. Cf. above, n. 34.
38. This translation follows the interpretation of Ventura (p. 186) rather than that of Guttmann (p. 114), who renders the passage "knowledge, although subtler than the soul, is stronger than the latter."

founded the earth; by understanding He established the heavens
(Prov. 3:19).

Nay even among the four elements can we observe this fact.
We see, for example, that the water, which is finer than the [ele-
ment of] earth, is nevertheless stronger than it, because it pene-
trates and pulls it away. Again the wind, although finer than the
water, is nevertheless more powerful than the latter, because it
moves it and even causes it to rise upward. Finally, the fire is the
most powerful of all the elements, because the sphere of fire encompasses all [others] and, by virtue of its perpetual motion, the
earth and what is upon it remains fixed in the center. As for the
celestial eastward motion that causes the highest sphere to make
its revolution, nobody knows of any cause that sets it in motion
other than the command of its Creator, blessed and exalted be He,
who is at the same time the most abstract and the most powerful
of all forces. It has thus become thoroughly clear that, the finer
one thing is in relation to another, the more powerful is it in proportion to the latter.

And now that these preliminary matters have been presented
by me, I see fit to follow them up with a discussion of the most
common descriptions and assertions about God concerning which
questions might be raised in this connection because of ideas [that
may have risen] in the mind or [because] of what is found [writ-
ten] in Scripture or of [some expression] heard from the mouth of
a believer. I preface my remarks with a general observation, and
say that whenever any reference is made in this connection to such
matters as substance or accident or the attribute of a substance or
an accident, neither "much" nor "little" thereof can be applied in
the case of the Creator. For it is our firm conviction that He is the
Creator of the universe. There does not, therefore, remain a substance or accident or attribute that was not acquired or discerned
or put together by Him or about which it is not certain that this
Creator was its maker. Hence it is out of question and impossible
to declare Him to be anything that He has Himself created. Consequently for all divine attributes pertaining to either substance

or accident that are encountered in the books of the prophets it is necessary to find in the language of Scripture nonanthropomorphic meanings that would be in keeping with the requirements of reason. Whenever, then, we the community of believers apply to God epithets that have the appearance of anthropomorphisms, <93> this is due to our endeavor to give a proximate and figurative description of deity. They are not to be taken in the material sense in which we would apply them to human beings.

Since, then, these three points have been cleared up by me, thou must no longer be led astray or thrown into uncertainty, Oh thou who studiest this book, by such statements that thou mayest make as "[God] was" and "[God] wanted" and "[God] was pleased" and "[God] was angry" and other such remarks and similar utterances that occur in the Scriptures. For these expressions are used by us only on the basis of the principle previously established by us, to which they must constantly be referred and related. An edifice, let t be noted, is always built from the foundation upward, never from the top down. Do not, therefore, become confused because of some anthropomorphic attribute of God that thou seest in the Scriptures, or of which thou findest us making common use, with the result that thou wouldst lapse back again, on its account, into doubt. But check it [39] against the principle, the true nature of which has already been clarified and firmly established.

CHAPTER IX

And now let me elaborate on these matters on the basis of the *ten categories*, discoursing about each as befits it. I say, then, that there are people who think that this being called "God" is a substance. However, their views in regard to the nature of this substance differ. One of them, for example, asserts [that it is that of] a human being.[40] Another says [it consists of] fire. Still another states [that it is] air. Again another affirms [that it is identical with]

---

39. "But check it"—added by Ibn Tibbon.
40. Such anthropomorphists existed among Jews, as well as among Mohammedans at the time of Saadiah. Cf. Ventura, p. 187, n. 56.

empty space,[41] while others make assertions other than these. Since, however, it has been clearly established that God is the Creator of all men, of all the air, and all fire, and space, and of everything that exists, and all knowledge, all these false impressions have by logical demonstration been proven null and void.

Now just as this is verified by reason, so does it become certain from the Scriptures. All existing things are namely divided into five principal groups: minerals, vegetables, animals, astral bodies, and angels, and the Scriptures exclude the idea that any of these five groups resembles the Creator or that He resembles them. For they say apropos of the most precious minerals, namely gold and silver: *Whom will ye liken unto Me, and make My equal, and compare Me to, that we may be like?* [42] *Ye that lavish gold out of the bag, and weigh silver in the balance?* (Isa. 46: 5, 6). His remark, magnified be His majesty: *Whom will ye liken unto Me, and make My equal* disproves the possibility of anything's resembling Him. His remark again: *And compare Me to, that we may be like* <94> disproves the possibility of His resembling anything else.

Furthermore the Scriptures say apropos of the most distinguished plants, namely the cedar and the plane tree: *To whom then will ye liken God? Or what likeness will ye compare unto Him? The image perchance, which the craftsman hath melted, and the goldsmith spread over with gold? . . . A holm-oak is set apart, he chooseth a tree that will not rot . . .* [43] (Isa. 40: 18-20). They say, moreover, in regard to all the animals: *Take ye therefore good heed unto yourselves—for ye saw no manner of form . . . lest ye deal corruptly, and make you a graven image, even the form of any figure, the likeness of male or female, the likeness of any beast that is on the earth, the likeness of any winged fowl that flieth in the heaven, the likeness of anything that creepeth on the ground, the likeness of any fish that is in the water under the earth* [44] (Deut. 4: 15-18). Again they say apropos of the stars: *To whom*

41. "empty space"—Ibn Tibbon translates "silver." Cf. Guttmann, p. 116, n. 2.
42. "Whom . . . like"—the usual translation is "To whom will ye liken Me, and make Me equal, and compare Me, that we may be like?"
43. This quotation follows the reading of Ibn Tibbon.
44. This quotation, too, follows the reading of Ibn Tibbon.

then will ye liken Me, that I should be equal? saith the Holy One.
Lift up your eyes on high, and see: who hath created these? He
that bringeth out their host by number (Isa. 40:25–26). Finally
they remark, apropos of the angels: *For who in the skies can be*
compared unto the Lord, who among divine beings [45] *can be*
likened unto the Lord? (Ps. 89:7).

Thus the Scriptures, taking into account [46] everything that exists,
exclude the possibility of its resembling the Creator or the Creator's
resembling it. These explicit statements are, then, to be regarded
as the basic principles that are to serve as the foundation of belief
to which every doubtful expression with a figurative meaning must
be referred in order to be brought into agreement with them.
Among the Biblical utterances, now, with a figurative meaning
is the statement of Scripture: *And God created man in His own*
image, in the image of God created He him (Gen. 1:27). This
[linking of the image with God], I must explain, is merely a way
of conferring honor. That is to say just as, even though all lands
belong to Him, God honored one of them by saying: "This is My
Land," and although all mountains are His, He honored one
mountain by saying: "This is My mountain," so did He, [although]
all forms are His, honor one of them by saying: "This is My
form," by way of distinction, not in a material sense.

Another one of these passages with a figurative meaning is the
statement of Scripture: *For the Lord thy God is a devouring fire*
(Deut. 4:24). Now I must explain that what Scripture means
hereby is that God is as punishing and destructive to unbelievers
and heretics as fire. I find, moreover, that in the language of Scripture comparisons are sometimes expressed without [the use of
the preposition] *kaf.* Thus we read: *And He brought you forth*
out of the iron furnace (Deut. 4:20), the meaning of which is
[really] *as out of an iron furnace.* [We read] also: <95> *after*
a dead dog? After a flea? (I Sam. 24:15), the actual meaning of
which is: *as after a dead dog and as after a flea.* Finally [we read]

---

45. "divine beings"—the usual translation is "the sons of might."
46. "taking into account"—literally "gathering" or "summing up."

concerning the Gadites that *Their faces were the faces of lions* (I Chron. 12:9), the meaning of which is [of course] *like the faces of lions*. Similarly must the meaning of *He is a devouring fire* be construed as: He is as punishing *as a devouring fire*.

[The] next [subject I shall discourse] about [in connection with the nature of God is that of] quantity. I say, then, that the concept of quantity calls for two things neither of which may be applied to the Creator. One of these is the measurement of length, width, and depth. The other is division and combination whereby things are divided from one another or combined with each other. None of these things can be asserted of the Creator, as it is proven by reason, Scripture, and tradition.

As far as the rational proof is concerned, it consists herein, that it was a Creator of these combinations and compositions, as demanded by our reason, that we were looking for and we found that there was nothing left of these [combinations] that would not be included in the concept that He was the author thereof.

As for the proof from Scripture, it is contained in the verse we have mentioned previously, namely: *Lest ye deal corruptly* (Deut. 4:16), and the rest of that passage.

As for the proof from tradition, again, we find that whenever our sages, who were considered trustworthy authorities in regard to our religion, encountered any such comparisons of God to physical beings, they did not translate them in an anthropomorphic sense, but rendered them in such a way as to correspond to the previously established principle. Now they were the disciples of the prophets and better acquainted than others with the speech of the prophets. If, therefore, it had seemed to them that these expressions were meant to be taken in their material sense, they would have translated them literally. However, they knew for certain from the prophets, aside from what their reason dictated to them, that by means of these anthropomorphic expressions they meant to designate lofty, exalted ideas. They therefore translated them in accordance with their clear understanding of the underlying thoughts.

One example of this type of translation is:

Behold, the hand of the Lord (Exod. 9: 3) = *Behold, a plague from before the Lord.*[47]

Another illustration of this sort of rendering is:

And under His feet (Exod. 24: 10) = *And under the throne of His glory.*

A further instance is:

According to the mouth [48] *of the Lord* (Exod. 17: 1) = *According to the word of the Lord.*

A still further sample of this mode of translating on their part is:

In the ears of the Lord (Num. 11: 18) = *Before the Lord.* Thus also did they translate all passages of a similar nature.

CHAPTER X

And now that I have made it clear that reason, Scripture, and tradition are in agreement <96> on the exclusion of any comparison from the personality of our Lord, I shall elaborate on these anthropomorphic terms, that are employed by Scripture in speaking of God, and say that there are ten of them, namely:

head, as in its statement: *And a helmet of salvation upon His head* (Isa. 59: 17);

eye, as in its statement: *The eyes of the Lord thy God are always upon it* [49] (Deut. 11: 12);

ear, as in its statement: *For ye have wept in the ears of the Lord* (Num. 11: 18);

mouth, as in its statement: *According to the mouth* [50] *of the Lord* (Exod. 17: 1);

lip, as in its statement: *Nor will I alter that which is gone out of My lips* (Ps. 89: 35);

face, as in its statement: *The Lord make His face to shine upon thee* (Num. 6: 25);

---

47. All these examples are taken from Targum Onkelos.
48. "mouth"—the usual translation is "commandment."
49. This quotation follows the reading of Ibn Tibbon.
50. Cf. above, n. 48.

hand, as in its statement: *Behold, the hand of the Lord* (Exod. 9:3);

heart, as in its statement: *And the Lord said in His heart* (Gen. 8:21);

entrails, as in its statement: *Therefore My entrails*[51] *yearn for him* (Jer. 31:20);

and *foot,* as in its statement: *And prostrate yourselves at His footstool* (Ps. 99:5).

Such statements, now, and others resembling them, are instances of the usage of language and its extension, each of them pointing to some idea [in connection with God]. As for their interpretation, it is such as we find it to be in matters other than those pertaining to the Creator. Thus we know that it is really of the nature and the peculiarity of language thus to extend and transfer meanings and employ figures of speech.

Such an extension of meaning is employed by the language of Scripture when it says

that heaven speaks: *The heavens declare the glory of God* (Ps. 19:2);

that the sea talks: *For the sea hath spoken, the stronghold of the sea, saying* (Isa. 23:4);

that death utters speech: *Destruction and Death say* (Job 28:22);

that stones can hear: *Behold, this stone shall be a witness against us; for it hath heard* (Josh. 24:27);

that the mountains speak: *The mountains and the hills shall break forth before you into singing* (Isa. 55:12);

and that the hills put on garments: *And the hills are girded with joy* (Ps. 65:13).

There are also other such passages that cannot be enumerated in haste.

Now if someone were to ask, "But what advantage is there in this extension of meaning that is practiced by language and that is calculated only to throw us into doubt? Would it not have done better if it had restricted itself to expressions <97> of unequivocal meaning and thus have enabled us to dispense with this burden of dis-

---

51. "entrails yearn"—the usual translation is "heart yearneth."

covering the correct interpretation?" my answer would be that, if language were to restrict itself to just one term, its employment would be very much curtailed and it would be impossible to express by means of it any more than a small portion of what we aim to convey. It therefore preferred rather to extend its use of words so as to transmit every meaning, relying for the correct interpretation upon reason and acquaintance with the texts of Scripture and with history. Were we, in our effort to give an account of God, to make use only of expressions that are literally true, it would be necessary for us to desist from speaking of Him as one that hears and sees and pities and wills to the point where there would be nothing left for us to affirm except the fact of His existence.

And now that I have made this clear, let me go back to the ten terms listed before in order to explain their actual meaning. I say, then, that [when they used the word] *head* [in connection with God], the prophets wished [to convey] the thought of distinction and elevation, as Scripture expresses itself elsewhere in regard to human beings: *My glory, and the lifter up of my head* (Ps. 3: 4). By *eye*, again, they meant solicitude, as in the statement found in Scripture: *That I may set mine eyes upon him* (Gen. 44: 21). By *face* [as applied to God] they meant either good will or anger. Thus Scripture says in one instance: *In the light of the king's countenance is life* (Prov. 16: 15); and in another: *And her countenance was no more sad* (I Sam. 1: 18). By *ear* they meant the acceptance of a plea, as Scripture says: *Let thy servant, I pray thee, speak a word in my lord's ears* (Gen. 44: 18). By *mouth* and *lip* they meant explanation and command, as in the statements of Scripture: *At the mouth* [52] *of Aaron and his sons* (Num. 4: 27), and *The lips of the righteous feed many; [but the foolish die for want of understanding]* (Prov. 10: 21). By *hand* they meant power, as in the statement of Scripture: *Therefore their inhabitants were short of hand* (II Kings 19: 26). By *heart* they meant wisdom, as in the statement of Scripture: *A young man void of heart* [53] (Prov. 7: 7). By *entrails* they meant tenderness, as in the statement of Scripture: *Yea, Thy Law is in my inmost parts* (Ps. 40: 9). By *foot*, finally, they meant domina-

52. "mouth"—the usual translation is "commandment."
53. "heart"—the usual translation is "understanding."

tion by force, as in the statement of Scripture: *Until I make thine enemies thy footstool* (Ps. 110:1).

Since, then, at certain times we find such expressions used of human beings, in a non-material sense <98> how much more fittingly should they be construed in this non-material sense when applied to the Creator! Furthermore I say that we find that expressions similar to these are used in speaking of inanimate things which cannot properly be said to possess any of these organs. We find, namely, that in the language of Scripture thirteen [54] such terms are applied to the earth and water.

The first of them is *head*—*Nor the head* [55] *of the dust of the world* (Prov. 8:26).

[Another is] *eye*, as in the statement of Scripture: *And they shall cover the eye* [56] *of the earth* (Exod. 10:5).

[A third is] *ear*, as in the statement of Scripture: *And give ear, Oh earth* (Isa. 1:2).

[A fourth is] *face*, as in the statement of Scripture: *Above the face of the earth* (Num. 11:31).

[A fifth is] *mouth*, as in the statement of Scripture: *And the earth opened her mouth* (Num. 16:32).

[A sixth is] *wing*, as in the statement of Scripture: *From the wing* [57] *of the earth* (Isa. 24:16).

[A seventh is] *hand*, as in the statement of Scripture: *By the hand* [58] *of the river* (Dan. 10:4).

[An eighth is] *lip*, as in the statement of Scripture: *By the river's lip* [59] (Exod. 2:3).

[A ninth is] *heart*, as in the statement of Scripture: *The deeps were congealed in the heart of the sea* (Exod. 15:8).

[A tenth is] *navel*, as in the statement of Scripture: *That dwell in the navel* [60] *of the earth* (Ezek. 38:12).

[An eleventh is] *belly*, as in the statement of Scripture: *Out of*

---

54. "thirteen"—the Arabic and Hebrew versions both read "twelve."
55. "head"—the usual translation is "beginning."
56. "eye"—the usual translation is "face."
57. "wing"—the usual translation is "uttermost part."
58. "hand"—the usual translation is "side."
59. "lip"—the usual translation is "brink."
60. "navel"—the usual translation is "middle."

*the belly of the netherworld cried I, and Thou heardst my
voice* (Jonah 2:3).

[A twelfth is] *womb,* as in the statement of Scripture: *Or who
shut up the sea with doors, when it broke forth, and issued out
of the womb* (Job 38:8).

[A thirteenth is] *thigh,* as in the statement of Scripture: *And I
shall gather them from the thighs* [61] *of the earth* (Jer. 31:8).

Thus we find that the language of Scripture employs these expressions in speaking of things, which, according to the testimony
of our senses, possess none of these organs, on which account they
must all be construed as merely figures of speech. It must, therefore, do the same for whatever our reason testifies possesses none
of these organs. In that case, too, these expressions can be only
figures of speech. He, therefore, who alleges that the language of
Scripture uses words only in their material sense, must find these
thirteen [62] organs for us in the earth and the water.

Now just as the above-mentioned terms for the organs of the
body [when applied to God] are used only figuratively, so also are
all acts connected with these organs. [This would hold true where
such words are addressed to God] as *incline Thine ear, open Thine
eyes, stretch forth Thy hand,* and the like. The same thing would
also apply to the <99> special functions ascribed to these organs,
[as when it is asserted of God] that *He hears and sees and speaks
and thinks* and the like. Each one of these has an interpretation
other than its literal sense. Hence even such a statement as *And
the Lord smelled,* the true implication of which is difficult to construe, would have the meaning of "to receive," which [the word
"smell" necessarily has] in the statement of Scripture: *Through the
smell* [63] *of water it will bud* (Job 14:9). [Such a construction would
be] in keeping with reason and Scripture and tradition.

Peradventure however, someone, attacking our view, will ask:
"But how is it possible to put such constructions on these anthropomorphic expressions and on what is related to them, when Scrip-

61. "thighs"—the usual translation is "uttermost parts."
62. "thirteen"—the Arabic and Hebrew versions both read "twelve."
63. "smell"—the usual translation is "scent."

ture itself explicitly mentions a form like that of human beings that was seen by the prophets and spoke to them and to which they imputed God's words, let alone the description by it of God's being seated on a throne, and His being borne by the angels on top of a firmament, as Scripture says: *And above the firmament that was over their heads was the likeness of a throne, as the appearance of a sapphire stone; and upon the likeness of the throne was a likeness as the appearance of a man above it?* (Ezek. 1:26.) Furthermore, this form is also mentioned as having been seen seated on a throne with angels on its right and its left, as Scripture says: *I saw the Lord sitting on His throne, and all the host of heaven standing by Him on His right hand and on His left"* (I Kings 22:19).

Our answer to this objection is that this form was something [specially] created. Similarly the throne and the firmament, as well as its bearers, were all of them produced for the first time by the Creator out of fire for the purpose of assuring His prophet that it was *He* that had revealed His word to him, as we shall explain in the third treatise of this book.[64] It is a form nobler even than [that of] the angels, magnificent in character, resplendent with light, which is called *the glory of the Lord*. It is this form, too, that one of the prophets described as follows: *I beheld till thrones were placed, and one that was ancient of days did sit* (Dan. 7:9), and that the sages characterized as *šĕkhinah*. Sometimes, however, this specially created being consists of light without the form of a person. It was, therefore, an honor that God had conferred on His prophet by allowing him to hear the oracle from the mouth of a majestic form created out of fire that was called *the glory of the Lord*, as we have <100> explained.

What further proves the correctness of our thesis is the statement of the prophet concerning this form: *And He said unto me: "Son of man, stand upon thy feet, and I will speak with thee"* (Ezek. 2:1). Now it is inconceivable that this interlocutor was the master of the universe, because the Torah says that the Creator has never spoken to anyone without an intermediary except to *our teacher Moses* alone. That is the import of its statement, *And there hath not*

64. Cf. below, p. 151.

arisen a prophet since in Israel like unto Moses, whom the Lord knew face to face [65] (Deut. 34:10). As for the rest of the prophets, however, it was only the angels that addressed them. When, then, we find the text directly mentioning the title *angel*, we have an explicit reference to a created being. If, again, it uses the phrase *glory of the Lord*, that too implies something created. If, however, it mentions the name *Lord* but does not attach to it the word *glory* or *angel* but only such expressions as *vision* or *throne* or some human attribute, there can be no doubt but that there is something suppressed in that utterance, the full form of which should be *glory of the Lord* or *angel of the Lord*, in accordance with the practice of the language of Scripture to leave out words by ellipsis.

CHAPTER XI

Next I shall discourse upon [the category of] *quality*, that is to say the accidents, [in their relationship to God]. I say, then, that in reality it cannot be asserted at all that accidents could apply to God, in view of the fact that He is the creator of all accidents. When, therefore, we find Him saying that He loves or hates a certain thing, what is meant thereby is that whatever He has commanded us to do is designated by Him as lovable in His sight, since He has made the love of that thing obligatory upon us. Thus, for example, Scripture says: *For the Lord loveth justice* (Ps. 37:28), and *For the Lord is righteous, He loveth righteousness* (Ps. 11:7), and the like. It also makes this assertion about the virtues in general, saying: *For in these things I delight, saith the Lord* (Jer. 9:23). Whatever, again, He has forbidden us to do is designated by Him as hateful in His sight, since He has made the hating of that thing obligatory upon us. Thus Scripture says: *There are six things which the Lord hateth* (Prov. 6:16), and *I hate robbery with iniquity* (Isa. 61:8). It also makes this assertion about vices in general, saying concerning them: *For all these are things that I hate, saith the Lord* (Zech. 8:17).

65. This quotation follows the reading of Ibn Tibbon.

Furthermore, whenever we note that, [according to Scripture], God says that He is pleased <101> or angry, what is meant thereby is that whenever happiness and reward are decreed for some of God's creatures, that is characterized as God's pleasure. This is illustrated in such statements of Scripture as *The Lord taketh pleasure in them that fear Him* (Ps. 147:11), and *Lord, Thou hast taken pleasure in Thy land* (Ps. 85:2). Again, when some of them are deserving of hardship and punishment, that is characterized as God's anger. This is illustrated in such statements of Scripture as *The anger of the Lord is against them that do evil* (Ps. 34:17), and *But His power and His wrath is against all them that forsake Him* (Ezra 8:22). As for physical anger and pleasure or physical love and hate, they can be possessed only by beings that desire and fear. It is out of the question, however, that the Creator of all things should entertain a desire for aught that He has created or be in fear of it. The same exegesis is to be given to all other apparently anthropomorphic descriptions of God occurring in Scripture that fall under the category of quality.

With respect to [the category of] *relation* I say that it would be improper to connect anything with the Creator in an anthropomorphic manner or to relate it to Him, because He has existed since eternity, [that is a time] when none of the things created were connected with Him or related to Him. Now, that they have been created by Him, it would be necessary to make the inadmissible assumption that a change has taken place in His essence, permitting them to become related to and connected with Him in an anthropomorphic fashion, subsequent to the existence of a contrary situation.

When, therefore, we note [66] that the Scriptures call God *king* and present human beings as His slaves and the angels as ministering to Him, as is done in the statements of Scripture: *The Lord is king forever and ever* (Ps. 10:16), and *Praise, O ye servants of the Lord* (Ps. 113:1), and *The flaming fire His ministers* (Ps. 104:4), all that is merely a means of expressing reverence and es-

66. "we note"—so Ibn Tibbon. The Arabic original reads "thou notest."

teem. For the human beings most highly esteemed by us are the kings. God is also called "king" in the sense that He can do whatever He wishes and that His command is always carried out, as Scripture says: *Forasmuch as the king's word has power; and who may say unto Him: "What doest thou?"* (Eccles. 8: 4.)

Again, when we find that the Scriptures ascribe to God friends and enemies, as is done in such statements of Scripture as *O ye that love the Lord, hate evil* (Ps. 97:10), and *The haters of the Lord should dwindle away before Him* (Ps. 81: 16), that is merely a metaphorical usage of these terms on their part for <102> the purpose of expressing esteem or disapproval. Esteem is shown of those men that obey God by applying to them the designation of *lovers* of God, whilst disapproval of the disobedient is expressed by the application to them of the designation of *haters*. In the same vein must everything else that falls under this category be interpreted.

Apropos of [the category of] *place,* I say that it is inconceivable for several reasons that the Creator should have need for occupying any place whatsoever. First of all He is Himself the Creator of all space. Also He originally existed alone, [that is, at a time] when there was [as yet] no [such thing as] place. It is unthinkable, therefore, that as a result of His act of creation He should have been transported into space. Furthermore, space is required only by a material object which occupies [67] the place of the object that it meets and comes in contact with, so that each one of the two contiguous objects forms the place of the other. This is, however, out of the question so far as the Creator is concerned.

As for the assertion of the prophets that God dwells in heaven, that was merely a way of indicating God's greatness and His elevation, since heaven is for us the highest thing we know of. This is borne out by such explanations offered by the Scriptures as *For God is in heaven, and thou upon earth* (Eccles. 5: 1); as well as *Behold, heaven and the heaven of heavens cannot contain Thee* (I Kings 8: 27). The same applies to statements to the effect that

67. "occupies"—Cf. Lane-Poole's *Arabic-English Lexicon* (London, 1863–1893), p. 1567, šagala.

God dwells in the Temple, such as *And I will dwell among the children of Israel* (Exod. 29:45), and *And the Lord dwelleth in Zion* (Joel 4:21). The purpose of all this was to confer honor upon the place and the people in question. Besides that it is to be remembered that God had also revealed in that place His specially-created light, of which we have made mention previously, that was called *šĕkhinah* and *glory*.

As regards [the category of] *time*, it is inconceivable that the concept of time could be applied to the Creator because of the fact that He is Himself the Creator of all time. Furthermore, He existed originally alone when there was as yet no such thing as time. It is, therefore, unthinkable that time should have effected any locomotion or change in Him. Moreover, time is nothing else than the measurement of the duration of corporeal beings. He, however, who has no body, is far removed from such concepts as time and duration. If, nevertheless, we do describe God as being enduring and permanent, that is done only by way of approximation, as has been stated by us previously.

Again, when we find the Scriptures making such statements as *Even from everlasting <103> to everlasting, Thou art God* (Ps. 90:2), as well as *Yea, since the day was I am He* (Isa. 43:13), and again, *Before Me there was no God formed, neither shall any be after Me* (Isa. 43:10), all the points of time referred to therein revert solely to God's acts. Those, therefore, who say *Even from everlasting to everlasting, Thou art God,* mean thereby: "From the beginning of time Thou hast always helped Thy servants." Thus Scripture expresses it elsewhere: *God is unto us a God of deliverances* (Ps. 68:21).

As for His statement, blessed be He, *Before Me there was no God formed,* that was meant to convey the thought: "Before I sent My messenger and after I sent Him there was no God outside of Myself." For immediately prior to this remark He says: *My servant whom I have chosen.* In the popular idiom, in fact, it is quite proper for a person to say "before me" when he means "before I act." This was done by Joab when he said: *I may not tarry thus before thee* (II Sam. 18:14). Also one may say "after me" when one means "after I have acted," as Nathan did when he said: *I also will come in after thee, and confirm thy words* [68] (I Kings 1:14).

Similarly is there, in the statement *Yea, since the day was I am He*, an allusion to some distinguished day, either the day of the revelation at *Sinai* or another such day. What God says, in effect, in this statement is: "From that time on have I been the one commanding you to do such and such a thing and forbidding you to do that, and saving you from this," because He concludes the statement with the remark: *I will work, and who can reverse it?*

As regards [the matter of] *possession*, inasmuch as all creatures are God's creation and handiwork, it is not seemly for us to say that He possesses one thing to the exclusion of another, nor that He possesses the one to a greater and the other to a lesser degree. If we, nevertheless, see the Scriptures assert that a certain people is His peculiar property and His possession and His portion and *inheritance*, [as they do in the statement]: *For the portion of the Lord is His people, Jacob the lot of His inheritance* (Deut. 32:9), that is done merely as a means of conferring honor and distinction. For, as it appears to us, every man's portion and lot are precious to him. Nay the Scriptures even go so far as to declare God, too, figuratively to be the lot of the pious and their portion, as they do in their statement: *O Lord, the portion of mine inheritance and of my cup* (Ps. 16:5). This is, therefore, also an <104> expression of special devotion and esteem.

It is also in this sense that one must construe the designation of God as the Master of the prophets and of [all] believers, as He is called in such expressions used by Scripture as *The God of Abraham, [the God of Isaac and the God of Jacob]* (Exod. 3:6), and *The God of the Hebrews* (Exod. 3:18). Such a designation is entirely in order, since God is the Master of all. This [special attachment of God's name] to the pious is, then, merely an expression of His esteem and high regard for them.

As for [the category of] *position* [in relation to God], inasmuch as the Creator, blessed and exalted be He, is not a physical being, it is unseemly [to speak] of Him as having any such position as

---

68. This quotation follows the reading of Ibn Tibbon.

sitting or standing or the like. Nay, it is impossible because He is not a physical being, and because originally there existed nothing outside of Himself. Also by position is meant the extension of one body over another. Finally the various positions assumed necessarily produce some change or alteration in him that assumes them.

If, nevertheless, the Scriptures make such assertions as *Yea, the Lord sitteth as king forever* (Ps. 29: 10), their object therein is solely to indicate the permanence of God's existence. Such statements on the part of the Scriptures, again, as *Rise up, O Lord, and let Thine enemies be scattered* (Num. 10: 35) mean nothing else than readiness for help and punishment. In such utterances, moreover, as *And He stood with him there* (Exod. 34: 5), the subject referred to is the divine light called *šĕkhinah*. Finally, by such Scriptural remarks as *And the Lord went His way, as soon as He had finished* (Gen. 18: 33) is meant the removal of that light. The same sort of exegesis must be given to any Scriptural statements resembling these.

CHAPTER XII

Apropos of [the category of] action, let me say that, even though we denominate the Creator "Maker" and "Agent," the meaning that we attribute to these terms must not be construed in a corporeal sense. A physical agent, namely, cannot produce an effect upon another before acting upon himself. He must first himself move. Having done that, he can then generate motion in others. As for God, however, exalted and magnified be He, He need but entertain the wish in order to have a thing come into being. And that is the manner in which He works always. Also every physical agent needs materials to work with, and time and place to work in, and an instrument to do his work <105> with. All this is, however, far removed from God, as we have explained before.

When, therefore, we find the Scriptures, in speaking of some of the works of God, make mention of an act and its opposite, and in speaking of others mention an act without its opposite, it must all be reduced to the fact that. when God creates anything, He brings it into being without actually taking it in hand or coming in contact with it. The Scriptures do, indeed, characterize the positive and negative acts of creation by saying: *And God made* (Gen. 1:7), *And He rested* (Gen. 2:2). However, just as the *And He made* was effected without motion or exertion, consisting only of the production of the thing created, so undoubtedly, when it is said *And He rested*, it was not relaxation from any kind of motion or exertion. It constituted merely the discontinuance of the production of what was to be created. Even though, then, the Scriptures say of God *And He rested* (Exod. 20:11), it means nothing further than that He discontinued His work of creation and production.

On the subject of prophecy, the Scriptures employ the expression *And the Lord spoke* (Num. 1:1). Now the ultimate meaning of this statement is that God created speech, which He conveyed through the medium of the air to the hearing of the prophet or the people in question. Apropos of the opposite of *speech* in relation to God, again, the Scriptures say: *I have long time held My peace, I have been still, and refrained Myself* (Isa. 42:14). But the actual meaning of this silence is postponement and the granting of respite. However, the Arabic language,[69] although it permits God's speech to be characterized in accordance with our interpretation, does not allow a similar characterization or interpretation of His silence. Yet when we apply to such Hebrew expressions as *I have held My peace* (heḥěšethi) the proper exegesis, what we have said at the beginning of our remark about its meaning "postponement" is completely borne out.

Again, the matter of the deliverance of the human world from a painful situation is designated by the Scriptures as *recollection* on the part of God. Thus they say: *And God remembered Noah* (Gen. 8:1), and *And God remembered Rachel* (Gen. 30:22), and the like. Now both languages employ the word "remember" in speaking of God. Neither of the two languages, however, permits the

69. Saadia has in mind the Koran and the theory of certain Mohammedan theologians, such as Ashari, to the effect that silence on the part of God would imply perfection in Him. God's word must, therefore, be forthcoming continually. Cf. Ventura, pp. 192 ff. and n. 74.

use of the opposite of remembering, namely the term "forgetful-ness," in connection with God's desisting from the deliverance of His creatures. In such cases they generally employ such expressions as *And He remembered not His footstool* (Lam. 2:1).

Furthermore, grace and mercy are attributed <106> to God, for He is called *A merciful and gracious God* (Exod. 34:6). So, too, are vengeance and punishment attributed to Him, for He is called *A jealous and avenging God* (Nah. 1:2). However, these concepts, also, revert to the creatures rather than the Creator. Thus Scripture says: *The Lord taketh vengeance on His adversaries; and He reserveth wrath for His enemies* (*ibid.*). It says also: *Who keepeth covenant and mercy with them that love Him and keep His commandments to a thousand generations* (Deut. 7:9).

Similarly do all other attributes of this class go back, so far as their ultimate meaning is concerned, to God's works. Herein, then, lies the difference between the essential and the active attributes of God, as we have also explained in the commentary on the book of Exodus.

As regards His being the recipient of action, there is no one who believes that that could apply to the Creator in any form other than that of visibility [in revelations]. It is necessary, therefore, for me to explain that this susceptibility to being seen does not [really] apply to Him either. Things are, namely, visible only by virtue of the colors appearing on their surfaces which are related to the four elements of nature. These colors are united with the faculty of their own species, lodging in the [organ of] sight through the medium of the air, from which vision follows as a result. So far as the Creator is concerned, however, who cannot possibly be supposed to possess any accidents, the [sense of] sight has no power to perceive Him. Thou notest, indeed, that even imagination has no means of picturing or forming an image of God. How, then, could the [sense of] sight have the means therefor?

Now some people are confused by the story related in Scripture that our teacher Moses requested of His Master: *Show me, I pray*

Thee, Thy glory (Exod. 33:18). They are even more confused by God's answer to Moses: *Thou canst not see My face, for man shall not see Me and live* (Exod. 33:20). And their confusion is doubled by God's subsequent remark: *And thou shalt see My back; but My face shall not be seen* (Exod. 33:23).

I say, then, invoking the aid of God in the effort to reveal and clarify all this, that God has a special light which He creates and makes manifest to His prophets in order that they may infer therefrom that it is a prophetic communication emanating from God that they hear. When one of them sees this light, he says: "I have seen *the glory of the Lord.*" Often, however, he would say simply: "I have seen God," by way of ellipsis. <107> Thou knowest also that about *Moses and Aaron, Nadab and Abihu, and seventy of the elders of Israel* (Exod. 24:9) Scripture says at first, *And they saw the God of Israel* (Exod. 24:10). This is explained afterwards as follows: *And the appearance of the glory of the Lord was like devouring fire on the top of the mount* (Exod. 24:17). However, when they beheld this light, they were unable to look upon it on account of its power and brilliance. Indeed whoever looked upon it incurred the disintegration of his entire makeup and the flight of his spirit from his body, as Scripture says: *Lest they break through unto the Lord to gaze, and many of them perish* (Exod. 19:21).

Moses, accordingly, asked his Master to give him the strength to look upon this light. The latter, however, answered him that the first rays of this light were so powerful that he would be unable to view them clearly with his naked eyes, lest he perish. He would rather cover him up with a cloud or the like until the first rays of this light have passed, because the greatest strength of every radiant body is contained in its initial approach. All this was implied in the statement of Scripture: *And I will cover thee with My hand until I have passed by* (Exod. 33:22). When, then, the first portion of the light had passed, God removed from Moses the thing that had covered him, so that he might be able to look at the back of the light, as Scripture says: *And I will take away My hand, and thou shalt see My back* (Exod. 33:23). As for the

Creator Himself, however, there is no means whereby anybody might see Him. Aye, that is in the realm of the impossible.

CHAPTER XIII

Next I would ask: "How is it possible to establish this concept in our minds—I mean that of the Creator, exalted and magnified be He—when none of our senses have ever perceived Him?" My answer is that it is done in the same manner in which such notions arise in them as the approbation of the truth and the disapproval of lying, although these matters are not subject to the perception of any of our senses. It is done also in the same way in which our minds recognize the impossibility of a thing's being existent and nonexistent at one and the same time, as well as of other such mutually exclusive phenomena, although these matters have never been observed by the senses. Furthermore, Scripture says: *But the Lord God is the truth* (Jer. 10:10).

Another question that I would ask is: "But how is it possible for our minds to conceive the thought of God's presence everywhere so that no place would be vacant of His presence?" My answer is that God existed before there was any such thing as space. If, therefore, the existence of many different localities could have brought about a division among the parts of the Creator's personality, He would not have created them. Again, if the various material objects <108> would have taken away space from Him or a certain amount of space, He would not have had to produce them. Since, then, that is the case, His existence after His creation of all the bodies must be exactly as it was before He had created them without any change or division or concealment or interruption, but, rather, as Scripture puts it: *Can any hide himself in secret places that I shall not see him? saith the Lord. Do not I fill heaven and earth?* (Jer. 23:24.)

Now let me make this a little more comprehensible, and say that if we had not been accustomed to noting that certain walls do not cut off sound, and had we not been in the habit of observing that glass does not screen the light, and had we not known that the light of the sun is not affected adversely by the filth that exists in the world, we would have been rather surprised at the above-mentioned. All these [commonplace] marvels serve, therefore, as a corroboration of the validity of our idea of God.

I would also ask this question, namely: "How is it conceivable by the mind that God knows everything that has happened in the past as well as all that will take place in the future, and that He knows both equally?" Let me explain, then, that the reason why this seems hard to understand is because God's creatures do not know what is to take place in the future, since their knowledge comes to them only through the medium of their senses. Whatever, therefore, has not come to their hearing or sight or their other senses cannot be apprehended by them. For the Creator, however, who requires no mediary cause for the acquisition of His knowledge, since it is rather by His essence that He is cognizant of things, the past and the future are both on the same level. He knows the one as well as the other without any mediary cause, as Scripture remarks: *Who declares the end from the beginning, and from ancient times things that are not yet done; saying: "My counsel shall stand, and all My pleasures will I do"* (Isa. 46:10).

Now when a person has achieved the knowledge of this lofty subject by means of rational speculation and the proof of the miracles and marvels [mentioned in Holy Writ], his soul believes it as true and it is mingled with his spirit and becomes an inmate of its innermost recesses. The result is then that, whenever the soul walks in its temple, it finds it, as the saint has said: *With my soul have I desired Thee in the night; yea, with my spirit within me have I sought Thee earnestly* (Isa. 26:9). Moreover his soul becomes filled with [70] completely sincere <109> love for God, a love which is beyond all doubt, as Scripture expresses it: *And thou shalt love the Lord thy God with all thy heart*, etc.[71] (Deut. 6:5.)

70. "filled with"—so according to Ibn Tibbon. There is an error of metathesis in the Arabic text.

71. This quotation follows the reading of Ibn Tibbon.

That servant of God will also grow accustomed to remembering God in the daytime when he does his work and at night when he lies on his bed, as Scripture says: *When I remember Thee upon my couch, and meditate on Thee in the night watches* (Ps. 63:7). Nay it will almost speak—I mean his spirit—moaning [72] at the recollection of God, out of longing and yearning, as Scripture says: *When I think thereon, O God, I must moan; when I muse thereon, my spirit fainteth* (Ps. 77:4). Nay more, the mention of God will nourish his soul more than fatty foods and His name quench its thirst better than the juiciest fruit, as Scripture says: *My soul is satisfied as with marrow and fatness; and my mouth doth praise Thee with joyful lips* (Ps. 63:6). The soul's attachment to God will become so great that it will refer all its affairs to Him, trusting and reposing complete confidence in Him always, as Scripture says: *Trust in Him at all times, ye people; pour out your heart before Him; God is a refuge for us* (Ps. 62:9).

The result of this is that when God affords it pleasure, the soul is grateful, and if He causes it pain, it endures it patiently, as Scripture says: *All the fat ones of the earth shall eat and worship* (Ps. 22:30). Aye, even if God were to separate the soul from its body, it would be indulgent toward Him and not entertain misgivings about Him on that account, as Scripture says: *Though He slay me, yet will I trust in Him* (Job 13:15).

The more it contemplates His being, the more does it fear and revere Him, as Scripture says: *Therefore am I affrighted at His presence; when I consider, I am afraid of Him* (Job 23:15). Also the more it considers His attributes, the greater becomes its praise of Him and the more does it rejoice in Him, as Scripture says: *Let the heart of them rejoice that seek the Lord* (Ps. 105:3).

Thus it reaches the point where it loves those that love Him and honors those that honor Him, as Scripture says: *How precious also are Thy friends* [73] *to me, etc.* (Ps. 139:17). On the other hand, it hates those that hate Him and is hostile to His enemies,

72. "moaning"—Ibn Tibbon. The Arabic original uses a word meaning "lovesick."

73. "How precious also are Thy friends . . ."—the usual translation is: "How weighty also are Thy thoughts . . ."

as Scripture says: *Do not I hate them, O Lord, that hate Thee, etc?* [74] (Ps. 139: 21). In this way is it induced to take up His cause and to refute everyone that raises arguments against Him, by the employment of reason and knowledge, not with harshness, as the saint has said: *I will fetch* <110> *my knowledge from afar, and will ascribe righteousness to my Maker. For truly my words are not false; one that is upright in mind is with thee* (Job 36: 3, 4).

It will furthermore laud and praise Him justly and uprightly, not by attributing to Him exaggerations and absurdities. Thus Scripture says, in regard to those that uttered God's praises: *And Hezekiah spoke encouragingly to all the Levites that showed good understanding for the Lord* [75] (II Chron. 30: 22). It will not, therefore, praise Him for being able to cause five to be more than ten without adding anything to the former, nor for being able to put the world through the hollow of a signet ring without making the one narrower and the other wider, nor for being able to bring back the day gone by in its original condition. For all these things are absurd.

Of course, certain heretics often ask us about such matters, and we do indeed answer them that God is able to do everything. This thing, however, that they ask of Him isn't anything because it is absurd, and the absurd is nothing. It is, therefore, as though they were to ask: "Is God capable of doing what is nothing?" which is, of course, a real question.

The soul [of the pious] will [therefore] rather praise Him for His essential attributes, such as that He is eternal, that He always was and that He will never cease to be, as Scripture says: *The eternal God is a dwelling-place* (Deut. 33: 27). [It will] furthermore [assert of Him] that He is truly one in essence, as Scripture says: *Thou are the Lord, even Thou alone* (Neh. 9: 6). [It will] also [affirm] that He is living and enduring, as Scripture says: *For I lift up My hand to heaven, and say: As I live forever* (Deut. 32: 40). [It will], moreover, [declare] that He is able to do everything, as Scripture says: *The God, the great, the mighty, and the awful*

74. This quotation follows the reading of Ibn Tibbon.
· 75. This quotation follows the reading of Ibn Tibbon.

(Neh. 9: 32). [It will say] besides, that He knows everything with a perfect knowledge, as Scripture says: *Dost thou know the balancings of the clouds, the wondrous works of Him who is perfect in knowledge?* (Job 37: 16). [It will affirm] in addition, that He is the original Creator of everything, as Scripture says: *Not like these is the portion of Jacob; for He is the former of all things* (Jer. 10: 16).

Furthermore, [this soul will allege] that God does not produce aught that is vain or wasteful, as Scripture says: <111> *He created it not a waste, He formed it to be inhabited* (Isa. 45: 18). [It will] also [say of Him] that He commits no injustice or violence, as Scripture says: *The Rock, His work is perfect, for all His ways are justice . . .*[76] (Deut. 32: 4). [It will] furthermore [declare] that He deals out unto His servants only what is good for them, as Scripture says: *The Lord is good to all . . . . All Thy works shall praise Thee . . . . They shall speak of the glory of Thy kingdom . . .*[77] (Ps. 145: 9–11). [It will state] moreover, that He is not subject to alteration or change, as Scripture says: *For I the Lord change not* (Mal. 3: 6).

Furthermore, [it will assert] that His kingdom will not cease nor disappear, as Scripture says: *Thy kingdom is a kingdom for all ages* (Ps. 145: 13). [It will] also [affirm] that His command is always obeyed, irreversible, as Scripture says: *The Lord hath established His throne in the heavens; and His kingdom ruleth over all* (Ps. 103: 19). [It will] also [assert] that it is obligatory to praise His good and exalted qualities, as Scripture says: *Yea, they shall sing of the ways of the Lord; for great is the glory of the Lord* (Ps. 138: 5). Yet [it will bear in mind the fact] that for all the laudatory descriptions given of Him and all the praise bestowed upon Him, He is elevated and exalted above and far removed from all that, as Scripture says, *And let them say: Blessed be Thy glorious Name, that is exalted above all blessing and praise* (Neh. 9: 5).

Now we find in certain places of the Scriptures that praise or encomium is related not to God but rather to an attribute of His, as in such statements of Scripture as *Blessed be the glory of the*

76. This quotation follows the reading of Ibn Tibbon.
77. This quotation follows the reading of Ibn Tibbon.

Lord from His place (Ezek. 3:12), and *Sing praises to His name* (Ps. 68:5). Nay, we find it at times applied to the attribute of an attribute, as in such statements of Scripture as *Blessed be the name of His glory* [78] (Ps. 72:19) and *And give thanks to the mention of His Holiness* [79] (Ps. 97:12). In fact, among the utterances of our forefathers there are some that give the impression of being praises applied to the attribute of the attribute of an attribute, for they used the formula, *Blessed be the name of the glory of His kingdom* (Mišnah Yoma 3:8).

Let me then say in regard to all that, that this is also a peculiarity of the usage of the language of Scripture. When, namely, it aims to exalt and magnify someone, it has the actual mention of the individual, who is thus to be glorified, preceded by a number of expressions. The greater the number of expressions <112> preceding the mention of his name, the greater the distinction conferred upon him. Thus the language of Scripture employs three such expressions [following each other] in the statement: *When he showed the riches of the glory of his kingdom* (Esther 1:4), as well as the phrase: *And the honor of the excellence of his majesty* (*ibid.*). All that it means to say there really is *his riches and his glory and his kingdom and his honor and his excellence and his majesty*. All these attributes are, however, synonymous.

Do, then, try to understand, may God guide thee aright, what we have noted down and put it into thy soul and grasp it with thy mind. Do not, however, hasten to judge the validity thereof on the basis of the particular expression used, but rather on that of the previously stated principles, considering the expression merely as a figure of speech and an approximate rendering of the thought, as we have explained.

The second treatise is hereby completed with the help of God's might.

78. "the name of His glory"—the usual translation is "His glorious name."
79. "the mention of His holiness"—the usual translation is "His holy name."

TREATISE III

CONCERNING COMMAND AND PROHIBITION

EXORDIUM

IT behooves me to preface this treatise with the remark that once it is realized that the Creator, exalted and magnified be He, is eternal, nothing having been [associated] with Him [originally], it must be recognized that His creation of all things was purely an act of bounty and grace on His part. Also, as we noted at the end of the first treatise of this book,[1] in regard to the motive of the Creator in creating the world, and in accordance with what is found written in the Scriptures, God is bountiful and a dispenser of favors. Thus Scripture says: *The Lord is good to all; and His tender mercies are over all His works* (Ps. 145:9).

Now His first act of kindness toward His creatures consisted in His giving them being—I mean His calling them into existence after a state of nonbeing. Thus did He also express Himself toward the elite of His creatures, saying: *Every one that is called by My name, and whom I have created for My glory . . .* (Isa. 43:7). In addition to that, however, He also endowed them with the means whereby they might attain complete happiness and perfect bliss, as Scripture says: *Thou makest me to know the path of life; in Thy presence is fulness of joy, in Thy right hand bliss for evermore* (Ps. 16:11). This means the commandments <113> and the prohibitions prescribed for them by God.

Now this remark is the first thing that strikes the attention of the reflecting mind, prompting it to ask: "Could ·not God have bestowed upon His creatures complete bliss and permanent happiness without giving them commandments and prohibitions? Nay it would seem that His kindness would in that case have contrib-

1. Cf. above, p. 86.

uted even more to their well-being, because they would be relieved of all exertion for the attainment of their bliss."

Let me, then, say in explanation of this matter that, on the contrary, God's making His creatures' diligent compliance with His commandments the means of attaining permanent bliss is the better course. For according to the judgment of reason the person who achieves some good by means of the effort that he has expended for its attainment obtains double the advantage gained by him who achieves this good without any effort but merely as a result of the kindness shown him by God. In fact, reason recognizes no equality between these two. This being the case, then, the Creator preferred to assign to us the ampler portion in order that our reward might yield us a double benefit, not merely a compensation exactly equivalent to the effort, as Scripture also says: *Behold, the Lord God will come as a Mighty One, and His arm will rule for Him; behold, His reward is with Him, and His recompense before Him* (Isa. 40:10).

CHAPTER I

Now that I have made this preliminary observation, let me state by way of introduction that our Lord, exalted and magnified be He, has informed us by the speech of His prophets that He has assigned to us a religion whereby we are to serve Him. It embraces laws prescribed for us by Him which we must observe and carry out with sincerity. That is the import of the statement of Scripture: *This day the Lord thy God commandeth thee to do these statutes and ordinances; thou shalt, therefore, observe and do them with all thy heart, and with all thy soul* (Deut. 26:16).

Moreover, in support of the validity of these laws, His messengers executed certain signs and wondrous miracles, with the result that we observed and carried out these laws immediately. Afterwards we discovered the rational basis for the necessity of their prescription so that we might not be left to roam at large without guidance.

Certain matters and classifications relative to this subject that reason makes imperative must now be explained by me. I say, then, that logic demands that whoever does something good be compensated either by means of a favor shown to him, if <114> he is in need of it, or by means of thanks, if he does not require any reward. Since, therefore, this is one of the general demands of reason, it would not have been seemly for the Creator, exalted and magnified be He, to neglect it in His own case. It was, on the contrary, necessary for Him to command His creatures to serve Him and thank Him for having created them. Reason also demands that he that is wise do not permit himself to be treated with contempt or to be insulted. It was, therefore, likewise necessary for the Creator to forbid His servants to conduct themselves in such a way toward Him.

Furthermore, reason demands that the creatures be prevented from wronging each other in all sorts of ways. Hence it was also necessary for the All-Wise not to permit them to do such a thing. Reason also deems it proper for a wise man to give employment to an individual who performs a certain function and to pay him a wage for it, merely in order to confer a benefit upon him, since this is something that redounds to the benefit of the worker without hurting the employer.

If, now, we were to combine these four classes of requirements, their sum-total would make up all the laws prescribed for us by our Lord. For example, He made it obligatory upon us to learn to know Him, to worship Him, and to dedicate ourselves wholeheartedly to Him, as the saint has said: *And thou, Solomon my son, know thou the God of thy father, and serve Him with a whole heart and with a willing mind* (I Chron. 28: 9). Next he forbade us to conduct ourselves in an ugly insulting fashion toward Him, even though it could not hurt Him, because it is not the way of divine Wisdom to permit it, as Scripture says: *Whosoever curseth his God shall bear his sin* (Lev. 24: 15). Nor would He permit one of us to wrong the other or commit violence against him, as Scripture says: *Ye shall not steal; neither shall ye deal falsely, nor lie to one another* (Lev. 19:11). These three classes of injunctions and whatever might be included in them constitute, then, the first of the two divisions of the laws of the Torah.

Now in the first of the [three] categories [we have mentioned above] there are to be included such acts as humble submission to God and serving Him and standing before Him and whatever resembles these, all of which are found in the text of Holy Writ. In the second class are to be included such injunctions as the one not to associate anyone else with God, nor to swear falsely in His name, nor <115> to describe Him with mundane attributes and whatever resembles these, all of which are [also] found in the text of Holy Writ. To the third division, again, are to be added the practice of justice, truth, fairness, and righteousness, and the avoidance of the killing of human beings, and [the observance of] the prohibition of fornication and theft and deception and usury. [There is to be appended] also the duty devolving upon the believer to love his brother like himself and whatever else is embraced in these paragraphs, all of which is found in the text of Holy Writ.

Now the approval of each of these classes of acts that we have been commanded to carry out is implanted in our minds just as is the disapproval of each of the classes of acts that we are forbidden to commit. Thus has Wisdom, which is identical with reason, said: *For my mouth shall utter truth, and wickedness is an abomination to my lips* (Prov. 8:7).

The second [general] division [of the precepts of the Torah, on the other hand,] consists of things neither the approval nor the disapproval of which is decreed by reason, on account of their own character, but in regard to which our Lord has imposed upon us a profusion of commandments and prohibitions in order thereby to increase our reward and happiness. This is borne out by the remark of Scripture: *The Lord was pleased, for His righteousness' sake, to make the Torah* [2] *great and glorious* (Isa. 42:21).

What is commanded of this group of acts is, consequently, [to

2. "Torah"—the usual translation is "teaching."

be considered as] good, and what is prohibited as reprehensible; because the fulfillment of the former and the avoidance of the latter implies submissiveness to God. From this standpoint they might be attached secondarily to the first [general] division [of the laws of the Torah]. Nevertheless one cannot help noting, upon deeper reflection, that they have some partial uses as well as a certain slight justification from the point of view of reason, just as those belonging to the first [general] division have important uses and great justification from the point of view of reason.

CHAPTER II

Now it is fitting that I proceed first to the discussion of the rational precepts of the Torah. I say, then, that divine Wisdom imposed a restraint upon bloodshed among men, because if license were to prevail in this matter, they would cause each other to disappear. The consequence would be, in addition to the pain experienced by the victims, a frustration of the purpose that the All-Wise had in mind with regard to them. For their murder would cut them off from the fulfillment of the function for which He had created them and in the execution of which He had employed them.

Furthermore [divine] Wisdom forbade fornication in order that men might not become like the beasts with the result that no one would know his father <116> so as to show him reverence in return for having raised him. [Another reason for this prohibition was] that the father might bequeath unto his son his possessions just as the son had received from his father the gift of existence. [A further reason was] that a human being might know the rest of his relatives, such as his paternal and maternal uncles, and show them whatever tenderness he was capable of.

Theft was forbidden by [divine] Wisdom because, if it were permitted, some men would rely on stealing the others' wealth, and they would neither till the soil nor engage in any other lucrative occupation. And if all were to rely on this source of livelihood, even stealing would become impossible, because, with the disappearance of all property, there would be absolutely nothing in existence that might be stolen.

Finally, [divine] Wisdom has made it one of its first injunctions that we speak the truth and desist from lying. For the truth is an assertion about a thing as it really is and in accordance with its actual character, whereas telling a lie is making an assertion about a thing that does not correspond to what it really is or to its actual character. Then when the senses, perceiving it, find it to be constituted in one form whilst the soul, reasoning about it, asserts that it is constituted otherwise, these two contrary views set up in the soul will oppose each other, and, on account of their mutual exclusion, the thing will be regarded by the soul as something grotesque.[3]

Let me say next that I have seen some people who are of the opinion that these four principal vices that have been listed above are not at all objectionable. Only that is objectionable in their view which causes them pain and worry and grief, whilst the good is what affords them pleasure and rest. This thesis will be refuted by me at considerable length in the fourth treatise of this book, in the chapter on "justice."[4] I shall, however, cite a portion of that refutation here, and say that whoever entertains such an opinion leaves out of account all the arguments we have produced here, and whoever leaves such matters out of account is an ignoramus about whom we need not trouble ourselves. Nevertheless I shall not be content until I have convinced him of the contradiction and the conflict inherent in his views.

I say, then, that the slaying of an enemy is an act that gives pleasure to the slayer but pain to the slain. Likewise the taking of another man's possessions or his wife gives pleasure to the robber but pain to the robbed. In the opinion of those who hold this view, however, each of these two acts would have to be regarded as wisdom and folly at one and the same time—as wisdom because it affords pleasure to the murderer or the thief or the adulterer, and

3. "grotesque"—cf. the discussion by Guttmann on this (p. 137, n. 1).
4. Cf. below, pp. 184 ff.

as folly because it inflicts pain on his opponent. Now any theory that leads to such internal contradiction and mutual exclusion must be false. In fact, there are instances in which two such contrary things can both befall <117> one and the same person, as when he eats honey into which some poison has fallen. This is something that gives pleasure and also causes death, and would consequently, according to their theory, have to be considered as wisdom and folly at one and the same time.

Let me proceed further now and discourse about the second general division of the laws of the Torah. This division consists of acts which from the standpoint of reason are optional. Yet the Law has made some of them obligatory and others forbidden, and left the rest optional as they had been. They include such matters as the consecration of certain days from among others, like the Sabbath and the festivals, and the consecration of certain human beings from among others, such as the prophet and the priest, and refraining from eating certain foods, and the avoidance of cohabitation with certain persons, and going into isolation immediately upon the occurrence of certain accidents because of defilement.

But even though the chief reason for the fulfillment of these principal precepts and their derivatives and whatever is connected with them is the fact that they represent the command of our Lord and enable us to reap a special advantage, yet I find that most of them have as their basis partially useful purposes. I see fit, therefore, to note some of these motivations and discuss them, although the wisdom of God, blessed and exalted be He, is above all that.

Now among the benefits accruing from the consecration of certain seasons, by desisting from work on them, there is first of all that of obtaining relaxation from much exertion. Furthermore it presents the opportunity for the attainment of a little bit of knowledge and a little additional praying. It also affords men leisure to meet each other at gatherings where they can confer about matters of their religion and make public announcements about them, and perform other functions of the same order.

Some of the benefits accruing from consecrating a particular person from among others are that it makes it possible to obtain more knowledge from him and to secure his services as an intercessor. [It] also [enables him] to imbue his fellow-men with the desire for righteousness so that they might thereby attain something like his own eminence. Finally [it permits him] to concern himself with the moral improvement of humanity, since he is qualified for such a task, and other things of this nature.

Among the advantages, again, that result from the prohibition against the eating of [only] certain animals [5] is the prevention of any comparison between them and the Creator. For it is inconceivable that God would permit anything resembling Him to be eaten or, on the other hand, that [the eating of such a being] could cause defilement to man. This precept also serves to keep man from worshiping any of these animals, since it is not seemly for him to worship what has been given to him for food, nor what has been declared unclean for him.

As for the advantages accruing from the avoidance of cohabitation with certain women, <118> those derived from observing this ruling in regard to a *married woman,* are such as we have stated previously. As far as the mother, sister, and daughter are concerned, since the relationship with them is necessarily intimate, the license to marry them would encourage dissoluteness on their part. There exists also the danger, if this were permitted, that men would be fascinated by those of their female relatives who have a beautiful figure, while those possessing homely features would be spurned even by strangers, since the latter would see that the male relatives [of these women] do not desire them.

Some of the benefits accruing from the observance of the laws of uncleanliness and cleanliness are that man is thereby led to think humbly of his flesh,[6] that it enhances for him the value of prayer by virtue of his being cut off therefrom for a while during the period of defilement, that it endears to him the Temple which he was prevented from entering in the state of impurity, and finally that it causes him to dedicate his heart to the fear of God.

5. i.e., while others are permitted. Cf. Guttmann, p. 138, n. 2.
6. "of his flesh"—Ibn Tibbon. The reading of the Arabic original is corrupt.

Similarly, if one were to follow up most of these revealed [7] precepts, one would discover that they are, to a large extent at least, partially justified and possess much utilitarian value, although the wisdom and the view that the Creator had in mind in decreeing them is far above anything that men can grasp, as Scripture says: *For as the heavens are higher than the earth, so are My ways higher than your ways* (Isa. 55:9).

CHAPTER III

Now that I have expressed myself in this summary fashion about the two general divisions of the precepts of the Torah, namely the rational and the revealed, it behooves me to explain why there should have been need for divine messengers and prophets. For I have heard that there are people who say that men have no need for such messengers because their reason is enough of a guide for them to distinguish between good and evil. I therefore went back to the touchstone of truth and I noted that, if the matter were really as they said it was, the Creator would have known it best and He would not have sent any messengers to mankind, since He does nothing that has no purpose. Then I pondered the matter deeply and I found that there was considerable need for the dispatch of messengers to God's creatures, not merely in order that they might be informed by them about the revealed laws, but also on account of the rational precepts. For these latter, too, are carried out practically only when there are messengers to instruct men concerning them.

Thus, for example, <119> reason calls for gratitude to God for His kindness, but does not define how this gratitude is to be expressed or at what time or in what form it is to be shown. There was, therefore, need for messengers who defined it and designated it as prayer and assigned to it certain set times and gave to it a particular formulation and [prescribed] a specific posture and direction.[8]

7. "revealed"—cf. Guttmann's rendering.
8. "direction," i.e., the *ḳiblah*, facing toward the Temple of Jerusalem.

Another illustration hereof is that, whereas reason regards fornication as reprehensible, it does not define how a woman is to be acquired by a man in order to be considered as belonging to him. [It does not state, for example,] whether that is to be effected by means of a word only, or by means of money only, or with her consent and the consent of her parents only, or by the testimony of two or ten witnesses, or by having all the inhabitants of the town bear witness thereunto, or by marking her with a sign or branding her. The prophets thereupon came along and prescribed the giving of a dowry and the use of a writ and the presence of two witnesses.

A further example is that, although reason considers stealing objectionable, there is nothing in it to inform us how a person comes to acquire property so that it becomes his possession. [It does not state, for instance,] whether this comes about as a result of labor, or is effected by means of barter, or by way of inheritance, or is derived from what is free to all, like what is hunted on land and sea. Nor [is one informed by it as to] whether a sale becomes valid upon the payment of the price or by taking hold of the article or by means of a statement alone. Besides these, there are many other uncertainties pertaining to this subject which would take too long and would be too difficult to enumerate. The prophets, therefore, came along with a clear-cut decision for each instance.

Another example is the question of the expiation of crime. Reason considers it proper, to be sure, that whoever commits a crime should expiate it, but does not define what form this expiation ought to take: whether a reprimand alone is sufficient, or a malediction should go with it, or flogging too should be added. In the event that the punishment take the form of flogging, again, the question is how much, and the same applies to the malediction and the reprimand. Or it is possible that no satisfaction will be obtained except by the death of the criminal. And again it might be asked whether the punishment should be the same for whoever commits a certain crime, or whether it should vary from person to person. Then the prophets came and fixed for each crime its own penalty, and grouped some of them with others under certain conditions, and imposed monetary fines for some. For these considerations, <120> then, that we have enumerated and other such reasons, is it necessary for us to have recourse to the mission of God's messengers. For if we were to defer in these matters to our own opinions, our views would differ and we would not agree on anything. Besides that, we are, of course, in need of their guidance on account of the precepts prescribed by revelation, as we have explained.

CHAPTER IV

And now that we have demonstrated clearly how necessity led God to dispatch messengers to mankind, it is fitting that this discussion be followed up with an explanation of how the authenticity of their mission was established among the rest of men. I say, then, that human beings realize that it is impossible for them, with such power and ability as they possess, to subdue the elements of nature or to transform the essences of things. They are, indeed, incapable of doing that because these are all the work of the Creator. For it is He that subdued the various elements of nature and created them in their composite form, although it is their natural tendency to fly apart. However, God so altered the character of their separate essences that as a result of their combination no essence of theirs appeared in its pure form any more, but always as something else than the unadulterated essence. I mean [that the elements of nature were combined so as to form] either a human being or a plant or other such corporeal things. [Since men recognized all this,] such feats of necessity had to be regarded by them as a sign of the work of the Creator.

Hence any messenger whom the Creator would choose to carry out His mission would, as a matter of course, have to be provided by Him with one of these signs. [This sign might consist] of the subjection of elements of nature, such as preventing fire from burning or keeping water from running or arresting a heavenly sphere in its course and the like. [It might] also [take the form of] the transformation of substances, such as the conversion of an animal into an inanimate object, or [the change of something] inanimate into a living thing, or [the transformation of] water into blood, or of blood into water. When, therefore, one of these signs is presented to the prophet, it becomes the obligation of those men that see it to regard him as holy and to lend credence to what he tells them, for the All-Wise would not have presented His sign to him unless he had been found trustworthy by Him.

Now although this account [of the authentication of a prophetic mission] is [sanctioned] by reason, it is also found in the texts of the Scriptures. This is known to thee from the story of *Moses our teacher,* and from the wondrous miracles that were shown to him. Hence I can dispense with mentioning them here. It has also been explained in the text of the Book of Exodus and elsewhere, as well as in the commentary thereon. It is illustrated furthermore by the remark, made by Moses to his people, of < 121 > *The great trials which thine eyes saw* (Deut. 7: 19).

Those of the servants of God, then, who believe the prophet and accept his words as the truth, are the virtuous, as Scripture says: *And he did the signs in the sight of the people. And the people believed* (Exod. 4: 30, 31). Those, on the other hand, who do not believe him and do not accept his words as true, are the erring. This, too, thou knowest from the case of those of whom it was said: *Because they believed not in God* (Ps. 78: 22).

At this point I find it necessary to make an observation for the purpose of safeguarding [our belief in] the [usual] fixity [of things]. What I have reference to is that the Creator, exalted and magnified be He, does not change the substance of anything unless He first calls the attention of the people to the fact that He is about to effect that change. For [God's] motive [in the performance of the miracle] is to have men lend credence to His prophet. Where, however, such a motive does not exist, there is no reason for changing any substance. For if we were to assume [purposeless change to be the rule], then our confidence in the fixity of things would be shaken. None of us could then be sure, upon returning to his dwelling and family, whether the All-Wise had not changed their essences, and whether they were not different from the way in which he had left them. The same applies to the deposition of testimony about a person or the issuance of a judgment concerning him. We must, therefore, take it for granted that all things that exist ordinarily retain their character, and that their Master does not alter them except after having first called attention to the fact.

Let me say, furthermore, that it would not have been seemly for [divine] Wisdom to allow God's messengers to mankind to be angels, because human beings are not acquainted with the extent of the power of the angels, [not knowing] what they are able or what they are unable to do. Consequently, if these [angels] had come before men with wondrous miracles, the latter might have thought that to perform such marvels was the nature of all angels, and they would have had no proof that these miracles were a sign hailing from the Creator. Since, however, the messengers sent by God were human beings like ourselves, and we nevertheless found them performing feats of which we are incapable and which, consequently, could only have been the work of the Creator, their mission as transmitters of the word of God was thereby authenticated.

I say, also, that it was for this very reason that God made the prophets equal to all other human beings so far as death was concerned, lest men get the idea that just as these prophets were capable of living forever, in contradistinction to them, so were they also able to perform marvels in contradistinction to them. For this reason, too, did God not nourish them without food and drink, nor restrain them from marriage [9] lest <122> any doubt arise in regard to the significance of their miracles. For men might have thought that such nourishment [without food and drink] was natural with them and that, just as that was possible for them, so too was it possible for them to perform miracles.

Thus, also, did God not guarantee to the prophets perpetual health of body or great wealth or posterity or protection from the violence of the violent, whether that violence consist of flogging or insults or murder. For if He had done that, men might have ascribed this fact to some peculiarity in the constitution of the prophets wherein they deviated from the rules applying to all other men. They would have said that, just as the prophets neces-

9 "not nourish . . . marriage"—Ibn Tibbon.

sarily deviated [from the character of the rest of humanity] in this respect, so too was it a foregone conclusion that they be able to do what we cannot.

I say, therefore—but of course God's wisdom is above aught that might be said—that God's purpose in letting the prophets remain in every respect like all other human beings, while singling them out from the totality of them by enabling them to do what was impossible for the whole of mankind, was to authenticate His sign and to confirm His message. I declare, moreover, that on this account, too, did God not allow the prophets to perform miracles at all times nor permit them always to know the secrets of the future, lest the uneducated masses think that they were possessed of some peculiarity which brought that about as a matter of course. He rather permitted them to perform these miracles at certain stated occasions and to obtain that knowledge at certain times, so that it might thereby become clear that all this was conferred upon them by the Creator and that it was not brought about by themselves. Praise be, then, unto the All-Wise and sanctified be He!

Now what impelled me to note down these points here is the fact that I have seen people whose preconceived opinions caused them to reject the assertions made above. One of them, for example, says: "I deny that the prophet dies like all other human beings." Another refuses to believe that he experiences hunger and thirst. Another rejects the idea that the prophet cohabits and begets offspring. Another denies that violence and injustice can have effect on him. Still another denies that anything in the world can be hidden from the prophet. However, I found all their allegations to be wrong, false, and unjust. On the contrary, it became certain to me that the wisdom manifested in what the Creator had done in the case of His messengers <123> was of an order similar to that inherent in the rest of His works, as it is expressed in the statement of Scripture: *For the word of the Lord is upright; and all His work is done in faithfulness* (Ps. 33:4). Scripture likewise says: *But they know not the thoughts of the Lord, neither understand they His counsel* (Mic. 4:12).

CHAPTER V

I also considered the question of how the prophet could be sure that the message that he heard came from God before ascribing it to his Lord in the presence of his people, and I arrived at the conclusion that this was effected by means of some sign that would appear to him at the beginning of the colloquy and remain until its termination. This sign could take the form of a pillar of fire or a pillar of cloud or a light that did not emanate from the ordinary luminaries. When, then, the prophet saw such a sign, he was certain that the message came from God.

Often the people, too, would see it, as did the followers of Moses. When, namely, he would leave them to betake himself to the scene of the revelation, they would stand up and look into the air and note that it was free from any cloud and their eyes would be fixed on Moses. Then as Moses would arrive at the scene of the revelation, a thin cloud would descend in the shape of a pillar and tarry until [10] God had spoken to Moses, whereupon it would go up again. Then Moses would return to them. All this is borne out by the statement of Scripture: *And it came to pass, when Moses went out unto the Tent, that all the people rose up, and stood, every man at his tent door* . . . (Exod. 33:8).

When he would come back to them, therefore, bringing his message, they would say: "Thou hast spoken truly. We noticed how clear the atmosphere was before thy arrival at the scene of the revelation and how the pillar of cloud made its descent at the time of thy arrival there. Also the time of its sojourn corresponded to the time which it took for thee to hear this communication which thou hast delivered unto us."

Yes, I find that even where in the account given of a certain prophet in one place it is not explicitly stated that God revealed Himself to him in a pillar of *cloud*, it is made clear about him in another book of the Scriptures that He did thus reveal Himself to him. Thus Samuel is included with Moses and Aaron in one

10. "until"—added by Ibn Tibbon and M.

passage of Scripture, which says of them all: *Moses and Aaron among His priests, and Samuel . . . He spoke unto them in the pillar of cloud* (Ps. 99: 6, 7). Since, then, I have found such a thing to hold true for Samuel, there can be no doubt about it but that the same would apply to many <124> other prophets.

If someone were to ask now how the magicians of Pharaoh could have performed miracles paralleling those wrought by Moses, we would say, in reply, that of the ten miracles that Moses performed; namely, the conversion of his cane into a serpent and the nine others, there were only three which the Torah mentions as having been duplicated by them. But even the reproduction by them of these three to parallel Moses' feat is not mentioned by the Torah for the purpose of showing that he and they were equals. It was done merely in order to differentiate between his feat and theirs. The Torah, namely, states explicitly that Moses had performed a patent act, *as the Lord had commanded* (Exod. 7: 20). These others, however, had done something clandestine, undercover, the cunning of which stood revealed once it was uncovered. Thus Scripture states, with reference to the three aforementioned miracles: *And the magicians did in like manner with their secret arts (bĕlaṭehem)* (Exod. 8: 3).

This [last] expression is used [11] in the language of Scripture solely to designate something hidden, covered, wrapped up. That is apparent from such statements as *Behold, it is here wrapped (luṭah) in a cloth* (I Sam. 21: 10); *The face of the covering that is cast (halloṭ halloṭ) over all peoples* (Isa. 25: 7); *That he wrapped (wayyaleṭ) his face in his mantle* (I Kings 19: 13), *And the king covered (la'aṭ) his face* (II Sam. 19: 5), *Speak with David secretly (ballaṭ)* (I Sam. 18: 22), and *And the word that dealeth quietly [12] (la'aṭ) with thee* (Job 15: 11).

Since, then, the Torah explicitly uses the phrase *with their secret arts (bĕlaṭehem)*, it is quite clear therefrom that it was meant as a rejection, not as an endorsement of their deed. This might be compared to thy saying: "Reuben hit the mark in his speech, whereas

11. "used"—Ibn Tibbon, literally "applies."
12. "quietly"—the usual translation is "gently."

Simon missed the mark in his speech," or to thy remarking: "Levy performed a good deed, whereas Zebulun committed a foul deed." Thy intention in both cases would be merely to differentiate between the two utterances or the two deeds, not to indicate that they are equal.

Inasmuch as I have now established this principle, it is not necessary for me to demonstrate any further how it was possible for the magicians, by the employment of cunning with small quantities of water, to change the hue of this water by means of dyes, and how they could throw something into certain bodies of water in order to cause the frogs to take flight from them, except that it is impossible to do with large bodies of water what can be done with such small portions. What Moses had done, however, was to change the water of the Nile in its entirety, and its measurement is a stretch of forty parasangs from 'al-'Allaki [13] to Mareotis.[14] Similarly he also caused the frogs to come up from the entire river, which was something that <125> neither ruse nor cunning was able to accomplish, but was solely the work of the Mighty, All-Wise and Omnipotent, as Scripture says: *To Him who alone doeth great wonders* (Ps. 136:4).

If, furthermore, one were to ask, "But how was it that Jonah was chosen to carry out a mission from which he ran away, when it would seem that the All-Wise would not choose anyone who would disobey him?" I would answer that I have gone over the story of Jonah repeatedly and yet have not found a single verse that would state explicitly that he did not fulfill his first mission. And although I have not found a definite indication that he carried it out either, yet I feel constrained to believe that he did, in the same manner in which all the prophets did. Another reason is

13. According to *Jacuts Geographisches Woerterbuch*, ed. F. Wuestenfeld (Leipzig, 1868), III, 710, this was a fortress in Southern Egypt (near the Nubian desert) in the district inhabited by the Buja (identical with the Beja? Cf. *Encyclopedia Britannica*, 14th ed. III, 334). There still exists today a Wadi Alagi, which is a tributary of the Nile flowing into it from the southeast. Cf. *idem*, Vol. XXIV, map no. 79.

14. According to *idem*, IV (1869), 517, this was a town near Alexandria, Egypt, on the Mediterranean coast.

that the All-Wise would not choose anyone to execute an errand of His who would not carry it out. Besides, I find Scripture saying constantly: *And the Lord spoke unto Moses, saying: Speak unto the children of Israel* (Lev. 23:1, 2). Yet it is only in a few instances that the comment is made that the command was carried out, as it is done [in the statement]: *And Moses spoke so unto the children of Israel* [15] (Exod. 6:9).

What Jonah fled from was only the possibility of his being sent on a mission a second time. For it seemed to him that his first mission constituted a warning, but that the second was an act of intimidation and a threat. He was, therefore, afraid that, after his having threatened them with some punishment or other, those to whom he would be sent would repent so that the threat would not be carried out and it would be said that it was due to his having lied. Hence he departed from the land which the Creator had appointed to be the seat of prophecy.

[All] this is explicitly stated at the end of Jonah's remark: *I pray Thee, O Lord, was not this my saying, when I was yet in mine own country? Therefore I fled beforehand unto Tarshish* (Jonah 4:2). No sin attached to him, therefore, since his Lord had not told him: "I am going to send thee a second time." That was merely a thought that had arisen in his mind, and he rejected what might perhaps come or not come to pass. Thereupon God made him return by compulsion to the country that had been singled out for prophecy, and brought him to the point of prophesying, and sent him forth on his mission and thus executed [the plan conceived by] His wisdom.

CHAPTER VI

Next let me explain the character of the Holy Scriptures and say that God has provided us with summary accounts of all that has transpired in the past in order that we might thereby be put into a fit condition for obeying Him. These accounts were incorporated by Him into His Holy Book. He attached to them also His pre-

15. This quotation follows the reading of Ibn Tibbon.

cepts and appended to the latter a statement of the rewards He would mete out for their observance. Thus this became a matter of permanent benefit [to mankind] for all time.

What I mean to say is that when we examine all the books written by the prophets and <126> the scholars of all peoples, however great their number might be, we discover that they all embrace no more than three basic themes. The first in rank is that of commandments and prohibitions. These constitute one classification. The second theme is reward and punishment, which represent the consequences [of the observance or nonobservance of the commandments and the prohibitions]. The third [theme consists of] an account of the men that lived virtuously in the various countries of the world and were, therefore, successful, as well as of those who dealt corruptly in them and perished as a result. The interests of human well-being can be served completely only by a combination of these three [themes].

[Let me cite, as] an illustration [of what I wish to convey,] the case of a physician who visits a person sick with fever. It is clear to him that the cause of the patient's illness is an overabundance of blood. Now, if he were to say to him: "Do not eat meat and do not drink wine," he would thereby be contributing to his recovery, but not completely. If, again, in addition to this prescription, he were to say: "Don't do it in order that thou mayest not be afflicted with a headache," he would be contributing still more to his recovery, although not yet completely, until he would say to him: "As it happened to so-and-so." For when he has done that, he has completed the process leading to the patient's cure. This is, then, the reason why the books referred to dwell on all of these three basic themes. However, I shall be brief and refrain from noting down anything further about these subjects, because they are far too extensive.

Furthermore, let me say that it was well known to the All-Wise, exalted and magnified be He, that His precepts and the accounts of His signs would in the course of time require transmitters, in order that these matters might seem as authentic to posterity as they did to the early ancestors. Therefore did He render the human mind susceptible to the acceptance of authenticated tradition and the human soul capable of finding repose therein, so that His Scriptures and traditions might be acknowledged as true.

I deem it proper also to call to mind the following details that lend color to the validity of tradition. For example, were it not for the fact that man felt satisfied in their hearts that there is such a thing in the world as authentic tradition, no person would be able to cherish legitimate expectations on the basis of the reports he receives about the success of a certain commercial transaction, or the usefulness of a specified art—and, after all, the realization of man's potentialities and the satisfaction of his needs depend upon enterprise. Nor would he heed the warnings about the dangers of a certain road, or the announcement of the prohibition of a certain act. [However,] without such expectations and apprehensions he would fail in his undertakings.[16]

Again, were it not for the assumption that there exists in the world [such a thing as] authentic tradition, <127> men would accept neither the command nor the interdict of their ruler, except when they saw him with their own eyes and heard his words with their own ears. In the event of his absence, however,[17] the acceptance on their part of his command and interdict would cease. But if things were like that, it would mean the end of law and order, and the death of many human beings.

Also, were it not for the existence in the world of such a thing as authentic tradition, no man would be able to identify the property of his father or his inheritance from his grandfather. Nay, he would not even be certain of being the son of his mother, let alone of his being the son of his father. The result would then be that the affairs of men would always be subject to doubt, to the point where human beings would believe only what they perceive with their senses at the time of perception. Such a viewpoint would be close to the theory of the Skeptics, whom we have mentioned in the first treatise.[18]

16. "However . . . undertakings"—Ibn Tibbon. The Arabic original is defective at this point.
17. "however"—added by Ibn Tibbon and M.
18. Cf. above, pp. 80 ff.

Now the Scriptures, too, assert that authentic tradition is as trustworthy as things perceived with our own eyes. That is the import of their statement: *For pass over to the isles of the Kittites, and see, and send unto Kedar, and consider diligently* (Jer. 2:10). But why, in the portion of this verse pertaining to the report, were the words *and consider diligently* added? My answer is that a report is subject to falsification in two directions from which direct observation is immune. It may be due either to false impression or else to deliberate misrepresentation. That is why Scripture says: *and consider diligently.*

Now when we ponder these two criteria of the trustworthiness of traditions, our reason arrives at the conclusion that it is only the individual who is subject to and fooled by false impression or deliberate deception. In the case of a large community of men, however, it is not likely that all of its constituents should have been subject to the same [19] wrong impressions. On the other hand, had there been a deliberate conspiracy to create a fictitious tradition, that fact could not have remained a secret to the masses, but wherever the tradition had been published, the report of the conspiracy would have been published along with it. When, therefore, a tradition is free from the above-mentioned two flaws, there is no third means of invalidating it. Accordingly, if the traditions transmitted to us by our ancestors are viewed in the light <128> of these [three] principles, they will be found to be proof against these arguments, correct and unshakable.

CHAPTER VII

After all the aforesaid, I deem it proper to have the remarks that have been made followed by a discussion of the subject of the abrogation of the Law, because this treatise is the appropriate place for it. I say, then, that the children of Israel have a general tradition to the effect that the prophets had informed them that the laws of the Torah were not subject to abrogation. They assert,

19. "should have been subject to the same"—cf. Guttmann, p. 147, n. 2.

furthermore: "We have heard this view expressed so explicitly as to brook no misunderstanding or misinterpretation."

By a careful study of the Scriptures I found considerable support for this thesis. First of all, I noticed that many laws had attached to them such phrases as *throughout their generations* (e.g., Exod. 31:16) and *for a perpetual covenant* [20] (*ibid.*). Again, there is the statement of the Torah: *Moses bequeathed* [21] *unto us a Law, an inheritance of the congregation of Jacob* [22] (Deut. 33:4).

Furthermore, our nation of the children of Israel is a nation only by virtue of its laws. Since, then, the Creator has stated that the Jewish nation was destined to exist as long as heaven and earth would exist, its laws would, of necessity, have to endure as long as would heaven and earth. That is, indeed, the import of the statement of Scripture: *Thus saith the Lord, who giveth the sun for a light by day, and the ordinances of the moon and the stars for a light by night, who stirreth up the sea, that the waves thereof roar, the Lord of hosts is His name: If these ordinances depart from before Me, saith the Lord, then the seed of Israel also shall cease from being a nation before Me forever* (Jer. 31:35, 36).

I noted also in the last of the prophecies a direct admonition [23] in regard to the observance of the Torah of Moses until the day of the resurrection, which latter would be preceded by the sending of Elijah. The statement I have reference to is: *Remember ye the Law of Moses My servant, which I commanded unto him in Horeb for all Israel, even statutes and ordinances. Behold, I will send you Elijah the prophet before the coming of the great and terrible day of the Lord* [24] (Mal. 3:22, 23).

I have also seen some of our nation who, in their effort to refute the theory of the abrogation of the Law, cite certain general considerations, alleging that the laws promulgated by God could at the time of their promulgation have been of one of four kinds only. <129> Either it was explicitly stated that they were meant to be

20. "attached . . . covenant"—the original reads literally: "written in them *a perpetual covenant* and have written in them *throughout your generations.*"
21. "bequeathed"—the usual translation is "commanded."
22. This quotation follows the reading of Ibn Tibbon.
23. "admonition"—Ibn Tibbon.
24. This quotation follows the reading of Ibn Tibbon.

eternal, in which case they could not possibly be abrogated. Or they were ordained by God to be operative for only a certain period of time, as if, for example, He had said: "Do such and such a thing for 100 years." In that case their dissolution during the one hundred years would be inconceivable, while after the hundred years were up [the term of its operation] would have expired, wherefore abrogation would not be applicable to it. Or else they might have been imposed only on a specific locality, as if, for example, God had said: "Do such and such a thing in Egypt." In that case it would be out of the question that it be abrogated by Him in Egypt, whilst the institution of another law elsewhere would not be tantamount to the abrogation [of the first]. The fourth possibility is that the law was ordained for a definite reason, as if, for example, God had said, "Do such and such a thing because the water of the Nile is flowing." In that case no dissolution of the law would be possible before the water of the Nile stops flowing, whereas the institution of another law after the water has stopped flowing would not constitute an abrogation of the original ordinance.

If objection were now to be raised against this assertion on their part by pointing out that there exists also a fifth category, namely that of a law for which no time limit has been set, so that men go on practicing it until they are ordered to do otherwise, their reply would be that, if this were so, it would also constitute legislation for a limited interval of time. The period of its validity would, of course, be fully known in advance by God, whereas it would become known to men at the time of the institution of the second law. In either case, however, there could be no talk of abrogation, since the law was intended, from the time when it was first instituted, to be of limited duration.[25] Some, again, would answer the objection by declaring that such a fifth classification is untenable for the reason that laws [26] had purposely been designated as permanent or temporary in order that none of them might remain unspecified.[27]

Now I have seen someone who presents seven arguments in

25. "since . . . duration"—cf. Guttmann, p. 149 and n. 2.
26. "laws"—Ibn Tibbon and M correctly.
27. "unspecified"—Ibn Tibbon.

favor of the possibility of the abrogation of the Law which, he maintains, are advanced by reason, and all of which would corroborate such a view. I, therefore, see fit to make note of them, as well as of what might be offered in the way of refutation against them. The first of these arguments, then, let me say, is the one drawn from the analogy with life and death. Just as it is possible for [divine] Wisdom to give life and to put to death again, asserts [the proponent], so, too, should it be possible for it to legislate and abrogate the laws instituted.

Upon careful consideration, however, I realized that there was a great difference between these two matters. For if God grants life only in order to put to death again, it is because death is the means of transition to future life, which is the ultimate goal of mortal existence. God did not, however, issue laws for the [sole] purpose of abrogating them again. For, <130> if He had done that, every law would have to be subject to abrogation. The first would then have been superseded by the second, and the second by the third, and thus ad infinitum, which is, of course, nonsense. Furthermore, if this were the case, there would always be inherent in the second law an inner antithesis and contradiction. What I mean is that the second law would be the means to an end that lies outside of itself, by reason of the fact that it is a law and that it lies in the character of every law [according to this assumption] thus [to serve as a means to an end, namely the law superseding it]. In addition, it would also constitute an end in itself because it supersedes the first law and it is of the nature of every supersedent to be an end to a means by virtue of the fact that it supersedes its antecedent. This is, then, a flimsy thesis.

The second [argument that is advanced in favor of the abrogation of the Law] is [derived] from the analogy to the fact that God permits those charged with the fulfillment of the Law to die and with their death allows the obligation resting on them to lapse. As I see it, however, the reason why death cannot do otherwise than remove the obligation of the law from the dead is that commandments and prohibitions do not apply to them altogether. One must not, therefore, compare the case in which an alternative is possible with one in which no such choice exists. For if it were to be assumed that [even for the living] the abrogation of the Law is an inevitability, then one would again be faced with that inner contradiction which I mentioned in connection with the theory that every law was subject to abrogation.

The third [argument] is [taken] from the analogy to the person who works one day and rests on another, or who fasts one day and breaks his fast on another, as the Law requires. This is, however, also due to compulsion. For since it is not within the power of a human being to fast every day or to rest every day, it would not have been seemly for the All-Wise to charge him therewith. Yet it is quite possible for a human being to carry the law out in every generation.

The fourth [argument] is [based] on the analogy to the fact that God makes men rich or poor, seeing or blind, each one at the time that it suits Him best to do it. I recognized, however, that there is a wide divergence between the phenomena compared. For good fortune might be God's reward for obedience, whereas hardship might be the retribution meted out by Him for disobedience. As far as the Law is concerned, however, it was not instituted by Him as a requital of either obedience or disobedience. If, nevertheless, such a claim be pressed, how is one to explain [28] [the < 131 > promulgation of the] first Law, since it could not possibly have been ordained as a reward for acts preceding its institution in view of the fact that there existed no law before it [which it was obligatory to obey]?

The fifth [argument in favor of the possibility of an abrogation of the Law] is [founded] on the analogy to the date, which turns red as it ripens after having been green, and similar phenomena. Now I considered all these matters very carefully and I noted that the changes were brought about either by the natural constitution of the subjects or by habit. The Law is, however, not of such a character. For had it been like that, every law would have been subject to abrogation and we would again have been confronted with the inner contradiction [that has been referred to previously].

28. "how is one to explain"—literally "it would have vitiated for him."

The sixth [argument runs] as follows: Just as work on the Sabbath was, from the standpoint of reason, originally considered permissible until revelation substituted for it restraint, even so should it be possible for another revelation to restore it to the status of permissibility. Let me say, then, in reference to this matter, that the analogy cited would have been complete only if reason had made work on the Sabbath day obligatory. Then it could have been said that revelation caused that obligation to be abrogated. Inasmuch, however, as reason merely regarded it as optional, the analogy does not hold. For human reason was always of the opinion that it was permissible for man to be idle on the Sabbath day or any other day, either in order to afford his body rest or on account of some other advantage that he would gain thereby, or for both reasons. It was under such conditions that revelation injected itself into something, which from the standpoint of man's reason was permissible, and said to man: "Rest in order to afford thy body relaxation and in order that thou mayest thereby gain some advantage and reward." That did not really constitute the abrogation of anything, even though it was decreed by God as a permanent institution. For it would have been perfectly proper, from the standpoint of his reason, for any person endowed with intelligence to order someone to remain idle on a specific day with the promise to give him a *denar* every day.

The seventh [argument] is to the effect that, just as it was permissible for the Law of Moses to be different from that of Abraham, so should it be permissible for a Law to come into being that is different from that of Moses. However, when we study the Law of Moses, we find that it is, in reality, identical with that of Abraham. To be sure, Moses added such precepts as those of the eating of unleavened bread on Passover and the Sabbath, on account of certain events that happened to his people, in the same manner in which a person would take a vow always to fast on the anniversary of the day on which he escaped death. If it is proper, then, for this individual to assume such an obligation of his own volition, it is also proper for his Lord to impose it upon him. And if this addition is <132> to be regarded as constituting an abrogation, then anyone who voluntarily obligates himself to pray or fast or give alms would thereby be abrogating the Law; and the author of the Law, who gave him license to do that, would, by the same token, have given him license to abrogate His Law. Similar objections apply also to all the previously mentioned arguments. These are, therefore, all, may God have mercy on thee, mere diversions which cannot stand up under a careful inquiry into the matter.

CHAPTER VIII

Having disposed of these seven arguments, I deem it proper to make note of a theory of theirs, which they propound with great loquacity. They assert, namely, that just as the belief in the mission of Moses was based on his performance of miracles and marvels, so too ought the belief in someone else's mission be based on that one's performance of miracles and marvels.

When I heard this, I was very much surprised, because the basis of our belief in the mission of Moses is not solely the miracles and marvels that he performed. The reason for our believing in him, and in every other prophet, is rather the fact that he first called upon us to do what is proper. Then, when we had heard his appeal and we saw that it was proper, we demanded from him miracles in support of it and, when he performed them, we believed in him. If, however, we had felt that the appeal he made at the beginning was not proper, we would not have demanded any miracles from him, because miracles are of no account in supporting the unacceptable.

The case might be compared to that of two litigants, Reuben and Simon, standing before a judge. If Reuben files a reasonable claim against Simon, saying, for example, "He owes me one thousand drachmas," the judge asks him for witnesses, and if they rise to testify on his behalf, the defendant becomes liable for the payment to him of the money. If, on the other hand, he files against him a claim that is not in the realm of possibility, saying, for example, "He owes me the Tigris River," his claim becomes completely null and void because the Tigris is not in any one man's possession.

It is, therefore, not seemly for the judge to ask him for testimony thereon.

The same procedure is to be followed in the case of every claimant of prophecy. If he says to us, "My Lord commands you to fast today," we ask him for a sign in support of his mission, and when he shows it to us, we accept it and fast. If, however, he were to say to us, "My Lord commands you to commit adultery and steal," or "He informs you <133> that He is about to bring a flood of water upon the world," or "He makes it known to you that He created heaven and earth thoughtlessly while He was asleep," [29] we would not ask him for any sign, since what he called upon us to do is not sanctioned by either reason or tradition.

Now I have seen one of the proponents of the theory that has just been discussed go further in the matter and say, "But suppose we note that the [pretended] prophet pays no attention to us but makes us witness the miracles and marvels so that we see them perforce. What shall we say to him in that case?" My answer was that our reply to him should be the same as that of all of us would be to anyone who would show us miracles and marvels for the purpose of making us give up such rational convictions as that the truth is good and lying reprehensible and the like. He was thereupon compelled to take refuge in the theory that the disapproval of lying and the approval of the truth were not prompted by reason but were the result of the commandments and prohibitions of Scripture, and the same was true for the rejection of murder, adultery, and stealing. When he had come to that, however, I felt that I needed no longer concern myself with him and that I had my fill of discussion with him.

Among the proponents of the theory of abrogation there are also some who cite in support thereof verses of the Bible. I therefore deem it fitting to make note of these verses, as well as of their interpretation of them and the objections against these interpretations.

The first of these is the statement of the Torah, *And he said: The Lord came from Sinai, and rose from Seir unto them; He*

29. "thoughtlessly while he was asleep"—Ibn Tibbon, but in reverse order.

shined forth from mount Paran, and He came from the myriads holy (Deut. 33:2). In reality, however, these three are all of them names applied to Mount Sinai. The reason for its having these different appellations is that whenever a mountain extends toward several countries, its nomenclature is divided according to the names of these countries, each division bearing the name of the country lying opposite it. Just as one and the same sea acquires from the countries bordering it many names corresponding to that of each adjacent country, so is *Mount Sinai* a mountain opposite the lands of *Sinai, Seir,* and *Paran,* called by the names of all three because it stands on something resembling a straight line.

The proof that *Sinai* and *Paran* meet one another is the statement of Scripture: *And the children of Israel set forward by their stages* <134> *out of the wilderness of Sinai; and the cloud abode in the wilderness of Paran* (Num. 10:12). The proof, again, that *Paran* and *Seir* are contiguous is the statement of Scripture: *And the Horites in their mount Seir, unto El Paran, which is by the wilderness* (Gen. 14:6). I have also found that in the other books of Holy Writ the name *Seir* is used in referring to *Sinai.* This is illustrated by the statement of Scripture: *Lord, when Thou didst go forth out of Seir . . . that is, Sinai,*[30] *at the presence of the Lord, the God of Israel* (Judg. 5:4, 5).

Now certain people, in their effort to prove from Scripture their belief in an abrogation of the original law, go further, pointing out that after having stated, *He shined forth from mount Paran* (Deut. 33:2), using the past tense, Scripture says: *God will come*[31] *from Teman, and the Holy One from mount Paran* (Hab. 3:3), employing the future form.

I have noted quite definitely, however, that whenever an enumeration of facts takes place, some of the verbs are put in the past tense whilst others are given a future form, as it were. Thus, for example, Scripture, enumerating the sins of our ancestors in the wilderness, lists them as follows: *But they were rebellious at the sea, even at the Red Sea. . . . They soon forgot His works. . . .*

30. "that is Sinai"—the usual translation is "even yon Sinai."
31. "God will come"—the usual translation is "God cometh,"

But lusted exceedingly in the wilderness (Ps. 106:7, 13, 14). Yet in speaking of some of them it uses future forms of expression, as it were, such as *They make (ya'asu) a calf in Horeb* (Ps. 106:19) and *The earth opens (tippathah) and swallows up (wĕthibhla')* *Dathan* (Ps. 106:17). Both these verbs seem, according to their form, to refer to the future, although in reality they stand for the past. For it is characteristic of the person who feels grateful to say: "So-and-so [32] *is* good to me, or useful to me, or kind to me," as it is also typical of one who has been wronged and who complains to say: "So-and-so [32] *is* wronging me, or betraying me, or doing me an injustice."

I have furthermore encountered people that asked: "Who is this person of whom it is said in Scripture: *And an ambassador is sent among the nations: 'Arise ye, and let us rise up against her in battle'?*" (Obad. 1:1). In reply thereto I informed them that the person alluded to was Jahaziel and that the battle was the one waged by Edom during the reign of Jehoshaphat, for Obadiah lived in his time. When, then, *the children of Ammon and Moab and mount Seir* (II Chron. 20:10) attacked him, as is explained in the Book of Chronicles, Jehoshaphat fasted <135> and prayed and called unto his Lord, as is clearly written. God thereupon sent to him Jahaziel on account of these *nations,* as is stated in Scripture: *Then upon Jahaziel the son of Zechariah, the son of Benaiah, the son of Jeiel, the son of Mattaniah, the Levite, of the sons of Asaph, came the spirit of the Lord in the midst of the congregation* [33] (II Chron. 20:14). That one said to them, "Stand aside, for God will deliver you from Edom." That is the import of his statement: *Ye shall not need to fight in this battle; set yourselves, stand ye still, and see the salvation of the Lord with you* (II Chron. 20:17).

The meaning, therefore, of the expression *Arise ye* in the utterance of Obadiah is identical with that of *Set yourselves, stand ye still* in the utterance of Jahaziel. When, then, they heard from him the exhortation of *Set yourselves,* they took counsel thereon with

---

32. "So and so"—added by Ibn Tibbon.
33. This quotation follows the reading of Ibn Tibbon.

one another, and the thought occurred to them that he had meant that they should rise to praise and laud God, as Scripture states: *And when he had taken counsel with the people, he appointed them that should sing unto the Lord* (II Chron. 20:21). That must have been in consonance with the pleasure of the Creator, since He delivered them from the enemy as they began to utter His praise, as Scripture states: *And when they began to sing and to praise, the Lord set liers-in-wait against the children of Ammon . . .* (II Chron. 20:22). But all this is long past already.

I also found still others who cited as proof of their theory the statement of Jeremiah: *Behold, the days come, saith the Lord, that I will make a new covenant with the house of Israel, and with the house of Judah* (Jer. 31:31). To these I said: "Why don't you look at what follows this verse, where it is explicitly stated that this new covenant that was mentioned before was the Torah itself?" Thus Scripture says: *But this is the covenant that I will make with the house of Israel after those days, saith the Lord, I will put My law in their inward parts . . .* (Jer. 31:33). It would only be different from the first covenant in this respect: that it would not be broken this time as it was the first time, as Scripture says: *Forasmuch as they broke My covenant, although I was a lord over them* (Jer. 31:32).

CHAPTER IX

After [disposing of] these theories, I found that the advocates of the doctrine of abrogation still cast doubts on [the meaning of certain passages of] the Bible in which they maintained that they saw evidence for the abrogation of the Law. These [passages to which they refer] are quite numerous and those <136> related to them even more so. However, I have confined myself to ten questions culled from among them. Should, therefore, any other present itself to the reader of this book, then let him give it careful consideration and the cause of the false impression or of the erroneous opinion entertained by him will be uncovered.

The first of these [problems presented by Scripture] is [that arising from] the marriage by the sons of Adam of Adam's daughters. This [violation of the law of incest], assert the proponents of the abrogation theory, is [proof that the later regulation constituted] an abrogation [of the original practice]. In reality [the license given to the sons of Adam to marry their sisters] was [no more than] a [special] dispensation. For we are quite certain that the marriage of sisters was forbidden even before the time of Moses, as we find Abraham saying to Sarah, [in order to give the impression that she was not his wife]: *Say, I pray thee, thou art my sister* (Gen. 12:13). The only reason why the sons of Adam married their sisters was because they were compelled to do so, since there were no human beings outside of their family.

However, as their offspring increased, this dispensation was rescinded and remained that way thenceforth. The case was analogous to that of a person who may break the fast while he is sick but whose exemption from fasting is rescinded when he gets well again. It might also be compared to that of the person who in the wilderness will eat carrion, in order not to starve to death, but whose exemption from observing the dietary laws ceases when he finds other [i.e., permitted] food.

The second [difficulty arises from] the fact that Cain was sentenced for slaying Abel to become *a fugitive and a wanderer* (Gen. 4:12), whereas thereafter the sentence imposed upon every slayer was death. But this, too, did not constitute abrogation, for when the All-Wise ordered the slayer to be slain, it was only by a judge and witnesses. Since, however, at the time when Cain slew Abel these were nonexistent, the death penalty could not be imposed on the former, and he therefore had to be punished by God in another way. Dost thou not see how God said to Noah: [34] *Whoso sheddeth man's blood, by man shall his blood be shed?* (Gen. 9:6.)

The third [problem is presented by] the fact that God commanded all men to offer up sacrifices and then forbade such activities to everyone except Aaron and his children. But this, too, did not constitute an abrogation, for there is not contained in Scripture a single text indicating that all men had been appointed

34. He also lived before Moses.

to perform the sacrificial rite. Before the appointment of Aaron it was only he who had been appointed to a position similar to his that performed this rite. One who had not been appointed, however, had no right to engage in the performance of the sacrificial rite, neither before nor after the election of Aaron.

The fourth [difficulty] is [due to the command for] the offering of sacrifices on the Sabbath, notwithstanding the fact that work had been previously forbidden on that day. This, too, did not constitute an abrogation. On the contrary, it helped to prevent <137> abrogation. For the law of sacrifice preceded that of the Sabbath, and it would, therefore, have been improper for the Sabbath law to interfere with it, since that would have been tantamount to abrogation. Hence, while all other forms of work were forbidden, the offering of sacrifices and circumcision, that antedated the Sabbath, were not.

The fifth [perplexity] is [caused by] the injunction of God, exalted be He, to Abraham in regard to Isaac: *And offer him there for a burnt-offering* (Gen. 22:2), and His injunction to him later on, *Lay not thy hand upon the lad, neither do thou anything unto him* [35] (Gen. 22:12). But this, too, did not constitute an abrogation either from our point of view or from that of the proponents of the doctrine of abrogation. For he who holds that abrogation is possible would not believe it to be so unless the law to be abrogated has been carried out at least once, lest it be thought that it had been ordained in vain. What God had really ordered Abraham to do was merely to reserve his son as a sacrifice. When, therefore, this reservation had been completed by him, as evidenced by his display of the fire and the wood and his taking in hand of the knife, God said to Abraham, "Enough for thee! I do not want any more from thee than this."

The sixth [uncertainty arises from] God's injunction to Balaam in regard to the emissaries of Balak: *Thou shalt not go with them* (Num. 22:12) and his [counter-]order to him later on: *Go with them* (Num. 22:20). But this, too, did not constitute an abrogation, because the people he went with were not the same as those

35. This quotation follows the reading of Ibn Tibbon.

with whom God had forbidden him to go. For Scripture states: *And Balak sent yet again princes, more, and more honorable than they* (Num. 22:15). God had, then, kept him from going with the base and given him leave to go with the distinguished emissaries, in order thereby to enhance Balaam's esteem, so that it might be said that God had delivered the children from the yoke of so-and-so of exalted station.

The seventh [problem] is [that presented by] the declaration of God, praise be His, to Hezekiah: *For thou shalt die, and not live* (Isa. 38:1), and His statement to him afterwards: *Behold, I will add unto thy days fifteen years* (Isa. 38:5). But this, too, did not constitute an abrogation, for God may issue a command to threaten or reprimand a human being, and if the latter pays attention to it and permits himself to be reprimanded, <138> the threat is removed from him, as we know from the story of the inhabitants of Nineveh and the case of every submissive penitent.

The eighth [perplexity arises from the implication of] the passage; *And I have taken the Levites instead of all the first-born among the children of Israel* [36] (Num. 8:18). But this, too, did not constitute an abrogation, for it is entirely in order for the heavenly Master to raise a servant of His in rank and, in the event of the latter's disobedience, to demote him again. It was precisely in this way that God had first caused Adam to dwell in the Garden [of Eden], and then, when he had sinned, He drove him out again. Thus also did He allow our ancestors to enter Palestine, but when they sinned, He dispersed them. A similar procedure is followed whenever punishment is meted out.

The ninth argument that they bring up is that Joshua waged war on the Sabbath day. That was not so, however, for it is not mentioned in Scripture that fighting went on every day. What did take place every day of the week was only the carrying of the *Ark* and the blowing of the trumpets, functions that were permissible on the Sabbath. The seventh day,[37] however, that is referred to as a day of battle, was not the Sabbath day.

36. This quotation follows the reading of Ibn Tibbon.
37. Cf. Joshua 6: 4, 15.

The tenth argument that they cite is that originally one had to turn in the direction of the *Tabernacle* [when one prayed]. Then God changed [the direction one was to face in prayer] and turned it toward the Temple. But this, too, did not constitute an abrogation, for it was in the direction of the *Ark* that the facing in prayer had been ordained. So long, therefore, as the *Ark* was in the wilderness, those who prayed had to face thither. Then when the Ark was removed to *Gilgal, Shiloh, Nob,* and *Gibeon,* and finally to the Temple [of Jerusalem], the direction one had to face in prayer changed accordingly. This is but another illustration of the true meaning of the maxim that the effect follows the cause.

Now some of the proponents of the theory of abrogation base their view on an analysis of the term "forever" ('*olam*) concerning which they assert that they note that it has in the Hebrew language a variety of meanings. Our rejoinder is: Yes, it has three possible meanings. One of these is "fifty years." The other is "the lifetime of the thing referred to." The third, again, is "as long as the world will exist."

Now when we apply this term to the Sabbath law, the first two possibilities are at once eliminated, only the last being retained. For we note that Jeremiah, although he lived something like nine hundred years after Moses and the lapse of many centuries and generations of the offspring of the children of Israel, exhorted them to observe <139> the Sabbath and to refrain from working on it. Thus Scripture says: *Neither carry forth a burden out of your houses on the sabbath day, neither do ye any work, but hallow ye the sabbath day, as I commanded your fathers* [38] (Jer. 17:22). Since, then, the period of fifty years, as well as that of the lifetime of the individuals in question, is eliminated, the only one of the [different] types [of meaning that can be applied to the term '*olam*] that remains is [that of] the duration of the world.

There are some, again, who question us about the exact formulation of the tradition received by us orally concerning the eternal validity of the legislation of the Torah, assuming that, whatever phraseology we might cite to them, they would interpret it differ-

38. This quotation follows the reading of Ibn Tibbon.

ently from our accepted interpretation. To such it is our habit to reply by asking, "Is there in the world any expression so explicit and
clear-cut as to dispel all ambiguity and doubt?" If they say: "No,"
then they thereby admit the impossibility of knowing the true
meaning of any word and they have declared everything to be
doubtful.[39] If, on the other hand, they say: "Yes," then it was in
those unequivocal terms that we heard that we must always observe the precepts of the Torah.

I have also seen one of the proponents of the abrogation theory
who said: "[What] if the Brahmins told you, 'We have a tradition
from Adam ordering us to wear garments made of a mixture of
wool and linen, and to eat meat-soup with milk, and to team up
an ox and a donkey'? Should you not, therefore, have rejected the
tradition of any prophet prohibiting these things, since Adam told
us that they would not be abolished?"

These are, however, may God guide thee aright, allegations
without any foundation. It is really they who put these allegations
into the mouth of the Brahmins. As for the Brahmins themselves,
they merely maintain that these things were permissible, and we,
too, admit that they were permissible at the time when they were
thus held to be, but that it was also fully in consonance with reason
to forbid them, when man was capable of voluntarily refraining
from them, on account of some advantage that he might attain
thereby. On the other hand, if a Brahmin were to go and make in
the future the [above-mentioned] allegation imputed to him, no
attention would be paid to him. For he who transmits a tradition
must make the same assertion on every [succeeding] day that he
made the day before. He is not like the person who expresses his
own opinion and who is permitted to say, "I have discovered today what I could not understand yesterday."

Now, then, may God have mercy on thee, that [all these arguments in support of the doctrine of] the abrogation [of the Torah]
have been removed from us and overthrown, <140> it would be
most surprising if we did not fulfill these precepts which we tried

39. "doubtful"—Ibn Tibbon and M.

with so much effort and zeal to confirm. Would not all this exertion have been as useless as that of those of whom Scripture says: *She is hardened against her young ones, as if they were not hers; though her labour be in vain, she is without fear?* (Job 39: 16.) We would, in that event, be like one who has neither intelligence nor knowledge, as Scripture says: *Because God hath deprived her of wisdom, neither hath He imparted to her understanding* (Job 39: 17). Against that sort of condition one must beware.

CHAPTER X

I have now discussed the various aspects of the subject of the abrogation of the Law insofar as I have noted it down, and given an account of the confusion aroused in the hearts [of men] by [such facts as] the mortality of the prophets and [the performance by them of such functions as] eating and drinking and cohabiting, and by the violence to which the prophets are subject. [All this was done by me] for the purpose of clearing men's minds of notions by which they had come close to being corrupted. I have furthermore made an exposé of the matter of *creatio ex nihilo,* as well as of such questions as chronology, space, and time, concerning which, too, defective ideas might have been entertained had I failed to discuss them. I have also touched on some of the attributes of the Creator in order to dispel the thought of any resemblance between God and other beings, as well as on the themes of God's omniscience and His omnipotence and other traits. My neglect to explain these would, I am afraid, have led men to unbelief. These things having been disposed of, I deem it proper also to append to this treatise an analysis of twelve problems, failure to discuss each one of which would, in my estimation, produce confusion in people's minds and corrupt their faith. An elucidation thereof by me, on the other hand, would cause the prevalence of the uncertainties inspired by them to cease and human minds to be ridded of them as they were ridded of the false notions referred to above.

I say, then, that there may be some men who would give up

their adherence to the Bible because many of the *commandments* are not clearly explained [40] in it. My answer to them is that the Bible is not the sole basis of our religion, for in addition to it we have two other bases. One of these is anterior to it; namely, the fountain of reason. The second is posterior to it; namely, the source of tradition. Whatever, therefore, we may not find in the Bible, we can find in the two other sources. Thus are the commandments rounded out quantitatively as well as qualitatively.

Secondly, there may be someone else who would question the reliability of the Bible on account of some <141> contradiction which it appears to him to contain. Thus, for example, Scripture states in the Book of Samuel: *And there were in Israel eight hundred thousand valiant men* (II Sam. 24:9), whereas in the Book of Chronicles it says: *And all they of Israel were a thousand thousand and a hundred thousand men* (I Chron. 21:5). My answer hereto is that something like three hundred thousand were entered in the register of the king, twenty-four thousand of whom took their turn every month. Thus Scripture states: *Throughout all the months of the year, of every course were twenty and four thousand* (I Chron. 27:1). These three hundred thousand were dropped from one of the two versions although entered in the other.

Thirdly, one might perhaps be impelled to abandon the Bible by some erroneous impression that it contains certain accounts that are untrue, such as one according to which a son would have been two years older than his father. For Jehoram, the son of Jehoshaphat, died when he was forty years old, whereupon his son Ahaziah sat in his place, anent whom it is written in the Book of Kings (II Kings 8:26) that he was twenty-two years of age. According to the Book of Chronicles, however, he was forty-two years old (II Chron. 22:2). My answer hereunto is that the entry of twenty-two years refers to his own life, whereas that of forty-two years refers to the age of his mother, the reason for using the

40. "clearly explained"—Ibn Tibbon. The reading of the Arabic text is to be corrected accordingly.

latter figure being that it was on account of his mother that he died.

If, however, someone were to challenge this interpretation, saying: "How can one credit a son with the chronology of a life preceding his own existence?" I might say that I have fathomed this subject and found that it used to be the custom for an Israelite who wanted to have a son to make a vow years before God would grant his wish. Then when he had been granted to him, he would call him "son of vows," as Scripture expresses it: *What, my son? and what, O son of my womb? and what, O son of my vows?* (Prov. 31:2). Thus do those that seek the truth probe deeply into things until the road becomes clear to them.

Fourthly, one might think frivolously of the Bible on account of the precepts pertaining to the sacrifices, either because they order the slaughtering of beasts or the shedding of blood and [the offering up] [41] of fat. I might make this a little more comprehensible by saying that the Creator had decreed that every living thing must die. Accordingly, he apportioned to every human being his alloted lifetime, whereas the period of life of the beasts was made by Him to extend until the time when they would be slaughtered, setting up slaughter in their case in place of death. Should <142> their slaughtering, however, entail pain over and above that which is experienced in natural death, God would be fully aware of it and He would, of course, in such an event compensate the beasts in accordance with the excess of the pain.

But this, we say, applies only if it could be proved by means of reason, not by prophecy, that there exists such an excess of pain. As for the endurance of pain [resulting from slaughtering] and the shedding of the animal's blood and [the offering up] [41] of its fat, the purpose of that, as is made clear in the Torah, was to make us pensive. For the blood is the dwelling-place of our souls, as Scripture says: *For the soul* [42] *of the flesh is in the blood* (Lev.

41. "offering up"—supplied from the expression "offering up" used by Ibn Tibbon in the place of "shedding."
42. "soul"—The usual translation is "life."

17: 11). Seeing that, then, we would repent, saying: "We shall not sin again lest our blood be shed and our fat be burned as, alas, we see it happen."

Fifthly, someone might wonder how it happened that the Creator should have caused His light to abide among men and have abandoned the pure angels. Our reply hereunto is: "How dost thou know that the angels are without such divine light when it is fully in the realm of possibility that God should have caused many times as much light to dwell in their midst as He had put among men?" But there is no need to bring up this argument in view of the fact that Scripture says: *A God dreaded in the great council of the holy ones and feared of all them that are round about thee* (Ps. 89:8), that is to say, "those that are round about this light of Thine."

Sixthly, someone might express surprise at the *construction of the Tabernacle,* saying, "What need has the Creator for a tent, and a curtain, and lamps, that give light, and sounds of music, and the offering of incense, and fragrant odors, and gifts of grain and wine, and oil and fruits, and other such things?" Our answer hereunto, and we invoke God's assistance herein, is that all these are forms of devotion not at all prompted by necessity. For reason has long since decided that God does not require anything, but that all things, rather, have need of God.

God's sole aim [in issuing the above-mentioned injunctions] was that His servants indicate their submissiveness to Him by [presenting [43] to Him] the best that they possessed, and the best that they possess is meat and wine and music and incense and grain and oil and things that are pleasant. Of this, however, they were to bring only a little bit, in accordance with their capacity. He, on the other hand, would recompense them amply in accordance with His ability, as Scripture says: <143> *Honour the Lord with thy substance. . . . So shall thy barns be filled with plenty* (Prov. 3:9, 10). He would also deliver them from misfortunes, as no one outside of Him could protect them, because of their obedience. Thus Scripture says: *Offer unto God the sacrifice of thanksgiving;*

43. "presenting"—the basis of this word is a variant in the original for "indicate their submissiveness," differing only in the order of two radicals.

and pay thy vows unto the Most High; and call upon Me in the day of trouble; I will deliver thee, and thou shalt honour Me (Ps. 50: 14, 15).

They were also bidden to honor the dwelling-place of that light which was called šĕḳhinah by means of their substance; namely, with silver and gold and precious stones and other things of value. In return therefor God was to recompense them by causing the divine revelation to manifest itself from that place, as Scripture says of the *Tabernacle: And there will I meet with the children of Israel* (Exod. 29: 43). Likewise was it destined to become a place for accepting the prayer of the nation in any mishap that might befall it. Thus Solomon enumerated, at the time when he built the Temple, the various instances [in which the prayers offered in it] were to be answered, whereupon God said to him: *I have heard thy prayer and thy supplication, that thou hast made before Me* (I Kings 9: 3).

In the seventh instance, one might wonder, apropos of the individual precepts, how it could be that so long as a man's body is in its complete natural state he is not perfect, whereas, when something is cut off from it, he becomes perfect. What I have reference to is the [rite of] *circumcision*.[44] Let me explain, then, that the perfect thing is one that suffers from neither superfluity nor deficiency. Now the Creator created this part of the body with a redundancy, with the result that, when it is cut off, the redundancy is removed and what is left is in a state of perfection.

In the eighth place, thinking about the case of the *red heifer,* one might wonder how it could have been ordained that this heifer was to purify the unclean and defile the pure.[45] Our answer hereunto is that it is by no means extraordinary that one and the same thing should produce two opposite effects, depending on the nature of the body that encounters it. For we note that fire liquefies lead while it solidifies milk, and that water moistens the wood of the pine while it dries that of the sycamore. We find, furthermore, that good food is beneficial to the person who is hungry but

44. The expression used in prescribing this rite to the patriarch Abraham was "Walk before Me, and be thou perfect (tamim)" (Gen. 17: 1).

45. Cf. Num. 19: 1 ff.

harmful to him that is sated, and that choice medicine might be of benefit to the sick and yet do harm to the person who is in good health. Hence it is not strange that <144> the same thing should have the effect of purifying the impure and defiling the pure.

The ninth problem is presented by the sacrifice the Israelites were wont to offer up to *Azazel* on the day of *Atonement*.[46] To certain people this name sounded like that of a demon. Our reply hereunto is that *Azazel* was the name of a mountain, and that names of this type were given to mountains is borne out by the statement of Scripture: *And he took the rock* [47] *by war, and called the name of it Joktheel* (II Kings 14:7). Similarly *Jabneel* (Josh. 15:11), *Irpeel* (*ibid.* 18:27), and *Jeruel* (II Chron. 20:16) were all of them localities.

Now one of the two heads [of cattle] was offered up by the *priests* in the sanctuary in view of the fact that most of their sins were committed in the sanctuary. The other, again, was offered up by the *nation* outside of the sanctuary because most of their sins were committed outside of it, preference being thereby shown to the priests. As for the casting of the lots, which was, as it were, the most objectionable feature of the whole affair, let me explain that that was not due to any variation in the recipient of the sacrifice, for both were offered up to the same Master. Lots were cast only on account of the difference in the persons in whose behalf the sacrifices were offered; namely, that they were offered for *priests and Israelites*. It was, therefore, necessary to throw lots first, so that whatever fell to each one's share might be offered up in his behalf with the assurance that it belonged to him.

In the tenth instance one might ask, in regard to the *heifer whose neck was broken,* how it was possible for the people thereby to be forgiven for a sin of which they had no knowledge? For it is stated previously, at the beginning of the passage concerning the man who was found slain: *And it be not known who hath smitten him* (Deut. 21:1). Let me reply, then, that just as it is necessary to chastise a human being for doing what he ought not to do, so is it

46. Cf. Lev. 16:8 ff.
47. "the rock"—the usual rendering is "Sela."

necessary to chastise him for failing to do what he ought to do. Now if the above-mentioned burghers had appointed watchmen, who made the rounds of the town, and night patrols,[48] there would not have arisen the situation of *And it be not known who hath smitten him*. Since they had not done this, however, they became liable to punishment, and not only to the extent of the price of that beast alone, but also by being prevented <145> from cultivating some of their fields.

The eleventh [problem arises from] the fact that one sees that this nation that clings to this Law is in a state of humiliation and contempt. Our answer hereunto is that if the adherents of the Law had been granted perpetual sovereignty, the nonbelievers might have said about them that the only reason they served their Lord was in order to preserve their favorable situation. This, thou knowest, was indeed said about *Job*.[49] Aye, these [infidels] might also have said [if they had been in such a position,] that the only reason why they themselves did not obey God but turned their backs to Him was that they had been brought low and were treated with contempt and were granted no sovereignty. Therefore did the All-Wise elevate the latter, and since they still did not believe, the verdict against them was sustained. Again He debased the former, and, since they nevertheless did not deny Him, the justice they were entitled to was confirmed. Thus [the believers] said: *Our heart is not turned back, neither have our steps declined from Thy path* (Ps. 44: 19).

The twelfth problem brought up is the fact that one does not find in the Torah any mention of reward or punishment in the world to come but only mundane recompense. In reply hereto let me say that I have dedicated a special treatise to this subject, namely the ninth treatise of this book, where I shall, with the help of the Merciful One, explain all that is required in connection with this theme.

The third treatise is hereby completed with the praise of God and His help.

48. "night patrols"—M.
49. Cf. Job 1: 10.

TREATISE IV

CONCERNING OBEDIENCE AND REBELLION AND PREDESTINATION AND [DIVINE] JUSTICE

EXORDIUM

I SHALL open this treatise with the introductory remark that, even though [1] we see that the creatures are many in number, nevertheless, we need not be confused in regard to, which of them constitutes the goal of creation. For there exists a natural criterion by means of which we can determine which one of all the creatures is the end. When, then, we make our investigation with this criterion [as a guide], we find that the goal is man.

We arrive at this conclusion in the following manner: Habit and nature place whatever is most highly prized in the center of things which are themselves not so highly prized. Beginning with the smallest things, therefore, we say that it is noted that the kernel lodges inside of <146> all the leaves. That is due to the fact that the kernel is more precious than the leaves, because the growth of the plant and its very existence depend upon it. Similarly does the seed from which trees grow, if edible, lodge in the center of the fruit, as happens in the case of the nut. But even if [a tree grows] from an inedible kernel, this kernel is located in the center of the fruit, no attention being paid to the edible portion, which is left on the outside to preserve the kernel. In the same way is the yolk of the egg in the center, because from it springs the young bird and the chicken. Likewise also is the heart of man in the middle of his breast, owing to the fact that it is the seat of the soul and of the natural heat of the body. So, too, is the power of vision located in the center of the eye because it is by means of it that one is able to see.

When, therefore, we see that this situation appertains to many

1. "even though"—Ibn Tibbon.

things and then find the earth in the center of the heaven with the heavenly spheres surrounding it on all sides, it becomes clear to us that the thing which was the object of creation must be on the earth. Upon further investigation of all its parts we note that the earth and the water are both inanimate, whereas we find that the beasts are irrational. Hence only man is left, which gives us the certainty that he must unquestionably have been the intended purpose of creation.

When we examine the Scriptures,[2] we likewise find in them a statement by God to the effect that *I, even I, have made the earth, and created man upon it* (Isa. 45: 12). In fact, at the very beginning of the Torah God listed all classes of creatures. Then, when He had completed them all, He said: *Let us make man* (Gen. 1: 26), like a person who builds a palace and, after having furnished and decorated it, brings its owner into it.

CHAPTER I

After this preliminary observation let me now proceed again and say that our Lord has informed us through His prophets that man has been shown preference by Him above all His creatures in His statement: *And have dominion over the fish of the sea, and over the fowl of the air* (Gen. 1: 28). Similarly Scripture remarks in the *psalm: O Lord, our Lord, how glorious is Thy name in all the earth! etc.* (Ps. 8: 2). <147> [God has] furthermore [told us] that He has granted to man the capacity to obey Him and has left it to him [to act upon it], and has given him freedom of choice, but enjoined him to choose the good. Thus Scripture says: *See, I have set before thee this day life and good, and death and evil* (Deut. 30: 15), which it follows up later with the remark: *Therefore choose life* (Deut. 30: 19). In corroboration of this statement miracles and marvels were wrought by the prophets, wherefore we accepted it [3] as binding.

Afterward, employing the speculative method, we inquired into

2. "Scriptures"—pl. according to M and Ibn Tibbon.
3. "it"—Ibn Tibbon and M.

what it could have been that distinguished man, and we found that his distinction above the rest of creation was due to the wisdom with which God had endowed him and which He had taught him, as Scripture says: *He that teacheth man knowledge* (Ps. 94: 10). By means of this wisdom he is able to retain all the events of the past and foresee many of the eventualities of the future, and achieve the subjugation of the animals so as to make them till the soil for him and transport to him its harvests. By means of it, too, he succeeds in extracting water from the depths of the earth to the point where it flows [4] on its surface. Nay, he makes himself water-wheels by means of which the soil is automatically watered. By dint of this wisdom he is furthermore able to build the most exquisite dwellings, wear the choicest garments, and prepare the most delicious foods. By means of it he becomes capable also of leading hosts and armies and of exercising governmental authority in such a way that men will allow themselves to be bound and ruled [5] thereby. By means of it, moreover, he attains to the knowledge of the disposition of the heavenly spheres and the course of the stars and the measurements of their masses and their distances and all the rest of their attributes. Should anyone, however, imagine that there exists some other being outside of man that is endowed with such superior qualities, then let him show us these qualities [6] or even some of them in another creature. Such a being, however, he will never discover.

In view of the above-mentioned considerations it is only right that man should be subject to commandments and prohibitions and reward and punishment, seeing that he is the axle of the world and its foundation, as Scripture says: *For the pillars of the earth are the Lord's,* <148> *and He hath set the world upon them* [7] (I Sam. 2: 8), and again: *But the righteous is the foundation of the world* [8] (Prov. 10: 25).

4. "flows"—M.
5. "ruled"—the term used in the Arabic text is borrowed from the Aramaic. Cf. Brockelmann's *Lexicon Syriacum* (Berlin 1895), p. 236, *sakkem*.
6. "qualities"—Ibn Tibbon and M.
7. This quotation follows the reading of Ibn Tibbon.
8. "the foundation of the world"—the usual translation is "an everlasting foundation."

When, therefore, I considered these principles and the inferences to which they were conducive, I realized that the superiority ascribed to man was not due to some false notion that struck our minds or to an inclination on our part toward favoring man, nor was it self-preference or conceit or boastfulness that induced us to arrogate this superiority unto ourselves. On the contrary, it was nothing but the unadulterated truth and plain veracity. Nor did the All-Wise endow man with superiority in these respects for any other reason than that He had made him the bearer of His commandments and prohibitions, as Scripture says: *And unto man He said: "Behold, the fear of the Lord, that is wisdom; and to depart from evil is understanding"* (Job 28:28).

CHAPTER II

It behooves me now to write down what is essential of the results of my investigations [9] appertaining to the present theme. I say, then, that I have thought to myself and asked myself the question of how everything in the world could have been made to depend upon man when we see that his body is so small and slight. So I pondered this matter thoroughly and I came to the conclusion that even though man's body is of small dimension, his soul is more extensive than heaven and earth because his knowledge embraces all that they contain. Aye, it goes so far as to know even that which is above heaven and earth and by virtue of which they exist, I mean the Creator, exalted and sanctified be He, as Scripture says: *Wonderful are Thy works; and that my soul knoweth right well* (Ps. 139:14).

I reflected also about the brevity of man's existence on earth and the fact that he does not live forever. But then I realized that this short life had been given to him by the Creator only in this nether abode, which is a world of care. He promised him, however, that, once he had been transferred [from it], life everlasting would be his, as Scripture also states: *He asked life of Thee, Thou gavest*

9. "investigations"—Ibn Tibbon and M.

it him; [even length of days forever and ever] (Ps. 21:5), and as I shall explain in the ninth treatise of this book.

Furthermore, I wondered why, with all the distinction accorded to man, he came to have this feeble frame of a body composed of blood and phlegm and two galls. Why was it not constituted of pure elements resembling each other? But then I rejected this idea, saying [to myself] that for us to insist upon such a thing would only be equivalent to demanding that man should have been created <149> as a star or an angel. For what is known as the human body is this thing, created of these mixtures, which is of all earthly beings the purest. Anything purer would have to be one of the two, either an angel or a star. Whoever, therefore, insists upon man's body's being composed of elements other than those of which it consists is only demanding his nonexistence, just as he does who demands that the heaven be made of nothing except dirt or that the earth consist solely of fire. That is, of course, demanding the absurd, which does not correspond to [the plans of divine] Wisdom, in regard to which Scripture says: *How manifold are Thy works, O Lord! In wisdom hast Thou made them all* (Ps. 104:24).

I thought also about those maladies that befall man and said to myself: "If only he could be protected against them or they would be warded off from him!" I found, however, that they were really salutary for him because they keep him away from sin, and render him submissive to his Master, and introduce balance into his affairs, as Scripture says: *He is chastened also with pain upon his bed* (Job 33:19).

I meditated, moreover, about the fact of man's being subject to heat and cold and his susceptibility to the poisons of reptiles and noxious animals. I recognized, however, that his ability to have such experiences redounded to his well-being. For had he felt no pain, he would not have been afraid of his Master's punishment, because if the latter had said to him, "I shall inflict pain on thee," he would not have known what pain was. God, therefore, enabled him to experience these aches in order that they might serve as a premonition to him of things to be, as Scripture says, with reference to the heat of hell-fire: *For, behold, the day cometh, it burneth as a furnace* (Mal. 3:19). It says also, likening God's punishment to poisons: *Their wine is the venom of serpents* (Deut. 32:33).

Then I thought about these urges with which man is endowed and the appetites, many of which are detrimental to him. I realized, however, that the All-Wise endowed him therewith only in order that he might employ each one in its proper place with the help of the reasoning faculty which God has granted him. Thus, for example, the craving for food [should be used] for the purpose of sustaining the individual organism, and the sex impulse for the maintenance of the human species as a whole. Each of them should receive the attention that it definitely requires and that is allowed it. If employed < 150 > to the extent to which it is permissible, pre-occupation therewith is excusable. To reach out to what is forbidden thereof, however, is reprehensible, as Scripture says: *The desire of the righteous is only good; but the expectation of the wicked is wrath* [10] (Prov. 11:23), and as it also states: *For the wicked boasteth of his heart's desire* (Ps. 10:3).

I wondered, moreover, how it came that God had prepared for man painful torment and perpetual sojourn in hell-fire. But I noted that that contrasted with the promise of perennial delight and per-petual reward. Also were it not for these two alternatives, there would have been nothing to imbue man with either aspiration or fear, as Scripture says: *Some to everlasting life, and some to re-proaches and everlasting abhorrence* (Dan. 12:2).

Finally, I meditated over the fact that, even before this retribu-tion in the future life, man was ordered to be put to death by means of four different forms of execution. I realized, however, that all this was for his benefit and that it was not contrary to reason. For it is in accordance with the verdict of reason that, just as the in-dividual recognizes that the cutting off of one of the members of his body, which has been rendered worthless by poison or disease, is a corrective necessary for the preservation of the rest of his body, so the human species must recognize that the slaying of one of its members who has become corrupted and is causing trouble

10. This quotation follows the reading of Ibn Tibbon.

on earth is a corrective necessary for preserving the rest of the species. Thus Scripture also says: *And those that remain shall hear and fear* (Deut. 19:20).

Having now demonstrated God's justice toward man in the seven instances I have enumerated, I may say that in the event of any misgivings that might be aroused in the mind of a believer by similar phenomena, he need but ponder the matter well. For if he were to do that, he would undoubtedly discover some basis for it in [divine] Wisdom, as Scripture says: *All the paths of the Lord are mercy and truth* (Ps. 25:10).

CHAPTER III

And now that I have explained how these different instances that are illustrative of the various aspects of God's justice are to be understood, I say that it is in keeping with [11] the justice of the Creator and of His tender solicitude for man that He gave him the power and ability to execute what He had commanded him and to refrain from what He had forbidden him. This is evident from the standpoint of reason as well as from the Scriptures.

As far as reason is concerned, it demands that the All-Wise <151> do not charge anyone with aught that does not lie within his competence or which he is unable to do. As for [the corroboration by] Scripture, again, it is found in such statements as *O My people, what have I done unto thee? And wherein have I wearied thee? Testify against Me* (Mic. 6:3). Scripture also says: *But they that wait for the Lord shall renew their strength* (Isa. 40:31), and *Keep silence before Me, O islands, and let the peoples renew their strength* (Isa. 41:1), as well as *When the morning is light, they execute it, because it is in the power of their hand* (Mic. 2:1).

I am also of the opinion that the ability [to act] must precede the act itself to the point where an equal opportunity would be granted to man either to act or desist from acting. For if the ability to act were completely synchronous with the act itself, [then there would be only one of two possibilities so far as their relationship

11. "in keeping with"—Ibn Tibbon.

to each other is concerned.] Either each is the cause of the other or neither is the other's cause. If, on the other hand, it be [assumed that the ability to act comes] after the act, then it would be possible for a person to render undone an act that has already been performed by him, which is absurd, as is also the previous assumption. It follows, therefore, of necessity that man's power to act must precede the act itself, in order that he may thereby be in a position to carry out the command of God, his Lord.

I deem it proper also to explain that, just as man's doing a thing constitutes an act, so does also his desisting therefrom constitute an act, for by desisting from it he only permits the opposite thereof to come about. Man's position in this respect cannot be compared to the desistence from the creation of things by the Creator, exalted and magnified be He, which, as we explained,[12] did not constitute an act. For when the Creator refrained from any further creation of substances and their contents, the latter had no counterparts to take their place. As far as man is concerned, however, since his action extends to the domain of accidents only, his sole reason for desisting from one thing is that he chooses to allow the opposite thereof to take place. Thus if he does not love, he hates; and if he is not well disposed, he is angry. Hence thou wilt not find a middle ground for him between these two alternatives. In a like vein do the Scriptures say: *Therefore shall ye keep My charge, that ye do not any of these abominable customs, which were done before you* (Lev. 18: 30); and also *Yea, they do no unrighteousness; they walk in His ways* (Ps. 119: 3).

It behooves me furthermore to explain that man cannot be considered as the agent <152> of an act unless he exercises freedom of choice in performing it, for no one can be held accountable for an act who does not possess freedom of choice and does not exercise this choice. On the other hand, the reason why, as we note, the Law did not impose any punishment upon the person who by oversight did something that was forbidden, was not that he did not exercise choice in committing the act, for such an act would have no significance that would make it subject to punishment. It

12. Cf. above, p. 86.

was rather because he was ignorant of the motive or reason for its prohibition. Thus, for instance, we say of him that *killeth any person through error* [13] that he is an individual who acts with deliberate intent and from choice so far as the cutting of the wood is concerned. He is only negligent in taking precautions against striking a passer-by. Similarly we say of him who profanes [14] the Sabbath that he is a person who acts with deliberate intent so far as *the gathering of sticks* [15] is concerned, but that he has forgotten that the day on which he does it is the Sabbath.

CHAPTER IV

After the aforementioned let me say next that the Creator, magnified be His majesty, does not in any way interfere with the actions of men and that He does not exercise any force upon them either to obey or disobey Him. For this I can adduce proof from the standpoint of the experience of the senses and of reason, as well as from the Scriptures and tradition.

As far as the attestation of our senses is concerned, I find that a human being feels conscious of his own ability either to speak or remain silent, or to take hold of things or desist from them, while at the same time he is not conscious of the existence of any other power that might at all prevent him from carrying out his will. All he has to do to gain his end is to allow his natural impulses to be directed by his intellect. If he abides by this rule, he is wise. If he does not, he is foolish.

As for the proof from reason, we have already previously presented arguments demonstrating the untenability of the theory that one act can have two authors.[16] Whoever, therefore, believes that the Creator, magnified and exalted be He, exercises force upon His servant in regard to anything, thereby attributes one and the same act to both of them? Furthermore, if God were to exercise force upon His servant, there would be no sense to His command

13. Cf. Deut. 19: 5.
14. "profanes"—Ibn Tibbon.
15. Cf. Num. 15: 32 and Mišnah Šab. 7: 1.
16. Cf. above, p. 60 and pp. 98 ff.

or His interdict. Also if God were to force him to perform some act, it would not be proper for Him to punish him for it.

Again, if men acted out of compulsion, the believer and the infidel would alike have to be rewarded, since each would be doing what is requested of him, just as any intelligent person, if he employed two workingmen, the first to build and the other to tear down, would be obliged to pay each of them his wage. Finally, if it were conceivable that man is subject in his action to <153> compulsion, he would always be able to present the excuse that he knew that he could accomplish nothing against the power of his Master. Under such circumstances, if the unbeliever were to offer as an alibi for his unbelief the fact that he is unable to believe in God, he would have to be considered justified and his alibi accepted.

As for the proof from Scripture, it consists [first of all] of what we have stated previously [17] apropos of [the injunction of] *Therefore choose life* (Deut. 30: 19). [It is made up], furthermore, [of] the statement made to the sinners: *This hath been of your doing— Will He accept any of your persons? etc.*[18] (Mal. 1: 9). [It is] also [contained in such] statements [of Scripture], in which the Creator explicitly clears Himself of all responsibility for the deeds of liars, as *I have not sent these prophets, yet they ran; I have not spoken to them, yet they prophesied* (Jer. 23: 21), and the like.

An example, again, [of the proofs furnished] by tradition is the [following] maxim transmitted by the ancients: *Everything is in the hands of heaven except the fear of heaven, as it is said: "And now, Israel, what doth the Lord thy God require of thee, but to fear . . . ?"* (Deut. 10: 12) (Běr. 33b).

However, notwithstanding the fact that after these explicit pronouncements on the subject there is nothing left to be asked about any more, Scripture takes occasion to deny the exercise of compulsion by God by employing three other basic [rhetorical] devices. The first of these denials is in the form of an expression of amazement whereby the astonishment of men over the matter is aroused.

17. Cf. above, p. 181.
18. This quotation follows the reading of Ibn Tibbon.

It says, namely: *Have I any pleasure at all that the wicked should die?* (Ezek. 18:23). The second is in the form of an assertion made by God that such a thing would not be. It says, namely: *Indeed* [19] *I have no pleasure in the death of him that dieth* (Ezek. 18:32). The third consists of an oath taken thereon by God. It is worded: *Say unto them: As I live, saith the Lord God, I have no pleasure in the death of the wicked* (Ezek. 33:11). Thus the subject has been treated from every possible aspect, [all of which was done for the purpose of] driving home the idea [20] [of man's complete freedom of choice].

After this explanation let me present the following questions. I say, that someone might perhaps ask: "If it be true, as has been explained, that God does not desire the rebellion <154> of the rebellious, how is it possible that there should exist in His world anything that He does not approve of or find pleasure in?" The answer to this is, however, [quite] simple. If it seems odd to us that one who is all-wise should permit anything to transpire in his domain that does not accord with his wishes or please him, that could apply only to man. For when a human being hates a thing, he does so usually because it harms him. Our Lord, however, does not hate anything [21] on account of His own personality, because it is impossible that He be affected by any of the accidents appertaining to mortals. He considers them objectionable, only on our account, because of the harm they might inflict upon us. For if we transgress against Him by failing to acknowledge our indebtedness to Him, we are guilty of folly. On the other hand, if we wrong one another, we bring about the destruction of our lives and our wealth.

In the light of this exposé of the matter, it is no longer strange that there could exist in God's world anything that we consider objectionable and which He made clear was objectionable in His sight on our account, out of pity for us. This has been made [completely] plain by Him in Scripture, where He says: *Do they pro-*

19. "Indeed"—the usual translation is "For."
20. "driving home the idea"—Ibn Tibbon and M.
21. "anything"—Ibn Tibbon.

voke Me? saith the Lord; do they not provoke themselves, to the confusion of their own faces? (Jer. 7:19).

Furthermore, one might perhaps also say: "Inasmuch as God knows what is to be before it happens, He must also know that man will rebel against Him. But in that case it would be impossible for man not to rebel, since otherwise what God foreknows would not be realized." The resolution of this doubt, however, is more obvious even than that of the first one. It need not be pointed out that the person who makes the above-mentioned assertion is really unable to prove that the Creator's foreknowledge of things is the cause of their coming into being. His assertion is, therefore, nothing else than an erroneous assumption or deliberate invention.

Its untenability is made clear by the realization that if God's foreknowledge of anything could be the cause of its coming into being, then all things would have to be eternal, having existed always since God has always known of them. What we profess, therefore, is that God has a knowledge of things as they are actually constituted. He also knows before anything happens to them that it will happen. Furthermore He is cognizant of what man's choice will be before man makes it.

Should it be asked, therefore: "But if God foreknows that <155> a human being will speak, is it conceivable that he should remain silent?" We would answer simply that, if a human being decided instead of speaking to be silent, we would merely modify our original [22] assumption by saying that God knows that that human being will be silent. It would not be proper to assume that God knows that that person will speak, because what God foreknows is the final denouement of man's activity as it turns out after all his planning, anticipations, and delays. It is that very thing that God knows, as Scripture says: *The Lord knoweth the thoughts of man* (Ps. 94:11), and also *For I know their imagination how they do even now* (Deut. 31:21).

22. Cf. Guttmann's interpretation of this passage (p. 170).

CHAPTER V

I have furthermore encountered men who asked in this connection: "What reason could have prompted [divine] Wisdom to issue commandments and prohibitions to the virtuous of whom God knew that he would not turn aside from serving Him?" For this I found four reasons. One of them is [that this was done] in order to inform the virtuous individual of what it was that God desired from him. Another was to pay him his full reward, for, if he were to serve God without having been commanded to do so, he would not receive any reward for it.[23] Thirdly, if it had been proper for God to reward him for the performance of a virtuous deed that He had not commanded him to do, it would likewise have been proper for Him to punish him for committing a misdeed that He had not forbidden him to do, which would have been an act of injustice on the part of God. Finally, the repetition by the prophets of the injunction already dictated by reason served to put man on his guard, and make him beware, and take the necessary precautions in the fulfillment of these precepts. Thus Scripture says: *Nevertheless if thou warn the righteous man, that the righteous sin not, and he doth not sin, he shall surely live, because he took warning* (Ezek. 3:21).

Men ask also: "What could have prompted [divine] Wisdom to send missions to the unbelievers, of whom God knew that they would not believe but that they would look upon all prophecy as idle play?"[24] For this I found six reasons. One of them is that, if God had not sent any mission to the unbelievers with the prescription to them that they believe, that would have furnished them with a good alibi. <156> For they might have said: "If a prophet had come to us, we would have believed in him." Another [reason for admonishing unbelievers] is that, if [the intentions of man] that were known [to God] had not been translated into action,[25] reward and punishment would have been meted out by Him on ac-

---

23. Cf. the Talmudic maxim: *He who is commanded and does stands higher than he who is not commanded and does* (Ḳidd. 31a).

24. "idle play"—Ibn Tibbon.

25. For this rendering cf. Guttmann p. 171 and n. 3.

count of His prescience rather than the actual deeds of His servants.

[Thirdly,] just as the sensual and rational proofs have been established in the world by God for the believer as well as the infidel, so was it necessary for the prophetic proofs to be shared by believers as well as infidels. [Fourthly,] just as it seems certain to us that he who gives someone an order to do something reprehensible, which the latter fails to execute, is nevertheless doing him harm and would be called a fool, so must he who orders someone to do a good deed be regarded as the latter's benefactor and be called a wise man even though the order has never been carried out by him to whom it was given.

[Fifthly,] if the injunction to do what is good were to be regarded, when he to whom it is addressed fails to accept it, as folly on account of this nonacceptance, then by the same token the injunction to do what is reprehensible, issued to a person who accepts it, would have to be considered wisdom because of this acceptance by the latter. But in that case the actual nature of good and evil would be variable, depending upon the contingency of being accepted, which is, of course, absurd.

Sixthly, just as God made no differences [26] between [the different types of] men so far as intelligence, power, and ability are concerned, so too could He make no distinction [27] between them in regard to His commands or His mission to them.

Furthermore let me say that only he can be considered wanton that does something which benefits no one. As far as God's mission to the unbelievers is concerned, however, if they choose not to benefit by it nor to be chastised, there are the believers and the remainder of men who are chastised thereby and induced to take heed. Thus, for example, thou seest how the servants of God relate to each other even unto this very day—and they will continue to do so forever—the story of the deluge and of the inhabitants of Sodom and of Pharaoh and the like.

Men also ask: "If it were to happen that God deliver up one of His servants to be slain either in punishment for sin or as a trial,

26. "made no difference"—literally "made equal."
27. "could He make no distinction"—literally "He had to make equal."

what shall we think of that act or to whom shall we ascribe it in the event that the slaying is carried out by a tyrant like Jezebel, who put some of the prophets to death?" [28] Our reply hereto is that the cutting off [decreed for the victim] is an act of God, but the manner of slaying is an act of the tyrant. For as long as <157> [divine] Wisdom demands the extermination of the individual in question, even if the actual slayer should not in his malice slay him, the victim might perish by some other means.

A similar question [29] is [raised] in regard to the thief who is permitted by God to sequester some of the property of men either in punishment or as a trial of the latter. Shall this theft be conceived of as an act of God? The answer is that the [decree concerning the] loss of the property is an act of God but the theft is an act of man. For as long as [divine] Wisdom demands the loss of that particular object, if the thief were not to steal it, it might be destroyed by other means. Thus, too, did Shemaiah and his brother answer one of the kings of Rome. They said, namely: *We, however, have been sentenced to death by heaven. If thou dost not slay us, God has many demons at His disposal to strike us* (Ta'ăn. 18b).

The question is also asked, "How comes it that in order to punish David, may peace be upon him, for a sin he had committed, Absalom was caused to commit a similar, nay an even greater, sin, as Scripture puts it: *For thou didst it secretly; but I will do this thing before all Israel, and before the sun?*" (II Sam. 12:12.) To this I reply that the message that was brought by Nathan to David falls into two parts. One of them pertains to the act of God; namely, that of making Absalom prevail, and permitting him to stretch forth his hands, and turning over to him all that belonged to David. In regard to that Nathan said: *Behold, I will raise up evil against thee out of thine own house* (II Sam. 12:11). The other concerns an act of Absalom's own choosing. It was to this that Nathan had reference when he said: *And he shall lie with thy wives in the sight of this sun* (*ibid.*). His object in giving David

---

28. Cf. Guttmann p. 173 for this rendering.
29. "question"—Ibn Tibbon and M.

advance information of the act of Absalom's voluntary choosing was to cause him heartache thereby.

People ask also, with reference to what is related about Sennacherib and Nebuchadnezzar and the death and destruction and other forms of violence that they brought into the world, how God, exalted be He, could have referred to the one as <158> His scourge, saying, in regard to Sennacherib: *O Asshur, the rod of Mine anger, in whose hand as a staff [is Mine indignation]* (Isa. 10:5), and to the other as His sword, saying, in regard to Nebuchadnezzar: *And I will strengthen the arms of the king of Babylon, and put My sword in his hand* (Ezek. 30:24).

Our comment hereon is that all that God, blessed and exalted be He, did in the case of these two individuals, as well as of others of their kind, was to give them strength and encouragement, as though it were with a sword and a scourge. Nevertheless whatever they and their armies did was done by their own choice, for which they merited God's retribution. Apropos of this retribution Scripture says: *I will punish the fruit of the arrogant heart of the king of Assyria* (Isa. 10:12), and *And I will render unto Babylon and unto all the inhabitants of Chaldea all their evil* (Jer. 51:24).

Men ask furthermore: "Inasmuch as all happenings take place because of God's command, then if God creates a situation whereby a believer is compelled to tell a lie, would not He be the one who forces him to lie?" To this question two answers may be offered. One of them is that if one were to inquire closely into the manner in which a human being comes to be forced to lie, he would discover that it is grounded in his sinful conduct in the past, which he attributes [30] to his Lord. This has been expressed by Scripture as follows: *The foolishness of man perverteth his way; and his heart fretteth against the Lord* (Prov. 19:3).

The other is that, thanks to the intelligence with which God has endowed man, the latter is never really compelled to tell an [outright] lie. For if he uses an expression which, when taken in its figurative sense, may be understood to refer to the actual state of affairs, he is being truthful, and it cannot be held against him if the

30. "attributes"—Ibn Tibbon.

person whom he encounters puts the wrong construction on his words.

As an illustration one might cite the statement of Abraham, peace be upon him, concerning Sarah: *She is my sister* (Gen. 20:2), taking the expression *my sister* [31] in the sense of "my kinswoman," just as we find that Lot, who was really Abraham's nephew, was by rhetorical license called *brother* (Gen. 14:14). The Gerarites thought, however, that she was his sister in the literal meaning of the word. No <159> sin, therefore, attached to Abraham; it attached rather to them because they did what was wrong. For it is considered proper etiquette to ask a stranger about his situation and well-being and his needs, but not what relationship his companions [32] bear to him.[33] Still less could Abraham be blamed for his deed, since he had already had a trying experience of such a nature with someone else, as he said: *Because I thought: Surely the fear of God is not in this place; and they will slay me* [34] (Gen. 20:11).

And now that I have discussed these questions sufficiently, it behooves the student of this book to apply [35] the answers given to them to all similar cases that he may find.

CHAPTER VI

My next step is to append to the statement I have made all those verses of the Bible that throw uncertainty and doubt on our theory about the compulsion [exercised by God on man]. However, on account of the large number of such verses by reason of the extension of meaning to which language lends itself—for, as I have noted in the treatise on the unity of God,[36] unless there existed the possibility of an extension of meaning in language, nothing more than the barest reference to substances would have been within

31. "my sister"—added by M.
32. "companions"—Ibn Tibbon and M.
33. "to him"—Ibn Tibbon and M.
34. This quotation follows the reading of Ibn Tibbon.
35. "apply"—Ibn Tibbon.
36. Cf. above, p. 118.

its competence—I have seen fit to indicate the various ways in which they are to be interpreted so as to harmonize with reason. When, therefore, I shall have enumerated as many different classes as there are and discussed several examples of each, let the student of this book attach every type, as well as every individual instance, to the class to which it belongs, as his reason and his understanding may dictate.

I say, then, that there are eight classes altogether. The first of them constitutes the category of "prohibition." People are under the impression that the prevention of an act by means of an interdict is identical with its hindrance by means of a [preventive] act. The fact is, however, that there is a great difference between them.

As an illustration hereof we might cite the statement made by God, exalted and magnified be He, to Abimelech: [37] *And I also withheld thee from sinning against Me* (Gen. 20:6). Now it was thought by some that it was an act of God's that had withheld him. In reality, however, it was by means of God's interdict that he was withheld and by His announcement that she was a *married woman,* as well as by the threat of punishment. Thus God said: *Behold, thou shalt die, because of the woman whom thou hast taken; for she is a man's wife* [38] (Gen. 20:3). God furthermore said to him: *And if thou restore her not, know that thou shalt surely die* (Gen. 20:7).

Now the withholding of Abimelech from that woman so that he was unable to come in contact with her, as God said: *Therefore suffered I thee not to touch her* (Gen. 20:6), was of the same order as the withholding of a divorced husband from taking back <160> his divorced wife after she had married another man, as [demanded by] the injunction of Scripture: *Her former husband, who sent her away, cannot* [39] *take her again* (Deut. 24:4). The husband would be quite capable [of taking back his former wife] if it depended on his own choice, but he is unable to do it because of the law. This [point] is illustrated also by the statement

37. "to Abimelech"—Ibn Tibbon and M.
38. This quotation follows the reading of Ibn Tibbon.
39. "cannot"—the usual translation is "may not."

of Scripture: *Thou canst not sacrifice the passover-offering within any of thy gates* (Deut. 16:5), and others resembling it.

The second group of verses is that speaking of obstruction [by God] of [man's] mundane well-being, a punishment which resembles the prevention of spiritual well-being. Hence it was believed by those who misunderstood it that this constituted compulsion [on the part of God]. An instance of verses harboring this implication is the statement: *Make the heart of this people fat, and make their ears heavy, and shut their eyes, etc.* [40] (Isa. 6:10).

What Scripture meant hereby, however, was that, on account of some obstruction that would arise, they would be unable clearly to recognize their mundane interests in the event of war or misfortune and the like. The result would be that they would be at a loss as to the correct course to take under the circumstances. Thus Scripture says: *And thou shalt grope at noonday, as the blind gropeth in darkness* [41] (Deut. 28:29). It says also: *He taketh the wise in their own craftiness; and the counsel of the wily is carried headlong. They meet with darkness in the daytime* (Job 5:13, 14). It states furthermore: *He taketh away the heart of the chiefs of the land, etc. They grope in the dark without light* (Job 12:24, 25).

Now the advocates of the doctrine of predestination thought that all the above referred to the spiritual status [of the people. In reality,] however, the meaning of *And it will return and be healed* (Isa. 6:10) is merely that they would return from waging war against their enemy and rest up therefrom, as Scripture says elsewhere, in speaking of war: *But he is not able to heal you, neither shall he cure you of your wound* (Hos. 5:13).

The third [class of Biblical passages] consists of [those which present God as] giving courage to men when they are struck by a devastating calamity or [when they receive a] report of such a disaster, in order that they may not die therefrom. Hearing of such Scriptural utterances, the advocates of predestination thought that they implied a hardening of the hearts in order to keep them from becoming subservient to God. [What] especially [misled them

40. This quotation follows the reading of Ibn Tibbon.
41. This quotation follows the reading of Ibn Tibbon.

was] the fact that Scripture itself ascribes this to hardening the heart, by reason of the fact that the soul has its seat in it. Instances hereof are such utterances of Scripture as: *And I will harden Pharaoh's heart* (Exod. 7: 3), and *And I will make strong* [42] *Pharaoh's* <161> *heart* (Exod. 14: 4), and *For I have made heavy his heart* (Exod. 10: 1). Similarly does Scripture say in regard to Sihon: *For the Lord thy God hardened his spirit* (Deut. 2: 30).

Now Pharaoh needed a bolstering of the spirit in order not to die from the plagues [43] [that befell the Egyptians], but remain alive until the rest of the punishment had been completely visited upon him. That was made clear to him by God when He said: *Surely now I had put forth My hand, and smitten thee, etc. But in very deed for this cause have I made thee to stand,* etc.[44] (Exod. 9: 15, 16).

As for Sihon, again, he needed such a bolstering in order not to die from the terror inspired by the report about the children of Israel, as Scripture says about others in his time: *Who, when they hear the report of thee, shall tremble, and be in anguish because of thee* (Deut. 2: 25). Similarly did the inhabitants of the land of Canaan require a bolstering in order not to perish from the fright inspired by the report of the Israelites, as Scripture says: *And as soon as we had heard it, our hearts did melt, etc.*[45] (Josh. 2: 11). That is why Scripture says later on: *For it was of the Lord to harden their hearts, to come against Israel in battle, that they might be utterly destroyed* (Josh. 11: 20).

The fourth [group of verses] consists of [those that speak of] the assignment [by God] of station or rank [to men.] Now certain people, seeing this recorded in the Bible, thought that that was [indicative of the] exercise of influence and the exertion of pressure [by God]. [In reality] this [act on the part of God is merely identical with that of] the expert in a given art [who] corroborates what is correct in it and rejects what is wrong. Thus we say that

42. "make strong"—the usual translation is "harden."
43. "plagues"—Ibn Tibbon and M.
44. This quotation follows the reading of Ibn Tibbon.
45. This quotation follows the reading of Ibn Tibbon.

the judge made out Reuben to be a truthful man and Simon to be a liar, or that he justified Levi and made out Zebulun to be unjust. Now we do not mean to say thereby that he induced any one of them or that he commanded them to do a certain thing, but merely that he made clear and exposed his character and put him in his place. The meaning is the same as that contained in the statement of the holy Torah: *And they shall make righteous the righteous and wicked the wicked* [46] (Deut. 25: 1).

Similarly is it said: "The judge made out such and such a writ to be genuine and such and such a writ to be forged." Now he did not actually himself cause it to be forged, but merely explained that it was of that character. It has furthermore been reported to me that the expression used in regard to two coins is that "the money-sorter made one good <162> and the other counterfeit." Now those who employ this expression do not mean thereby that he himself counterfeited it but merely that he reported that it was counterfeit.

When, then, the ideas behind this figure of speech are carefully examined and [47] definitely determined, it becomes clear that it is in this sense that one must understand what is spoken of by the Scriptures as an act of God. When, for example, Scripture states: *If it concerneth the scorners, He maketh them scornful,*[48] *but unto the humble He giveth grace* (Prov. 3: 34), it means that "He puts the latter in the ranks of the *humble*." Similarly it says: *And when the prophet is enticed and speaketh a word, I the Lord have enticed that prophet* (Ezek. 14: 9), meaning "I have made it clear that he is enticed." Likewise God's statement: *Who shall entice Ahab, that he may go and fall?* (I Kings 22: 20) means "Who shall make it plain that he is enticed?"

Thus, too, did the statement of the prophet Jeremiah: *Surely Thou hast greatly deceived this people and Jerusalem, saying: Ye shall have peace* (Jer. 4: 10), merely charge, by exposure, the speech of those who had prophesied about Jerusalem with being un-

46. "and they shall make . . . wicked"—the usual translation is: "by justifying the righteous, and condemning the wicked."

47. "and"—added by Ibn Tibbon and M.

48. "He maketh them scornful"—the usual translation is "He scorneth them."

authentic. So also is the question of the people: *Why dost Thou make us err from Thy ways?* (Isa. 63: 17) to be understood in the sense of "Do not make us err by condemning us as men that err, but forgive us and have mercy on us." He, however, who does not understand correctly this and similar utterances thinks that they are [indicative of divine] compulsion.

The fifth group is that which comes under the heading of forgiveness. It is noted that the servant of God says: "Incline me toward Thee" and "Do not turn me away from Thee" in such utterances as *Incline my heart unto Thy testimonies, and not to covetousness* (Ps. 119: 36), and *Incline not my heart to any evil thing* (Ps. 141: 4). Consequently the impression arises that by these two types of inclination he has reference to [divine] compulsion. In reality, however, it is merely God's forgiveness [that he has in mind]. He means to say: "By forgiving me Thou inclinest me toward Thee, so that I do not sin against Thee again. On the other hand, if Thou shouldst not forgive me, Thou wouldst hurl [49] my soul into despair. Forgiveness [50] would, therefore, bring it about that I incline toward serving Thee." It is in this vein, too, that he says elsewhere: *Then will I teach transgressors Thy ways; and sinners shall return unto Thee* (Ps. 51: 15).

The sixth [group of verses] is that which describes God's work in shaping man's basic nature. This is erroneously believed [by some] <163> to be tantamount to inspiring and influencing man's will. An instance of this type is such a statement of Scripture as *The preparations of the heart are man's, but the answer of the tongue is from the Lord* (Prov. 16: 1). Hereby, however, is meant only man's basic nature, as it [certainly] is in such statements as *The hearing ear, and the seeing eye, the Lord hath made even both of them* (Prov. 20: 12).

The seventh group consists of hyperboles [51] which create in the mind of the hearer the false impression of the production by God of some special faculty. An instance hereof is such a statement of

49. "hurl"—Ibn Tibbon and M.
50. "Forgiveness"—Ibn Tibbon.
51. "hyperboles"—Ibn Tibbon and M.

Scripture as *The king's heart is in the hand of the Lord as the watercourses; He turneth it withersoever He will* (Prov. 21:1). Herefrom it is falsely inferred that a special faculty is possessed by kings whereby God puts into their minds whatever He wishes. In reality, however, this statement is merely a hyperbole saying, in effect, that even so far as the king is concerned, the course taken by his heart in the matter of serving God is like that of bodies of water in God's own [52] hand. However the *king* wishes, he may turn and employ it.

The eighth group consists of verses speaking of the creation by God of certain means, coincidental with man's choice, to perform a certain act. These means are of three different types. The first is deliverance from enemies, which leaves the servant of God free to carry out a certain task. Hence it is said figuratively that He who delivered him from his enemies was the cause of the act in question. Thus Scripture says: *And the God of Israel stirred up the spirit of Pul king of Assyria* (I Chron. 5:26); also *The Lord stirred up the spirit of Cyrus king of Persia* (II Chron. 36:22); and *And the Lord stirred up against Jehoram* (II Chron. 21:16); and *For the Lord had made them joyful, and had turned the heart of the king of Assyria unto them* (Ezra 6:22); and also *But Amaziah would not hear; for it was of God* (II Chron. 25:20); and finally *So the king hearkened not unto the people; for it was a thing brought about by the Lord* (I Kings 12:15). All these passages deal with deliverance from the enemy or some other evil.

The second [type] is the clearing of the mind and the refinement of the thinking faculties through the adjustment of the temperament, leading to the understanding on the part of the servant of God of the religious and scientific subjects that he hears while he is in that condition. This gives the impression of being [an act of divine] compulsion. Illustrative hereof are such statements of Scripture as *Show me Thy ways, O Lord; teach me Thy paths* (Ps. 25:4); and <164> *Teach me, O Lord, Thy way, that I may walk in Thy truth* (Ps. 86:11); and *Turn away mine eyes from beholding vanity* (Ps. 119:37); and *And also in Ju-*

---

52. Cf. Gersonides' interpretation of this passage in his commentary, *ad loco.*

dah was the hand of God to give them one heart (II Chron. 30: 12).

The third [type] is [some] extraordinary miracle produced by the Creator [to serve] as a means for inspiring a multitude of people with faith. This influence wielded upon the public [53] may be erroneously construed by him who hears about it as [divine] compulsion. An instance [of the above] is [given in] the statement of Elijah: *Hear me, O Lord, hear me, that this people may know that Thou, Lord, art God, for Thou didst turn their heart backward* (*'ăhoranith*) (I Kings 18: 37). He meant to say that when this fire would descend and burn up the *offering*, the hearts that had been *backward* (*'ăhoranith*) would thereby be inclined toward God again. Nothing else, therefore, has to be supplied in this utterance but the letter *he*, which would make the word backward (*'ăhoranith*) an attributive adjective, modifying the noun *heart*, as though the reading had been *ha'ăhoranith*. Similarly, [speaking] about the era of Israel's salvation, about which it is said: *And I will put My spirit within you, and cause you to walk in My statutes* (Ezek. 36: 27), what Scripture has in mind thereby is nothing else than the manifestation of miracles and marvels.

And now that these eight principal classes of verses have been disposed of, all that remain to be considered are verses the meaning of which is misunderstood on account of an improper construction of their sequence. As an instance we might cite a Scriptural statement like *Against Thee, Thee only, have I sinned, and done that which is evil in Thy sight; that Thou mayest be justified when Thou speakest* (Ps. 51: 6). He who hears this utterance might think that what this penitent says is that the reason he sinned was in order that His master's verdict concerning him might be carried out. In reality, however, the clause *that Thou mayest be justified* is not related to *have I sinned*. It goes back rather to the penitent's previous remark: *And cleanse me from my sin* (Ps. 51: 4). He says, in effect: "Pardon my sin, so that there may be confirmed what Thou hast said and decreed that whoever returns penitently unto Thee would be forgiven by Thee."

53. "This influence wielded upon the public"—Ibn Tibbon.

This is the [regular] usage [in the style [54] of Scripture], as it is illustrated in such statements as *They cried, and the Lord heard, and delivered them out of all their troubles* (Ps. 34: 18). This last remark, too, does not revert to the verse immediately preceding: *The face of the Lord is against them that do evil* (Ps. 34: 17). It goes back rather to the one before that; namely, *The eyes of the Lord are toward the righteous* (Ps. 34: 16).

As a result of this elucidation <165> the uncertainties about the meaning of certain Scriptural utterances that lend color to the theory of compulsion [exercised by God on man's conduct] disappear, and the claim of our Creator on His servants, so far as their obedience or disobedience of Him is concerned, is upheld, whereas any claim they might have upon Him becomes null and void. This is borne out by Scripture's remark: *Shall mortal man be more just than God?* (Job 4: 17), and the testimony of the miracles and marvels, as well as of prophecy.

The fourth treatise is hereby completed.

54. "usage in the style"—Ibn Tibbon.

TREATISE V

CONCERNING MERITS AND DEMERITS [1]

CHAPTER I

OUR Master, exalted and magnified be He, has made it known to us that, when the instances of obedience on the part of His servants predominate, they are accounted [2] unto them as merits, whereas when those of disobedience are predominant, they are accounted as demerits. Furthermore, a record is kept by Him of all this in regard to all of His servants. This is borne out by the statement of Scripture: *Great in counsel, and mighty in work; whose eyes are open upon all the ways of the sons of men* (Jer. 32: 19). Scripture says also: *For His eyes are upon the ways of a man, etc.*[3] (Job 34: 21.)

Moreover, these activities of men leave their traces upon the latter's souls, rendering them pure or sullied. Thus Scripture says, apropos of [the effect of] sin: *Then he shall bear his iniquity* (Lev. 5: 1), *And he shall bear his sin* (Lev. 24: 15), *And they set their soul* [4] *on their iniquity* (Hos. 4: 8), and *Its iniquity shall rest on that soul* [5] (Num. 15: 31).

Now even though these facts be hidden from the views of men and not evident to them, they are perfectly clear to God, blessed and exalted be He, as Scripture says: *I the Lord search the heart, I try the reins* (Jer. 17: 10). God has furthermore produced, in support of these matters, miracles and marvels, wherefore we have accepted them as true.

1."Merits and Demerits"—Ibn Tibbon. Cf. Henry Malter, *Saadia Gaon, His Life and Works* (Philadelphia, 1921), p. 217.

2. "accounted"—literally "designated."

3. This quotation follows the reading of Ibn Tibbon.

4. "soul"—the usual translation is "heart."

5. "Its iniquity shall rest on that soul"—the usual translation is: "His iniquity shall be upon him."

This conclusion having been reached by us, I proceeded to inquire further into this matter in accordance with my previous practice, and I noted that there exist in the world many fine arts that are unknown to the majority of men. The result is that they mistakenly identify what is good with what is bad in them until recourse is had to an expert who is able to make the distinction. One of these fine arts is that of numismatics. Thou seest that the <166> layman who is not well versed in this art will mistakenly identify good money with bad until the expert separates them.

Another illustration is furnished by the art of healing. Thou wilt find laymen feeling the pulse of the sick, not knowing the predominant form of the dilation and contraction of the arteries of the particular body, whereas the expert practitioner does. A further example is presented by the science [6] of the physiognomists, who look at the lines of the faces and of the feet of men and classify them by means of criteria that are unknown to others who are non-professionals. The same applies to the art of jewelry, such as precious stones and pearls and other such things. Only the expert knows them well. Thus in general does every fine art have its flaws which escape the detection of laymen but are patent to the specialists.

When, then, I found this to be true in the case of the arts, as I have just described, I felt encouraged in adhering to my theory that even though the flaws of the souls, such as sins and iniquities, might not be obvious to human beings because they are incapable of perceiving them with their senses, they are nevertheless evident to their Maker, since it is He that created them and brought them into being.

The reason for this is that the soul is made of a pure spiritual substance, finer even than that of the stars and the heavenly spheres. It is impossible for us to see it with our senses. How, then, could we discern what might affect and render turbid its substance? Only its Creator, who is also the Creator of the heavenly spheres,[7] can discern these things. That is why Scripture uses the

6. "science"—Ibn Tibbon.
7. "spheres"—M.

stars and the heavens as analogues of the soul in this matter, saying as it does: *And the stars are not pure in His sight* (Job 25:5),
and *Yea, the heavens are not clean in His sight* (Job 15:15).

It states furthermore that the soul has a light like the light of a
candle by which all hidden things and dark recesses are sought out
and whatever is concealed is revealed. It says, namely: *A lamp
of the Lord is the soul of man,*[8] *searching all the inward parts*
(Prov. 20:27). It states also that the soul has a fire like that which
causes the gold <167> and the silver to melt in the crucible and
thus refines them. Thus it says: *The refining pot is for silver, and
the furnace for gold; but the Lord trieth the hearts* (Prov. 17:3).

So I said [to myself]: "Isn't it remarkable! A human being may
eat two kinds of food, permitted and forbidden, and find them both
nourishing. He may indulge in two types of cohabitation, one of
which is permissible whilst the other is prohibited, and find that
both give him pleasure, on which account he thinks that they are
one and the same thing. Yet the [divine] numismatist distinguishes
between the varying effects that the two different classes have upon
the spirit of man, as we have explained above, and as Scripture
says: *Every way of a man is right in his own eyes!*" (Prov. 21:2.)

Thereupon I realized that when the merits predominate in the
soul, the latter is thereby purified and rendered luminous. This is
borne out by such statements of Scripture as *And his life beholdeth
the light* (Job 33:28), and *That he may be enlightened with the
light of the living* (Job 33:30). On the other hand, when the
demerits are in the majority in it, the soul becomes turbid and
darkened, as Scripture does indeed say of those who are in such a
state: *They shall never see the light* (Ps. 49:20).

Furthermore, we have been informed by God that He keeps a
record of these merits and demerits for all of His servants. They
are noted by Him just like the things written down by us. Thus
Scripture remarks apropos of the virtuous: *And a book of remembrance was written before Him, for them that feared the Lord,
and that thought upon His name* (Mal. 3:16). In regard to the

8. "A lamp . . . man"—the usual translation is: "The spirit of man is the lamp
of the Lord."

wicked, again, it says: *Behold, it is written before Me; I will not keep silence, except I have requited* (Isa. 65:6).

Now when I regarded this metaphor,[9] employed with respect to the All-Wise, I found it to be extremely well chosen and appropriate. For if we, who are but an aggregation of God's creatures, are capable, thanks to the faculty with which we have been endowed by the All-Wise, of producing the sounds of speech and of creating for each sound a special written character so that we might thereby keep a record of our thoughts as well as of those events of which we need to take cognizance, all the more so must divine Wisdom be in possession of the means of recording all our <168> doings without a book or archives. The only reason for using the figure of a book, in referring to God's record, is that that is how we are accustomed to keep accounts, the purpose being to make the idea more comprehensible to us,[10] as we have explained previously.

God has also informed us that during our entire sojourn in this workaday world He keeps a record of everyone's deeds. The recompense for them, however, has been reserved by Him for the second world, which is the world of compensation. This latter world will be brought into being by Him when the entire number of rational beings, the creation of which has been decided upon by His [divine] Wisdom, will have been fulfilled. There will He requite all of them according to their deeds. This is borne out by the statement of the saint: *I said in my heart: "The righteous and the wicked God will judge"* (Eccles. 3:17). He said also: *For God shall bring every work into judgment concerning every hidden thing, whether it be good or whether it be evil* (Eccles. 12:14). About this time of recompense I shall discourse in the ninth treatise in the appropriate manner.

Notwithstanding this, however, God does not leave His servants entirely without reward in this world for virtuous conduct and without punishment for iniquities. For such requitals serve as a sign and an example of the total compensation which is reserved

9. "metaphor"—Ibn Tibbon and M.
10. "how we are . . . comprehensible to us"—Ibn Tibbon and M.

for the time when a summary account is made of the deeds of God's servants. That is why we note that He says of such *blessings* as those listed by Him in the section of the Torah [beginning with the words] *If in My statutes* (Lev. 26: 3): *Work in my behalf a sign for good* (Ps. 86: 17), and again of the *curses* listed in the section [beginning with the statement] *But it shall come to pass, if thou wilt not hearken* (Deut. 28:15): *And they shall be upon thee for a sign and for a wonder, and upon thy seed for ever* (Deut. 28: 46).

It is, therefore, only a specimen and a sample of these rewards and punishments that is furnished in this world, while the totality of their merits is stored for the virtuous like a treasure. Thus Scripture says: *Oh how abundant is Thy goodness, which Thou hast laid up for them that fear Thee* (Ps. 31: 20). Similarly the totality of their demerits is laid up and sealed for the wicked, as Scripture says elsewhere: *Is not this laid up in store with Me, sealed up in My treasuries?* (Deut. 32: 34).

CHAPTER II

After these preliminary observations I consider it proper to enumerate the various gradations <169> into which God's servants may be divided according to the variety of their merits and demerits, as these are exposed in Scripture and tradition. Each of them will thus be assigned by me to the place in which he belongs, for the sake of the guidance of the masses of God's servants. I say, then, that God's servants may be classified with respect to their merits and demerits into ten categories; namely, pious and impious, obedient and disobedient, perfect and imperfect, sinful and corrupt, renegade and penitent. There are also those whose merits and demerits are evenly balanced. They constitute a class apart and we shall discourse about them separately.

It behooves me now to dwell on each of these categories and what it embraces. I say then that he is to be called "pious" in whose conduct the good deeds predominate, and that he is to be designated as "impious" in whose conduct evil deeds are predominant. The situation in this case is analogous to that which obtains in the world of nature. Scientists would, namely, refer to a thing as "hot" when the heat in it exceeds the cold, and call it "cold" when the cold in it predominates over the heat. Furthermore they would say that a body is healthy when the health in it predominates and sick if sickness is predominant in it. In similar fashion did prophetic nomenclature designate a servant of God as "virtuous" when most of his conduct was of a virtuous nature. That is why Jehoshaphat and Hezekiah were referred to by it as virtuous men even though some of their acts were tainted by sin. Thus it was said [11] to Jehoshaphat: *Shouldest thou help the wicked, and love them that hate the Lord? for this thing wrath is upon thee from before the Lord* (II Chron. 19:2). Similarly was it said [12] about Hezekiah: *But Hezekiah rendered not according to the benefit done unto him; for his heart was lifted up; therefore there was wrath upon him* (II Chron. 32:25). On the other hand, Jehu was designated by it as impious although he had abolished the worship of *Baal*,[13] and similarly was Zedekiah called impious notwithstanding the fact that he had rescued Jeremiah.[14]

It is furthermore a [general] rule laid down in this matter by the All-Wise to requite His servants in this world for the minority of their deeds and leave the majority for the next world,[15] since it would not be seemly <170> to transfer them in that other world from one status to another. For each group of those who are to be recompensed remains eternally in its particular position, as Scripture says: *Some to everlasting life, and some to reproaches and everlasting abhorrence* (Dan. 12:2). He therefore instituted recompense in this world only for the lesser [portion of man's conduct], as He also explained that the totality of his merits is reserved for a far-off time, whereas the small proportion of his

---

11. "it was said"—Ibn Tibbon and M.
12. "was it said"—Ibn Tibbon and M.
13. Cf. II Kings 10:28.
14. Cf. Jer. 38:10 ff.
15. For the Talmudic basis of this view, cf. the references in Guttmann, p. 180, n. 1.

demerits [16] is dealt with in this world. That is the implication of His statement: *Know therefore that the Lord thy God, He is God; the faithful God, who keepeth covenant and mercy with them that love Him . . . and repayeth them that hate Him to their face, to destroy them* (Deut. 7:9, 10).

A specific illustration of this truth is presented by the fact that the two princes of Israel, Moses and Aaron, were requited in this world for a slight failing of which they were guilty, as is stated by Scripture: *Because ye believed not in Me, to sanctify Me [in the eyes of the children of Israel], therefore shall ye not bring this assembly . . .* (Num. 20:12). Another example is furnished by the compensation of Abijah the son of Jeroboam in this world for the one good deed that he had performed, as Scripture says: *For he only of Jeroboam shall come to the grave; because in him there is found some good thing* (I Kings 14:13).

On the basis of this principle it often happens that a generally virtuous person may be afflicted with many failings, on account of which he deserves to be in torment for the greater part of his life. On the other hand, a generally impious individual may have to his credit many good deeds, for the sake of which he deserves to enjoy well-being for the greater part of his earthly existence. That is the tenor of the statement of tradition to the effect that *anyone whose sins exceed his merits is rewarded for the latter so that he resembles one that has fulfilled the entire Torah, whereas he whose merits exceed his sins is punished for the latter so that he resembles one that has burned up the entire Torah* (Kidd. 39b).

The aforegoing statement about the performer of good and <171> evil deeds applies, of course, only to him who at the moment when he does the good deed does not regret the evil and who at the moment when he does the evil is not sorry over the good. He, however, who, after having performed many good deeds, regrets having performed them, forfeits by regretting them the reward for them all. Of such a one does Scripture say: *But when the righteous turneth away from his righteousness, and committeth iniquity . . . none of his righteous deeds that he hath*

16. "demerits"—Cf. Landauer's correction of the text.

done shall be remembered (Ezek. 18:24). Similarly he that has committed many wrongs and regrets having committed them and carries out the rules of repentance, has [thereby] removed them from himself. Of him does Scripture say: *Again, when the wicked man turneth away from his wickedness that he hath committed . . .* (Ezek. 18:27). Furthermore it says: *None of his transgressions that he hath committed shall be remembered against him* (Ezek. 18:22), which tradition construes as referring *to one that regrets his past doings* (Kidd. 40b).

On the basis of this principle it is quite possible for a virtuous servant of God whose good deeds were destined for recompense in the next world but who regrets them to forfeit the right of their reservation for the next world. He would, on the contrary, be rewarded for a portion of them in this world, with the result that men, noting that the beginning of his prosperity coincided with that of his unbelief, would be emboldened [17] thereby to follow his example. In reality, however, this well-being that he enjoys is not due to his assumption of unbelief, but is merely the reward of his good deeds that has been reserved for later but is now paid out to him immediately. On the other hand, it is possible for an impious [18] servant of God, whose evil deeds were destined for punishment in the next world but who regrets them and repents, to be absolved from being punished for them in the next world but rather to receive in this world such terrestrial retribution as is unavoidable, as I shall explain later. As a consequence, men, noting how sorrows and misfortunes befell such a one at the moment in which he began to turn back from his sinful career, might be astonished, not knowing that what had come upon him was not due to the new course which he had begun to follow but was rather a holdover from that which he had abandoned.

Once, then, the existence of <172> these various classifications is understood by men, doubts will disappear from their minds and their hearts will be confirmed in the service of God, as Scripture says: *Yet the righteous holdeth on his way, and he that*

17. "emboldened"—Ibn Tibbon.
18. "impious"—this is how the text should read.

hath clean hands waxeth stronger and stronger (Job 17:9).

Now it should not be alleged that one evil deed is capable of offsetting many good deeds. Such an effect could be produced by the former only if it were coupled with regret of the latter and because of this regret, not on account of the evil deed itself. Nor must it be believed that one good deed is capable of making up for many evil deeds. Such an effect could be produced by the former only in conjunction with repentance and on account of this repentance, not on account of the good deed itself.

I have been compelled by necessity to make this explanation, for I have found that certain people, by the use of sophistry, assert that if it is within the competence of one act of unbelief to annul much belief, it cannot be within the power of one act of unbelief to cancel much belief. The consequence of this argument is that the believers are confused by it.

CHAPTER III

Next let me say that I find that the sufferings to which the virtuous are subjected in this world fall into two categories. One of these constitutes the penalties for slight failings, as I have explained previously. The second consists of incipient trials with which God tests them, when He knows that they are able to endure them,[19] only in order to compensate them for these trials later on with good. Thus Scripture says: *The Lord trieth the righteous; but the wicked and him that loveth violence His soul hateth* (Ps. 11:5).

It is not, however, His wont to act in this fashion with him who cannot bear these trials, since there would be no benefit therein. For the whole purpose of the suffering of the upright is that the rest of God's creatures might know that He has not chosen the former for nothing. This is known to thee from the case of Job and his suffering. Hence, if the pain to which the servant of God is subjected constitutes punishment and he asks his Master to en-

19. Cf. the simile of the potter and the pot in Genesis Rabba chap. lxxxii and Tanḥuma on Gen. 22:1.

lighten him thereon, it is a rule with Him to do so. Thus Scripture says: <173> *And it shall come to pass, when ye shall say: "Wherefore hath the Lord our God done all these things unto us?" then shalt thou say unto them* . . . (Jer. 5:19).

This also has the salutary effect of inducing him to abandon his sinful conduct. On the other hand, if the pain to which the servant of God is subjected serves as a form of trial and he asks his Master to inform him why He has brought this trial upon him, it is a rule with Him not to inform him. Thus when *our teacher Moses* said: *Wherefore hast Thou dealt ill with Thy servant? and wherefore* . . . (Num. 11:11), no clarification was given to him. Likewise when Job asked: *Make me know wherefore Thou contendest with me* (Job 10:2), no explanation was offered to him. This, too, has the salutary purpose of making certain that the patience of the virtuous person be not lightly esteemed by men, who [20] might [otherwise] say that the only reason for his patience is that he knows that he will be amply rewarded for it.

I will go still further and say that it is even possible for a completely guiltless individual to be subjected to trials in order to be compensated for them afterwards, for I find that children are made to suffer pain, and I have no doubt about their eventual compensation for these sufferings. The sorrows brought upon them by the All-Wise might, therefore, be compared to the discipline that their father might administer to them in the form of flogging or detention in order to keep them from harm, or to the repulsive, bitter medicines that he might make them drink in order to put an end to their illness. Thus it is stated in the Torah: *And thou shalt consider in thy heart, that, as a man chasteneth his son, so the Lord thy God chasteneth thee* (Deut. 8:5). Scripture also says in regard to such matters: *For whom the Lord loveth He correcteth, even as a father the son in whom he delighteth* (Prov. 3:12).

Should someone object now and say, "But why could not God be gracious to them right from the start in the same measure that He compensates them for their pains afterward, without first sub-

20. "who," i.e., these observers—M.

jecting them to suffering?" we would offer in reply the first answer we gave in regard to God's original purpose in creating the
next world,[21] and say that God was eager to grant us the greatest
possible good, for the favors conferred upon man by way of compensation are more highly prized than those conferred upon him
purely as an act of divine grace.

Next let me say that, so far as the well-being of the godless in
this world and the respite granted to them are concerned, that may
be accounted for in six different ways. One reason may be that
God knows that the individual in question will <174> eventually repent. He therefore gives him enough time to carry out
his repentance. Thus, for example, we find that God granted
Manasseh twenty-two years of grace [22] in order that he might repent during the remaining thirty-three years of his reign, notwithstanding the fact that his repentance was not carried out by
him.

Another reason why the godless is permitted to linger on earth
may be on account of a pious offspring that is expected to issue
from him. Thus God allowed Ahaz to live, with the result that
Hezekiah sprang from him, and He permitted Amon to live with
the result that Josiah sprang from him.[23]

A third reason for allowing the godless to linger on earth may
be to recompense him for the few good deeds that he has performed in the sight of God, as we have explained previously.

Again, respite may be granted to a certain unbeliever in order
that he may serve as an instrument for punishing malefactors that
are even worse than he. Thus Scripture says in regard to Assyria:
*I do send him against an ungodly nation, and against the people
of My wrath do I give him a charge, to take the spoil, and to take
the prey . . .* (Isa. 10:6).

Furthermore God may allow an unbeliever to linger on earth
on account of the request of a certain virtuous person to whose
advantage it would redound. Thus the angel of God said to Lot:

21. Cf. beginning of the third treatise, p. 137. See also p. 323, the beginning of
the ninth treatise.
22. Cf. II Chron. 33: 1 ff.
23. Cf. Cant. Rab., beginning.

See, I have accepted thee concerning this thing also [24] (Gen. 19: 21).

Finally the godless may be permitted to linger on earth merely in order that his punishment be made more severe. Thus God saved Pharaoh from the ten *plagues* only to drown him in the sea, as Scripture says: *But He overthrew Pharaoh and his host in the Red Sea* (Ps. 136: 15). This was also the tenor of the question posed by Jeremiah to his Master when he asked to be informed by Him on what grounds He tolerated sinners. By no means did he intend to express his disapproval of divine justice when he said: *Wherefore doth the way of the wicked prosper? Wherefore are all they secure that deal very treacherously?* (Jer. 12: 1). God informed him thereupon that the reason for this was the one last mentioned; namely, that He might punish them more severely. This is borne out by the remark of the prophet in the section immediately following: *How long shall the land mourn, and the herbs of the whole field wither? For the wickedness of them that dwell therein* (Jer. 12: 4).

And now that I have presented all the necessary explanations apropos of the subject of the pious and the impious, let me say, by way of postscript, that, when we note Scripture making such statements as *But one sinner destroyeth much good* (Eccles. 9: 18), comparing the latter to a fly that has fallen into perfumed oil, as it says immediately thereafter: <175> *Dead flies making the ointment of the perfumer fetid and putrid, etc.* (Eccles. 10: 1), [we must realize that] it is solely a question of nomenclature that is involved. Thus if a servant of God were to have to his credit two hundred and one acts, one hundred of which are good and another hundred evil, which would render his record evenly balanced, then, if the additional single act be good, he would on its account be called "virtuous," whereas if it be evil, he would be called "impious." [25]

24. The reference is to the sparing of the city of Zoar, which was requested in the preceding verse.
25. Cf. Bĕr. 61a and Kidd. 40b.

CHAPTER IV

As for the "obedient" individual, it is he who will not transgress as long as he lives over a particular precept that he has prescribed for himself, so that, whether he demeans himself affirmatively or negatively toward others, he never fails in its execution. Thus, for example, a person may take it upon himself not to miss his prayers or not to be remiss in honoring his parents or not to acquire wealth by any dishonest means whatever or not to lie and the like. Whoever conducts himself in this manner acts in accordance with the maxim cited in rabbinic tradition to the effect that *Whoever performs but a single commandment, good is done unto him and his days are increased and he inherits the earth* (Mišnah Ḳidd. 1:10), which was further interpreted by our sages *such as one who singles out for performance a commandment like that of honoring father and mother* (Pal. Talm. Ḳidd. 61d). He, however, who does not have to his credit at least one commandment that he has never at any time neglected, cannot be called "obedient."

The "disobedient," again, is he who has made it a rule for himself always to defy a certain precept. In the rabbinic tradition such a one is called *apostate*. For the sake of illustration let me conceive the case of a human being who thinks that a certain precept exceeds his means so that he abstains therefrom, or that there exists a certain precept which he is incapable of performing, wherefore he neglects to observe it. Thus he may find it difficult to observe the precept of usury or the dietary laws, wherefore he conducts himself vis-a-vis either of them in the way in which it seems right to him. This is the basis of the proverb: "Every man has his own law, <176> in accordance with the difference of opinions existing among men."

As for the "perfect" man, it is he who has succeeded in fulfilling all commandments, positive as well as negative, so that he is not remiss in any of them. Such a one is called *completely righteous*. Now even though in the opinion of men the probability of the existence of such a person who is blameless in every respect appears to be extremely remote, I yet consider it possible. For were it not so, the All-Wise would not have prescribed such a goal.

Now if someone were to argue: "Since we find in the very source of the Law the injunction to offer *in addition one he-goat for a sin-offering to make atonement for you* (Num. 28:22), we know that sin is inescapable," our answer thereto is that this law is posited on the contingency that if a sin be [committed], atonement would be achieved for it by means of the sacrifice. Should there be none, on the other hand, we would receive reward for the offering.

Again if one were to ask, "But how, if this be so, could Ecclesiastes declare: *For there is not a righteous man upon earth, that doeth good, and sinneth not?*" (7:20) we would reply that this assertion had reference only to the capacity possessed by those in question. What was meant by it was that there is not a single pious person possessing the faculty of doing what is good who does not also have the power to do evil. However, he prefers the good to the evil.

The "imperfect" individual, again, is he who is negligent in regard to the performance of the practical precepts. He is designated *a transgressor of a positive commandment*. Therefore he who is remiss in the matter of *fringes,* and *phylacteries,* and the *booth* [of the feast of tabernacles], and [the use of] the *palm-branch* and the *ram's horn* and the like belongs to this category of sinfulness.

As for the [ordinary] "sinner," it is he who transgresses negative precepts, such as are, however, not of a serious nature, as indicated by the fact that they are not severely punished in this world. Such a one is referred to as a *transgressor of a negative commandment*. By this term are characterized those who are lax in regard to the eating of *carrion and* [*the flesh of*] *organically defective beasts*, and in regard to the wearing of *mixed fibers,* and soothsaying and augury and the like. All these belong to this category of sinfulness.

As for the [morally] "corrupt" individual, it is he that commits serious transgressions that are punishable by *extirpation at the hand of God or death at the hand of God or one of the four types of death penalty executed by the court.* <177> That is how we recognize their seriousness. Included in this class of trespasses are such sins as *incest,* and the desecration of the Sabbath, and the breaking of the fast of the day of *atonement,* and the use on *Passover* of *what is leavened.* Whoever perpetrates any violation of this order belongs to this category of sinfulness.

The "renegade," again, is he who abandons the basic principle of the faith,[26] that is, the belief in the one, all-encompassing God, blessed and exalted be He. There are three different forms [27] that this abandonment of God may take. It may be either that of the worship of someone else than God, such as some pictured likeness or some human being or the sun or the moon. This is implied in the injunction: *Thou shalt have no other gods before Me* (Exod. 20:3). Or the renegade may worship neither someone else than God nor God Himself. In other words, he worships no being at all, real or unreal. It is this category that is referred to in the passage of Scripture that says: *Yet they said unto God: "Depart from us; for we desire not the knowledge of Thy ways"* (Job 21:14).

Or else he may be in doubt about his religious creed while bearing the name of an adherent of the faith. He may even participate in prayer and supplication although in his heart of hearts there is no firm conviction or certainty. Such a one is really mendacious and deceitful in his utterance as well as in his professed belief. He belongs to that group of men of whom Scripture says: *But they beguiled Him with their mouth, and lied unto Him with their tongue. For their heart was not steadfast with Him, neither were they faithful in His covenant* (Ps. 78:36, 37). Such a one is called *a person through whom the name of heaven is desecrated,*[27a] and he belongs to this category of sinfulness.

26. Cf. B.B. 16b and Sanh. 38b.
27. "forms"—M.
27a. Cf. Tosephta Yoma 5:8.

Now all the aforementioned are, if they repent, forgiven in both worlds. The only exception is the case of those [28] of whom God has written that *He will not hold guiltless* (Exod. 20:7), for these cannot possibly escape being overtaken by mundane misfortune, as I shall explain.

CHAPTER V

The tenth [class], finally, is that of the "penitent" who carries out the terms of repentance. Now these terms are four in number, to wit: (a) the renunciation of sin, (b) remorse, (c) the quest of forgiveness, and (d) the assumption of the obligation not to relapse into sin. All four of these conditions are mentioned in one place in the *Bible;* namely, in the statement: *Return, O Israel, unto the Lord thy God; for thou hast stumbled in thine iniquity. Take with you words, and return unto the Lord; say unto him: "Forgive all iniquity, and accept that which is good; so will we render for bullocks the offering of our lips. Asshur shall not save us; we will not ride upon horses; neither will we call any more the work of our hands our gods"* [29] (Hos. 14:2–5).

The exhortation *return* signifies [of course]: "Turn back from the course that thou art at present pursuing," which is <178> the category of the renunciation of sin. The statement again of *For thou hast stumbled in thine iniquity* implies remorse. It says, in effect: "These sins constituted stumbling-blocks and evil." Furthermore the exhortation: *Take with you words* implies the quest of forgiveness.

Now there occurs in the aforementioned passage a strange expression; namely, *Forgive all [kol] iniquity, and accept that which is good,* the meaning of which is, "In return for Thy pardoning us we thank Thee and say: *Good and upright is the Lord; therefore doth He instruct sinners in the way*" (Ps. 25:8). A similar use of the expression *kol* (*all*) occurs in the verse: *They shall*

---

28. "those," i.e. individuals, by substitution of the personal for the impersonal indefinite pronoun used in the text.

29. This quotation follows the reading of Ibn Tibbon.

all be ashamed of a people that cannot profit them (Isa. 30:5).
Now ultimately this usage of the word *kol* is derived from that of
kol kobhel (Dan. 2:8), which has in the Aramaic language the
meaning of "over against." A similar [syntactical] combination of
this word in Hebrew is also found in the statement of Scripture: *In
all points as he came (kol 'ummath šebba), so shall he go* (Eccles.
5:15).

The passage in question includes, furthermore, the statement:
So will we render for bullocks (parim) the offering of our lips
(Hos. 14:3), which may be construed either as a metaphor, that
is as though the wording had been *So will we render like bullocks
(kĕpharim) the offering of our lips,* or as an ellipsis for *So will we
render the bullocks which were offered ('ăšer paṣu) by our lips.*

Again the prophet's declaration: *Asshur shall not save us; we
will not ride upon horses; neither will we call any more the work
of our hands our gods* [30] (Hos. 14:4) constitutes a resolve not to
relapse into sin. Now the sole reason for the enumeration of these
three items, namely, *Asshur, horses,* and *idolatry,* was that they
were the most apparent of the various types of sin that the people
had committed, as is made clear in the earlier part of the book by
the statement: *For they are gone up to Assyria, like a wild ass
alone by himself* (Hos. 8:9), as well as the further remark: *For
Ephraim hath multiplied altars to sin* (Hos. 8:11). Similarly if
their most manifest sin had consisted of *killing, stealing,* and *committing adultery* (Hos. 4:2), the prophet would have expressed
the resolve to abandon it by saying: *Innocent blood we shall not
spill, nor shall we commit adultery nor steal anything.* When, then,
these four conditions have been fulfilled,[31] the terms of repentance
have been met.

Now I have no fears, so far as the majority of our people are
concerned, in regard to their being remiss in their fulfillment of
any of the conditions of repentance except this fourth category—
I mean that of lapsing back into sin. For I believe that at the
time when they fast and pray, they sincerely mean to abandon

---

30. This quotation follows the reading of Ibn Tibbon.
31. "fulfilled"—Ibn Tibbon.

their sinful way and experience remorse and seek God's pardon. It seems to me, however, that they are [really] resolved to lapse back into sin.

So I ask myself: "What device is there for eradicating <179> from men's hearts the thought of lapsing back into sin?" My answer is: "Thinking up reasons for holding this world in contempt." [32] Let a person remind himself of his condition of impotence, misery, exertion, and disillusionment, of his eventual death and the decomposition of the parts of his body, of the vermin and the putrefaction that are destined for him, of the accounting he will have to give for his conduct and the torments to which he will be subjected and whatever appertains to any of these matters. The result of such reflection would be contempt for this world, and once all mundane things are held in contempt by him, his sins would be included in the totality of things to be abstained from and his resolve to abandon them would be intensified.

I say, furthermore, that it was precisely for the above-mentioned considerations that I find that the sages of Israel introduced the custom of reciting on the Day of Atonement such liturgical selections as "Thou discernest the thoughts of the heart," "Oh God, if Thou comest with rebukes," "Lord of all that is done," and the like.[33]

To the four conditions of repentance listed previously should be added the following further aids; namely, more extensive prayer, increased charity, and the endeavor to restore [other] men to the path of virtue. In regard to prayer and the dispensing of charity, Scripture says: *By mercy and truth iniquity is expiated, and by the fear of the Lord men depart from evil* [34] (Prov. 16:6). Apropos of the endeavor to make men return to the path of virtue again, it says: *Then will I teach transgressors Thy ways, etc.* [35] (Ps. 51:15).

32. "for holding . . . contempt"—Ibn Tibbon.
33. These selections are not quoted in the *Siddur of Saadia*. Cf. the edition of Davidson, Assaf and Joel (Jerusalem, 1941). Cf. Guttmann, p. 187, n. 1, for them.
34. This quotation follows the reading of Ibn Tibbon.
35. This quotation follows the reading of Ibn Tibbon.

Let me explain also that if the resolve on the part of a servant of God not to lapse into sin again is sincere, his repentance is accepted, so that if, as a result of temptation, he falls once more,[36] his repentance is not thereby forfeited. What happens is rather that the iniquities he committed before his repentance are canceled, only those committed by him thereafter being charged against him. The same would apply even if this were to occur several times; namely, that he repent and lapse back into sin. Only the wrongs perpetrated by him after his repentance would count against him, that is, provided he has been sincere each time in his resolve not to relapse.

As for the statement thou findest made by Scripture to the effect of: *For three transgressions of Israel, yea, for four, I will not reverse it* (Amos 2:6), that has nothing to do with the acceptance of repentance. It refers rather to the question of whether punishment can be warded off after the dispatch of a summons. God might, for example, send a warning to a people, saying: "Repent, or I shall exact retribution from you by means of the sword and bring famine upon you as a punishment." If, now, they repent after the first or the second or the third message of this kind, the threatened punishment is canceled. If they do not, however, it becomes irrevocable. And even <180> though they repent at the fourth [warning], their repentance no longer avails to divert from them the punishment in question in this world. It does, however, avail to save them from the torment of the next world.

CHAPTER VI

Inasmuch as this thesis has now been fully discussed by me, let me append thereto an enumeration of other considerations on account of which prayer may not be accepted. I say, then, that there are seven of these. One reason might be that the prayer was offered after the decree was issued against the servant of God with reference to a certain matter. Thus thou knowest that in reply to

36. "his repentance is accepted . . . reverts"—added by Ibn Tibbon.

the prayer uttered by Moses, [namely] *And I besought the Lord* (Deut. 3:23), God answered: *Let it suffice thee; speak no more unto Me of this matter* (Deut. 3:26).

The second might be that sincere intention was absent from the prayer. An illustration hereof is presented by the statement of Scripture: *But they beguiled Him with their mouth, and lied unto Him with their tongue* (Ps. 78:36). A third might be that the individual who utters the prayer does not heed the words of the Torah, as Scripture says: *He that turneth away his ear from hearing the law, even his prayer is an abomination* (Prov. 28:9). A fourth reason may be inattention on the part of him who prays to the requests of the needy, as Scripture says: *Whoso stoppeth his ears at the cry of the poor, he also shall cry himself, but shall not be answered* (Prov. 21:13). The fifth is allowing oneself the use of forbidden wealth, as is stated in Scripture: *Who also eat the flesh of My people, and flay their skin from off them . . . .*[37] *Then shall they cry unto the Lord, but He will not answer them* (Mic. 3:3, 4). The sixth is praying in a state of impurity, as Scripture says: *Yea, when ye make many prayers, I will not hear; your hands are full of blood* (Isa. 1:15). The seventh is praying without having repented, notwithstanding the multitude of one's sins. Thus Scripture says: *And it came to pass that, as He called, and they would not hear; so they shall call, and I will not hear* (Zech. 7:13).[38]

At this point I must explain that absolution by means of repentance is possible for all sins with the exception of three. One of these is leading people astray by establishing an evil practice or issuing a wrong decision, since the damage done cannot be repaired. Of one who commits such a sin Scripture says: *Whoso causeth the upright to go astray in an evil way, he shall fall himself into his own pit* (Prov. 28:10). The second is spreading <181> evil reports about a believer, which it is impossible to recall. Of one who perpetrates such a crime Scripture says: *Lest he that heareth it revile thee, and thine infamy turn not away*

37. This quotation follows the reading of Ibn Tibbon.
38. Cf. the reference in Malter, p. 219, n. 491.

(Prov. 25: 10). The third is having in one's possession something wrongfully acquired which one does not return to its rightful owner, as Scripture says: *Then it shall be, if he hath sinned, and is guilty, that he shall restore that which he took by robbery* (Lev. 5:23). Scripture says also: *If the wicked restore the pledge, give back that which he had taken by robbery, walk in the statutes of life* [39] *. . . he shall not die* (Ezek. 33:15). Should he who was robbed die, however, then the robber must return the stolen goods to his heirs, as Scripture says: *Unto him to whom it appertaineth shall he give it* (Lev. 5:24). In the event, again, that he does not know who the owner is, let him declare the property ownerless, so that it will thereby become permissible to everybody.

Let me also fulfill the promise I have made to explain the nature of those sins for which punishment in this world is inevitable, notwithstanding the repentance for them by the servant of God. I say, then, that they are four in number. The first of these is perjury, of which Scripture says: *For the Lord will not hold him guiltless that taketh His name in vain* (Exod. 20:7). The second is the shedding of innocent blood, about which Scripture says: *And as for holding innocent their blood, I shall not hold it innocent* [40] (Joel 4:21). The third is adultery with a married woman, of which Scripture says: *So he that goeth in to his neighbor's wife; whosoever toucheth her shall not go unpunished* (Prov. 6:29). The fourth, finally, is bearing false testimony, of which Scripture says: *A false witness shall not be unpunished* [41] (Prov. 19:5). To these should be added that transgression for which punishment has already been decreed, as happened in the instance in which God said to Moses: *Let it suffice thee; speak no more unto Me* (Deut. 3:26) according to the explanation we have given thereof above. [42]

Now repentance is acceptable in the case of these five categories

39. This quotation follows the reading of Ibn Tibbon.

40. "And as for . . . innocent"—the usual translation is: "And I will hold as innocent their blood that I have not held as innocent."

41. Cf. Tosephta Pe'ah 1:2 and Palestinian Talmud Pe'ah 15d for the source of the entire remark.

42. Cf. pp. 223 ff,

of sin. However, on account of the rule of *He shall not leave un-punished,* there is no means of preventing misfortune from be-falling the servant of God in this world.

As for him who has wronged his fellow in respects other than his property, such as, let us say, by insulting or striking him, his pardon depends on the injured one. If the latter forgives him, the punishment of the offender is canceled, as Scripture says: *So shall ye say unto Joseph: "Forgive, I pray thee now, the transgression of thy brethren, etc."* [43] (Gen. 50:17). He must, however, ask him three times, as it is said: *I pray thee ('ana), forgive, now* [44] *(na) . . . And now, we pray thee (na), forgive (ibid.).* In the event, however, that he that was insulted [45] or struck has died, the offender must <182> apply for forgiveness in a corresponding manner. He must, namely, say three times in the presence of ten persons: "I have sinned against so and so." [46] For if he had made such a request of the injured party whilst the latter was still alive, he would have obtained his pardon even though the offended had not acceded to his request.

I must furthermore make it clear that there are, on the other hand, certain good deeds which are perforce requited in this world, even though he that performs them is an unbeliever. These, I say, are three in number. The first of them is a loving demeanor toward parents, as Scripture says: *Honor thy father and thy mother, that thy days may be long* [47] (Exod. 20:12). A second is pity on animals, as Scripture says: *Thou shalt in any wise let the dam go, but the young thou mayest take unto thyself; that it may be well with thee, and that thou mayest prolong thy days* [48] (Deut. 22:7). The third, again, is dealing honestly,[49] as Scripture says: *A perfect and just weight shalt thou have; a perfect and just measure shalt thou have; [that thy days may be long]* (Deut.

43. This quotation follows the reading of Ibn Tibbon.
44. "I pray thee, forgive, now"—the usual translation is: "Forgive, I pray thee now."
45. "insulted"—Ibn Tibbon.
46. Cf. Yoma 87a.
47. This quotation follows the reading of Ibn Tibbon.
48. This quotation follows the reading of Ibn Tibbon.
49. "dealing honestly"—Ibn Tibbon.

25: 15). To these is to be added the case where the promise of well-being in this world has already been definitely decreed. Thus, for example, Jehu was categorically told by God: *Thy sons to the fourth generation shall sit upon the throne of Israel* (II Kings 15: 12)—even though he and his children sinned against Him— because the promise made to them had to be fulfilled.[50]

Now it must not be thought that the statement of Scripture in regard to certain sins: *It will then be sin in thee* [51] constitutes proof positive that punishment of these sins in this world is unavoidable. For this statement is made only with reference to three matters. [It is made apropos of the] delay in the fulfillment of vows,[52] and since these are dedicated to God, it is likely that He might pardon the delay. [It is] furthermore [made] with reference to refraining from lending [to the poor],[53] which is also forgiven as soon as repentance has taken place. Finally, it is applied to deferment in [paying] the hired man his wages,[54] which falls under the heading of robbery.[55]

Let me also note that there are distinguishable five different degrees of repentance, each of which is superior to the next in the order of their enumeration. The first consists of a person's repenting at the epoch and in the locality in which he has committed his sin, and whilst the details of his transgressions are still present before him. It is with reference to this sort of repentance that Scripture says: *Cast away from you all your transgressions, wherein ye have transgressed; and make you a new heart and a new spirit* (Ezek. 18: 21).

The second [degree of repentance] is that which is carried out after the epoch in which the sin was committed has passed and the penitent has moved from the scene of his transgression and the <183> details of his sinful conduct are no longer present before him. With reference to this type of repentance Scripture says:

50. "because the promise . . . fulfilled"—Ibn Tibbon.
51. e.g., Deut. 23: 22. The usual translation, instead of "It will then be sin in thee" is: "And it will be sin in thee."
52. Cf. Deut. 23: 22.
53. Cf. Deut. 15: 9.
54. Cf. Deut. 24: 15.
55. "robbery"—Ibn Tibbon.

Turn ye unto Him against whom ye have deeply rebelled, O children of Israel (Isa. 31:6).

The third [degree] is that which is effected [by the sinner] only when he is threatened with impending disaster, as was said to the inhabitants of Nineveh: *Yet forty days and Nineveh shall be overthrown* (Jonah 3:4). The fourth is that which is not undertaken until part of the threatened disaster has already descended upon the sinner, as Scripture says: *Ye children of Israel, turn back unto the Lord, the God of Abraham, Isaac and Israel, that He may return to the remnant that are escaped of you out of the kings of Assyria* (II Chron. 30:6).

The fifth [degree, finally,] is that which is carried out at the moment when the soul passes out. He that repents at that time is also called "penitent," as Scripture says: *Yea, his soul draweth near unto the pit, and his life to the destroyers* (Job 33:22), and further on: *He prayeth unto God, and He is favorable unto him* (Job 33:26). That is why it is our practice to exhort a person who is fatally ill, at the approach of his death, with the following words: Say *I have sinned. I have been iniquitous. I have been faithless. May my death be an atonement for all my iniquities.*[56]

CHAPTER VII

Having discussed exhaustively the aforenamed ten [categories of servants of God], I shall now speak about the middling individual whose vices are exactly equal to his virtues.[57] This type of person is, if he is the recipient of God's mercy, reckoned among the righteous. It is to be borne in mind, of course, that when the attribute of mercy is mentioned in connection with the Creator, exalted and magnified be He, it must necessarily be thought of as reverting to His creatures, since it cannot possibly apply or appertain to Him inasmuch as He is free from all affect, as we have stated previously. It is, therefore, merely one of the predicates of God's activity.

56. Cf. Šab. 32a and Mišnah Sanh. 6: 2.
57. Cf. R.H. 17a.

Now we discern altogether three domains in which this mercy is exercised. [It is done firstly] in the acceptance of repentance, as Scripture says: *And let him return unto the Lord, and He will have compassion upon him* (Isa. 55:7). [It is displayed] also in answering the prayer of him who is in distress, as Scripture says: *In wrath remember compassion* (Hab. 3:2). [It is evinced] furthermore in attaching the middling person to the company of the righteous, as Scripture says: *Gracious is the Lord, and righteous; yea our God is compassionate* (Ps. 116:5).

Rabbinic tradition, moreover, interprets the words *And abundant in goodness* (Exod. 34:6) as meaning *He inclineth the scales toward goodness,* <184> *so that if it was evenly balanced, it tips in that direction* (R. H. 17a). That is why at the time of retribution there will be found no more than two groups of servants of God to the exclusion of a third, namely, righteous persons and evil-doers only, as Scripture says: *Then shall ye again discern between the righteous and the wicked, between him that serveth, etc.* (Mal. 3:18).

I consider it proper now, at the end of this treatise, to make the following observation; namely, that the higher the rank of human beings, the greater the value that attaches to the obedience they give to God, as Scripture says: *Rejoice in the Lord, O ye righteous, praise is comely for the upright* (Ps. 33:1). By the same token also are the sins they commit more serious, as Scripture says: *For both prophet and priest are ungodly* (Jer. 23:11).

Furthermore the service rendered in the distinguished place is rated more highly than any other, as Scripture says: *For in My holy mountain, in the mountain of the height of Israel, saith the Lord God, there shall all the house of Israel serve Me* [58] (Ezek. 20:40). Rebellion, on the other hand, in this distinguished place is accounted as greater sin, as Scripture says: *Yea, in My house have I found their wickedness* (Jer. 23:11).

A life of devotion to God is most highly prized in youth, as Scripture says: *And I raised up of your sons for prophets, and of your young men for Nazirites* (Amos 2:11). Licentiousness, on

58. This quotation follows the reading of Ibn Tibbon.

the other hand, is more reprehensible when found in old men, as Scripture says: *Yea, gray hairs are here and there upon him, and he knoweth it not* (Hos. 7:9).

Honesty is of greater worth when practiced by the poor, as Scripture says: *Better is the poor that walketh in his integrity, than he that is perverse in his ways, though he be rich* (Prov. 28:6). Per contra is deception more serious a crime when perpetrated by the rich, as Scripture says: *And there came a traveler unto the rich man, and he . . . took the poor man's lamb* [59] (II Sam. 12:4), and so forth. Graciousness has greater significance when shown toward an enemy, as Scripture says: *For if a man find his enemy, will he let him go well away?* (I Sam. 24:20). On the other hand, injury is more difficult to endure when done to a friend, as Scripture says: *He hath put forth his hands against them that were at peace with him; he hath profaned his covenant* (Ps. 55:21).

Humility, to go further, is more highly rated when displayed by the great, as Scripture says: *Now the man Moses was very meek, above all men* [60] (Num. 12:3). Conceit is, on the other hand, considered a most serious fault when found in the lowly, as Scripture says: *When <185> the base* [61] *among the sons of man are exalted* (Ps. 12:9). Oppression is most unendurable when practiced on the poor, as Scripture says: *To devour the poor from off the earth, and the needy from among men* (Prov. 30:14). Hurting the learned and anyone that benefits mankind is the gravest wrong, as Scripture says: *For I know how manifold are your transgressions, and how mighty are your sins; ye that afflict the just* (Amos 5:12).

Furthermore, the greater the multitude of those that have been wronged, the more serious the crime, for it is worse if a thousand men are robbed of a thousand drachmas than when five hundred [62] are robbed of that amount of money, as Scripture says: *By reason of the multitude of oppressions they cry out* (Job 35:9).

59. This quotation is supplemented by the reading of Ibn Tibbon.
60. This quotation is based on the reading of Ibn Tibbon.
61. "base"—the usual translation is "vileness."
62. "five hundred"—so Ibn Tibbon and M. The Arabic text reads: "one."

Also is it the gravest offense to sin on the most distinguished day of the year, as Scripture says: *Behold, in the day of your fast ye pursue your business* (Isa. 58:3).

Likewise is charity most highly prized when given by the needy, as Scripture says: *Better is little with the fear of the Lord* (Prov. 15:16). Fasting is most meritorious when practiced by the self-indulgent, as Scripture says: *Let the bridegroom go forth from his chamber, and the bride out of her pavilion* (Joel 2:16).

For the same reason also did God command us to consecrate the first-born and the first-fruits and to pray early in the morning at sunrise, precisely because all these things are so precious to us, as Scripture says: *And all your choice vows which ye vow unto the Lord* (Deut. 12:11).

CHAPTER VIII

After the aforegoing it behooves me now to discourse about [this subject as it applies to men's] thoughts. I say, then, that a person receives much reward for the rejection of [unwholesome] ideas [63] that arise, as Scripture says: *Let the wicked forsake his way, and the man of iniquity his thoughts* (Isa. 55:7). To him, however, who yields to these evil ideas, planning how to execute them, but not carrying them out, to such a one there attaches the guilt of the intent although not that of the act, as Scripture says: *The thoughts of wickedness are an abomination to the Lord* (Prov. 15:26). There is indeed no instance in which a human being is punished for his intention or his [inner] conviction [64] except for denying the existence of God, since that is a conclusion reached only by the mind. With reference thereto does Scripture say: *That I may take the house of Israel in their own heart, because <186> they are all turned away from Me through their idols* (Ezek. 14:5).

I say,[65] furthermore, that those who interpret the verses of Sacred Writ allegorically fall into four categories. They may do so

63. "ideas"—Ibn Tibbon.
64. "inner conviction"—Ibn Tibbon.
65. "I say"—correctly added by Ibn Tibbon.

either to (*a*) harmonize a verse with the evidence of the senses, or (*b*) with the testimony of reason, or (*c*) with other Biblical passages, or (*d*) with tradition. Whoever is successful herein is rewarded for it. Of such a one does Scripture say: *If thou seek her as silver, and search for her as for hid treasures; then shalt thou understand the fear of the Lord, and find the knowledge of God* [66] (Prov. 2: 4, 5). Should he, however, not succeed herein, he receives neither reward nor punishment for it.

He, again, who imputes allegorical meanings to the precepts of the Torah, thereby fostering heresy,[67] borders on the category of the *false prophets,* of whom Scripture declares that they are people *that follow their own spirit, and things which they have not seen* (Ezek. 13: 3). Likewise he who, by means of his speculations about the attributes of the Creator, fosters heretical opinions, borders on the category of unbelievers. To this group belong those, for example, who interpret the passage: *Let us make man in our image* (Gen. 1: 26) as implying that some angel had created Adam and likewise also the rest of the world. Of such individuals does Scripture say that they are persons *who utter Thy name with wicked thought, they take it for falsehood, even Thine enemies* (Ps. 139: 20).

I say, moreover, that even the judge, who decrees chastisement and punishment on his own authority, if his aim in issuing these decrees is the preservation and confirmation of religion, is rewarded therefor. This is borne out by the dictum of our early teachers, who said: *The court have a right to flog and decree punishments unauthorized by the Torah. But they may do this not in order to transgress the words of the Torah, but merely* [68] *in order to make a fence around the Torah* (Sanh. 46a). If, however, his aim thereby is tampering with the scales of justice or the satisfaction of personal whim, then he brings about his own perdition, as Scripture says: *To punish also the righteous is not good, nor to strike the noble for their uprightness* (Prov. 17: 26).

66. This quotation is based on the reading of the Arabic text supplemented by that of Ibn Tibbon.
67. "fostering heresy"—M and Ibn Tibbon.
68. "merely"—so correctly M and Ibn Tibbon, omitting the word "even."

Let me state also that when uneducated people who, upon finding that they do not understand what they read in the Torah, consult about its meaning the most learned and pious of their contemporaries and act upon the latter's recommendations, they comply fully with the requirements of their religion, as Scripture says: *The lips of the righteous feed many* (Prov. 10:21). If they <187> fail to act thus, on the other hand, they are not excused for the sins committed out of ignorance. It is of such persons that Scripture says: *A scorner loveth not to be reproved; he will not go unto the wise* (Prov. 15:12).

Furthermore I would say that the needy, who are compelled by circumstances to default in their prayers and divine service, are excused only to the extent of the requirements of their livelihood. For aught that exceeds these limits, however, they are held accountable, as Scripture says: *He delivereth the poor by his poverty* [69] (Job 36:15). Similarly I declare that persons who are in pain are not excused on account of their illness for railing against divine justice. Thus, too, does Scripture say: *And they have not cried unto Me with their heart, though they wail upon their beds* (Hos. 7:14).

Let me say, furthermore, in regard to drunkards, that they are not excused for any crime committed by them in their state of drunkenness, for the law says: *The purchase and sale made by a drunkard are valid. If he is guilty of a transgression that is punishable with death, he is put to death; of one that is punishable by flogging, he is flogged* ('Erubh. 65a). Also, with reference to Jews who are oppressed by *Gentiles,* I would say that their distress is no excuse for disloyalty to their faith, but that they must be patient, as Scripture says: *Let him give his cheek to him that smiteth him, let him be filled full with reproach* (Lam. 3:30).

As for those who constantly lapse back into sin, to them I say that it is more difficult for them to repent than it is for others, as Scripture says: *As a dog that returneth to his vomit, so is a fool that repeateth his folly* (Prov. 26:11). In the same vein did our

69. "the poor by his poverty"—the usual translation is: "the afflicted by his affliction."

early teachers say: *He that says: "I shall sin and repent, sin and repent," is not given the opportunity to do repentance* (Mišnah Yoma 8:9).

I say also concerning those who rely upon the atonement of the *Day of Atonement* that it will not profit them aught without repentance. This is borne out by the remark of our early teachers: *I might have thought that it atones for those that repent as well as for those that do not repent. The text, therefore, reads: "Only [70] on the tenth"* (Lev. 23:27). *Hence it atones only for those that repent* (Šĕbhu. 13a).

Furthermore I declare that, so far as those that have corrupted other men are concerned, their repentance can, as a rule, not be effectuated.[71] To them is applicable the statement of Scripture: *How trimmest thou thy way to seek love! Therefore—even <188> the wicked women hast thou taught thy ways* (Jer. 2:33). In regard to those, again, who endeavor to direct their fellowmen to the path of virtue I say that they can, as a rule, not fall entirely into sin, as Scripture says: *My foot hath held fast to His steps, His way have I kept, and turned not aside. I have not gone back from the commandment of His lips; I have treasured up the words of His mouth* (Job 23:11, 12).

In conclusion, let me state that I realize that, even if I had collected many more data on this subject, I would not have exhausted all that might have been said in order to call the attention of human beings to what their religion requires of them. Nevertheless the easily understood general principles that I have outlined will be of some benefit to humankind with the help of the Merciful.

The fifth treatise is hereby completed.

70. "Only"—the usual translation is "Howbeit."
71. Cf. Mišnah 'Abhoth 5:18.

TREATISE VI

CONCERNING THE ESSENCE OF THE SOUL AND DEATH AND WHAT COMES AFTER DEATH

CHAPTER I

OUR Lord, blessed and exalted be He, has informed us that man's soul has its origin in his heart simultaneously with the completion of the formation of his body. This is illustrated by such statements of Scripture as *The burden of the word of the Lord concerning Israel. The saying of the Lord, who stretched forth the heavens, and laid the foundation of the earth, and formed the spirit of man within him* (Zech. 12:1). He has told us, furthermore, that He has appointed a period during which the soul and the body remain united and at the conclusion of which He separates them again. In this latter state they remain until the number of the souls which His wisdom has deemed necessary to create has been fulfilled. When this has taken place, He will again unite these souls with their bodies and requite them for their conduct. These sundry theories have been supported for us by means of miracles and marvels produced by the prophets, wherefore we have readily accepted them. However, we also endeavored, in addition, to reach these conclusions by means of rational speculation, pursuing the method followed by us in the preceding treatises.

Now the first point which it behooves me to investigate is the nature of the essence of the soul. I have, namely, found a bewildering variety of opinions to exist among men regarding its nature, differences that distract the mind. The majority of these I would rather not mention,[1] but limit myself to noting seven of the most important <189> theories outside of the four that have been listed previously. That would make a total of eleven altogether.

1. "mention"—added by Ibn Tibbon and M.

As for those four other theories, I have already tested and examined them thoroughly, and they have turned out to be defective and thus been refuted. What I have reference to is (*a*) the theory of the spiritual elements,[2] (*b*) the doctrine that all things emanated from the substance of the Creator,[3] (*c*) the view that they were derived from Him and something else,[4] and (*d*) the theory of the dualists.[5] But since the soul constitutes one of the objects of [human] cognition, it is, to the extent to which it has been included by them in the generality of these objects, subject to the refutation already presented of the said theses, so that we may dispense with going over these matters again.

I shall, however, at this point record the following seven theories and say, first of all, that I have found people who think the soul is merely an accident among accidents. What led them to this conclusion is, in my estimation, the circumstance that they have never seen the soul itself but only the effects of its operation. On account of its being too subtle to be perceived by the senses, it seemed to them that it had to be an accident, since accidents are of such a subtle and fine character.

Yet those that hold this theory differ among themselves, falling into five distinct groups. Some of them believe that the soul is a self-moving number.[6] Others believe it constitutes the completion of the natural body. Still others are under the impression that it consists of a combination of the four elements of nature. A further group imagines it to be a juncture of the senses. Finally there are those who conceive of it as an accident originating from the blood.

Now when I considered carefully these theses, all of which have in common the allegation that the soul is an accident—for the concepts of number and completion and combination and juncture and derivation refer to accidents—I found them all untenable from

2. Cf. above, pp. 50 ff.
3. Cf. above, pp. 55 ff.
4. Cf. above, p. 58.
5. Cf. above, pp. 59 ff.
6. "number"—so M. Ibn Tibbon and Arabic text read "accident." Cf. Ventura, p. 228, n. 3.

several points of view. One reason is that something accidental cannot be the source of that great wisdom and remarkable understanding that are the basis of the world's existence, as I have noted in a [7] treatise preceding this one.[8] Then, too, one accident could not be the bearer of another, because that would be entirely unsound. Yet we find that the soul is the bearer of many accidents. One speaks, for example, of an ignorant soul and a knowing soul, and of [9] a pure soul and a wicked soul. Thou dost also ascribe <190> to the soul love and hate and good will and anger and the other well-known traits. Possessing these characteristics, it cannot possibly be construed as being a mere accident. On the contrary, since we note that it is susceptible to such opposite attributes, it is more likely that it be a substance.

Secondly, I have seen people who are under the impression that the soul is made of air, and, in the third place, some who think that it consists of fire. These last two theories I also find to be unsound, for if the soul had been made of air, it would have been of a hot and humid nature, and if it had consisted of fire, it would have been of a hot and dry nature, whereas we do not find it to be of such a character.

A fourth theory, again, is to the effect that the soul consists of two parts, one of which is intellectual, rational, intransient, with its seat in the heart, while the other is the source of vitality that is spread over the rest of the body and of a transient nature. I ascertained, however, that this view, too, was erroneous, for if the rational portion of the soul were distinct from that which is spread throughout the body, they could not mingle with each other, by virtue of the fact that the one is uncreated and the other is created, and that the latter is transient whereas the former is not transient. Furthermore, if the rational part of the soul were something separate from that which is spread throughout the body,[10] it could not hear or see or be capable of other sensations.

7. "a"—the Arabic text reads "the."

8. He has reference to his discussion at the beginning of the fourth treatise, p. 182.

9. "and of"—the Arabic text reads "and thou sayest."

10. "separate . . . body"—added correctly by Ibn Tibbon.

Now one cannot resolve the difficulty in this instance by replying, as I explained in the first treatise [11] of this book, that the various sense perceptions converge in reason, which discourses about them all. I declare, rather, that this theory clearly implies the existence of two distinct souls, since each portion stands by itself.

A fifth theory is to the effect that the soul consists of two kinds of air, one of which is internal while the other is external to the body. Now what compelled the proponents of this theory to resort to it was the fact that they found that the soul could be maintained only by the inhaling of air from without. They therefore thought that this was effected by means of one half of the soul. In reality, however, the purpose of this respiration is to temper the natural heat of the heart wherein the soul has its seat, just as one blows on a fire in order to drive the offensive smoke away from it—I mean from the fire.

A sixth view is that the soul is pure blood. This view is propounded only by Anan,[12] as he states expressly <191> in his book. He was led to this erroneous conclusion by the statement of the Torah:[13] *For the blood is the soul*[14] (Deut. 12:23), not remembering that this Torah had previously said: *For the soul*[15] *of the flesh is in the blood* (Lev. 17:11). From this, however, it is obvious that the blood is only the seat and center of the soul, the force of which reveals the soul's strength while its weakness makes apparent its feebleness.

Furthermore, when the soul rejoices and is anxious to display its gladness over the object of its joy, it causes the blood to appear, whereas when it endeavors to flee in fear from something which it is afraid of, it withdraws the blood together with it into the interior. If, then, the Torah states: *For the blood is the soul*[16]

11. Cf. p. 64 of the Arabic text.

12. i.e., the founder of the Karaite schism. Cf. H. Graetz, *History of the Jews* (Philadelphia, 1894), III, 128 ff. As Malter notes (p. 223), Saadia was wrong in ascribing this theory to Anan alone. It was subscribed to by several of the Greek philosophers and even by the Midrash.

13. This quotation follows the reading of Ibn Tibbon.

14. "soul"—the usual translation is "life."

15. "soul"—the usual translation is "life."

16. "soul"—cf. above, n. 14.

(Deut. 12:23), it is only in keeping with the common usage of language which designates an object by the name of the place in which it is located. Thus wisdom is called *heart,* as, for example, in the statement of Scripture: *A young man void of heart* [17] (Prov. 7:7), because the heart is the seat of wisdom. Language, again, is called *lip,* as in the statement of Scripture: *And the whole earth was of one lip* [18] (Gen. 11:1), because it is by means of the lip that speech becomes possible.

CHAPTER II

The seventh is the correct theory, and with the help of God I shall explain it. My object in prefacing it by the exposition of the six aforementioned theories was merely to make it clear to whoever may read this book that this inquiry into the science of the soul is an inquiry into a profound, abstract, and subtle subject. Just as I remarked with reference to the truth apropos of the doctrine of *creatio ex nihilo* [19] and with regard to the Creator of all that exists,[20] so is the investigation of the nature of the soul fraught with subtleties that confuse many persons. That is why I say that thou findest the sage bestowing honor on him who understands correctly the meaning of the rational soul possessed by man, when he says: *Who knoweth the spirit of man whether it goeth upward, and the spirit of the beast whether it goeth downward to the earth?* (Eccles. 3:21).

Now I must make it clear that his remark *Who knoweth* is not an expression of doubt as to whether certain souls are elevated and noble and others are lowly and base. It is merely <192> an expression of esteem for him who knows [that] such [differences exist among] them. I say, furthermore, to him who hears this statement that it is analogous to such a question as: "Who knows the learned Reuben?" and "Who knows the devout Simon?" By ask-

17. "heart"—the usual translation is "understanding."
18. "lip"—the usual translation is "language."
19. Cf. the beginning of the first treatise, pp. 39 ff.
20. Cf. the beginning of the second treatise, pp. 87 ff.

ing this very question the questioner indubitably attributes learning to Reuben and devoutness to Simon. The whole object of asking "Who knows them?" is to confer upon them honor or distinction or something similar.

Likewise when the sage remarks: "Who knows the noble soul that rises upward and the lowly soul that sinks downward?" that remark indubitably constitutes nothing more than an affirmation that these two types of soul are of such a character. As for his intention in expressing this idea by saying *Who knoweth,* it is to indicate that whoever understands this matter has reached the goal of his striving for the truth.

I will say also that this remark on his part—I mean *Who knoweth*—might be construed as an expression of admiration and praise on noting how two types of soul are attached to two similar bodies. Consequently what he says is: "We find that these two bodies are perceptibly alike in their physical constitution and their accidents. Yet we have no doubt, on the other hand, that there exists a difference between the two spirits. Now who is capable of fathoming and understanding this?" That is indeed the import of his statement preceding this one: *For that which befalleth the sons of men befalleth beasts; even one thing befalleth them; as the one dieth, so dieth the other; yea, they have all one breath* (Eccles. 3:19).

What corroborates the view that this statement is to be understood as we have interpreted it is his added remark: *So that man hath no preëminence above a beast* (*ibid.*). Now the sage could not possibly have meant to imply hereby that the soul of man had no [21] preëminence whatever over that of the beasts. For no wise man would make such an assertion, since he would thereby be denying the reality of all wisdom. Another reason why this could not have been his intention is that an ignoramus who has but a smattering of intelligence would not make such an assertion either. For the latter regards himself as superior to <193> the beasts in various respects which it would take too long to explain, such as the fact that he makes them subservient to him and rides upon them and uses them for whatever purpose he pleases. What he

21. "no"—correctly added by M and Ibn Tibbon.

meant by this statement was, then, rather merely that the *body* of man is in no way superior to that of the beast, since it is composed, like that of the latter, of four elements, as he says subsequently: *All go unto one place; all are of the dust, and all return to dust* [22] (Eccles. 3:20). Nevertheless man has spiritual preeminence. *Who knoweth the spirit of man?* (Eccles. 3:21.)

This statement on the part of the sage might, moreover, be compared to the assertion of a person who says that there is no difference between a precious stone and an ordinary rock so far as stoniness is concerned, for the one is as much a stone as is the other. Yet he who knows the bright sparkle contained in the precious stone and the opaqueness of the rock recognizes [their distinctive qualities].

Furthermore I would say that the sentence *Who knoweth* might quite properly be construed as an affirmation, just like the statement found elsewhere in the Bible: *Who knoweth will return* [23] *and repent* (Joel 2:14); that is, "Whoever knows that he is sinning, will repent." Likewise does the sage say here: "He that knows, understands that the one soul rises upward while the other goes down."

CHAPTER III

Having made these prefatory remarks, it behooves me now to present the seventh theory. I say, then, that the truth, so far as the nature of the soul is concerned, is that it is created. This view accords with my previous demonstration that all things existing in the world have been created [24] and that it would be wrong to ascribe eternity to aught except the Creator. It is prompted furthermore by the declaration of God [that He was the one] *Who formed the spirit of man within him* (Zech. 12:1).

Now this creation of the soul by our Lord first takes place simultaneously with the completion of the bodily form of the human

22. This quotation follows the reading of Ibn Tibbon.
23. "will return"—the usual translation is "whether He will not turn."
24. Cf. the first treatise.

being, for it is stated in the above-quoted remark that it is created *within him,* which corresponds to the wording of the oath generally employed by our forefathers; namely, *As the Lord liveth that made us this soul* (Jer. 38:16).

As for the quality of its substance, it is comparable in purity to that of the heavenly spheres. Like the latter, it attains luminosity as a result of the light which it receives from God, except that its substance becomes, in consequence hereof, even finer than that of the spheres.[25] That is how it came to be endowed with the power of speech.

< 194 > This conclusion I reached on the basis of two important fundamental premises. The first is a proof of a rational character. When, namely, I considered the evidences of the soul's wisdom and its conduct aside from the body, and noted how the body is deprived of all these advantages once the soul is separated from it, I realized that if its substance were of the same nature as that of terrestrial things, it could not perform any of these lofty functions. Again, if it were of the consistency of the heavenly spheres, it would no more be endowed with reason than any of the latter. Consequently it must be a fine substance that is clearer and purer and simpler than that of the spheres.

The second proof is derived from the statement of Scripture to the effect that the virtuous souls shine like the heavenly spheres which are illuminated by the stars. This is expressed in the words: *And they that are wise shall shine as the brightness of the firmament* (Dan. 12:3). The wicked souls, on the other hand, do not shine, but are on a lower level than the unspecified [26] spheres, as Scripture says: *Behold, He putteth no trust in His holy ones; yea, the heavens are not clean in His sight. How much less one that is abominable and impure, man who drinketh iniquity like water* [27] (Job 15:15, 16). Now it must be realized by thee that the Scriptures would not have compared the former to the luminous spheres and the latter to something below the unspecified spheres unless

25. "spheres"—M and Ibn Tibbon.
26. "unspecified"—Ibn Tibbon.
27. This quotation follows the reading of Ibn Tibbon.

it were for the reason that there exists a similarity between their respective substances. These two similes also bear out the declaration made by the sage: *Whether it goeth upward . . . whether it goeth downward* (Eccles. 3:21).

Next I say, pursuing this subject further, that the statement made by the sage at the end of his book: *And the spirit returneth unto God who gave it* (Eccles. 12:7), serves as a confirmation and a verification, proving the correctness of the interpretation given by me to the sentence *Who knoweth* (Eccles. 3:21). Should anyone insist, however, that this latter remark implies doubt on the part of the sage, as the sequel would seem to indicate, the sage's passage from original uncertainty to final certainty is made clear by his statement: *And the spirit returneth unto God* (Eccles. 12:7), as well as by his pronouncement about the spirit of man made at the end of the passage: *But know thou,* <195> *that for all these things God will bring thee into judgment* (Eccles. 11:9).

Next I ascertained that for sundry reasons this soul of man must perform the act of cognition by means of its essence. One of these is that it is inadmissible that it acquire its knowledge from the body, since the latter is not a function of the body. Moreover, it is known for certain that a blind man is able to see in his dream as though he possessed the power of sight. But since he does not owe this perception to his physical faculties, it must be due to his soul. Herein is evident also the error of those who regard the soul as a union and a mingling and a juncture of the sense perceptions,[28] when, as a matter of fact, it is the soul that provides the various sense organs with their sense faculties. How, then, can it be asserted that it is they that give to it its essence? Whoever makes such an assertion perverts all judgment and distorts the truth.

Furthermore, I ascertained that the soul performs its functions only by means of the body, since the act of every created being requires for its execution some instrument. When, now, the soul is united with the body, three faculties belonging to it make their appearance; namely, the power of reasoning, the power of appetition, and that of anger. That is why our language applied to

28. Cf. above, p. 236.

them three distinct appellations, to wit: *nepheš, ruaḥ, and nĕšamah.*

By the appellative *nepheš* it alludes to the soul's possession of an appetitive faculty. This is borne out by such statements of Scripture as *Because thy soul (naphšĕkha) desireth* (Deut. 12:20) and *And his soul (naphšo) desirable* [29] *food* (Job 33:20).

By the appellative *ruaḥ,* again, it alludes to the soul's possession of the power to become bold and angry. This is illustrated by such statements of Scripture as *Be not hasty in thy spirit (ruḥăkha) to be angry* (Eccles. 7:9) and *A fool spendeth all his spirit (ruḥo)* (Prov. 29:11). By means of the appellative *nĕšamah,* finally, it refers to the soul's possession of the faculty of cognition. This is evident from such statements of Scripture as *And the breath (nišĕmath) of the Almighty, that giveth them understanding* (Job 32:8), and *And whose spirit (nišĕmath) came forth from thee?* (Job 26:4).

Now it is a mistake to apportion these [three] faculties among two distinct [psychic] elements, one of which has its seat in the heart while the other is located in the rest of the body. All three powers belong rather to one soul, to emphasize which fact the language of Scripture has coined two additional designations, besides those previously listed; namely, *ḥayyah* (living) and *yĕḥidhah* (unique). It is called *ḥayyah* (e.g., Job 33:20) because of its capacity to survive when its Creator grants it survival. It is also *yĕḥidhah* (e.g., Ps. 22:21) because <196> there exists nothing comparable to it among all creatures, either celestial or terrestrial.

It has furthermore become clear to me that, so far as the human soul is concerned, its seat is in the heart, since it is definitely known that the nerves,[30] which endow the body with the powers of sensation and motion, all have their roots in the heart. I do, indeed, find that the great ramifications of nerves do not issue from the heart, but originate rather from the brain. However, these ramifications have no connection with the soul as such. They are merely the sinews and ligaments of the body. That is why Scripture in-

---

29. "desirable"—the usual translation is "dainty."

30. "nerves"—cf. Ventura, p. 240, who calls attention to the fact that no distinction was made by Saadia between veins and nerves.

variably mentions heart and soul together. It does this in such statements as *With all thy heart, and with all thy soul* (Deut. 6:5), *With all your heart and with all your soul* (Deut. 11:13), and the like.

CHAPTER IV

And now that I have presented these theories, let me inform the reader that I have encountered certain people who asked how it was compatible with the wisdom of the Creator, magnified and exalted be He, to place a being as noble as the soul, which exceeds in purity even the heavenly spheres, in something as turbid as the body In fact, they began to think in their hearts that God had wronged the soul by so doing. I feel compelled, therefore, to pause[31] at this point and explain it clearly.

Let me, however, preface my remark at the outset with the observation that it is absolutely absurd to assert of the Creator, magnified be His majesty, of whose essence we have discoursed previously, that He would wrong or deal unjustly with any creature of His. For in the first place, all accidents are excluded from His Being. Furthermore, all acts attributable to Him are good and beneficent. Besides, He created His creatures only for the purpose of benefiting, not of hurting them. This is what I would say in general and by way of summary.

To explain this in greater detail and be more specific, let me add that injustice is due to one of three causes, there being no fourth. However, none of these three is applicable to the Creator. The first of these [three possible causes of injustice] is the subject's fear of the object of his injustice. A second cause [that might prompt it] is greediness for something that might be obtained from the latter. <197> A third is ignorance of the truth concerning the victim. Since, however, it cannot be asserted about the Creator that He is afraid or desires[32] or is ignorant of anything that is the object of knowledge, all these causes are removed from Him.

31. "pause"—Ibn Tibbon.
32. "or desires"—correctly added by Ibn Tibbon.

I next applied myself to an investigation of the Scriptures and I found that they bore testimony to God's justice in all these three respects. This is illustrated by the declaration concerning God on the part of the saint that He is one *That respecteth not the persons of princes, nor regardeth the rich more than the poor. For they all are the work of His hands* (Job. 34:19). By means of his statement: *That respecteth not the persons of princes,* he refers to the category of fear. With his declaration, again, *Nor regardeth the rich more than the poor,* he points to the category of desire. His remark, finally, *For they all are the work of His hands,* hints at the category of knowledge, for since God is well acquainted with the character of His creatures, all the more would He be conversant with their deeds and their requirements and needs.

Since, then, I have hereby established justice as a basic attribute of God, I can refer and direct any question that might be asked by men in regard to the soul to the principle laid down here.

I will also say that inasmuch as the soul cannot, by virtue of its constitution, function by itself, it must needs be united with something that will enable it to work toward its improvement. For it is such actions alone that are conducive to permanent well-being and perfect bliss. All this is in keeping with our explanation in the fifth treatise to the effect that obedience [to God's commandments] increases the luminosity of the soul's substance, whereas sin renders its substance turbid and black.[33] This is evidenced by such pronouncements of Scripture as *Light is sown for the righteous* (Ps. 97:11), and *The light of the righteous rejoiceth; but the lamp of the wicked shall be put out* (Prov. 13:9).

Now He that subjects the soul to its trials is none other than the Master of the universe, who is, of course, acquainted with all its doings. This testing of the soul has been compared to the assaying by means of fire of [lumps of metal] that have been referred to as gold or silver. It is thereby that the true nature of their composition is clearly established. For the original gold and silver remain, while the alloys [34] that have been mingled with them are

33. He refers to the beginning of that treatise, p. 205.
34. "alloys"—Ibn Tibbon?

partly burned and partly take flight. This is illustrated by such statements of Scripture as <198> *The refining pot is for silver, and the furnace for gold, and a man is tried by his praise* (Prov. 27:21), and again: *And I will refine them as silver is refined, and will try them as gold is tried* (Zech. 13:9).

The pure, clear souls that have been refined are thereupon exalted and ennobled,[35] as Scripture says: *For He knoweth the way that I take; when He hath tried me, I shall come forth as gold* (Job 23:10). Those that resemble dross and base metals, on the other hand, are degraded and debased, as Scripture says: *In vain doth the founder refine, for the wicked are not separated. Refuse silver shall men call them* (Jer. 6:29, 30). Nevertheless even the soiled souls are capable, so long as they are within the body, of being purified and cleansed again. That is why repentance is accepted so long as the human being is alive. Once, however, the soul has departed from him, it is incapable of being cleansed any longer of the corruption that has accumulated in it. In fact, nothing of the kind is to be expected for it any more, as Scripture says: *when a wicked man dieth, his expectation shall perish* (Prov. 11:7).

By means of the aforementioned reasons, then, we make it clear and evident [36] to him who asserts that it would have been best for the soul if God had left it in its state of isolation, so that it would have been relieved of sin and defilement and pain, that if such isolation had been the best thing for the soul, its Creator would have fashioned it in such a state. However, from what we know, if God had allowed the soul to remain unattached, it would not have been able to attain well-being or bliss or life eternal. For the attainment of all these things can be effected by it only by serving its Master, and the soul has no means, by virtue of its nature, of rendering this service except through the instrumentality of the body.

The reason for this is that the soul carries out all its activities in conjunction with the body, just as fire can make an appearance only by being attached to something else and just as other com-

35. "exalted and ennobled"—Ibn Tibbon and M.
36. "we make it clear and evident"—Ibn Tibbon and M.

posite organisms fulfill their functions jointly only. If, therefore, the soul were to be left by itself, it would not be able to do anything. Still less could the body do anything. And if they were both thus deprived of activity, there would be no sense to their creation. But if the creation of these two have no meaning, <199> then the creation of heaven and earth and what is between them too would be futile, since the entire universe was created only on account of man, as we asserted at the beginning of the fourth [37] treatise.

[This thesis is] furthermore [supported] by the fact that in [the description of God's role as Creator] He is referred to as one *Who stretched forth the heavens, and laid the foundation of the earth* for the purpose implied in the sequel; namely, *And formed the spirit of man within him* (Zech. 12:1). Similarly it has been remarked by us, in connection with *the story of the creation of the world,* that that act was motivated by the thought of *Let us make man* (Gen. 1:26).

Now someone might, of course, say: "But why not leave the soul in its original unattached state and endow it with the power to act in such a way as to attain the object for which it has been created?" To such a one we must point out that this demand on his part resembles his first demand, which we mentioned in connection with the human body; namely, that it be composed of a substance similar to that of the stars and the angels. We tell him, moreover, that to insist upon this demand is to ask that the soul be no soul, because the intellectual soul is capable of carrying out its activities only in conjunction with the body of man. For if it did not function within a human body, it would have to be either a star or a celestial sphere or an angel. In that case, however, it would no longer possess the real nature of a human soul.

Such a demand is, therefore, merely equivalent to abrogation in all except the name. It is like demanding that fire tend downward and water rise upward by nature, which would be an abrogation of their essential characters; or like desiring that the fire cool and

37. "fourth"—i.e., beginning with p. 180. Both the Arabic and the Hebrew versions mistakenly read "third."

the snow give warmth, which would also constitute an abrogation of their essential character. To make such a request is to do violence to wisdom, for wisdom consists in knowing things as they are in their real, observable character, not as someone would desire or like them to be. This is also borne out in Scripture by the statement: *Woe unto him that striveth with his Maker, as a potsherd with the potsherds of the earth! Shall the clay say to him that fashioneth it: "What makest thou?" etc.*[38] (Isa. 45:9).

As for the objection one might raise against the fact that sins are permitted to become attached to the soul, it must be realized that such an eventuality would be due solely to the bad choice that is exercised by the soul in opposing the intentions of its Creator concerning it. This thought is also implied in the statement of Scripture: <200> *Behold, this only have I found, that God made man upright; but they have sought out many inventions* (Eccles. 7:29).

As for the objection that is raised against the defilement and the contamination of the soul consequent upon its union with the body, we say, in reply thereto, that the body of man contains no impurity in and by itself.[39] It is, on the contrary, entirely pure, for defilement is neither a thing that is subject to sense perception nor a requirement of logic. It is purely a decree of the law of the Torah. This law has declared unclean certain secretions of human beings after their discharge from the body, although they do not defile while they are within the body. The aforementioned allegation can be maintained only if he that makes it will impose upon us rules that he has invented out of his own mind and make it obligatory upon us to consider as reprehensible what he so regards. That, however, we shall not permit him to do.

As for the pains with which the soul is afflicted because of its connection with the body, they are due inevitably to one of two causes. If, for example, they are aches that it has contracted by exposure at the time of darkness or of excessive heat or cold, the fault is its own and not that of its Master. For He has endowed

38. This quotation is based on the reading of the Arabic original supplemented by that of Ibn Tibbon.
39. Saadia expressed the same idea in his refutation of Ḥiwwi the Balchite. Cf. Ventura, p. 241, n. 78.

the soul with intelligence and enjoined it to beware of such evils, but it disregarded the injunction. [It is,] as Scripture declares: *A prudent man seeth the evil, and hideth himself; but the thoughtless pass on, and are punished* (Prov. 27: 12).

On the other hand, if these pains have been brought upon it by its Master, the only possible explanation, in view of God's justice and mercy, is that He permitted them to come upon it as a discipline in order that He might, in return therefor, requite the soul with good. This is borne out by such statements of Scripture as: *That He might afflict thee, and that He might prove thee, to do thee good at thy latter end* (Deut. 8: 16), and *Happy is the man whom Thou instructest, O Lord, etc. . . . that Thou mayest give him rest from the days of evil.*[40] (Ps. 94: 12, 13).

CHAPTER V

Furthermore let me explain that the soul and the body constitute one agent, as it is remarked at the very beginning of man's creation: *Then the Lord God formed man of the dust of the ground, and breathed into his nostrils the breath of life* (Gen. 2: 7). Similarly are they both either rewarded or punished together.

Now the reason why thou findest many persons confused in regard to this subject, one of them believing that reward and punishment apply to the soul only, while another <201> thinks they apply solely to the body and still another imagines that they appertain to the bones alone—as, for example, Benjamin [41] does—is simply that they were led astray by lack of acquaintance with the language of Scripture.

When, for instance, some of them found Scripture making use of the expression *If a soul* [42] *shall sin* (Lev. 4: 2), or *If any soul* [43] *commit a trespass* (Lev. 5: 15), or *The soul that sinneth, it shall die* (Ezek. 18: 4), they thought that these functions belonged to

40. This quotation is based on the reading of Ibn Tibbon.
41. He has reference to the Karaite scholar, Benjamin Nahawendi. Cf. Graetz III, 149 ff.
42. "a soul"—the usual translation is "anyone."
43. "soul"—the usual translation is "one."

the soul exclusively. They did not note that Scripture likewise says: *And when a soul* [44] *shall touch any unclean thing* (Lev. 7:21) and *But the soul that eateth of the flesh* (Lev. 7:20), where the expression "soul" can refer only to the body.

On the other hand, when another one among them observed in the usage of the language of Scripture such statements as *And it shall come to pass, that from one new moon to another . . . shall all flesh come to worship before Me* (Isa. 66:23) and *And let all flesh bless His holy name* (Ps. 145:21), and the like, he thought that such activities were performed by the body, not realizing that the functions involved in them, namely speech and eloquence, appertain to the soul.

Benjamin, again, found such expressions as *And whose iniquities are upon their bones* (Ezek. 32:27), and also *All my bones shall say: "Lord, who is like unto Thee?"* (Ps. 35:10). He therefore thought that everything depended upon the bones. To be sure, the books of anatomy [45] do, indeed, declare that the bodily frame of man consists of the bones and that the flesh, the arteries, the nerves, and the muscles are only their servants and guardians. I know, however, that he did not make the allegation he did out of unawareness of the fact that every science has a method different from that of another, and that the science of the Law bears no relationship whatever to that of anatomy. [He did so] rather [out of a misunderstanding of Scripture,] not realizing that the [psalmist's] declaration: *Lord, who is like unto Thee* was not made by the bones.

But he was not content with [the misinterpretation of the expression in] this [instance]. He went so far as to add [on the basis of the same misunderstanding] that the bodies of Saul and of his children were burned by the inhabitants of Jabesh, because of the statement *And they came to Jabesh and burned them there* (I Sam. 31:12). [He asserted] also that their bones alone were buried, as is stated by Scripture: *And they took their bones and buried them under the tamarisk-tree in Jabesh* (I Sam. 31:13).

But in that case, when thou notest Scripture <202> saying:

---

44. "a soul"—the usual translation is "anyone."
45. He is evidently referring to the books of Galen. Cf. Guttmann, p. 206, n. 1.

And Moses took the bones of Joseph with him (Exod. 13:19), who, pray, burned his body? And would that I knew who burned the body of *The man of God that came from Judah* (I Kings 13:21) [leaving his bones untouched] so that he declared: *Lay my bones beside his bones!* (I Kings 13:31.) The remark made by Scripture in regard to Saul and his children: *And they burned them* (*'otham*) *there* (I Sam. 31:12) must, therefore, be taken as being equivalent to *And they made a burning for them* (*'alehem*) there, as is said elsewhere: *And with the burnings of thy fathers, the former kings that were before thee, so shall they make a burning for thee* [46] (Jer. 34:5). Incidentally it is to be noted that, in the usage of the language of Scripture, the expression *And his father wept for him* (*'otho*) (Gen. 37:35) is employed in place of *And he wept over him* (*'alaw*).

In general, however, it may be remarked that whoever attributes actions to the soul only, or to the body alone or to the bones exclusively, does so out of ignorance of the rules of the language of Scripture and its usage. It is, namely, one of the peculiarities of the style of Holy Writ that an act that is performed by three or four or five different things is sometimes related by it to the first alone, and sometimes to the second alone, and sometimes to the third alone.

Thus we know that the function of speech is carried out by five organs; namely, *the mouth and the tongue and the lip and the palate and the throat.* The language of Scripture consequently abounds in such expressions as *My mouth shall tell of Thy righteousness* (Ps. 71:15); *And my tongue shall speak of Thy righteousness* (Ps. 35:28); *My lips shall praise Thee* (Ps. 63:4); *Set the horn to thy palate* [47] (Hos. 8:1); and *Cry with the throat,* [48] *spare not* (Isa. 58:1). In each case, then, it is just one of the five organs employed that is mentioned explicitly, the other four being merely implied.

Similarly, therefore, here it is sometimes the soul alone that is mentioned, or the body alone, or the bones, or the skin, when in

46. This quotation is based on the reading of Ibn Tibbon.
47. "palate"—the usual translation is "mouth."
48. "with the throat"—the usual translation is "aloud."

reality all of them are meant. It even happens that a function pertaining only to the body or the soul is attributed to one member of the body alone. Thus it is said: *Her feet abide not in her house* (Prov. 7:11), *And she worketh willingly with her hands* (Prov. 31:13), *And mine eye abideth in their provocation* (Job 17:2), *Cannot my palate* [49] *discern crafty devices?* (Job 6:30), and the like.

Having made it clear, then, from the standpoint of reason as well as Scripture, <203> that the soul and the body constitute a single agent, we might add a further support derived from rabbinic tradition. I have reference to the statement: *If someone were to assert: "The body and the soul can have themselves exempted from being judged,"* . . . *one could cite the parable of the king who had an orchard in which he stationed two watchmen, one a lame man and the other a blind man* (Sanh. 91a), and so forth until the end of that story.

CHAPTER VI

Next let me discuss the matter of the time limit and say that the Creator of body and soul has set a certain fixed measure of time for their union. Thus He said: *The number of thy days I will fulfill* (Exod. 23:26). He likewise said to the prince of men: *Behold, thy days approach that thou must die* (Deut. 31:14). Furthermore he said to one of the saints: *When thy days are fulfilled, and thou shalt sleep with thy fathers* (II Sam. 7:12).

I say, furthermore, that God may either increase this measure of time or diminish it. In my opinion, however, it is not God's knowledge of how long He will allow the soul to remain within the body that determines the duration of their union, for God's knowledge exercises no direct influence on the reality of things. The measure of time that is subject to increase and diminution is, in my estimation, due rather to that of the vitality with which the body has been endowed.

There can, namely, be no doubt that the body is provided by

49. "palate"—the usual translation is "taste."

God, from the very beginning of its creation, with a certain basic potentiality, either great or small. Now the extent of the duration of this potentiality is what is called the "time limit" of man's existence. God can, however, add to it and strengthen it so that it will last, in addition to the usual seventy years, for thirty years longer; or He may weaken and soften it, so that it will dissolve at the age of forty. It is along these lines that we conceive of the increase or the diminution in man's life span.

Now the net age attained by man after the increase to or the deduction from his life expectancy is the one that is known by his Creator as being the actual number of years that he is destined to live. This is to be explained as follows: God knows that the basic life expectancy of the body is set at seventy years. He might increase this by thirty or diminish it by thirty.

But what are the causes of this increase or diminution? [The answer is given] in <204> such statements of Scripture as *The fear of the Lord prolongeth days; but the years of the wicked shall be shortened* (Prov. 10:27). God said, moreover, to one of the pious: *And I will add unto thy days fifteen years* (II Kings 20:6). He said, furthermore, with reference to the nature of many of the rewards for virtuous conduct: *That thy days may be long* (Exod. 20:12 and Deut. 25:15), and the like. About some of the wicked, again, Scripture says: *And the Lord smote all the first born in the land of Egypt* (Exod. 12:29) and *And those that died by the plague were. . . .* (Num. 25:9) and the like. Now if these last-mentioned had died in accordance with the potentiality of the time limit fixed for them, there would have been no *plague* by reason of their sins, nor would aught have been removed through the act of Phineas.

It has also been definitely indicated by the prophet that the *plague* produces death at a time other than the regular age limit set to man's life. He said, namely: *Nay, but the Lord shall smite him; or his day shall come to die; or he shall go down into battle, and be swept away* (I Sam. 26:10).

On the other hand, however, let me say that not every virtuous man has his life increased, nor is every sinner's life diminished.

Everything depends rather upon the choice of the Creator and upon what is salutary in each case. Those virtuous individuals, therefore, whose life is not increased, can look forward to reward in the world to come. Again the wicked who have not been cut off before their time in this world have punishment awaiting them in the world to come. This is borne out by the statement of Scripture: *For there is a time there for every purpose and every work* (Eccles. 3: 17).

CHAPTER VII

And now that I have made all these matters clear, it behooves me to explain the state in which the soul finds itself at the time when it leaves the body. I say, then, that our forebears have informed [50] us that the angel who is dispatched by the Creator for the purpose of separating the soul and the body appears to man in the form of a figure of yellowish fire filled with eyes composed of bluish fire and holding in his hand a drawn sword aimed at him. Upon seeing him thus, the person shudders and his spirit separates from his body.

Now when I regarded carefully what is written in Scripture, I found the circumstances described there to correspond exactly to the information they have transmitted to us. For Scripture remarks, apropos of the time of the plague: *And David lifted up his eyes, and saw the angel of the Lord standing between the earth and the heaven, having a sword drawn <205> in his hand stretched out over Jerusalem* (I Chron. 21: 16). Then, after David had prayed and offered sacrifices, Scripture states: *And the Lord commanded the angel; and he put up his sword back into the sheath thereof* (I Chron. 21: 27).

I furthermore found support for the view that the body of the angel [51] is composed of a yellowish fire in the statement of Scripture: *As for the likeness of the living creatures, their appearance was like coals of fire, burning like the appearances of torches* (Ezek,

50. Cf. 'Ābh. Zarah 20b.
51. "angel"—Ibn Tibbon.

1: 13). For the belief, again, that he [52] is completely full of eyes, I can adduce the statement: *And their whole body, and their backs, and their hands, and their wings, and the wheels were full of eyes round about* (Ezek. 10: 12). The indication, moreover, that the light of the eyes is blue is presented by the fact that, if they were yellow like the body, it would be impossible to recognize them as eyes. It is only by a distinction of their color that they are recognizable. Now the color blue has the appearance of the *electrum* which is mentioned in the text (Ezek. 1: 4, 27).

Thou knowest also that at the sight of the great fire our ancestors almost died, as Scripture relates: *Now therefore why should we die? for this great fire will consume us* [53] (Deut. 5: 22). All the more would this happen if such a fiery figure were directed against a human being with a drawn [54] sword. Thou knowest, too, that when the master, *David, peace be upon him,* beheld that angel, even though the latter had no evil intentions so far as he himself was concerned, he was afraid and frightened and made to tremble by him, as Scripture says: *For he was terrified because of the sword of the angel of the Lord* (I Chron. 21: 30). Nor did he cease shivering from that day on until he died, as is attested by Scripture: *And they covered him with clothes, but he could get no heat* (I Kings 1: 1). All the more would this apply to a person for whom [the vision of the angel of death] is intended.

If now someone were to remark, "But we never see the soul depart from the body," our reply would be, "That is due to its transparency and to its resemblance to the air in its fineness, just as we are unable to see the heavenly spheres on account of the purity of their substances and their transparency. In keeping with my custom, let me cite the following example: If a person were to take ten lamps of transparent glass and put one inside the other and place a candle in the innermost of them, he who would see the candle from a distance would not know that it is inside ten lamps,

52. "he"—Ibn Tibbon.
53. This quotation follows the reading of Ibn Tibbon.
54. "drawn"—Ibn Tibbon.

<206> because the light penetrates the substances of these lamps and the vision of the beholder penetrates to the light." This is, then, all very clear.

Next I shall put the question: "But what is the status of the soul after its exit from the body?" and I shall reply, as I have already previously indicated; namely, that it is stored up until the time of retribution, as is stated in Scripture: *And He that keepeth thy soul, doth not He know it? And shall not He render to every man according to his work?* (Prov. 24: 12.)

The place, however, where the pure souls are kept is up on high, while that of the turbid is down below. This corresponds fully with the construction I have put previously [55] on the expression *As the brightness of the firmament* (Dan. 12: 3) and on the statement *Whether it goeth upward* (Eccles. 3: 21). It agrees also with the remark of our early teachers: *The souls of the righteous are stored beneath the throne of glory whilst those of the wicked wander* [56] *about in the world* (Šab. 152b). This and similar distinctions constitute the difference between them.

During the first period after its separation from the body, however, the soul exists for a while without a fixed abode until the body has decomposed; that is to say, until its parts have disintegrated. It consequently experiences during this period much misery, occasioned by its knowledge of the worms and the vermin and the like that pass through the body, just as a person would be pained by the knowledge that a house in which he used to live is in ruins and that thorns and thistles grow in it.

Now this painful experience comes to the soul in varying degrees according to its desert, just as does its rank in the world below. The misery it experiences is, then, in proportion to its deserts. It is with reference to that that our early teachers say: *Vermin are as painful to the dead as a needle to the flesh of a living person* (Šab. 152a). They base this remark on the statement of Scripture:

55. Cf. above, pp. 242 ff.
56. The reading in the common editions of the Babylonian Talmud varies somewhat from that given here.

But his flesh grieveth for him, and his soul mourneth over him (Job 14:22). That is what I understand is called *the judgment of the grave* or *the chastisement of the grave.*[57]

Next let me say that the duration of its existence apart from the body extends until the time when all the souls, the creation of which has been decreed by the wisdom of <207> the Creator, have been collected; [58] that is to say, until the end of the existence of this world. When, then, their number has become full and they have been collected, the souls and their respective bodies will be united again, as I shall explain in the treatise following this one,[59] whereupon God will recompense them according to their deserts.

This thought, as well as the thesis that we have made clear prior to it, is also evident from the statement of the sage. For after declaring: *And the spirit returneth unto God who gave it* (Eccles. 12:7), he informs us that the process through which it passes ends in retribution. For he says after this remark: *The end of the matter, all having been heard. . . . For God shall bring every work into the judgment* (Eccles. 12:13, 14). When he says *every work,* he has reference, of course, to both the body and the soul. When, again, he employs the expression *concerning every hidden thing* (Eccles. 12:14), he means thereby that any misrepresentation or forgery on the part of the soul that might be hidden from us is revealed to God. At that time, then, God will bring the soul from heaven and the body from the earth and give them both their recompense, as Scripture says: *He calleth to the heavens above, and to the earth, that He may judge His people* (Ps. 50:4). Praised, therefore, be the All-Wise and blessed be He, and let us ask Him to lead us on the road [60] of virtue. So far as the nature of the reward and the punishment destined for man in the hereafter is concerned, however, I shall, with the help of the Merciful One, explain that in the ninth treatise.

57. Cf. Ta'ān. 11a.
58. Cf. the references to the Talmudic sources, Guttmann, p. 211, n. 1.
59. Cf. pp. 264 ff.
60. "road"—added by Ibn Tibbon,

CHAPTER VIII

Now I deem it proper to append to these observations a reference to the point of disagreement existing among those who differ about the nature of the substance of the soul and who have
expressed themselves in regard to its fate after death. For I find
that those who assert that it is a material thing of airy [61] or fiery [62]
substance and most of those who affirm that it is an accident [63] all
maintain that the soul decomposes and disintegrates and disap-
pears.[64] Those, again, who are of the opinion that it is derived
from spiritual beings, or from its Creator only, or from Him and
something else, or from two principles existing since eternity,[65]
maintain unanimously that the soul returns after death to the
source from which it originated. However, I have already demonstrated the untenability of all these theories and refuted them.

Yet I must say that I have found certain people, who call themselves Jews, professing the doctrine of metempsychosis, <208>
which is designated by them as the theory of the "transmigration"
of souls. What they mean thereby is that the spirit of Reuben
is transferred to Simon and afterwards to Levi and after that to
Judah. Many of them would even go so far as to assert that the
spirit of a human being might enter into the body of a beast or
that of a beast into the body of a human being, and other such
nonsense and stupidities.

Now I have studied the considerations which, they maintain,
led them to accept this doctrine, and found that they consisted of
four mistaken premises, which I deem it proper to list now and refute. The first is that they adhere to the theory of the spiritualists
and the three other theories,[66] or they are unaware of the fact that
the advocates of the doctrine of transmigration have derived it
from the theory of the dualists and the spiritualists. However, the

61. Cf. p. 237.
62. Cf. p. 237.
63. Cf. p. 236.
64. Cf. Guttmann, p. 211.
65. Cf. p. 236 and notes 2–5.
66. Cf. above, n. 65.

arguments against all these views have already been set forth and noted by me.

The second basis of their conclusion is that they observed [67] the traits of many human beings and found them to resemble those of the beasts. [They saw, for example, that there were] persons [68] who were gentle like sheep, and others who were violent like wild animals, and such as were malicious and contemptible like dogs, and others, again, who were flighty like birds, and so forth. These observations provided support for their view that the aforementioned traits were acquired by the persons in question by virtue of their possessing the souls of the respective beasts.

This in itself, however, indicates how very foolish they are. For they take it for granted that the body of man is capable of transforming the essence of the soul so as to make of it a human soul after having been the soul of a beast. They assume, furthermore, that the soul itself is capable of transforming the essence of the human body to the point of endowing it with the traits of the beasts even though its form be that of men. It was not sufficient for them, then, that they attributed to the soul a variable nature by not assigning to it an intrinsic essence, but they contradicted themselves when they declared the soul capable of transforming and changing the body and the body capable of transforming and changing the soul. But such reasoning is a deviation from logic.

The third [argument they present] is in the form of a logical argument. They say, namely: "Inasmuch as [69] the Creator is just, it is inconceivable that He should occasion suffering to little children, unless it be for sins committed by their souls during the time that they were lodged in their former <209> bodies." This view is, however, subject to numerous refutations.

The first is that they have forgotten what we have mentioned on the subject [70] of compensation in the hereafter for misfortunes experienced in this world.[71] Furthermore we should like to ask

67. "they observed"—Ibn Tibbon.
68. "persons who"—Ibn Tibbon.
69. "inasmuch as"—Ibn Tibbon.
70. "subject"—Ibn Tibbon.
71. He is referring to the theory mentioned in the fifth treatise, p. 214.

them what they conceive the original status of the soul to be—we mean its status when it is first created. Is it charged by its Master with any obligation to obey Him or not? If they allege that it is not so charged, then there can be no punishments for it either, since it was not charged with any obligations to begin with. If, on the other hand, they acknowledge the imposition of such a charge, in which case obedience or disobedience did not apply to the soul theretofore,[72] they thereby admit that God charges His servants with obligations on account of the future [73] and not at all on account of the past. But then they return to our theory of compensation and are forced to give up their insistence on the view that man's suffering in this world is due solely to his conduct in a previous existence.

The fourth [cause of their mistaken conclusions] is their dependence on faulty interpretations of the Bible. Of these I consider it appropriate to mention a few examples. As one of these I might cite the statement made by Moses, peace be upon him: *But with him that standeth here with us this day before the Lord our God, and also with him that is not here with us this day* (Deut. 29: 14). This, they say, proves that the souls of the latest generations were identical with those of the earliest, wherefore those present and those absent were one and the same. However, the simple meaning of that verse negates their viewpoint, because it states explicitly that he who is present is someone else than he who is absent. Its import, in fine, is that those to whom the message of Moses has come by tradition are just as much obliged to accept it as those that were present to receive it.

Another instance of misinterpretation is that of the Biblical verse: *Happy is the man that hath not walked in the counsel of the wicked* (Ps. 1: 1). They say, namely, that the fact that Scripture uses the expression *hath not walked* and not that of *will not walk* indicates to us that the punishment is meted out for evil done by the soul in the past while it was in its first body. But this is a grave error on their part, because Scripture can decree that the person

72. "obedience or . . . theretofore"—Ibn Tibbon, and M as corrected in the notes to the Arabic text.

73. i.e., for the sake of future compensation. Cf. Guttmann, p. 213.

in question will be *happy* only after *he hath not walked*. It cannot do so before *he will not walk*. The explicit meaning of the verse, therefore, refutes their view.

Furthermore, if it were as they put it, then reward would be conferrable only for future good deeds, not for those of the past, by reason of the fact that the expression used by Scripture in the sequel is *And in His law he shall* [74] *meditate* (Ps. 1:2) and not that of *he hath meditated,* <210> by the same token that they concluded that punishments are meted out for past evils and not those of the future from the fact that the phraseology employed by Scripture is: *Happy . . . is he that hath not walked* and not *that will not walk*.

Another verse that has been misinterpreted by them is: *It is changed as clay under the seal; and they stand as a garment* (Job 38:14). They namely construed the expression *It is changed* as referring to the soul, asserting that this proves that it alternates continually between men and beasts. They did not realize, however, the fools, that this predication was in reality made of the earth, for the statement immediately preceding is: *That it might take hold of the ends of the earth, and the wicked be shaken out of it* (Job 38:13). It is about the earth [75] that the assertion is made that it is transformed by virtue of the misfortunes, due to the *wicked*, like clay under the seal, and that they cling to it as though they were its garment, unable to be stripped off from it until God's sentence concerning them has been executed.

A further misunderstanding on their part is that applying to the remark of the saint: *He will restore* [76] *my soul* (Ps. 28:3). They thought, namely, that this implied a shuttling from body to body, not recalling, ignoramuses that they are, that it referred to the relaxation and rest and repose of the soul from the excitement experienced by it, not to a restoration after its departure from a body.

The meaning of the expression in the language of our early an-

74. "he shall"—the usual translation is "doth he."
75. "about the earth"—Ibn Tibbon.
76. "will restore"—the usual translation is "restoreth."

cestors is quite clear and evident. Thus they said [77] of Samson, when he was thirsty and his Master gave him water to drink: *His spirit came back and he revived* (Judg. 15: 19), although it had actually never departed from him. Similarly they said of the Egyptian who was hungry and who was fed by David, peace be upon him, *And his spirit came back to him* (I Sam. 30: 12). Again Scripture says of the faithful messenger: *So is a faithful messenger to him that sendeth him; for he restoreth [78] the soul of his master* (Prov. 25: 13). It also says of the Law: *The law of the Lord is perfect, restoring the soul* (Ps. 19: 8). I would have bewared of discussing the error of their theory and guarded against discoursing about its worthlessness were it not that I was afraid of the evil influence [of this viewpoint upon others].

Lastly [I must cite of the examples of misunderstanding] their quotation [in support of their theory] of the Scriptural statement: *Come from the four winds, O spirit,[79] and breathe upon these slain, that they may live* (Ezek. 37: 9). I ask, however: <211> "What is there in [all] this that points conclusively to [the doctrine of] metempsychosis?" The only reason this thought has been expressed as it is here is that the winds have their fixed abode in the upper and lower regions. In whichever of these two sides they might be, therefore—aye, even if they should be in their four directions—they must come forward when their Master calls them. This is also borne out by the statement of the saint: *Thou wouldst call, and I would answer Thee; Thou wouldst have a desire to the work of Thy hands* (Job 14: 15).

The sixth treatise has hereby been completed.

77. "they said"—Ibn Tibbon.
78. "restoreth"—the usual translation is "refresheth."
79. "spirit"—the usual translation is "breath."

TREATISE VII

CONCERNING THE RESURRECTION OF THE DEAD IN THIS WORLD

CHAPTER I

THE author of this book declares that, as far as the doctrine of the resurrection of the dead is concerned—which we have been informed by our Master will take place in the next world in order to make possible the execution of retribution—it is a matter upon which our nation is in complete agreement. The basis of this conclusion is a premise mentioned previously in the first treatises of this book: namely, that man is the goal of all creation.[1] The reason why he has been distinguished above all other creatures is that he might serve God, and the reward for this service is life eternal in the world of recompense. Prior to this event, whenever He sees fit to do so, God separates man's spirit from his body until the time when the number of souls meant to be created has been fulfilled, whereupon God brings about the union of all bodies and souls again, as I have explained.

We consequently do not know of any Jew who would disagree with this belief. Nor is it hard for him to understand how his Master can bring the dead to life, since he has already accepted as a certainty the doctrine of *creatio ex nihilo*. The restoration by God of aught that has disintegrated or decomposed should, therefore, present no difficulty to him.

Furthermore God has transmitted to us in writing the fact that there would be a resurrection of the dead at the time of the [Messianic] *redemption*, which has been borne out by means of miraculous proofs. It is in regard to this point that I have found a difference of opinion to exist: namely, as to whether there will be a

1. Cf. pp. 180 ff.

resurrection of the dead in this world.[2] For the masses of our nation assert that it will come about at the time of the *redemption*. They namely interpret all verses of the Bible in which they find references to the resurrection of the dead in their exoteric sense and set the time to which they refer as being unquestionably that of the *redemption*.

I have noted, moreover, <212> that some few of the Jewish nation interpret every verse in which they find mention made of the resurrection of the dead at the time of the *redemption* as referring to the revival of a Jewish government and the restoration of the nation. Whatever, on the other hand, is not dated as taking place at the time of the *redemption* is applied by them to the world to come. I have, therefore, dedicated the present treatise specifically to this subject.

Let me say here, then, that I have inquired and investigated and verified the belief of the masses of the Jewish nation that the resurrection of the dead would take place at the time of the *redemption*. I have, therefore, seen fit to write it down in order that it might serve as direction and guidance like the preceding observations of this book.

CHAPTER II

And so I declare, first of all, that it is a well-known fact that every statement found in the Bible is to be understood in its literal sense except for those that cannot be so construed for one of the following four reasons. It may, for example, either be rejected by the observation of the senses, such as the statement: *And the man called his wife's name Eve; because she was the mother of all living* (Gen. 3:20), whereas we see that the ox and the lion are not the offspring of womankind. Hence we must needs conclude that the implication of the statement embraces human descendants only.

Or else the literal sense may be negated by reason, such as that

2. Cf. the differences of opinion among the teachers of the Talmud in Běr. 34b and Šab. 63a.

of the statement: *For the Lord thy God is a devouring fire, a jealous God* (Deut. 4:24). Now fire is something created and defective, for it is subject to extinction. Hence it is logically inadmissible that God resemble it. We must, therefore, impute to this statement the meaning that God's punishment is like a consuming fire, in accordance with the remark made elsewhere in Scripture: *For all the earth shall be devoured with the fire of My jealousy* (Zeph. 3:8).

Again, [the literal meaning of a Biblical statement may be rendered impossible] by an explicit text of a contradictory nature, in which case it would become necessary to interpret the first statement in a non-literal sense. Thus, for example, it is said in Scripture: *Ye shall not try the Lord your God, as ye tried Him in Massah* (Deut. 6:16). And it is also said, on the other hand: *And try Me now herewith . . . if I will not open you the windows of heaven* (Mal. 3:10). Now the point wherein these two statements agree is that we must not test our Lord as to whether He is able to do a certain thing, as they did of whom it is reported: *And they tried God in their heart by asking food for their craving. Yea, they spoke against God;* <213> *they said: "Can God prepare a table in the wilderness?"* (Ps. 78:18, 19.) It is to these that the remark *as ye tried Him in Massah* refers. It is, however, permissible for a servant of God to test his Master's power by asking whether it be possible for Him to create a miracle in his behalf. Such a request was indeed made by Gideon, who said: *Let me make trial, I pray Thee, but this once with the fleece* (Judg. 6:39). It was also done by Hezekiah (II Kings 20:8) and others.

Finally any Biblical statement to the meaning of which rabbinic tradition has attached a certain reservation is to be interpreted by us in keeping with this authentic tradition. Thus it has been transmitted to us that the punishment of stripes consists of thirty-nine blows, although Scripture states: *Forty stripes he may give him* (Deut. 25:3). We therefore adopt the view that this is just a rough way of saying that there be thirty-nine stripes. The text of Scripture has merely expressed this thought in round numbers, as it has done in the statement: *After the number of the days in which ye spied out the land, even forty days, for every day a year shall ye bear your iniquities, even forty years* [3] (Num. 14: 34). For in reality there were only thirty-nine years, since the first year of Israel's sojourn in the wilderness did not enter into this punishment.

There exist, then, only these four possible reasons for a non-literal interpretation of the verses of Sacred Writ, there being no fifth. So far as the resurrection of the dead is concerned, however, we have seen it [take place], and there is no eyewitness to contradict it, for we do not allege that they will come to life of their own accord but merely that their Creator will bring them to life. Furthermore, there is no rational objection to the doctrine [of resurrection] because the restoration of something that has once existed and disintegrated is more plausible logically than *creatio ex nihilo.* Moreover, there is no other pronouncement of Scripture to contradict the belief in resurrection, but, on the contrary, the text of Sacred Writ confirms it by expressly citing the resurrection in this world of the son of the *Zarephite* (I Kings 17: 22) and that of the *Shunammite* (II Kings 4: 35) woman. Finally, there exists no rabbinic tradition necessitating the non-literal interpretation of this concept, but, on the contrary, all traditions corroborate it.

Hence we must let this belief stand as it is according to the explicit statement of the text of Scripture that God will bring the dead of His nation to life again at the time of the *redemption,* and it is not to be interpreted otherwise. How, indeed, could that be done when the passages in which the resurrection of the dead is mentioned [in Scripture] indicate specifically that it is to take place in this world?

CHAPTER III

After these prefatory remarks let me say that [for example] the poem *Give ear* (Deut. 32: 1 ff.), which reviews in chronological order the fortunes of the *children of Israel,* starts out with the time when our Master first elected us. It says, namely: *Remember*

3. This quotation is based on the reading of Ibn Tibbon.

<214> *the days of old, consider the years of many generations,* . . . . *When the Most High gave to the nations their inheritance.* . . . *For the portion of the Lord is His people* (Deut. 32:7–9). It then points out, in the second place, how God favored us, saying: *He found him in a desert land* (Deut. 32:10). Thereupon, in the third strophe, it speaks of our haughtiness and our sins, saying: *But Jeshurun waxed fat, and kicked* (Deut. 32:15). The fourth strophe deals with our punishment. It says, namely: *And the Lord saw, and spurned* (Deut. 32:19), and all that follows. Then the fifth strophe speaks of the punishment of our enemies, saying: *For their vine is of the vine of Sodom* (Deut. 32:32). The sixth, again, dwells on our consolation and the help to be extended to us, by telling us: *See that I, even I, am He* (Deut. 32:39), and so forth until the end of the poem.

Now according to this chronological order, God's statement: *I kill, and I make alive; I have wounded, and I heal* (*ibid.*) applies to the days of the *redemption.* Lest, however, we get the impression that the meaning hereof is the putting to death of certain people and the bringing to life of others, in accordance with the nature of the world, He goes on to say: *I have wounded, and I heal* (*ibid.*). [This is done] in order to inform us that, just as the body that has been made sick is the same as that which is healed, so the body that has been put to death is the one that is to be brought back to life.

It is, furthermore, indicated to us that all this is to transpire at the time of the *redemption,* for He states in the sequel: *For I lift up My hand to heaven,* . . . . *If I whet My glittering sword.* . . . *I will make Mine arrows drunk with blood.* . . . *Sing aloud, O ye nations, of His people* (Deut. 32:40–43), i.e., in the sense of *Sing with gladness for Jacob* . . . [*Announce ye,* . . . *and say: "O Lord, save Thy people, the remnant of Israel"*] (Jer. 31:6).

Furthermore let me say that because the Creator was aware of the scruples aroused in our hearts by the difficulty we have in accepting the doctrine of the resurrection of the dead, He apprised His prophet Ezekiel thereof in advance, saying to him: *Son of man, these bones are the whole house of Israel; behold, they say:*

Our bones are dried up, and our hope is lost; we are clean cut off (Ezek. 37: 11). Then He ordered him to bring us the good tidings of our resurrection from our graves and of the resuscitation of all our dead, by saying to him immediately thereafter: *Therefore prophesy, and say unto them: . . . Behold, I will open your graves, and cause you to come up out of your graves, O My people* (Ezek 37: 12).

Lest, however, we think that this promise was made only for the world to come, He added at the end of the statement the words *And I will bring you into the land* <215> *of Israel (ibid.)* in order to assure us that it was meant to take place in this world. The object to be attained thereby is that each one of us will, when God has brought him back to life, make mention of the fact that it is he that was alive and died and was then resurrected That is the import of His statement: *And ye shall know that I am the Lord, when I have opened your graves* (Ezek. 37: 13). The mention of the resurrection [4] in the land of Palestine is then repeated by Him a second time in order to confirm for us the thought that it is to take place in this world, as He says: *And I will put My spirit in you, and ye shall live, and I will place you in your own land; and ye shall know that I the Lord have spoken, and performed it, saith the Lord* (Ezek. 37: 14).

I say, moreover, that the prophet *Isaiah* [5] announced something similiar to this promise when he said: *Thy dead shall live, my dead bodies shall arise* [6] (Isa. 26: 19), which corresponds to the statement made by God [in the book of Ezekiel]: *Our bones are dried up, and our hope is lost* (Ezek. 37: 11). Again, the prophet's likening this situation to that of a person who awakes from his sleep, as he says: *Awake and sing* (Isa. 26: 19), corresponds to God's statement in the book of Ezekiel: *And ye shall know that I am the Lord, when I have opened your graves* (Ezek. 37: 13). The comparison of resurrection, furthermore, to *the dew of light* (Isa. 26: 19) is prompted by the fact that this process involves the use

4 "resurrection"—Cf. Lane-Poole, p. 1296, *sab'*.
5. "Isaiah"—added by Ibn Tibbon.
6. This quotation follows the reading of Ibn Tibbon.

of four elements. The dust is, of course, already present. As for the moisture, that is added by our Lord and is implied in the word *dew*. Next God endows the dead with the spirit, which is implied in the expression *light*, because the soul is luminous like light,[7] as we have explained previously.

And the earth shall cause the shades to fall [8] (*ibid*.) means that the godless will fall to the ground and be degraded, as we have explained before. The same applies to those that do not know what their Master has commanded or forbidden. This is borne out by the statement of Scripture: *The man that strayeth out of the way of understanding shall rest in the congregation of the shades* (Prov. 21:16).

Next let me state that I find that Daniel was informed by our Lord about what was to come to pass at the end of time in forty-seven verses. Among these there is one verse that speaks of what was to transpire at the end of the rule of the Persians; that is to say, the [very] first. Thirteen of these verses again deal with the history of the kingdom of the Greeks, i.e., beginning with [the words]: *And a mighty king shall stand up, that shall rule with great dominion, and do according to his will* (Dan. 11:3), and extending up to *But he that cometh against him shall do according to his own will* (Dan. 11:16). Twenty other verses dwell on the history of the empire of the Romans, i.e., beginning with [the words]: *But he that cometh against him shall do according to his own will* (*ibid*.), and extending up to *And the king shall do according to his will* (Dan. 11:36). Ten further verses constitute the history of the dominion of the Arabs, <216> i.e., beginning with [the words]: *And the king shall do according to his will; and he shall exalt himself, and magnify himself* (*ibid*.) up to *And at that time shall Michael stand up, the great prince* (Dan. 12:1). The last three verses, finally, deal with the subject of the *redemption*.

Now one of these last three verses declares: *And many of them*

7. Cf. pp. 242 ff.
8. "cause the shades to fall"—the usual translation is: "bring to life the shades."

that sleep in the dust of the earth shall awake, some to everlasting life, and some to reproaches (Dan. 12:2). Note that it says specifically: *And many of them that sleep,* not *All of them that sleep in the dust of the earth,* because *All of them that sleep in the dust of the earth* would have implied that all the sons of Adam were included, whereas this promise was valid for the children of Israel only. That is why it says *many.*

Furthermore the statement: *Some to everlasting life, and some . . .* (*ibid.*) does not mean that some of those that are resurrected are destined for reward and some for punishment, since no one will be resurrected at the time of the *redemption* who is subject to punishment. It means rather, by division of the statement, that those that *will awake* will do so *to everlasting life,* whereas those that *will not awake* are destined *for reproaches and everlasting abhorrence.* For all the virtuous and penitent persons will be alive and there will remain only the godless and whoever died impenitent, and all that at the time of the *redemption.*

Now there may, of course, be those who would resort to a nonliteral interpretation of these verses who would construe them as referring to something else than the resurrection of the dead. They might, for instance, say that we find that in the language of Scripture a person of lowly fortunes who has been uplifted by God is spoken of as having been raised by Him from the dust. Thus it is stated: *Who raiseth up the poor out of the dust . . . that He may set him with princes* (Ps. 113:7, 8). Scripture likewise speaks of a commoner who has been given a position of leadership in such terms as the statement: *Forasmuch as I exalted thee out of the dust* (I Kings 16:2). On the other hand, it compares the multiplicity of misfortunes and adversities to the dead, for it says: *Set apart among the dead, like the slain that lie in the grave* (Ps. 88:6). Man's release from his misfortunes, again, is likened to resurrection, as Scripture says: *Thou, who hast made me to see many and sore troubles, wilt quicken me again* (Ps. 71:20). It says, furthermore: *Wilt Thou not quicken us again, that Thy people may rejoice in Thee* (Ps. 85:7)?

CHAPTER IV

To him who presents such arguments we wish to point out that his method is erroneous because it is not admissible that a verse [of Scripture] be construed <217> in any other than its literal sense except for one of the four reasons mentioned by us previously.[9] Where, however, none of these reasons exists, the verses are to be taken in their explicit meaning. For if it were necessary to construe every verse of Sacred Writ in whatever figurative sense is possible without compelling proof, not a single revealed law would be maintained, since they are all capable of such non-literal interpretation.

Let me present several detailed illustrations of the above and say that, for example, the statement of the Torah: *Ye shall kindle no fire [throughout your habitations upon the sabbath day]* (Exod. 35:3) might allegorically be taken to mean "Do not set up armies in battle array on the Sabbath day," corresponding to Scripture's remark elsewhere: *For a fire is gone out of Heshbon, a flame [from the city of Sihon; it hath devoured Ar of Moab]* (Num. 21:28).

The injunction, again, of *There shall no leavened bread be eaten* (Exod. 13:3) might be construed allegorically as signifying refraining from fornication, in keeping with the statement made by Scripture elsewhere: *They are all adulterers, as an oven heated by the baker, who ceaseth to stir from the kneading of the dough until it be leavened* (Hos. 7:4).

Furthermore the commandment, *Thou shalt not take the mother* [10] *with the young* (Deut. 22·6) would be interpreted as meaning, "Do not kill an old man and his children in war," just as it does in the statement of Jacob: *Lest he come and smite me, the mother with the children* (Gen. 32:12), and as Scripture says elsewhere: *The mother was dashed in pieces with her children* (Hos. 10:14).

Also, if this kind of interpretation is necessary for the legal sec-

9. Cf. p. 265.
10. "mother"—the usual translation is "dam."

tion of Scripture, it must likewise apply to the narrative portion. Consequently the statement of the Torah: *And the children of Israel went into the midst of the sea upon dry ground; and the waters were a wall unto them* [11] (Exod. 14:22) might be interpreted allegorically to mean that they entered midway between the armies, since in the language of Scripture armies are compared to bodies of water. Thus Scripture says: *Behold, waters rise up out of the north, and shall become an overflowing stream, and they shall overflow the land and all that is therein* (Jer. 47:2). It says also: *Now therefore, behold, the Lord bringeth up upon them the waters of the River, mighty and many, even the king of Assyria and all his glory* (Isa. 8:7).

Similarly the statement of Scripture: *And the sun stood still, and the moon stayed, until the nation had avenged themselves of their enemies* (Josh. 10:13) could be interpreted allegorically to mean that the government would be firmly established and the kingdom maintain itself, in accordance with the statement made elsewhere: <218> *Thy sun shall no more go down, neither shall thy moon withdraw itself* (Isa. 60:20).

The only correct principle on which to proceed, therefore, is that a verse is not to be diverted from its obvious and generally recognized meaning except on the ground of one of the four reasons that I have described. Wherever such grounds do not exist, however, the verse is to be taken in its simple sense.

CHAPTER V

Yet there are still likely to arise in somebody's mind uncertainties in regard to the meaning of certain verses, leading him to think that they negate the idea of a resurrection of the dead in this world. I have, therefore, deemed it proper to mention them and make clear the purpose they have in view. I say, then, that there are three types of uncertainties, each one of which is to be clarified in its own specific manner. The first of these is of the order of the statement of the servant of God who said: *Oh remember that*

11. This quotation follows the reading of Ibn Tibbon.

my life is a breath. . . . The eye of him that seeth me shall behold me no more; while Thine eyes are upon me, I am gone. As the cloud is consumed and vanisheth away, so he that goeth down to the grave shall come up no more. He shall return no more to his house (Job 7: 7–10). He asked also: *If a man die, may he live again?* (Job. 14: 14.) Furthermore he declared: *So man lieth down and riseth not* (Job 14: 12).

Now the saints do not mean to imply, when they make such remarks, that the Creator is incapable of bringing the dead to life. How, indeed, can one reproach Him therewith when it is known that He is omnipotent? Hence their intention in making the above-mentioned statements could only have been to describe man's impotence after his descent into the grave and his inability to resurrect his soul or to awake from his sleep or to return to his dwelling. They say in effect: "O God, have pity on a servant who is so helpless and in need of Thy mercy."

The second [type of verses requiring elucidation] is of the order of such statements of Scripture as: *So He remembered that they were but flesh; a wind that passeth away, and cometh not again* (Ps. 78: 39); and *As for man, his days are as grass; as a flower of the field, so he flourisheth. For the wind passeth over it, and it is gone* (Ps. 103: 15, 16).

Now the object of these verses is to indicate that one of the reasons for God's mercy on His servants is His knowledge of their weakness and of the inability on the part of their spirits to return to their bodies or their dwellings of their own accord. It is by no means, however, intended thereby to imply that their Creator is unable to restore them. On the contrary, the more this condition of impotence is described as applying to men, the greater, as a consequence, does the ability of the Creator to do these things loom. <219> Utterances of this nature are of the same tenor as the expression of amazement on the part of Scripture over the assembly at Mount Sinai, when it says: *For ask now of the days past, which were before thee, . . . whether there hath been any such thing as this great thing is, or hath been heard like it, etc*

(Deut. 4:32). In fact, it is chiefly through the impotence of His creatures that the omnipotence of God becomes evident.

[An example,] again, of the third type [of verses presenting difficulty so far as the doctrine of resurrection is concerned] is such a statement as: *For him that is joined to all the living there is hope; for a living dog is better than a dead lion. For the living know that they shall die; but the dead know not anything,* etc. . . . *As well their love, as their hatred and their envy, is long ago perished,* etc. (Eccles. 9:4-6). Now although these three verses were pronounced by the sage, they do not represent his personal opinion. They are rather a quotation of the view of the foolish, because they are preceded by an account of the agitation aroused in the hearts of the foolish by this condition. He says, namely: *Yea also, the heart of the sons of men is full of evil, and madness is in their heart while they live, and after that they go to the dead* (Eccles. 9:3).

Then, after having first stated that men have *evil and madness* in their hearts by reason of their life as well as of death, he explains what is actually in their hearts by expressing it in the three [subsequent] verses. The import of these verses is that, in the opinion of these fools, a living dog is better than a dead lion and that the living know what they are going forward to but the dead do not know anything, for all their activities are over and they have no more portion in this world.

Since, however, the sage does not make these statements before prefacing them with the observation that they represent the agitations of the fools and their evils, therefore whoever adheres to these views is a fool, a person who does not turn toward God and does not prepare to meet, aye who does not draw near, the presence of the light of his Master. For men of *evil and madness* stand aside from God, as it is said: *Evil shall not sojourn with Thee. Madmen* [12] *shall not stand in Thy sight* (Ps. 5:5, 6).

12. "Madmen"—the usual translation is "The boasters."

CHAPTER VI

I next inquired into what has been transmitted by rabbinic tradition, and I learned that it presented a view similar to this: namely, that anyone that does not profess the belief in the resurrection of the dead in this world will not be resurrected together with the totality of the Jewish nation at the time of the *redemption*. That is the import of the dictum of our sages: *Since he does not believe in the resurrection <220> of the dead, therefore he shall have no portion in it, because in all His dealings the Holy One, Blessed Be He, metes out measure for measure. For it has been said: "Then the captain on whose hand the king leaned answered the man of God, and said: 'Behold, if the Lord should make windows in heaven, might this thing be?' And he said: 'Behold, thou shalt see it with thine eyes, but shalt not eat thereof.' (II Kings 7:2)"* (Sanh. 90a).

It is also reported in the traditions of our sages in explanation of the prophetic utterance: *Then shall we raise against him seven shepherds, and eight princes among men* (Mic. 5:4), that the *seven* were *David in the center, Adam, Seth, and Methuselah on his right, and Abraham, Jacob, and Moses on his left;* and that the *eight princes* were *Jesse, Saul, Samuel, Amos, Zephaniah, Hezekiah, Elijah, and the Messiah* (Suk. 52b).

It has furthermore been transmitted by rabbinic tradition that when the dead are resurrected by their Creator, their clothes will also be put on them again,[13] which is no more remarkable than the restoration to the dead of their souls. Now when this report became widespread among the masses of our nation, people went to such excesses in their expenditures for the burial garments of their deceased that the burden became too heavy for them, until one of the scholars alleviated it by asking for moderation in the shrouds to be used for him. That is the import of the statement of our teachers: *At the beginning the expenditure on behalf of the dead used to weigh so heavily upon those who were charged therewith, that they would abandon the body and run away. Then*

13. Cf. Kĕth. 111b.

came Rabban Gamaliel and set the example of the disregard of custom through himself when he had himself carried out in ironed linen garments, whereupon all the people followed his example (M.Ḳ. 27b).

CHAPTER VII

Having elaborated on the aforementioned statements, let me now say, by way of pressing further my inquiry into the subject of the resurrection of the dead, of those to be resuscitated at the time of the *redemption* as well as of those to be resurrected in the world to come, that perhaps someone might wonder, saying: "[It is maintained] that, when the first generation of men dies, the elements of which their bodies are composed disintegrate, each part returning to its original source—I mean that the heat rejoins the [element of] fire and becomes mingled with it, and the moisture with the air, and the coldness with the [element of] water, while the dryness remains dust. Thereupon [it is believed] the Creator puts together the bodies of the second generation out of the source materials <221> with which the disintegrated parts of the first generation have been mingled. Then the second generation of men dies and their parts mingle with the sources of the elements too. After that the Creator makes up out of them a third generation and the same thing happens to it that happened to the two preceding ones, and so for the fourth and the fifth. [If all this be so,] how is it conceivable that the first generation could be completely restored by Him and thus also the second and the third, when a part of each generation has already entered into the other?"

Now I can explain this very satisfactorily by saying that the employment of the decomposed portions of the bodies of the first generation in composing the bodies of the second would be necessary only if it were those parts alone that remained in existence. In that case they would have to be used over again perpetually. Let me cite as a parable hereof the case of a person who has in his possession silver vessels worth a thousand drachmas and [suppose] that there are no others in existence. Whenever they would be broken, he would bring them back to the foundry and the silversmith's shop. On the other hand, however, he who possesses treasure houses and gives the assurance that he will take away the fragments of any vessels that may break so as to make them over again into the selfsame vessels—such a person would take from his treasure house the new things produced and not mix therewith the fragment of any broken vessel. Nay he would set aside the latter until he had made them over as he had promised.

On the basis of this assumption, then, I made my investigation and I found that the sources of air and fire that are located between the earth and the first part of the heavens were equivalent in volume to 1008 times the entire mass of the earth and its mountains and seas. With such latitude there was certainly no reason for the Creator to compose the bodies of any second generation out of the decomposed parts of the first. Nay, He would merely set the latter aside until He would fulfill for them what He had promised.

However, someone might also wonder and ask: "But suppose a lion were to eat a man, and then the lion would drown and a fish would eat him up, and then the fish would be caught and a man would eat him, and then the man would be burned and turn into ashes. Whence would the Creator restore the first man? Would He do it from the lion or the fish or the second man or the fire or the ashes?"

Now it seems to me that this is a matter that causes confusion to believers, and I therefore deem it proper to preface my answer by a preliminary observation. I say, then, that it is necessary <222> for us to know that there exists no object in the world that could completely annihilate another. Even fire, which causes things to be burned so quickly, merely effects a separation of the parts of a thing and a reunion between each part and its original element, causing the dust part to turn into ashes. It does not, however, bring about the annihilation of anything. Nor is it conceivable that anyone should have the power to annihilate anything to the point where it would vanish completely except its Creator, who produced it out of nothing. Since, then, this theory is undoubtedly correct, any animal that has devoured a certain body has not thereby annihilated it but merely brought about a disintegration of its component parts.

I say, moreover, that the cause which compels every animal to seek nourishment is the fact that the air withdraws from the body the three constituent elements: namely, the heat, the moisture, and the coldness. Nor is it in animals alone that this withdrawal is effected by the air, but also in every vegetable. The proof hereof is that, if we were to leave a flat-cake of bread in a house for a long period of time, we would find the air to have withdrawn from it the three above-mentioned elements, leaving in it only the element of earth. Hence the bodies of animals are always in need of nourishment in order that there may be a material reserve within them that the air will not draw out. For if the air did not find any food particles to draw from, it would draw upon the basic elements of the body and the body would perish.

I say, furthermore, that when a person eats an apple, the air extracts from his body the heat and the moisture and the coldness that were contained in the apple and only the earthy part remains, which turns into refuse that is excreted. It thereby becomes clear that the constituent parts of the apple disintegrate, three of them being absorbed by the air whilst the fourth is taken up by the earth. Inasmuch, however, as the apple has not been promised by its Creator that it will be restored, its parts become mingled with the great sources, each part rejoining its original element.

As for man, on the other hand, by reason of the fact that he has been promised by his Creator that his constituent parts will be gathered and restored to their former position, these parts of his body are set aside, not being mixed with the elemental masses. Rather they remain separate until the time of the resurrection, so much so that even the earthy portion of the human body that has been absorbed <223> by the earth, although it may seem to us as though it has become mingled with the general mass and is thus hidden from us, is yet not hidden from the view of the Creator.

Since, then, the matter can be thus explained, in view of the fact that none of the constituent parts of the human being who has been devoured could have been annihilated, they must all have been set aside, wheresoever they may have been taken up, whether it be on land or in the sea, until such time as they are to be restored in their entirety. Nor would such a restoration be any more remarkable than their original creation.

However, one might perhaps wonder and ask: "Will these individuals who are destined to be resurrected in this world eat and drink and marry, or will they not do any of these things?" Our reply hereto is that it must be realized by us that they will eat and drink as we do and that they will also marry. This is evident from the fact that the son of the *Zarephite* [14] and the one of the *Shunammite* [15] woman, who were brought back to life in this world, both ate and drank after their revival and were in a fit state for marriage.[16] It has also been stated by one of the scholars of the Talmud that he was a descendant of some of these [persons who had been resurrected in this world] (Sanh. 92b).

A convincing proof of the resurrection of the dead in this world was furthermore furnished by that miracle, which was seen by the master Ezekiel, the priest, and which is published at the beginning of the Biblical passage commencing with the words *The hand of the Lord was upon me* (Ezek. 37: 1), and so forth. The fact, moreover, that these dead appeared to the prophet [in their resuscitated state], as Scripture states: *And the breath came into them, and they lived, and stood up upon their feet, an exceeding great host* (Ezek. 37: 10), served as conclusive evidence to the prophet. So must also the rest of the nation consider it positive evidence of the truth of this doctrine when they see anyone of these resurrected persons with whom they are acquainted, live and stay alive.

Now the life span of these whom God brought back to life, according to Ezekiel, was probably approximately of the same dura-

14. Cf. I Kings 17: 23 ff.
15. Cf. II Kings 4: 35.
16. According to Pirke Rabbi Eliezer, chap. xxxiii, the son of the Zarephite was the prophet Jonah, whose wife (cf. 'Erubh. 96b) is reputed to have made the pilgrimage to the Temple of Jerusalem. The son of the Shunnamite, according to Zohar (I, 7b. Introduction) was the prophet Habakkuk.

tion as that of the son of the Zarephite and of the son of the Shunammite woman. As for those who are destined to be resurrected at the time of the *redemption,* it has been transmitted to us concerning them, by rabbinic tradition, that they will not die again. It has, namely, been remarked by our forebears: *The dead whom the Holy One, Blessed Be He, is destined to resuscitate will not return to their dust again* (Sanh. 92a). Also, when we scrutinize Scripture carefully, we note that it confirms this view, for it declares that the heaven and the earth will disappear, but that the *redemption* will remain. That is the import of its statement: *Lift up your eyes to the heavens, and look upon the earth beneath; for the heavens shall vanish away like smoke, and the earth* <224> *shall wax old like a garment, and they that dwell therein shall die in like manner; but My salvation shall be forever, and My favour shall not be abolished* (Isa. 51:6). Now we know, of course, that the *redemption* is not a substance so that [one could say of it] that it is itself subject to survival. What is, therefore, meant by *the redemption* is rather the persons [who are to be the beneficiaries] of the *redemption,* just as in the statement of Scripture: *The wisdom of women* [17] *buildeth her house* (Prov. 14:1), it is the [human] possessors of wisdom that are referred to.

One might, however, wonder and ask: "How will these [individuals who are resurrected at the time of the redemption] be transported to the next world?" [In reply thereto,] let it be stated that we must realize that the road which will be followed by these who will be brought back to life will be the same as that of all other men for whom the second locality in which they will have their being will be created, so that they will be transferred with the least effort from their first location.

Now one might furthermore remark: "These individuals who are to be resurrected performed while they were alive in this world the functions of eating and drinking and marriage. After their resurrection, however, they will be transferred to the next world and, although they will retain their original nature, they will no longer eat or drink. How is this to be explained?" To

17. "The wisdom of women"—the usual translation is "Every wise woman."

render this comprehensible we need but point to the example of *Moses, our teacher,* of whom we know that he ate and drank like any other human being, and yet, while he was tarrying on the mountain for forty days, he neither ate nor drank (Exod. 34:28), although his physical constitution had undergone no change.

Another question that might be asked is: "In the case in which those to be resurrected were married while they were alive in this world, will each man's wife return to him because of the fact that she had formerly lived with him, or does death dissolve all marital ties?" Our reply thereto is that it was similarly asked by one of the scholars of the Talmud as to whether or not those who will be resurrected will have to have *water of purification* sprinkled on them, and the answer given to him was that, inasmuch as *our teacher Moses* will be with them, it is not necessary for us to rack our brains about the matter.[18] Likewise, apropos of the subject of marriage, I will say that our minds are capable only of grasping our present state. As for what is forbidden or permitted in a situation that has no parallel at all in our earthly existence, such as whether or not marriage bonds will be abrogated for those who are resurrected, we need not concern ourselves therewith, since there will be available in the beyond prophets and prophetic inspiration and divine guidance.

The observation might also be made that, in connection with the first redemption—I mean *the deliverance from Egypt*—we do not find that anyone who was dead was to come to life again. Our reply thereto is that that was due to the fact that the Creator had not included with the promise of redemption that of resurrection, for if He had made such a promise to them, He would have carried it out. He had said only: *And afterward they shall come out with great substance* (Gen. 15:14). In connection with the final redemption, however, the promise of resurrection has been made by Him. There is, therefore, no doubt that it will be fulfilled.

<225> At this point I declare that the reason that prompted [divine] Wisdom, to the extent to which our intellect is able to

18. Cf. Niddah 70b.

fathom it, not to include the promise of resurrection in the first redemption while it did include it in the last, was that the first *enslavement* of Israel was lighter than that to which it is subjected at present. Also its duration was briefer, nor were the masses of Israel dispersed in the manner in which they are now scattered. They were, rather, all of them in one place. Hence even if they were promised but little, they were satisfied and looked forward to it. So far as our present *enslavement* is concerned, however, our Master, exalted and magnified be He, knew that on account of its arduousness and the length of its duration we would not be able to bear up under it without great promises and many good tidings. That is why He rendered the second redemption superior to the first in several respects, one of them being this one—I mean the resurrection of the dead.

To this I might, of my own accord, add certain other advantages. Thus I might point out that, whereas the first redemption was carried out in *haste* (Deut. 16:3) and speed, the last will not take place in such a manner. On the contrary, concerning it Scripture says: *For ye shall not go out in haste* (Isa. 52:12). Also, when our people was redeemed the first time, divine revelations were transmitted to us by the speech of the prophets. In consequence of this last redemption, however, each one of us will be the recipient of such inspiration, so that we would no longer be dependent on one another in the matter of religion, as Scripture says: *And they shall teach no more every man his neighbour* (Jer. 31:34) Moreover, the first redemption was succeeded by Israel's *subjection* to foreigners, whereas the last will not be followed by any such *subjection,* as is said by Scripture: *And there shall no strangers pass through her any more* (Joel 4:17). There are also other similar respects in which the last redemption will surpass the first.

CHAPTER VIII

If someone were to ask now and say, "Whom will those who are destined to be resurrected include?" our answer would be that it will embrace the entire Jewish nation, the virtuous thereof as well as whoever died repentant. This may be inferred from the statement of Scripture: *And I will cause you to come up out of your graves, O My people* (Ezek. 37:12). Anyone, therefore, to whom the designation of *My people* could be applied would be included in this promise. Now I do actually find that the virtuous are called *My people.* Thus Scripture says: *And to say unto Zion: "Thou art My people"* (Isa. 51:16). Of the sinful, again, the impenitent are not called *My people.* This is borne out by the statement of Scripture: *For ye are not My people* (Hos. 1:9). The penitent among them, on the other hand, are called My people, as Scripture says: *And I will say to them that were not My people:* <226> *"Thou art My people"* (Hos. 2:25).

Furthermore, our early teachers declared,[19] when they enumerated the various types of sinners: *One might think that if a person transgressed positive and negative commandments, such as are punishable by extirpation and such as are punishable by the four forms of death sentences to be carried out by the court, or if a person desecrated the name of heaven, his death would not atone for him. Hence the text of Scripture teaches: "Behold, I will open your graves"* (Ezek. 37:12). They have thus informed us that anyone that has repented from whatever sin it be, even from that of unbelief, is included in this promise.

Next let me ask this general question: "Do not we, the congregation of monotheists, acknowledge that the Creator, magnified be His Majesty, will resurrect all the dead in the world to come for the occasion of their retribution?" But what is there in this that would contradict the view that this nation would enjoy an advantage in being granted an additional period during which our dead would be resurrected by God prior to the world to come, that new life of theirs being extended by Him up to the time of the life of the world to come? Why again should there be any cause to prevent this or distrain therefrom, or why should it not be considered as a mere act of justice whereby whoever has been tried

19. Saadia follows the reading of Mĕkhilta on Exod. 20:7, quoting the view of Rabbi.

receives compensation in proportion to his trials, since this nation of ours has been subjected by God to great trials, as Scripture says: *For Thou, O God, hast tried us; Thou hast refined us?* (Ps. 66: 10.) It is most fitting, therefore, that He should grant to it this additional period prior to the world to come so that it might have an advantage over all those who have conducted themselves well in this world, just as its patience and its trials have exceeded those of the others.

Again, if someone were to ask, "If it should happen that God resurrect all the dead of this nation, how would the earth have enough space to contain them?" we would say, in reply thereto, that we tried to figure this matter out and found that from the time that our nation emerged upon the world of men until that of the *redemption* a period of some 2,200 odd years would have elapsed, constituting approximately thirty-two generations, each of which would consist of 1,200,000 men and women. Now even if we were to concede that all of them would be virtuous or penitent so that they would be deserving of being resurrected at the time of the *redemption,* we would find that they would fill up only $\frac{1}{150}$th part of the earth; that is, after allocating to each one of them more than 200 cubits for his dwelling and his fields and his business and other [20] needs. Now if we were to multiply 1,200,000, which is the approximate [average] size of [the population of] the Jewish nation throughout <227> the ages, by 32 generations, which is the number of the generations, the product would be 38,400,000. If, furthermore, we were to cut off for them from the earth a strip of 200 by 200 parasangs, which constitutes $\frac{1}{150}$th part of the earth's area, and we were to compute it in cubits, assuming that every parasang is made up of three miles and that every mile consists of 4,000 cubits, the standard being the Ethiopian cubit which measures two and a half and a third of the ordinary cubit, there would be an area of 288 cubits in breadth [by 500 in length] [21] for each of those to be resurrected. This is, then, some-

20. "other"—Ibn Tibbon.
21. This is the emendation suggested by Solomon Gandz, *Saadia Anniversary Volume* (New York, 1943), p. 189 and notes 165 and 168.

thing that can remain unknown only to those who are not disciples of the learned.

CHAPTER IX

Should someone ask, again, whether the members of their families and their kinsmen would recognize the resurrected and whether they would recognize each other, I might say that I have considered this matter and have arrived at an affirmative conclusion. For the *shepherds* and the *anointed* and the prophets will certainly be recognized [22] by the nation [at the time of the resurrection]. Hence the rank and file will also have to be distinguishable so that the difference between the former and the latter may become evident.

Besides, Scripture has definitely stated that every man will be attached to his tribe, as is explained in the chapter of the book of Ezekiel beginning with the words *Now these are the names of the tribes* (Ezek. 48:1). In fact, even the converts to Judaism will each be related to the tribe whose clients they have become, as it is stated: *And it shall come to pass, that in what tribe the stranger sojourneth, there shall ye give him his inheritance, saith the Lord God* (Ezek. 47:23).

Should the question be asked now as to whether persons afflicted with a blemish will be resurrected with their blemish still attaching to them or whether they will be cured thereof, we would reply that they will be cured. This is borne out by the statement of our forebears to the effect that *They will rise from their graves with their blemish attached to them and then be cured* (Sanh. 91b). It is, furthermore, based on the statement of Scripture: *I kill, and I make alive; I have wounded, and I heal* (Deut. 32:39), as well as on the declaration: *Then the eyes of the blind shall be opened, [and the ears of the deaf shall be unstopped.] Then shall the lame man leap as a hart, and [the tongue of the dumb] shall sing* (Isa. 35:5, 6).

One might ask, moreover, whether those who are destined to be

22. Cf. Suk. 52b.

resurrected at the time of the *redemption* will be capable of rebellion against God or not. For, if they should not be invested with the power to do that, they would be subject to duress. On the other hand, if they should possess that power, the question arises as to what would happen to them in such an event. Would they die and be punished or not?

Now our answer to questions of a similar nature is well known. [I have in mind] particularly three other questions. <228> The first is whether those who are to be rewarded with life in the world to come will be able to sin there or not. The second is whether prophets are capable of adding or subtracting aught from their message. The third is whether angels are able to rebel against their Master or not.

Now the answer to these three questions, as well as to the fourth here propounded, is one and the same. We must, namely, declare that, inasmuch as it seems plausible to reason that the Creator of all things knows what will happen to them before it comes to pass, we must needs assume that He would create as an angel only such a being as He knows will obey and not rebel against Him. Nor would he select as a prophet anyone except him who He knows will choose to be truthful in his mission and not tell lies. Nor again would He promise reward in the world to come to those who are to be resurrected unless He knew that they would then choose to obey and not rebel against Him. Similarly He would not have promised His nation that it would be brought back to life at the time of the *redemption* except that He knew for certain that it would choose to obey Him after the resurrection and not rebel against Him. For nothing that is destined to happen is in its true essence hidden from Him.

Our reply, again, to the question that might be asked as to whether those to be resurrected will receive any reward for the services they will render to God at the time of the *redemption* is: "Yes," just as reason demands that those who are destined to live in the world of retribution receive reward for the services they will perform in the world to come. This reward will constitute an addition that they will receive over and above what they have earned by virtue of their previous conduct. Now there is no hesitancy about asserting that there is such a thing as the performance of service to God. Why, then, should there be such hesitancy about declaring that there is in the world to come such a thing as the earning of reward?

Finally, if the question were to be asked as to what would happen to those individuals in whose lifetime the *redemption* would take place, whether they would die or not, we would reply that, when this matter was considered by the thinkers, they arrived at three different conclusions. Some of them said that these persons would live and not die, but be transported to the next world in the same manner as the resurrected. Others stated that they would live for only a short while and die, and then immediately [23] be revived in order to be on a par with those destined to be resurrected at the time of the *redemption*. Still others declared that they would live a long life <229> but that they would not live until the time for their transference to the world to come.

In choosing among these views, I found the third most plausible. For the only reason why those members of the Jewish nation that had died had been promised resurrection was in order that they might witness the *redemption*. Those, however, who will be alive when it occurs, will have seen it in their lifetime. There would, therefore, be no need of bringing them back to life [except] at the time of the world to come.

Now a proof of the fact that lives will be long at the time of the *redemption* is presented by the statement of Scripture: *They shall not build, and another inhabit, they shall not plant, and another eat; for as the days of a tree shall be the days of My people, etc.* (Isa. 65:22). As for this remark that thou seest made by Scripture, namely: *For the youngest shall die a hundred years old, and the sinner being a hundred years old shall be accursed* (Isa. 65:20), that is to be regarded only as an approximation and to be interpreted in a relative sense. What I mean is that, considering the fact that in our age the life span of man is close to

23. "immediately"—so with a slight emendation of the Arabic text by the addition of the definite article *'al*. Cf. Guttmann, p. 228, n. 2.

one hundred years, a person who dies at the age of twenty would be said by us to have died a young man. Since, however, in the era of the redemption the life span will be approximately five hundred years, the individual who would die at the age of one hundred would, by comparison, be said to have died young.

As for the *sinner* who is mentioned in this verse, he is not one who sinned against God, for as regards one who sins against his Master, it makes no difference whether he be *twenty* or *a hundred years old*. This *sinner* is rather one who wronged human beings, for human beings are accustomed to being indulgent toward an old man who has sinned against them. [In this instance,] however, a person who is one hundred years old will, in relation to the life span of 500 [which will prevail at the time of the redemption,] not be regarded by men as being old. They will, therefore, not be respectful of him, but curse him and treat him with contempt because he will occupy in their sight the position of youth.

Mayest thou, then, share in this promise—Oh, how excellent it is!—since all the prophets and the virtuous and the rest of the nation will participate in it.

The seventh treatise has hereby been completed with the grace of God.

TREATISE VIII

CONCERNING THE REDEMPTION

CHAPTER I

OUR Master, magnified and exalted be He, has informed us, the congregation of the children of Israel, that He would deliver us from our present state, and gather our scattered fragments from the east <230> and the west of the earth, and bring us to His holy place and cause us to dwell therein, so that we might be His choice and peculiar possession. Thus it is stated in Scripture: *Thus saith the Lord of hosts: Behold, I will save My people from the east country, and from the west country; and I will bring them, and they shall dwell in the midst of Jerusalem, etc.* (Zech. 8:7, 8).

This subject has been enlarged upon by His prophets to such an extent that they wrote many books about it. Nor is it from His latest prophets alone that this knowledge has come to us. Nay, this promise had already, prior to that, been brought to our attention by the messenger of God and master of all prophets, *our teacher Moses.* He remarked, namely, in the Torah: *That then the Lord thy God will turn thy captivity* (Deut. 30:3) and whatever else he said in that passage until its end. This has, furthermore, been supported by them for us by means of miracles and marvels, wherefore we accepted the doctrine.

Now I also began to inquire into this matter and subject, making use of the speculative method. There was, however, nothing in it that stood in need of investigation and analysis [1] except one item, which I shall mention when I shall come to the middle [2] of this treatise.

As for the principle of the redemption itself, that is something

1. "analysis"—Ibn Tibbon and M.
2. Cf. pp. 312 ff.

that must be accepted for several reasons. Among these are the validation presented by the miracles performed by Moses, who was the first to speak of these things. There are also the signs produced for the prophet *Isaiah* and other prophets who announced the redemption as well as the fact that He that sent them would undoubtedly carry out [3] His promise, as is stated by Scripture: *That confirmeth the word of His servant, and performeth the counsel of His messengers* (Isa. 44:26).

Another [reason why Israel's ultimate redemption must be accepted as a matter of course] is that God is just, doing no injustice, and He has already subjected this nation to a great and long-protracted trial, which undoubtedly serves partly as punishment and partly as a test for us. Whichever happens to be the case, however, there must be a limitation of time, for [such operations] cannot <231> proceed endlessly. Once, then, the end has been reached, there must needs be a cessation of the punishment of those punishable and compensation for those subjected to trial. This would be in accordance with the statement of Scripture: *That her guilt is paid off; that she hath received of the Lord's hand double for all her sins* (Isa. 40:2).

A [third] reason [for having faith in Israel's redemption] is that God is trustworthy in His promise, His utterance standing firm and His command enduring forever, as is said in Scripture: *The grass withereth, the flower fadeth, but the word of our God shall stand for ever* (Isa. 40:8).

A [fourth] reason [for believing in our people's final redemption] is the parallel we can make between the promises concerning it and God's first promise, the one He had made to us at the time when we were in Egypt. He had then promised us only two things; namely, that He would execute judgment upon our oppressor and that he would give us great wealth. That is the import of His statement: *And also that nation,* whom they shall serve, will I judge; and afterward shall they come out with great substance* (Gen. 15:14). Yet our eyes have seen what He has done for us besides that; namely, the cleaving of the sea, and the

3. "carry out"—Ibn Tibbon and M.

Manna and the quail, and the assembly at *Mount Sinai,* and the arresting of the sun and other such things. All the more certain, therefore, [must the ultimate redemption be]. For God has made us great and liberal promises of the well-being and bliss and greatness and might and glory that He will grant us twofold [in return] for the humiliation and the misery that have been our lot. Thus it is said in Scripture: *For your shame which was double, and for that they rejoiced: "Confusion is their portion"; therefore in their land they shall possess double* [4] (Isa. 61:7).

Furthermore, what has befallen us has been likened by Scripture to a brief twinkling of the eye, whereas the compensation God will give us in return therefor has been referred to as His great mercy. For it says: *For a small moment have I forsaken thee; but with great compassion will I gather thee* (Isa. 54:7).

If, then, what has happened to us in the past can be used as a proof and an example, God will assuredly do for us in the future doubly double above what He has promised us, so that we will be unable quickly and entirely to compute it, as Scripture says: *And He will do thee good, and multiply thee above thy fathers* (Deut. 30:5).

This is also the reason why the mention of the exodus from Egypt is repeated for us by God in many places in the Torah, where we are reminded by Him of what we have seen. If, again, anything that <232> was wrought [5] by Him for us in connection with the redemption from Egypt has been left unexpressed in regard to this [last] redemption, it is implied in God's statement: *As in the days of thy coming forth out of the land of Egypt will I show unto him marvellous things* (Mic. 7:15).

Therefore, also, dost thou find us patiently awaiting what God has promised us, not entertaining any doubts concerning it, nor worrying or despairing. On the contrary, our courage and tenacity increase constantly, as is expressed in Scripture: *Be strong, and let your heart take courage, all ye that wait for the Lord* (Ps. 31:25).

4. This quotation is based on the reading of Ibn Tibbon.
5. "wrought"—Ibn Tibbon and M.

Now whoever sees us behaving in this fashion may be surprised at us or regard us as fools for the simple reason that he has not experienced what we have nor believed as we have believed. He resembles a person who has never seen how wheat is sown, wherefore, when he sees someone throw it into the cracks of the earth in order to let it grow, he thinks that that individual is a fool. It is at the time of the threshing, when every measure yields twenty or thirty measures, that he first realizes that it is *he* who has been the fool. This type of metaphor is also employed by Scripture in such statements as *They that sow in tears shall reap in joy* (Ps. 126:5).

Or else [the position of him who does not appreciate our behavior is] like that of a person who has never seen how a child is raised and who consequently ridicules him who raises a child and endures all the burdens imposed upon him by the latter's needs, asking: "What is it that can be expected from [6] this child?" However, when the child has grown up and acquired knowledge and wisdom and become a king and a leader of armies, that person realizes that it was himself that he had ridiculed. It is in this vein that Scripture compares the expectations cherished by us to [the birth of] a man child. Thus it says: *Before she travailed, she brought forth; before her pain came, she was delivered of a man-child* (Isa. 66:7).

CHAPTER II

Furthermore I ask: "How can it be difficult for Him, in whose sight the heavens have approximately the dimension of a span, to send us prophetic revelations from them? Or why should it be hard for Him, for Whom the measurement of the seas [7] is like the stretch of a hand, to gather our scattered fragments out of them? Or should it not be easy for Him, in whose sight the dust of the earth is like something <233> measurable, to bring us from the extremities thereof? Again, how could it not be a simple mat-

6. "be expected from"—Ibn Tibbon and M.
7. "seas"—Ibn Tibbon and M.

ter for Him, in Whose sight the mountains are like something weighed, to build His holy mountain? That is indeed the reason why, at the beginning of those prophetic *messages of consolation* the question is asked: *Who hath measured the waters in the hollow of His hand, and meted out heaven with the span, and comprehended* [*the dust of the earth in a measure, and weighed the mountains in scales?*] (Isa. 40: 12).

"Furthermore could not He, in whose presence the nations are like the drop of a bucket or like the small dust of a balance, humble them before us, as Scripture expresses it: *Behold, the nations are as a drop of a bucket, and are counted as the small dust of the balance?* (Isa. 40: 15.) Aye, why should this be difficult for one who shakes the earth off from them as we gather the ends of a cloth and shake it out, as Scripture puts it: *To take* [8] *hold of the ends of the earth, and the wicked be shaken out of it?"* (Job 38: 13.)

The fact is that, even if I had merely pointed out that God is He that created everything out of nothing, it would have sufficed to prove my point. However, I presented in my exposition all these other matters because He Himself had presented them. It is, therefore, not permissible for us to entertain the thought that He is not aware of our situation or that He does not deal fairly with us or that He is not compassionate, as indeed He has rebuked us, saying: *Why sayest thou, O Jacob, and speakest, O Israel: "My way is hid from the Lord, etc?"* (Isa. 40: 27). Nor is it right to think that God is unable to help us or to answer our prayer, for, as Scripture says: *Behold, the Lord's hand is not shortened, that it cannot save, neither His ear heavy, that it cannot hear* (Isa. 59: 1). Nor finally is it proper to believe that He has forsaken us and cast us off. The truth is, rather, as it has been expressed by Scripture: *For the Lord thy God is a merciful God; He will not fail thee, neither destroy thee* (Deut. 4: 31).

What we believe, on the other hand, may God have mercy on thee, is that God has set two different limits to our state of *subjection*. One is the limitation produced by repentance, whereas the

8. "to take"—the usual translation is: "that it might take."

other is that occasioned by the *end*. Whichever of these happens to come first will draw after it the redemption. If, therefore, our repentance be completed, no regard would be had for the *end*. Rather what would happen would be as it has been said in the Torah [with reference to our repentance; namely,] <234> *And it shall come to pass, when all these things are come upon thee, the blessing and the curse, . . . and thou shalt return unto the Lord thy God, and hearken to His voice . . . that the Lord thy God will turn [thy captivity], etc.*[9] (Deut. 30: 1–3) and the remainder of the ten verses of that passage.

Should our repentance, on the other hand, fall short, we would have to linger until the period of the *end* is fulfilled,[10] some of us being subjected to punishment and others to trials. This is, as it is well known, a rule that applies to every universal catastrophe occurring at different times, such as famine, war, and pestilence. These serve as punishment for some and as a trial for others. Certainly there must have been in the world at the time of the deluge young children and babes whose death can be conceived of only as a trial for which they were to be compensated.

Similarly we do not doubt but that there were among our forefathers in Egypt many righteous persons who had to endure their trials until the period of that *end* was fulfilled. Hence, let no one say to us: [11] "Had there been any righteous persons among you, the redemption would have come to you." For we note that our masters and crowns, *Moses, Aaron, and Miriam*, lingered in the *servitude* [of Egypt] for over eighty years until the period of that *end* was fulfilled, and so did also many other righteous persons like them.

CHAPTER III

It behooves me now to dwell on the duration of the *end*. I say, then, that our Lord, magnified and exalted be He, revealed to His

---

9. This quotation is based on the reading of Ibn Tibbon.
10. "is fulfilled"—Ibn Tibbon and M.
11. "to us"—added by Ibn Tibbon and M.

prophet *Daniel* three angels. One of them was suspended [12] above the water of the Tigris, whilst the other two, who were standing on its two banks, asked the one who was suspended above the water when the redemption would take place. That is the import of the prophet's statement: *Then I Daniel looked, and, behold, there stood other two, the one on the bank of the river on this side, and the other on the bank of the river on that side* (Dan. 12:5).

Then the angel that was suspended above the water of his own accord swore to him concerning the limit that he had fixed, even though Daniel had demanded no oath from him. *Daniel* said; namely: *And I heard* <235> *the man clothed in linen, who was above the waters of the river, when he lifted up his right hand and his left hand unto heaven, and swore by him that liveth for ever that it shall be for a time, times, and a half* (Dan. 12:7). Now the other two angels heard from him the words *a time, times, and a half,* and they were satisfied therewith because they recognized its meaning. Daniel, however, did not know what was meant by *a time, times, and a half.* Hence he asked the angel who was suspended above the water concerning it,[13] for he said: *And I heard, but understood not; then said I: "O my Lord, what shall be the latter end of these things?"* (Dan. 12:8).

Thereupon the angel of his own accord, before giving him the explicit answer, prefaced his remarks to him by mentioning the reason on account of which he had veiled this answer in obscure terms. He told him, namely, that he had thus obscured it only in order that the common people and the ignorant might not understand and be worried. For the desires and apprehensions of these individuals do not correspond to those entertained by the wise; that is [to say], the reward of the world to come and life eternal. They desire, rather, the possessions of this world and its glory that can be acquired immediately. The wise, however, will understand the answer, as he said: *Go thy way, Daniel; for the words are shut up*

12. "suspended"—Ibn Tibbon and M.
13. "concerning it"—Ibn Tibbon and M.

and sealed till the time of the end. Many shall purify themselves, and make themselves white, and be refined; [but the wicked shall do wickedly; and none of the wicked shall understand; but they that are wise shall understand] (Dan. 12:9, 10).

Thereupon he explained to him that the period would be one of 1335 years. [He did this] in his statement: *Happy is he that waiteth, and cometh to the thousand three hundred and five and thirty days* (Dan. 12:12). The term *days* in this sentence stands for a cycle of years, as it does in the Scriptural statement: *Days* [14] *shall he have for its redemption* (Lev. 25:29), which is followed immediately by the remark: *And if it be not redeemed within the space of a full year* [15] (Lev. 25:30).

Now we find that whenever the *end* set by our Lord to the existence of a kingdom is spoken of, it is said to be in periods of years, not of days. Sometimes, however, this is expressed in terms of years. This is illustrated in such statements of Scripture as: *And it shall come to pass after the end of seventy years, that the Lord will remember Tyre* (Isa. 23:17), as well as *At the end of forty years will I gather the Egyptians* (Ezek. 29:13). On other occasions, again, although the cycles of time referred to are *years*,[16] they are called *days*, as, for example, in God's statement to the master: *Ezekiel, <236> the priest, peace be upon him: For I have appointed the years of their iniquity to be unto thee a number of days* (Ezek. 4:5). Now the promiscuous use in this case of the expressions *years* and *days* indicates that *days* are here equivalent to *years*. The same applies, therefore, to the aforementioned passage [in the book of Daniel].

Daniel understood, then, how the expression *a time, times, and a half* could come to mean 1335 years. That is why he refrained from asking further questions.[17] We, however, may God direct thee aright, must make strenuous mental efforts to fathom the

---

14. "Days"—the usual translation is "For a full year."
15. This quotation follows the reading of Ibn Tibbon.
16. "the cycles . . . years"—so correctly according to Ibn Tibbon.
17. "from asking . . . questions"—Ibn Tibbon.

meaning of *a time, times, and a half* so that the total will correspond to 1335 years. For so far as the expression *a time* is concerned, it has only the value of a modifier, as in the phrase, *In the time appointed in the month Abib* (Exod. 23: 15). The actual figure is implied in the words *times and a half*.[18]

It was, therefore, the meaning of *times and a half* that we investigated, and we found that it would tally, if it were to be assumed by us that he meant by the word *times* the period of the duration of the government of the children of Israel. In that event the interval of time covered by the *end* would undoubtedly be about one and a half times as long as the number of years that their rule lasted. That.is [to say, considering the fact] that the total of the period of their rule amounted to 890 years, neither more nor less, [being made up of the] 480 [years] before the building of the Temple and the 410 [years] of the existence of the Temple. Half of this sum would be 445. The result would be a grand total of 1335, neither more nor less.

According to the aforementioned calculation, the statement by Daniel: *And from the time that the continual burnt-offering shall be taken away, and the detestable thing that causes appalment set up, there shall be a thousand two hundred and ninety days* (Dan. 12: 11), concerning the date of an event which occurred at the time of the *second Temple,* when it was first built, would refer to something that happened forty-five years after the previously mentioned remark was made to *Daniel.*

Furthermore, from [the figure quoted in] his statement: *Unto two thousand and three hundred evenings and mornings; then shall the sanctuary be victorious* (Dan. 8: 14) a half must be deducted, because the number of diurnal cycles is here multiplied by the days and the nights. Now half of this sum would be 1150 years, which would make the date referred to herein 185 years after that in which the original remark, that we have mentioned above, was made to *Daniel.* Thus the termination of the three periods discussed would occur in one and the same year.

18. "We, however, . . . times and a half"—this entire passage is corrupt in the Arabic text of Landauer. It has been corrected according to Ibn Tibbon and M.

CHAPTER IV

Let me say, moreover, that, on account of <237> the seeming contradictions among the three periods of the *end* set by God to our present state of *subjection,* our Lord has also made the time limits of the first two *subjections* seemingly contradictory, lest we imagine that such an uncertainty applies only and solely to this last *end* by reason of its being spurious. But when we note that similar contradictions prevailed in the data pertaining to the two previous periods, which we know to have been genuine, doubt is removed from our minds.

Let me now explain this by saying that the difficulty pertaining to the *enslavement* of Israel *in Egypt* arises from the fact that one time [19] the period during which the *descendants of Abraham* were strangers, humiliated and enslaved is stated to have been 400 years. Thus it is said in Scripture: *Know of a surety that thy seed shall be a stranger in a land that is not theirs, and shall serve them; and they shall afflict them four hundred years* (Gen. 15:13), that is [to say counting] from the birth of Isaac. Another time,[20] again, mention is made of a period of 430 years, in which are included the *thirty* additional *years* during which Abraham was a stranger in a foreign land. For Abraham's age at the time of his departure from Haran to Palestine is explicitly stated [21] (Gen. 12:4). The date of his departure from Kutha to Harran, however, is not explicitly mentioned. The thirty years must, therefore, embrace the period of Abraham's journeying. All this is implied in the observation made by Scripture: *Now the time that the children of Israel dwelt in Egypt was four hundred and thirty years* (Exod. 12:40). As for the questions of how the name of *the children of Israel* came to be applied to Abraham and how Harran and Palestine could be called *Egypt,* they have their explanations which it is not appropriate to mention here.

19. "one time"—Ibn Tibbon and M.
20. "another time"—Ibn Tibbon and M.
21. He was then 75 years old. Five years are allowed by Saadia for his journey from Kutha to Harran.

Notwithstanding the aforementioned [figures], however, the total number of years spent by our forefathers [22] in Egypt was 210. No one can, namely, maintain that they stayed there four hundred years, because it is impossible that Kehath, Amram, and Moses should have lived so long—and this is not the place to expatiate on this matter. At all events, we now have three figures: namely, 400 years and 430 years and 210 years.[23]

As for the *subjection* of the Israelites *by the Babylonians,* two figures are cited for its duration. One of them is 52 years. This is borne out by the statement of Scripture: *After seventy years are accomplished for Babylon, I will remember you* (Jer. 29:10). <238> The other figure, again, is seventy years, as indicated by its statement: *That He would accomplish for the desolations of Jerusalem seventy years* (Dan. 9:2). Now between the beginning of the rule of Babylon and the *destruction of Jerusalem* there was an interval of eighteen years. This is borne out by the statement of Scripture: *Now in the fifth month, on the seventh day of the month, which was the nineteenth year of King Nebuchadnezzar* (II Kings 25:8), and the rest of that passage. Thus there was an interval of fifty-two years from the time of that event until that of the reign of Cyrus. The latter gave them permission to build the Temple, in the construction of which they engaged in that year. Then they remained idle for seventeen years until the period of seventy years was completed, as [24] it is stated in Scripture: *Then ceased the work of the house of God which is at Jerusalem; and it ceased unto the second year of the reign of Darius king of Persia* (Ezra 4:24).[25]

Now just as [the realization of] the first *end* was not jeopardized by the fact that three varying figures were assigned to it: namely, 400, 430, and 210; and just as the assignment of two different figures: namely. 52 and 70, to the second *end* did not jeopardize its [realization] either, so, too, the third *end* will not be jeopardized

---

22. "our forefathers"—M.

23. For this computation cf. Sedher 'Olam Rabba, chap. iii, and other references quoted by Guttmann, p. 234, n. 2.

24. "as"—Ibn Tibbon.

25. For the computation cf. Sedher 'Olam Rabba, chap. xxix.

by the application to it of three divergent figures: namely, 1150, 1290, and 1335, so long as the All-Wise has granted His nation the wisdom whereby they can discern the meaning of them all.

CHAPTER V

Having, then, explained these *ends* and made them clear, I now say that we already know that, should our repentance not be completed previously, we would linger in exile until the fulfillment of the *end*. If, on the other hand, the *end* be fulfilled without our having repented, it is inconceivable that the *redemption* come about while we are still steeped in the sins for the sake of which God had exiled us. Hence, if after our having lingered in exile for a long time without returning to God, God would bring us back to our land even though we should not have improved, [might one not ask whether] our exile has [not] been in vain?

However, it has been transmitted by the traditions of the prophets that God would cause misfortunes and disasters to befall us that would compel us to resolve upon repentance so that we would be deserving of redemption. That is the sense of the remark of our forebears: *If the Israelites will repent, they will be redeemed. If not, the Holy One, Blessed Be He, will raise up a king whose decrees will be even more severe than those of Haman, whereupon they will repent and thus be redeemed* (Sanh. 97b.)

<239> [Our forebears] also tell us that the cause of this [visitation] will be the appearance in *Upper Galilee* of a man from among the descendants of *Joseph,* around whom there will gather individuals from among the Jewish nation.[26] This man will go to Jerusalem [27] after its seizure by the Romans and stay in it for a certain length of time. Then they will be surprised by a man named Armilus,[28] who will wage war against them and conquer the city and subject its inhabitants to massacre, captivity, and dis-

26. Saadia is the first to mention this tradition. Cf. *Jewish Encyclopedia* article "Armilus." Cf. also Guttmann, p. 236, n. 4.

27. Jerusalem—M.

28. Armilus—Ibn Tibbon and M, as against the reading Armilius in Landauer's manuscript.

grace. Included among those that will be slain will be that man from among the descendants of *Joseph*.

Now there will come upon the Jewish nation at that time great misfortunes,[29] the most difficult to endure being the deterioration of their relationship with the governments of the world who will drive them into the wildernesses to let them starve and be miserable. As a result of what has happened to them, many of them will desert their [30] faith, only those purified remaining. To these *Elijah the prophet* will manifest himself and thus the redemption will come.

After hearing about these misfortunes, I looked into Scripture and I found in it supports for each point in the account. The first, namely, that the Romans will take Jerusalem at the time of the *redemption,* is borne out by the Scriptural statement: *And saviors shall come up on mount Zion to judge the mount of Esau* (Obad. 21). That, again, the war against them will be conducted by one of the descendants of *Rachel* is supported by the Scriptural statement: *Therefore hear ye the counsel of the Lord, that He hath taken against Edom; and His purposes, that He hath purposed against the inhabitants of Teman: Surely the youngest* [31] *of the flock shall drag them away* (Jer. 49:20).

Furthermore, that only a few from among the Jewish nation— not many—will gather about him is attested by the statement of Scripture: *And I will take you one of a city, and two of a family, and I will bring you to Zion* (Jer. 3:14). That, moreover, the attacker will seize them and take them captive and put them to death is borne out by the statement of Scripture: *Behold, a day of the Lord cometh, when thy spoil shall be divided in the midst of thee* (Zech. 14:1). It states, furthermore: *For I will gather all nations against Jerusalem to battle;* <240> *and the city shall be taken, and the houses rifled, [and the women ravished; and half of the city shall go forth into captivity], etc.*[32] (Zech. 14:2).

29. "misfortunes"—Ibn Tibbon.

30. "their"—Ibn Tibbon and M.

31. "youngest"—The usual translation is "least." Note that "Rachel" means "ewe" in Hebrew.

32. This quotation follows the reading of Ibn Tibbon.

Also that the man at the head of the Jewish nation will be among the slain and that people will weep over him and bewail him is attested by the Scriptural statement: *And they shall look unto Me because they have thrust him through; and they shall mourn for him, as one mourneth for his only son* (Zech. 12:10), and the rest of that passage. That, furthermore, great misfortune will befall the Jewish nation at that time is substantiated by the statement of Scripture: *And there shall be a time of trouble, such as never was since there was a nation even to that same time* [33] (Dan. 12:1).

That, again, enmity will spring up between them and many of the nations, with the result that the latter will drive them into the many wildernesses is supported by the Scriptural remark: *And I will bring you into the wilderness of the peoples, and there will I plead with you face to face* (Ezek. 20:35).[34] That the Jews will experience hunger and thirst and hardship, such as it was the lot of their early ancestors to endure, has its basis in the subsequent declaration: *Like as I pleaded with your fathers in the wilderness of the land of Egypt, so will I plead with you* (Ezek. 20:36).

That, moreover, they will be purified and sorted like silver and gold, so that their patience and [the strength of] their belief will become known, is borne out by the statement of Scripture: *And I will cause you to pass under the rod, and I will bring you into the bond of the covenant* (Ezek. 20:37).

That, furthermore, these matters will cause those whose faith is weak to desert their religion, saying, "This is what we have hoped for and this is what we have attained thereof," is implied in the statement which follows next, namely: *And I will purge out from among you the rebels, and them that transgress against Me* (Ezek. 20:38).

That, finally, *Elijah the prophet* will appear to those who will remain is borne out by the declaration: *Behold, I will send you Elijah the prophet. . . . And he shall turn the heart of the fathers to the children* (Mal. 3:23, 24).

The chief points of these matters are, then, all of them exposed

---

33. This quotation follows the reading of Ibn Tibbon.
34. This quotation follows the reading of Ibn Tibbon.

in the Bible, while their further ordering and arrangement is carried out in systematic fashion in the works of tradition. Praised be He who in His graciousness gave unto us advance notice of these misfortunes, lest they come upon us suddenly <241> and cause us to despair. In reference to the occurrence of these misfortunes Scripture also says: *From the uttermost parts of the earth have we heard songs: "Glory to the righteous,"* (Isa. 24:16) until the end of that passage.

CHAPTER VI

Next let me say that in either case—I mean whether we do not repent and the events associated with the *Messiah descended from Joseph* come to pass, or we do repent and are able to dispense with them—*the Messiah descended from David* will manifest himself to us suddenly. Should there be, however, [in the second eventuality] a *Messiah descended from Joseph* who would precede him, he would serve as his herald and as one who puts the nation in proper condition and clears the way, as Scripture says: *Behold, I send My messenger, and He shall clear the way before Me* (Mal. 3:1). Or he might be compared to one who purges with fire those members of the nation who have committed grave sins, or to one who washes with lye those of its constituents who have been guilty of slight infractions, as Scripture remarks immediately thereafter: *For he is like a refiner's fire, and like fullers' soap* (Mal. 3:2).

In the event, however, that the *Messiah descended from Joseph* does not come, so that the *Messiah descended from David* makes his arrival to us unheralded, as Scripture says: *And the Lord, whom ye seek, will suddenly come to His temple* (Mal. 3:1), and he will bring with him a retinue of people and go to Jerusalem,[35] then if it be in the hands of Armilus,[36] he will kill him and take it from him. That is the implication of the statement of Scripture: *And I will lay My vengeance upon Edom by the hand of My*

---

35. "Jerusalem"—Ibn Tibbon.
6. "Armilus"—Ibn Tibbon. The Arabic text of Landauer reads "Armilius."

people Israel (Ezek. 25: 14). Should it be in the hands of someone else, again, he would also be of *Edom*.

Furthermore, inasmuch as [37] *the descendant of Joseph* would not come, the appearance of the *descendant of David* would have upon those to be redeemed the effect of encouraging them and healing their breach and consoling their souls, as Scripture says: *The spirit of the Lord God is upon me; because the Lord hath anointed me to bring good tidings unto the humble; He hath sent me to bind up the broken-hearted, to proclaim liberty to the captives, etc. . . . to proclaim the year of the Lord's good pleasure* (Isa. 61: 1, 2). At this point the prophet expatiates on the various types of compensation that God would bestow upon His people; namely; the distinction and honor and glory that would be conferred upon them. For he says immediately after the preceding: *To appoint unto them that mourn in Zion, to give unto them* <242> *a garland for ashes* (Isa. 61: 3). They will also rehabilitate the land and dwell in it, as he says: *And they shall build the old wastes* (Isa. 61: 4).

Then Gog and Magog will hear about the *descendant of David* and the excellence of his people and country and the abundance of their wealth, and how they feel themselves secure without locks or fortifications or aught resembling them. They will, therefore, covet them, as is stated in the account given of Gog: *And thou shalt say: I will go up against the land of unwalled villages; I will come upon them that are at quiet, that dwell safely, all of them dwelling without walls, and having neither bars nor gates* (Ezek. 38: 11).

He will thereupon gather around himself people from sundry nations, crossing [38] countries in order to reach them, as Scripture says: *And thou shalt come from thy place out of the uttermost parts of the north, thou, and many peoples with thee* [39] (Ezek. 38: 15). Now the folk that will be assembled about him will be divided into two categories, one consisting of notorious sinners marked out for perdition, the other of people who have mended

---

37. "inasmuch as"—Ibn Tibbon and M. Landauer's Arabic text reads "if."
38. "crossing"—Ibn Tibbon.
39. This quotation follows the reading of Ibn Tibbon.

their ways in order to enter the faith. In regard to those who are destined for perdition Scripture says: *I will gather all nations, and will bring them down into the valley of Jehoshaphat* (Joel 4:2). It says also: *Proclaim ye this among the nations, prepare war; stir up the mighty men; let all the men of war draw near, let them come up. Beat your ploughshares into swords. . . . Haste ye, and come, all ye nations round about. . . . Let the nations be stirred up, and come up to the valley of Jehoshaphat . . . . Put ye in the sickle, for the harvest is ripe . . . . Multitudes, multitudes in the valley of decision* (Joel 4:9–14).

As for those who will have mended their ways, on the other hand, they are the ones of whom it has been said: *For then will I turn to the peoples a pure language, that they may all call upon the name of the Lord* (Zeph. 3:9).

Now there will descend upon the prodigals on that day four [40] types of misfortunes: (*a*) Some will perish from the fire and the sulphur and the stones of clay baked in hell that will rain down [41] upon them, as is said in Scripture: *And I will cause to rain upon him . . . an overflowing shower, and great hailstones, fire and brimstone* (Ezek. 38:22). (*b*) Some will die by each other's sword, as is stated by Scripture: *And I will call for a sword against him through all My mountains . . . every man's sword* <243> *shall be against his brother* (Ezek. 38:21).

(*c*) Of some, again, the flesh will rot and the bones disintegrate, as is said in Scripture: *And this shall be the plague wherewith the Lord will smite* [*all the peoples that have warred against Jerusalem:*] *Their flesh shall consume away while they stand upon their feet* [42] (Zech. 14:12). The decomposition will be so far-going that if one of them were to stretch out his hand to the other in order to grasp it, it would wrench out [43] his hand, as is said in Scripture: *And it shall come to pass in that day, that a great tumult from the Lord shall be among them; and they shall lay hold every one on*

40. "four"—Ibn Tibbon, correctly, as against "three," which is the reading of the Arabic text.

41. "rain down"—Ibn Tibbon.

42. This quotation is based on the reading of Ibn Tibbon.

43. "wrench out"—literally "bring up."

the hand of his neighbor, and his hand shall rise up against the hand of his neighbor (Zech. 14: 13).

(*d*) The rest, finally, will bear the marks of the blows endured by them, such as the gouging out of an eye or the mutilation of the nose or the cutting off of a finger. Thus will they go forth into the wide world [44] in order to report what they have seen, as Scripture says: *And I will work a sign among them, and I will send such as escape of them unto the nations, to Tarshish, etc.* (Isa. 66: 19).

As for those that will mend their ways, they, too, will fall into four classes: (*a*) Some will serve as domestics in the homes of the *children of Israel.* These will be the most distinguished among them, as Scripture says: *And kings shall be thy fosterfathers, and their queens thy nursing mothers* [45] (Isa. 49: 23). (*b*) Some will be made to serve in the cities and villages. Of them does Scripture say: *And the house of Israel shall possess them in the land of the Lord for servants and for handmaids; and they shall take them captive, whose captives they were; and they shall rule over their oppressors* (Isa. 14: 2). (*c*) Some, again, will serve in the fields and steppes, as is said in Scripture: *And strangers shall stand and feed your flocks, and aliens shall be your plowmen and your vine-dressers* [46] (Isa. 61: 5).

(*d*) The remainder, finally, will return to their countries and be submissive to Israel, and the *descendant of David* will decree it upon them that they come every year to celebrate the feast of tabernacles,[47] as Scripture says: *And it shall come to pass that every one that is left of all the nations that came against Jerusalem shall go up from year to year to worship the King, the Lord [of hosts, and to keep the feast of tabernacles]* (Zech. 14: 16).

For any nation, however, that will not make the pilgrimage, there will be no rainfall, as is stated in Scripture: *And it shall be, that whoso of the families of the earth goeth not up unto Jeru-*

---

44. "into the wide world"—cf. Ibn Tibbon.
45. This quotation follows the reading of Ibn Tibbon.
46. This quotation follows the reading of Ibn Tibbon.
47. "and the descendant . . . tabernacles"—added by Ibn Tibbon.

salem to worship . . . upon them there shall be no rain (Zech. 14:17). And if the Egyptians shall say, "We need no rain because our Nile waters our land," their Nile will not rise, as Scripture says: *And if the family of Egypt go not up, and come not, [they shall have no overflow]* [48] (Zech. 14:18).

Then the nations will see that the best means they have of winning the favor <244> of the *Messiah* is to bring members of the latter's nation that live in their midst to him as a gift. Thus Scripture states: *And the peoples shall take them, and bring them to their place* (Isa. 14:2). It says also: *And they shall bring all your brethren out of all the nations for an offering unto the Lord* (Isa. 66:20).

Now every nation will execute this in accordance with its ability. The wealthy among them will, namely, transport the Israelites on horses and mules and in litters and on dromedaries [49] in the most distinguished fashion, as is said in Scripture: *And they shall bring all your brethren . . . upon horses, and in chariots, and in litters, and upon mules, and upon swift beasts* (*ibid.*). The poor [50] among them, again, will bear them on their shoulders and their children in their bosoms, as is said in Scripture: *Thus saith the Lord God: Behold, I will lift up My hand to the nations, and set up Mine ensign to the peoples, and they shall bring thy sons in their bosom, [and thy daughters shall be carried upon their shoulders]* (Isa. 49:22).

Moreover, any Israelite dwelling on the isles [51] of the seas will be borne by them in ships accompanied by silver and gold, as Scripture says: *Surely the isles shall wait for Me, and the ships of Tarshish first, [to bring thy sons from far, their silver and their gold with them]* (Isa. 60:9).

Should an Israelite happen to be in the land of Ethiopia, again, he will be transported by them in boats of bulrushes until he arrives in Egypt. For in the upper regions of the Nile there are

48. "and if . . . overflow"—added by Ibn Tibbon.
49. "dromedaries"—cf. Dozy's *Supplement aux Dictionnaires Arabes* (Leyden, 1881), II, 171, *'amariyyah*.
50. "poor"—Ibn Tibbon.
51. "isles"—added by Ibn Tibbon.

mountains that protrude in the water which the ordinary vessels cannot pass lest they be broken in pieces. The boats of bulrushes covered with pitch, however, merely bend but do not break. Thus Scripture says: *Ah, land of the buzzing of wings, which is beyond the rivers of Ethiopia; that sendeth ambassadors by the sea, even in vessels of papyrus upon the waters!* (Isa. 18: 1, 2). The implication of the expression *the buzzing of wings,* by the way, is that its terrain is shaded and covered over by the multitude of men, as is stated at the end of the passage: *In that day shall a present be brought unto the Lord [of hosts of a people,] etc.* (Isa. 18: 7). Scripture also says elsewhere: *From beyond the rivers of Ethiopia shall they bring My suppliants, even the daughter of My dispersed, as Mine offering* (Zeph. 3: 10).

Any Israelite, again, who will remain in the desert or who will have no one of the nations to bring him to Jerusalem, will be brought so speedily by our Lord as though a cloud had lifted him up and carried him, as is stated by Scripture: *Who are these that fly as a cloud, and as the doves to their cotes?* (Isa. 60: 8.) Or it would seem as though the winds had borne him, as is said by Scripture: *I will say to the north-wind:* [52] *"Give up," and to the south-wind:* [53] *"Keep not* <245> *back, bring my sons from far, etc."* (Isa. 43: 6).

When, then, those [of the nations of the world] who are alive unite with the living among the Jewish [54] believers, as I have described, *the resurrection of the dead* will take place in the manner in which I have explained in the preceding treatise. At the helm and head of them will stand *the descendant of Joseph,* by virtue of his being a righteous and well-tried servant of God, greatly rewarded by his Master. Then, too, will our Lord, magnified and exalted be He, restore His sanctuary, as has been described for us: *When the Lord hath built up Zion, When He hath appeared in His glory* (Ps. 102: 17).

The structure [of the city] and the Temple will be of the form

52. "north-wind"—the usual translation is "north."
53. "south-wind"—the usual translation is "south."
54. "Jewish"—added by Ibn Tibbon.

explained by Ezekiel [in the passage beginning with the words]:
In the five and twentieth year of our captivity (Ezek. 40:1). They
will be studded with jewels and precious stones, as Isaiah said:
*And I will make thy pinnacles of rubies, and thy gates of car-
buncles* (Isa. 54:12). The entire land will be inhabited so that no
place in it will remain a desolation or a wilderness, as is said in
Scripture: *And the parched land shall become a pool, and the
thirsty ground springs of water* (Isa. 35:7).

Then the light of [God's] *Presence* will appear shining upon the
Temple with such brilliance that all lights will become faint or
dim in comparison with it, for I have already explained in the second treatise that this light [of God's Presence] is brighter than
any [55] other. Thus Scripture says: *Arise, shine, for thy light is
come, and the glory of the Lord is risen upon thee. For, behold,
darkness shall cover the earth . . . but upon thee the Lord will
arise, etc.* (Isa. 60:1, 2). So brilliant will that light be that anyone
who does not know the road to the Temple will be able to travel
by its brightness, for it will extend from heaven to earth, as it has
been said: *And nations shall walk at thy light, and kings at the
brightness of thy rising* (Isa. 60:3).

Then prophecy will be so widespread among our nation that
even our children and our slaves will prophesy,[56] as has been stated
in Scripture: *And it shall come to pass afterward, that I will pour
out My spirit upon all flesh; and your sons and your daughters
shall prophesy, etc. . . . and also upon the servants and upon the
handmaids* (Joel 3:1, 2). Such will be their endowment that if one
of them were to journey to any country and say: "I am one of
the believers," the people would ask him to tell them what happened the previous night or what would happen on the morrow
in regard to something that was a secret to them. From his reply
it will then become evident to <246> them that he belongs to
the Jewish people, as it has been said in Scripture: *And their seed
shall be known among the nations, and their offspring among the
peoples* (Isa. 61:9).

55. Cf. above, p. 121.
56. "will prophesy"—added by Ibn Tibbon.

This will, then, be the position that will be held by the believers as long as the world exists, without any change, as it has been said in Scripture: *O Israel, thou art saved by the Lord with an everlasting salvation; ye shall not be ashamed nor confounded world without end* (Isa. 45: 17). Now it occurs to me that the only reason Scripture employs the expression *world without end* in this one of all places is in order to confirm for us the certainty of the *redemption* by using the strongest [word] to be found [57] in [the vocabulary of] the [Hebrew] language. Another [reason] is to counteract the allegation that it will be limited or transitory.

Furthermore, Scripture informs us that the people that have been redeemed will choose to serve God and not to rebel against Him, as is explained in the passage [beginning with the words] *And the Lord thy God will circumcise thy heart* (Deut. 30:6), as well as in that [which commences with the statement]: *A new heart also will I give you, and a new spirit, etc.* (Ezek. 36:26).

This choice on their part will be due to several causes. It will be brought about by the fact that they will see the light of [God's] *Presence* and their endowment with divine inspiration, and their enjoyment of sovereignty and well-being, and the fact that there will be no hand that will oppress them and no need that they will experience, and that they will be generally successful in the rest of their undertakings.

We are also informed by Scripture that all pestilence, diseases, and infirmity [58] will disappear, and similarly sadness and sorrow. Their world will rather be one that is replete with joy and gladness, so that it will seem to them as though their heaven and their earth have been renewed for them. Thus it is expressly stated in the passage [of Scripture beginning with the words]: *For, behold, I create new heavens and a new earth, etc. . . . . But be ye glad and rejoice for ever. . . . And I will rejoice in Jerusalem, and joy in My people; and the voice of weeping shall be no more heard in her, nor the voice of crying* (Isa. 65: 17-19).

What an age that will be—one that is all joy and gladness, all

57. "to be found"—Ibn Tibbon.
58. "infirmity"—Ibn Tibbon.

obedience and service of God, all reward and saved-up wealth! It is to that age that the description of Scripture applies: <247> *We whose sons are as plants . . . whose garners are full, affording all manner of store; . . . whose oxen are well laden; with no breach, and no going forth* (Ps. 144: 12–14).

CHAPTER VII

Having presented these explanations, I shall next discuss the report that has reached me that certain people, who call themselves Jews maintain that the aforementioned promises and *consolations* applied, all of them, to the time of the *second Temple,* and that they were fully realized then so that there was nothing further left to be fulfilled. They arrived at this conclusion on the basis of a false premise on which they built their argument. They assert, namely, that all such extraordinary happenings as we see attributed to the *redemption,* in such statements of Scripture as *Thy sun shall no more go down, neither shall thy moon withdraw itself* [59] (Isa. 20: 20) and *It shall not be plucked up, nor thrown down any more for ever* (Jer. 31: 40), were intended to take place only on the condition that the obedience by the people of God be complete. These prophecies, they declare, are to be understood in the same sense as the statement made by *our teacher Moses, peace be upon him,* to Israel: *That your days may be multiplied, and the days of your children* (Deut. 11: 21). For when they sinned, their sovereignty came to an end and their rule ceased. Similarly, during the time of the *second Temple,* some of these promises were realized and then came to an end, while others were never carried out because the people had sinned.

Now I took, may God direct thee aright, the basic assumption of the thesis propounded by these individuals: namely, that these [promises appertaining to the redemption] were meant only conditionally, and subjected them to careful scrutiny, and I found it to be untenable for sundry reasons.

One of these is that the promises made by *Our teacher Moses,*

59. This quotation follows the reading of Ibn Tibbon.

peace be upon him, were explicitly stated to have been conditional. He said, namely: *For if ye shall diligently keep all this command-ment which I command you . . . then will the Lord drive out all these nations* [60] (Deut. 11:22, 23); and also: *But if thou shalt in-deed hearken unto His voice, and do . . . then I will be an enemy unto thine enemies* (Exod. 23:22); as well as: *And it shall come to pass, because we hearken* (Deut. 7:12), and the like. So far as the *consolations* [pertaining to the redemption] that have just been listed are concerned, however, there is nothing conditional in them at all. They are, in fact, absolute promises.

Furthermore *Moses, peace be upon him,* was not satisfied with merely stating the condition of their reward to his followers by saying, [as he did]: *If ye shall keep* <248> and *if ye shall hearken,* leaving it to their reason to infer that, if on the contrary they should not fulfill their pledges, God would not fulfill His promises either. Nay, he stated the converse of the agreement definitely and made it clear to them that if they would not fulfill their obligations, the situation would be reversed so far as they were concerned.

Thus he told them: *And it shall be, if thou shalt forget the Lord thy God, etc. . . . As the nations that the Lord maketh to perish before you, so shall ye perish* (Deut. 8:19, 20). He said also: *When thou shalt beget children and children's children, [and ye shall . . . deal corruptly] . . . I call heaven and earth to witness against you this day, [that ye shall soon utterly perish]* (Deut. 4:25, 26). Furthermore he said: *But if thy heart turn away, and thou will not hear . . . [I declare . . . that ye shall surely perish]* (Deut. 30:17, 18), and the like. In the *consolations applying* [to the redemption], however, no condition is stated, not to speak of the converse of a condition.

Another reason [why the thesis referred to above is untenable] is that God's promises in regard to Israel's redemption have been put by Him on a par with His statement in regard to the deluge that occurred in the days of *Noah, peace be upon him.* He said,[61] namely: "Just as, no matter how grievously My servants might sin,

60. This quotation follows the reading of Ibn Tibbon.
61. "He said"—added by Ibn Tibbon.

I shall not bring a deluge upon them because I have sworn that it would not come to pass but that I would punish them in some other way, so have I sworn insofar as you are concerned, that I shall no more abolish your rule." That is the sense of the statement of Scripture: *For this is as the waters of Noah unto Me; for as I have sworn that the waters of Noah should no more go over the earth, so have I sworn that I would not be wroth with thee, nor rebuke thee* (Isa. 54:9). Even, therefore, if the people were to sin, God would punish them in whatever manner He pleased, but not by the abolition of their government [, such as happened in the days of the second Temple].

A further reason [for the inadmissibility of the aforementioned hypothesis] is that Scripture reports that the people who will be redeemed will, as we have explained, choose to obey God and not to rebel against Him. Now God is, as we have previously demonstrated, aware of all that is to be.[62] It is, therefore, untenable that there should prevail [at the time of the redemption] any iniquity or sin of which He has no knowledge. If there be no sin, then, even though a condition be attached to their well-being, that condition could not harm them, still less if there is no condition.

Finally [the conditions that are to prevail at the time of the redemption] are presented in the Torah as resembling creations[63] decreed by God. <249> They must, therefore, inevitably come to pass, as we have explained[64] in the seventh treatise. Thus He took a solemn oath,[65] saying: *For I lift up My hand to heaven, and say: As I live for ever, if I whet My glittering sword . . . I will make Mine arrows drunk with blood . . . Sing aloud, O ye nations, of His people* (Deut. 32:40–43). By means of this explanation, then, all the confused and false notions entertained by them on the subject of underlying stipulations or provisos are refuted.

62. Cf. above, pp. 132 and 191.
63. "creations"—added by Ibn Tibbon and M.
64. Cf. above, p. 268.
65. "in the seventh treatise. Thus he took a solemn oath"—added by Ibn Tibbon and M.

CHAPTER VIII

And now that I have removed the foundation upon which they built their edifice, let me present, in addition, the following fifteen refutations of their view. Five of these consist of arguments from the text of Sacred Writ. Five others are proofs derived from history. Five more, again, are arguments that can be grasped by personal observation.

As for the five arguments taken from the text of Scripture, the first is that, according to the *messages of consolation* [which picture the conditions that are to prevail at the time of the redemption] all Israelites are supposed to foregather in the Holy Land, not a single one of them remaining in foreign parts. Thus it has been said in Scripture: *And I will gather them from the countries, and will bring them into their own land* [66] (Ezek. 34: 13). At the time of the *second Temple,* however, only 42,360 of them returned. Thus Scripture reports: *The whole congregation together was forty and two thousand three hundred and threescore* (Neh. 7: 66).

The second [refutation of the theory that the messages of consolation referred to the time of the second Temple] is that [according to these messages] the Israelites were destined to be gathered from the islands of the sea, as has been stated in Scripture: *And from Elam, and from Shinar, and from Hamath, and from the islands of the sea* (Isa. 11: 11). However, when the Israelites went into exile for the first time, they traveled to none of these islands of the sea, not to speak of returning from them.

Thirdly [according to the prophecies of consolation], the nations were to build the walls of Jerusalem, as is stated in Scripture: *And aliens shall build up thy walls, and their kings shall minister unto thee* (Isa. 60: 10). But not enough that they did not build anything for us at the time of the *second Temple,* but they even hindered us, so that we were constantly at war with them during the period of construction. Thus it is related in Scripture: *They that builded the wall and they that bore burdens . . . and the*

66. This quotation follows the reading of Ibn Tibbon.

builders, every one had his sword girded by his side, and so builded (Neh. 4: 11, 12).

In the fourth place, [at the time of the redemption] the gates of the city were to be <250> open day and night on account of the security felt by its inhabitants and the incoming and outgoing traffic, as is stated in Scripture: *Thy gates shall be open continually, day and night, they shall not be shut*[67] (Isa. 60: 11). We find, however, that at the time of the *second Temple* the gates used to be locked before sunset and would not be opened before late in the forenoon, as Nehemiah reports: *And I said unto them: "Let not the gates of Jerusalem be opened until the sun be hot"* (Neh. 7: 3).

In the fifth place, [it has been stated] that [at the time of the redemption] there would not remain a nation that would not be subservient to Israel as is said in Scripture: *For that nation and kingdom that shall not serve thee shall perish* (Isa. 60: 12). However, we have no doubt that both the Israelites themselves, as well as their fields, were subject to the kings during the time of the *second Temple*, as is stated in Scripture: *Behold, we are servants this day, and the land, etc.* (Neh. 9: 36). This constitutes the exposition of the five [refutations] from the standpoint of the text of Sacred Writ.

As for the arguments derived from history, it is to be remembered that in the first instance [according to prophecies concerning the redemption] the people were supposed to kindle fires with the wood of the implements of the war of Gog for a period of seven years, as it is stated in Scripture: *And they that dwell in the cities of Israel shall go forth, and shall make fires of the weapons and use them as fuel, both the shields and the bucklers, the bows and the arrows, and the handstaves, and the spears, and they shall make fires of them seven years*[68] (Ezek. 39: 9).

Secondly, [according to the predictions pertaining to the redemption] the Nile of Egypt is supposed to run dry in one place and the Euphrates in seven places, so that the people would be able to walk across them. Thus it is said in Scripture: *And the*

67. This quotation follows the reading of Ibn Tibbon.
68. This quotation follows the reading of Ibn Tibbon.

Lord will utterly destroy the tongue of the Egyptian sea; and with His scorching wind will He shake His hand over the River, [and will smite it into seven streams, and cause men to march over dryshod.] And there shall be a highway for the remnant of His people (Isa. 11:15, 16).

Thirdly, the *Mount of Olives* is supposed to split in twain from east to west so that one half of it will lie to the north and the other half to the south, with a large valley between them. Thus it is said in Scripture: *And the mount of Olives shall be cleft in the midst thereof toward the east and toward the west, [so that there shall be a very great valley; and half of the mountain shall remove toward the north, and half of it toward the south]* (Zech. 14:4).

In the fourth place the Temple was to be built in accordance with the [prophet Ezekiel's] *plan of the house* (Ezek. 43:11) from beginning to end.

Fifthly, a spring was to issue from the Temple and then broaden out until it would become a great river that no one could cross. Thus it is stated in Scripture: *And behold, waters issued from under the threshold* <251> *of the house eastward* (Ezek. 47:1), and so forth until the end of that passage. *Afterward he measured a thousand; and it was a river that I could not pass through* (Ezek. 47:5).

On the two banks of that river, furthermore, there was to be every kind of food-tree, that would constantly bear fruit and the leaves of which would be perennial and would thus be a source of nourishment as well as of healing. Thus it is stated in Scripture: *And by the river upon the bank thereof, on this side and on that side, shall grow [every tree for food, whose leaf shall not wither, neither shall the fruit thereof fail . . . and the fruit thereof shall be for food, and the leaf thereof for healing]* (Ezek. 47:12). However, no report has ever come down to us that any of these five things happened [during the days of the second Temple]. On the contrary, history states definitely that nothing of the kind took place [in that period].

As for the five other [arguments, which are based on facts] that can be grasped by personal observation, the first is that, according to the prophets, all creatures would eventually believe in and profess the unity of God, as has been said by Scripture: *And the Lord shall be King over all the earth* (Zech. 14:9). Yet we see them at present steeped in their error and unbelief.

Secondly, it has been foretold that the believers would be exempted from the defraying of taxes and the purveying of money and food to others, as is stated in Scripture: *The Lord hath sworn by His right hand, and by the arm of His strength: Surely I will no more give thy corn to be food for thine enemies* [69] (Isa. 62:8). Yet here we see an entire nation defraying the tax and being obedient and subservient to any nation under whose power it happens to fall.

In the third place, [the prophecies concerning the redemption speak about] the abolition of wars from among men so that they would no longer bear arms against each other, as is stated in Scripture: *And they shall beat their swords into ploughshares, and their spears into pruning-hoooks; nation shall not lift up sword against nation* [70] (Isa. 2:4). Yet what we actually see is that the nations are warring and fighting with each other as violently as possible. Should someone interpret the above-mentioned statement to mean that they would no longer wage war against each other on account of religion, his attention must be called to the fact that they are in reality quarreling and contending over their religions as fiercely as ever.

A fourth [condition attributed to the age of the redemption] is that the animals would be at peace with each other, so much so that the wolf and the lamb would graze together, and the lion would eat straw, and the young child would play with serpents and vipers, as has been stated by Scripture: *And the wolf shall dwell with the lamb. . . . And the cow and the bear shall feed. . . . [And the lion shall eat straw like the ox. And the sucking child shall play on the hole of the asp]. . . . They shall not hurt nor destroy* (Isa. 11:6–9). Yet we see that at present they

---

69. This quotation follows the reading of Ibn Tibbon.
70. This quotation follows the reading of Ibn Tibbon.

behave in accordance with their nature and their evil [tendencies], no change whatever having taken place in them.

Should someone, again, interpret this also as a parable, saying that it was meant solely to affirm that the wicked would make peace with <252> the virtuous among men, [it is to be noted that] the situation is really the reverse. Greater injustices and wrongs are committed nowadays by the strong against the weak than ever.

The fifth prediction [in regard to the period of the redemption concerns] the resettlement of the region of Sodom and its restoration to its former state. Thus Scripture says: *And I will turn their captivity, the captivity of Sodom and her daughters* (Ezek. 16: 53), and also: *And thy sisters, Sodom and her daughters, shall return to their former estate* (Ezek. 16: 55).

Furthermore the Torah states expressly that its sea was a sweet-water lake which watered the land by flowing over the surface. Thus Scripture says: *And Lot lifted up his eyes, and beheld all the plain of the Jordan, that it was well watered every where, etc.* (Gen. 13: 10). It says also [that the region of Sodom was] *Like the garden of the Lord (ibid.);* that is [to say] like that of which it is expressly stated: *And a river went out of Eden to water the garden* (Gen. 2: 10).

Finally, it declares [that this region was] *Like the land of Egypt* (Gen. 13: 10); that is, as is said elsewhere in Scripture: *It is not as the land of Egypt . . . where thou didst sow thy seed, and didst water it with thy foot, as a garden of herbs* (Deut. 11: 10). Yet we see that Sodom is today a land of desolation, a repository of salt, and that its sea is salty and terrifying in its present state. All these facts that have been listed prove conclusively that the *prophecies of consolation* [pertaining to the redemption] have not yet been fulfilled.

CHAPTER IX

Now all the arguments that we have presented against the view [that the messages of comfort on the part of the prophets referred to the period of the second Temple] apply also to [the belief of] the Christians; that is, except for our note in regard to the building of the *second Temple*. These Christians, namely, do not maintain that the fulfillment of these promises had its beginning at the time [of the construction of the] said [Temple]. They fix the date rather at 135 years before the destruction of the *second Temple*. There applies to them, therefore—I mean to the Christians in particular—another refutation; namely, that which is alluded to by the prophet, *peace be upon him,* in the passage *seventy weeks* (Dan. 9:24). In our opinion that is to be interpreted as meaning 490 years.[71] This would include the forty-nine from the time that the people was exiled until they began to build the *second Temple*, as is stated in the verse following: *Know therefore and discern, that from the going forth of the word to restore and to build Jerusalem unto one anointed, a prince, shall be seven weeks* (Dan. 9:25). Also to be included in this figure are the 434 years of the existence of the edifice of the [second] Temple. In that [sum allowance must be made for a period of] idleness during which the building operations were interrupted and suspended, as it is stated: *And for threescore and two weeks, it shall be built again,* <253> *with broad place and moat, but in troublous times*[72] (*ibid.*). This coincides exactly with the comment made by us in reference to the passage *Then ceased the work of the house of God* (Ezra 4:24).

The last week, finally, will be a period partly of peace between the Jewish nation and some of the kings, and partly one of the violation of treaties,[73] and of war among them all. Thus it is stated in Scripture: *And he shall make a firm covenant with many for one week; and for half of the week he shall cause the sacrifice and the offering to cease* (Dan. 9:27). The land will then be made desolate and many of its inhabitants perish, as is stated there: *And upon the wing of detestable things shall be that which causeth appalment; and that until the extermination wholly determined be poured out upon that which causeth appalment* (*ibid.*).

This period of seventy weeks embraces, therefore, eras of pros-

71. "years"—added by Ibn Tibbon.
72. This quotation follows the reading of Ibn Tibbon.
73. "of treatises"—added by Ibn Tibbon and M.

perity and well-being as well as those of the abolition of Jewish self-government and the functioning of the *priesthood* and the prophets. For Scripture makes at the beginning of the passage quoted above, the statement: *To finish the transgression, and to make an end of sin, and to forgive iniquity, and to bring in everlasting righteousness, and to seal vision and prophet, and to anoint the most holy place* (Dan. 9:24). One might compare this statement to that of a person who says: "I spent altogether fifty days of a mixture of good and evil between marriage,[74] sickness, and trade," and then gives the details.

[After this general statement,] then, Scripture informs us that at the end of the period every anointed *priest* will be cut off so that there will be none in existence. It says, namely: *And after threescore and two weeks shall an anointed one be cut off, and be no more* (Dan. 9:26). Now Scripture does not mean to refer, when it makes this statement, to any one specific person. It has in mind thereby every *anointed priest,* in the sense in which this term is used in the *Torah* when it says: *If the anointed priest* (Lev. 4:3); *And the anointed priest shall bring* (Lev. 4:16); *And the anointed priest that shall be in his stead* (Lev. 6:15), and the like.

High priests will, then, be cut off from the Jewish people after this period as our Lord, exalted and magnified be He, has informed us. Now these people maintain that by the statement of Scripture, *An anointed one shall be cut off, and be no more* (Dan. 9:26) is meant one specific individual. But this is untenable for sundry reasons. One of them is that the term *anointed* (mašiah) does not refer exclusively to one particular person, but may be applied to any *priest or king.* Furthermore, whenever the expression <254> *shall be cut off* (yikkareth) is used with the meaning of "to kill," it is employed only for one who is put to death deservedly, as in the statement of Scripture: *Whosoever eateth it shall be cut off* (Lev. 17:14). Moreover, this event is supposed to take place simultaneously with the destruction of the sanctuary, which is associated with it: *And the people of a prince that shall come shall destroy the city and the sanctuary; but his end shall be with a flood* (Dan. 9:26).

74. "marriage"—Ibn Tibbon and M.

However, the clearest [refutation] of all lies in the fact that from the time when this revelation was made to *Daniel* until the date which they believe [to have been the time of the fulfillment of the prophecies regarding the redemption], only 285 [75] years had elapsed. Now the total sum [mentioned in the book of Daniel] is 490 years. Of this number of years 70 were taken up by the period preceding the building of the second Temple, and 420 by that of its existence.

I have found, then, that the advocates [of the Christian doctrine] had no other means [of supporting their theory] except the contention that an addition is to be made in the chronological calculation. They maintain, namely, that the government of the Persians over Palestine existed for a period of something like 300 years before that of the Greeks and that the number of their kings during this period was seventeen. However, I have refuted this contention on their part from the text of the book of *Daniel* itself, [pointing out] that it was impossible that between the time of the government of Babylon and that of the Greeks more than four Persian kings should have ruled over Palestine. For the angel said to *Daniel, peace be upon him: And as for me, in the first year of Darius the Mede, I stood up to be a supporter and a stronghold unto him. And now I will declare unto thee the truth. Behold, there shall stand up yet three kings in Persia; and the fourth shall be far richer than they all; and when he is waxed strong through his riches, he shall stir up all against the realm of Greece* (Dan. 11: 1, 2). The above statement has thus been explained from every aspect.

These are, then, the arguments that may be offered in refutation of the doctrine of the Christians aside from the objections to be raised against their theory of the suspension of the laws [76] of the Torah and those that might be urged against them on the subject of the unity of God,[77] and other matters, which cannot properly be presented in this book.

The eighth treatise has hereby been completed.

75. "285"—Cf. Guttmann, p. 239 and n. 3.
76. Cf. the third treatise, pp. 157 ff.
77. Cf. the second treatise, pp. 103 ff.

TREATISE IX

<255> CONCERNING REWARD AND PUNISH-
MENT IN THE WORLD TO COME

CHAPTER I

O UR Lord, blessed and exalted be He, has informed us that He has set aside a time for recompensing the righteous, in which, moreover, he will make a distinction between them and the godless. This is borne out by His statement: *And they shall be Mine, saith the Lord of hosts, in the day that I do make, even Mine own treasure; and I will spare them, etc. Then shall ye again discern between the righteous and the wicked* [1] (Mal. 3:17, 18). It has furthermore been supported by miracles and marvels presented by the prophets,[2] wherefore we have acknowledged it [as a fact].

It behooves me now to list the considerations leading to the assumption of a period of time, which has been termed by us that of "the world to come," on the basis of rational arguments, Scripture, and tradition, in the same manner in which I have previously demonstrated the reality of prophecy at the beginning of this book [3] by means of logical proof. I say, then, first of all, that it has been conclusively proven in the course of the thesis presented in the third,[4] fourth,[5] and sixth [6] treatises [of this book] that the heaven and the earth and whatever lies between them have all been created solely on account of man. That is why God placed man in the center of the universe surrounded by everything.[7] For that reason, too, did He endow the human soul with superior qualities of intellect and wisdom and charge it with the observance of com-

1. This quotation follows the reading of Ibn Tibbon.
2. "prophets"—added by Ibn Tibbon and M.
3. Cf. the third treatise, pp. 145 ff.
4. Cf. pp. 137 ff.
5. Cf. pp. 180 ff.
6. Cf. p. 248.
7. Cf. p. 181.

mandments and prohibitions [8] by dint of which it might be fitted for life eternal.

[It has] also [been shown in these treatises] [9] that this life will commence when the number of human souls, the creation of which has been decreed by divine Wisdom, has been fulfilled. God will thereupon cause them to dwell in another abode so that He may recompense them therein. All this, that has been supported by logical, Biblical, and historical proofs presented by us there, is quite adequate as groundwork and introduction to this present treatise. I therefore intend to add to the previous allegations at this point only such observations as would confirm and corroborate and elucidate them more fully than they have been by the afore-mentioned three sources [of knowledge].

I say, then, that a further conclusion that reason forces upon us, in view of what we know of the wisdom and omnipotence <256> and kindness to His creatures on the part of the Creator, exalted and magnified be He, is that it is incompatible with His character, that the measure of happiness reserved for this human soul be restricted to the mundane well-being and pleasure it finds in this world. For all well-being in this mundane world is bound up with misfortune, and all happiness with hardship, and all pleasure with pain, and all joy with sorrow.

In fact, I find that these individual fortunes of which life is made up are either evenly balanced or that the things of a depressing nature outweigh those of a cheering nature. Since this is undoubtedly so, it is inconceivable that the All-Wise, may His greatness be magnified, should have set up these contradictory conditions as the highest goal of the soul's aspirations. It must, therefore, perforce be assumed that He has set aside for it a place in which it can lead an untroubled existence and attain pure happiness.

I find, furthermore, that none of God's creatures known to me feel secure and tranquil in this world, even when they have reached the most exalted ruling position and the highest station therein. Now this feeling is not something natural to the soul.

8. Cf. p. 137.
9. Cf. the beginning of the sixth treatise, p. 235.

It is due, rather, to its consciousness of the fact that there is reserved for it an abode that is superior to all the excellencies of its present dwelling. That is why it yearns for that abode and why its eyes look forward longingly to it. Were it not so, the soul would have felt secure and have been at rest.

Another consideration [necessitating the assumption of the existence of a world to come] is the fact that man's reason has been made to regard as reprehensible things which he desires by nature. These include such matters as adultery, stealing, bragging, the satisfaction of one's thirst for vengeance by murder, and the like. But, when man abides by the dictates of reason in regard to the aforementioned, he is overcome by feelings of regret and depression and sadness that pain him and cause him heartache. Now it would not have been right that this should happen to him were it not for the fact that he was to be compensated therefor by God.

Similarly, inasmuch as man's reason has been made to approve of truthfulness and justice, to demand what is acknowledged as good and prohibit what is forbidden, and since the carrying out of these things earns for him the enmity and hatred of those persons from whom payment has been exacted[10] or of those who have been prevented by his edict and interdict from realizing their desires, and since he might even be abused and flogged and killed, it would certainly not have been fair to expose him to such perils because of the things which his reason has been made to approve, were it not for the fact <257> that God intended to give him ample reward in return therefor.

A further proof is presented by the violence which we see men committing against each other resulting in the well-being of the one who committed the wrong and the misery of the wronged respectively.[11] Then they die. But since God, magnified be His majesty, practices justice, He must perforce have reserved for them a second abode in which justice would be restored in their relationship to each other, reward being remitted to the one corresponding

10. "payment has been exacted"—cf. Ibn Tibbon.
11. The text is defective. This interpretation is based on the rendering of Guttmann, p. 243.

to the pain he has suffered at the hand of him that wronged, and punishment being brought down upon the other corresponding to the pleasure derived by his nature from his wrongdoing and violence.

Again, we see the godless prospering in this world while believers are in misery therein. There can, therefore, be no escaping the belief that there exists for the former, as well as for the latter, a second world in which they will be recompensed in justice and righteousness.

Moreover, we find that he who has killed but one person suffers the penalty of death just as one does who has slain ten, and, similarly, he who has committed adultery once is punished once [by] the government, by flogging or the payment of a monetary fine, or the like, as is he who has done that twenty times. It must, therefore, perforce be assumed that the remainder of the punishment of which each of these sinners is deserving will befall him in another world. The same applies to whatever is of this order.

If someone were to ask, however, "But why, then, did not the All-Wise, magnified be His Majesty, from the very start create man in the world to come and thus spare him all these sorrows and the compensation therefor?" we would answer him as we have explained previously in the third treatise.[12]

CHAPTER II

I shall now give a résumé of thirteen instances from Scripture that bear out this doctrine of reward and punishment in the world to come. The first of these, I might say, is the case of *Isaac*, peace be upon him. Thou notest how he delivered up his soul as a *sacrifice* and *offering* in order to comply with the bidding of his Master. Now if he had been of the opinion that retribution is restricted to this world, what sort of requital could he have aspired to after his death? The All-Wise, magnified be His majesty, would certainly not have made so difficult a demand of him if he were not destined to be recompensed for it.

12. Cf. pp. 138 ff.

I find, furthermore, that *Hananiah, Mishael, and Azariah,* peace be upon them, delivered themselves up <258> to the fire rather than serve an idol instead of their Master.[13] Now if it had been their conviction that retribution is confined solely to this world, what would there have been left for them to aspire to or desire after having been burned to death?

I find also that *Daniel, peace be upon him,* delivered himself up to the lions on account of the prayer [14] that he had uttered to his Master. Now if it had been his conviction that there was no reward except that which is obtained in this world, what would there have been left for him to look forward to [15] after being devoured by the lions?

All these instances indicate, may God have mercy on thee, that the prophets, peace be upon them, were all agreed upon this: that the reward for man's behavior is not meted out in this world but is only given in that which comes after it. Should someone object, however, saying, "But we do not find any explicit mention in the Torah of retribution anywhere else than in this world alone, as is, for example, written in the *section* of *If in My statutes* (Lev. 26: 3 ff.) and the chapter of *And it shall come to pass if ye shall hearken diligently*" (Deut. 11: 13), our reply would be that the All-Wise did not completely omit from Scripture all references to reward and punishment in the world to come, as we shall explain later.

If, on the other hand, the express statements of Holy Writ dwell on this-worldly prosperity and hardship only, it is for two reasons. One of these is that, inasmuch as the reward of the world to come is demonstrable only rationally, as we have explained, the Torah was terse in its explanation. Such brevity was exercised by it in the statement: *And the Lord God commanded the man, saying* (Gen. 2: 16). It did not state there that the charge included such commandments as *I am the Lord thy God* (Exod. 20: 2), *Thou shalt not murder* (Exod. 20: 13), *Thou shalt not commit adultery* (Exod.

13. Cf. Dan. 3: 18 ff.
14. Cf. Dan. 6: 11 ff.
15. "to look forward to"—added by Ibn Tibbon.

20:14), [and] *Thou shalt not steal* (Gen. 20:15),[16] because reason points to the cogency of all these. It was explicit only with reference to the injunction *But of the tree of the knowledge of good and evil, thou shalt not eat* (Gen. 2:17), because that is not something indicated by reason. Similarly was it outspoken in regard to mundane retribution because reason does not point to its cogency, while it was terse in its explanation of the reward in the hereafter, relying on its being pointed out by reason.

Secondly, it is the characteristic of prophecy to enlarge upon events of immediate urgency and to be brief in regard to those of remote contingency. Inasmuch, therefore, as the people [of Israel] had greater need, at the time the Torah was written for them, to become acquainted with <259> the nature of the land of Palestine toward which they were traveling, the Torah dwelt at length upon the description thereof, as well as on the effect of their obedience or disobedience of God's commandments upon its fertility. That is why it began by speaking about the rainfall and whatever else is mentioned in the passage: *For the land, whither thou goest in to possess it, is not as the land of Egypt . . . where thou didst sow thy seed, and didst water it with thy foot* (Deut. 11:10), and so forth. Distant matters, on the other hand, were alluded to by it briefly, without going into lengthy explanations.

Among the most convincing proofs supporting our contention is the fact that we find that *Moses, our teacher, may peace be upon him,* who was the most pious and virtuous of men, did not attain, by virtue of the fact that he had not been permitted to enter Palestine,[17] any of the great mundane rewards, such as those promised in passages of Sacred Writ like *Then I will give your rains in their season* (Lev. 26:4), *And your threshing shall reach unto the vintage* (Lev. 26:5), *And I will give peace in the land* (Lev. 26:6), *And I will make you fruitful, and multiply you* (Lev. 26:9), and *And ye shall eat old store long kept* (Lev. 26:10). Now if the only rewards to be expected by the righteous were those enumerated in

16. Cf. the baraytha quoted in Sanh. 56a, in which the verse in Genesis is interpreted as harboring these implications.

17. Cf. Num. 20:12 and Deut. 3:27.

If in My statutes (Lev. 26: 3 ff.), then most of them should have been conferred on our teacher Moses. This, therefore, serves as further [18] proof that the greater portion of his reward is meted out to man in the world to come. Hence the aforementioned earthly rewards constitute only indications and symbols, as I have explained previously.[19]

Another instance supporting our thesis of reward in the world to come is the fact reported to us that *Elijah, may peace be upon him,* whose prayer to his Master resulted in other persons' being blessed by Him with fine flour and oil,[20] himself had to go looking for a loaf of bread without being able to obtain it.[21] Again, there is the case of *Elisha, peace be upon him,* on account of whom, when he was already dead, God brought back to life the man who had been cast into his grave.[22] Now certainly, if reward had been confined strictly to this world, he who would not have been deserving of attaining thereto could not have enabled others to realize anything thereof.

There is, furthermore, what we are told about the inhabitants of *Sodom*—that when their iniquities had become exceedingly great, God overturned their land and rained fire and brimstone upon it. Now if it were true that no punishment takes place outside <260> of this world, then whoever sins excessively should meet with a similar fate in proportion to his sinfulness. Yet we find nothing like that actually happening.

Another argument in favor of retribution in the hereafter is presented by the fact that whenever *the children of Israel* served other gods, their Lord caused one of the nations to rule over them, punishing them and taking them captive and leading them into exile. Yet we see in our own time many of the nations of the world serving other gods without being taken captive and led into exile. But if punishment were confined to this world only, a similar fate should have befallen them.

18. "further"—added by Ibn Tibbon and M.
19. Cf. pp. 208 ff.
20. Cf. I Kings 17: 15 ff.
21. Cf. I Kings 17: 11 and 19: 4 ff.
22. Cf. II Kings 13: 21.

Again we are confronted by the fact that God,[23] the just, ordered the killing of the young children of the *Midianites* and the extermination of the young children *of the generation of the deluge*. We note also how He continually causes pain and even death to little babes. Logical necessity, therefore, demands that there exist after death a state in which they would obtain compensation for the pain suffered prior thereto, as we have explained.[24]

CHAPTER III

Having mentioned these six instances, it behooves me now to add seven proofs furnished by the text of Scripture. I might say that these seven points are referred to and alluded to in the Torah and stated more explicitly and clearly in the other books of the prophets.

The first of these is the fact that what man acquires through wisdom and through compliance with the Law is called "life." Thus Scripture says: *Which if a man do, he shall live by them* (Ezek. 20: 21). On the other hand, what the fool achieves as a result of his folly is called "death." This is borne out by such statements of Scripture as *The soul that sinneth, it shall die* (Ezek. 18: 20); also *For whoso findeth me findeth life. . . . But he that misseth me wrongeth his own soul; all they that hate me love death* [25] (Prov. 8: 35, 36); also *The path of life goeth upward for the wise, that he may depart from the netherworld beneath* [26] (Prov. 15: 24); also *Her house is the way to the netherworld, going down to the chambers of death* [27] (Prov. 7: 27); also *If I had not believed to look upon the goodness of the Lord in the land of the living* (Ps. 27: 13); also *For Thou wilt not abandon my soul to the nether-world . . . Thou makest me to know the path of life* (Ps. 16: 11); and finally *Steadfast righteousness tendeth to life* (Prov. 11: 19). Since, however, it is out of the question that any of these expressions refer

23. "God"—added by M.
24. Cf. above, p. 214.
25. This quotation follows the reading of Ibn Tibbon.
26. This quotation follows the reading of Ibn Tibbon.
27. This quotation follows the reading of Ibn Tibbon.

to the life of this world in which the righteous and the wicked are equal, <261> they must, of necessity, refer to the life of the here-after. There is, moreover, much to be said about each of the verses quoted above.

The second [proof] is the declaration that bounty is treasured up before God for the righteous, while evil is reserved for the wicked. With reference thereto Scripture says: *The memory of the righteous shall be for a blessing; but the name of the wicked shall rot* (Prov. 10:7). Furthermore *Nehemiah* said: *Remember unto me, O my God, for good* (Neh. 5:10). About the wicked, on the other hand, he said: *Remember, O my God, Tobiah and Sanballat according to these their works* (Neh. 6:14). These utterances merely second such statements made in the *Torah* as *And it shall be righteousness unto us, if we observe to do . . .* (Deut. 6:25); and *And it shall be righteousness unto thee before the Lord thy God* (Deut. 24:13); as well as that of the prophet: *And thy righteousness shall go before thee* (Isa. 58:8). Each verse bearing on this subject, however, stands in need of extensive explanation.

The third [point] is the declaration that God has books and archives in which are recorded the deeds of the righteous as well as of the wicked. There is, for example, the statement made by *Moses, our teacher, peace be upon him: And if not, blot me, I pray Thee, out of Thy book, which Thou hast written* (Exod. 32:32). Scripture says, furthermore: *Let them be blotted out of the book of the living, and not be written with the righteous* (Ps. 69:29); also: *Then they that feared the Lord spoke one with another; and the Lord hearkened, and heard, and a book of remembrance was written before Him, for them that feared the Lord, and that thought upon his name* (Mal. 3:16); as well as *Behold, it is written before Me; I will not keep silence, except I have requited, yea, I will requite into their bosom* (Isa. 65:6). Each one of these utter-ances, moreover, entails [28] extensive explanations.

The fourth [point] is the admonition that God, magnified and exalted be He, will conduct a hearing for the requital of every human act, good or evil. This is borne out by such statements of

28. "entails"—literally "embraces."

Scripture as *If thou doest well, shall it not be lifted up? And if thou doest not well, sin coucheth at the door* [29] (Gen. 4:7); as well as *For there is a time there for every purpose and every work* (Eccles. 3:17); also *There are they in great fear* (Ps. 14:5); and *There are the workers of iniquity fallen* (Ps. 36:13); <262> and finally *There they cry, but none giveth answer* (Job 35:12). Each of these utterances, moreover, also embraces a host of explanations.

The fifth [general division] consists of extensive remarks found in the books of Sacred Writ to the effect that God, magnified and exalted be He, is a just judge who rewards every man for what he does. Thus they say on this subject: *The Rock, His works is perfect; for all His ways are justice; a God of faithfulness and without iniquity, etc.*[30] (Deut. 32:4). It is remarked, furthermore: *The Lord is righteous in all His ways* (Ps. 145:17); as well as *But the Lord is enthroned forever; He hath established His throne for judgment. And He will judge the world in righteousness* (Ps. 9:8, 9).

There are also such statements of Scripture as *They stand this day according to Thine ordinances* (Ps. 119:91); and *Though it be given him to be in safety, whereon he resteth, yet His eyes are upon their ways*[31] (Job 24:23); and *For His eyes are upon the ways of a man* (Job 34:21); and *For the ways of man are before the eyes of the Lord* (Prov. 5:21); and *Even to give every man according to his fruit, etc.* (Jer. 17:10); and, finally: *For God shall bring every work into the judgment* (Eccles. 12:14). Each verse, moreover, enfolds a multitude of explanations.

The sixth [general division] dwells on the warning concerning a day reserved by God for retribution. In regard thereto Scripture says: *The great day of the Lord is near, it is near and hasteth greatly*[32] (Zeph. 1:14); *That day is a day of wrath* (Zeph. 1:15); *And I will bring distress upon men, that they shall walk like the blind, etc.* (Zeph. 1:17); *Neither their silver nor their gold shall be able to deliver them in the day of the Lord's wrath* (Zeph. 1:18);

29. This quotation follows the reading of Ibn Tibbon.
30. This quotation follows the reading of Ibn Tibbon.
31. This quotation is found only in the Hebrew version of Ibn Tibbon.
32. This quotation follows the reading of Ibn Tibbon.

and *Gather yourselves together, yea, gather together, O shameless nation; before the decree bring forth . . .*[33] (Zeph. 2:1, 2). Each one of these verses, moreover, has explanations the mention of which I am cutting short in order not to extend unduly the length of this book.

The seventh [general division], finally, consists of [passages in which man's] reward is called good and [in] which [it is stated that] the wicked are excluded therefrom. Thus Scripture states: *That it might be well with them, and with their children for ever* (Deut. 5:26); and also *Oh how abundant is Thy goodness, which Thou hast laid up for them that fear Thee* (Ps. 31:20); as well as *Though yet I know that it shall be well with them that fear God, that fear before Him; but it shall not be well with the wicked, neither shall he prolong his days* (Eccles. 8:12, 13). Moreover, each verse of the above has its explanations.

Should it, <263> however, be thought by anyone that these passages were capable also of other constructions that would invalidate their use as proof of [the doctrine of] a world to come, we might explain to him that he is mistaken in his belief because reason demands retribution in another [34] world. Now any interpretation that agrees with reason must be correct, whereas any that leads to what is contrary to reason must be unsound and fallacious. These are, then, in brief, the proofs adducible from the written text of Scripture.

CHAPTER IV

As for tradition, the evidence that might be cited from that source in support of our theory is too extensive to be noted in its totality. Nevertheless we shall make mention of some of the most important utterances pertinent to this subject occurring therein.

Let us say, then, that our predecessors of *blessed memory* report on the basis of a tradition received from the prophets, *peace be upon them,* that this world stands in the same relationship to the

33. This quotation follows the reading of Ibn Tibbon.
34. "another"—Ibn Tibbon.

world to come as a vestibule to the palace of the king. It goes without saying, of course, that a person must put himself in a fitting condition in the former before entering into the palace in the presence of the ruler. This is explicit from their dictum: *This world is like a vestibule over against the world to come. Prepare thyself in the vestibule that thou mayest enter the main hall* (Mišnah 'Abh. 4:16).

They have said, furthermore, that one hour of penitence in this world is more profitable than the whole of the world to come since penitence is impossible in the latter. For, as we have explained previously, the filth and smut that becomes attached to the soul in this world can be removed from it only by means of penitence. On the other hand, one hour of repose in the world to come is preferable to the entire life of this world, since, as we have explained previously, the souls perpetually look forward to and long for it. *Better one hour of repentance and good deeds in this world than the life of the world to come, and better one hour of serenity in the world to come than the entire life of this world* (Mišnah 'Abh. 4:17).

They transmit, furthermore, that life in the world to come consists exclusively of light, and that eating and drinking and fatigue and procreation and buying and selling and all other mundane occupations are eliminated from it, the reward of the righteous [35] therein being comprised of enjoying the brilliance of the Creator, exalted and magnified be He. Such is the import of their dictum: *In the world to come <264> there will be neither eating nor drinking nor trade nor procreation. But the righteous will sit with their crowns on their heads and enjoy the splendor of the divine Presence* (Běr. 17a). As for the nature of the reward of the righteous, I shall return to the exposition and the explanation thereof later.

The extent to which they clung to the belief in this exalted state, which is to characterize the condition of the righteous in the world to come, is evidenced by the tradition reported by the sages to the effect that whoever does not believe in the reward of

---

35. "the righteous"—added by Ibn Tibbon.

the hereafter and the revelation of the *Torah* and the truthfulness of the transmitters of tradition will not be rewarded in the world to come, even though he be righteous in all other respects. That is the import of their dictum, *blessed be their memory: And the following have no share in the world to come: he that asserts there will be no resurrection of the dead and that the Torah is not of divine origin and the atheist* (Mišnah Sanh. 10:1).

They enumerated, furthermore, seven individuals from among those human beings who, it had been reported to them, would not receive any reward in the world to come on account of their having corrupted other people and having caused them to deviate from obedience to God without being able to repair the damage done by them. That is the import of their dictum: *Three kings and four commoners have no share in the world to come. The three kings are Jeroboam the son of Nebat and Ahab and Manasseh. The four commoners are Balaam and Doeg and Ahitophel and Gehazi* (Mišnah Sanh. 10:2).

Furthermore, when the sages translated the Torah [into Aramaic] for us, on the basis of traditions of the prophets, peace be upon them, they spoke explicitly in its *translation* about the resurrection of *Moses, peace be upon him,* and his heading the Jewish nation again. They, namely, translated the passage: *And he chose a first part for himself, [for there a portion of a ruler was reserved; and there came the heads of the people (wayyar rešith lo [ki šam helkath měhokek șaphun wayyethe raše 'am])* (Deut. 33:21) as denoting: *To him shall be assigned a share in the foremost part of it, for there in his portion Moses the great teacher of Israel is buried. He will come out and go at the head of the people.*[36]

Similarly did they express themselves clearly on the matter of life in the hereafter in the translation of *Let Reuben live, and not die* (Deut. 33:6), rendering it as *Let Reuben live the life of eternity and not die a second death.*[37] As for the translations of the Prophets, the references in them to the reward in the hereafter are too numerous to be quickly enumerated.

36. Cf. Targum Onkelos, *ad loc.*
37. Cf. Targum Onkelos, *ad loc.*

And now that I have explained in my discussion how the doctrine of reward and punishment in the world to come is supported by the three sources of knowledge, namely: reason, Scripture, and tradition, <265> let me say that our nation is fully agreed upon this matter. The tradition concerning it is most firmly established and not subject to being explained away or changed,[38] as I have remarked apropos of the [question of the] suspension of the Law.[39]

CHAPTER V

Having now properly clarified the aforegoing principles, let me say next that the reward and punishment in the hereafter is meted out upon the body and soul unitedly, since they constitute together a single agent. This has already been explained [40] and made clear by me. I have likewise made it evident and clear how God would revive the dead and unite every soul with its body.[41] I have, furthermore, answered the questions pertaining to this subject and resolved such doubts as might possibly arise in connection with it. It behooves me, therefore, at this point to endeavor to explain the nature of the reward and the punishment and describe [42] the locale in which they are to be executed and the time in which they are to take place. I must also demonstrate the necessity of the perpetuity of the status of those who are to be rewarded, as well as of those who are to be punished, and whether their reward and punishment will be equal in any respect or whether there will be a difference [43] between them.

I ought to indicate, furthermore who it is that is deserving of everlasting punishment, and whether those who are to be rewarded and those who are to be punished will be gathered together, and

38. "fully agreed . . . changed"—so according to Ibn Tibbon.
39. Cf. pp. 157 ff.
40. Cf. p. 253.
41. Cf. pp. 264 ff.
42. "describe"—Ibn Tibbon and M.
43. "difference"—Ibn Tibbon, correctly by omitting one diacritical point in the original.

whether it will be compulsory for them to render service to their Master or whether they will also have the right to choose to rebel against Him, and what, in the event that they obeyed Him, would be their recompense. Once I have dealt with ten of these subjects,[44] explaining each of them in turn, I shall have fulfilled the requirements of this treatise.

Let me, therefore, begin by giving an exposition of the nature of the reward and the punishment in the hereafter. In part, this subject has already been treated in what preceded.[45] Here, however, I shall elucidate more fully and say that this reward and punishment will take the form of two very fine substances that our Master, exalted and magnified be He, will create at the time of the retribution, applying them to each of His servants in accordance with his desert. They will both consist of the same essence, an essence resembling the property <266> of burning, luminous fire, that will shine for the righteous but not for the sinful, whilst it will burn the sinful but not the righteous. In reference thereto Scripture has expressly stated: *For, behold, the day cometh, it burneth as a furnace; and all the proud, and all that work wickedness, shall be stubble; and the day that cometh shall set them ablaze, etc. . . . . But unto you that fear My name shall the sun of righteousness arise with healing in its wings, etc. . . . . And ye shall tread down the wicked; for they shall be ashes under the soles of your feet,*[46] *etc.* (Mal. 3: 19–21).

How apt, indeed, is this likening of the retribution in the hereafter to the two activities of the sun, which is the cause of the heat of the day as well as of brilliant light! For [47] when Scripture employs the expressions *the day burneth* and *the sun of righteousness,* it refers to one and the same thing. Seest thou not that it is the usage of the language of Scripture to refer to the sun by means of the term *day (yom)*? It says, namely: *When they were by Jebus —the day (hayyom) was far spent* (Judg. 19: 11). It says further-

---

44. "ten of these subjects"—reading necessitated by the sequel.
45. Cf. above, p. 333.
46. This quotation follows the reading of Ibn Tibbon.
47. "For"—Ibn Tibbon.

more: *Behold, now the day (hayyom) draweth toward evening* (Judg. 19:9).

Basically, then, this substance that the Creator, exalted and magnified be He, will create resembles the sun, except that there will be this difference between it and the latter: namely, that the heat and the light of the sun are inseparable companions, whereas so far as this substance is concerned, the light can, through the omnipotence of the Creator, magnified be His Majesty, be drawn off for the sake of the righteous and its heat collected for the sinful.

This will be accomplished either by means of a special property with which it will be endowed or by means of an accident whereby the ones will be protected against the heat and the others will be screened from the light. However, the second theory is the more probable of the two. Now we note that God acted in this fashion in Egypt. He namely extracted the light for the believers and the darkness for the infidels by means of an accident produced at His behest.

Having established this principle, then, I say, further, that it was for the aforegoing reason that the Scriptures designate the reward of the righteous as light and the entire punishment of the wicked as fire. [The application of] the former to the reward of the righteous is made in such passages as <267> *For with Thee is the fountain of life; in Thy light do we see light* (Ps. 36:10); and also *Light is sown for the righteous, and gladness for the upright in heart* (Ps. 97:11); and again: *The light of the righteous rejoiceth; but the lamp of the wicked shall be put out* (Prov. 13:9). Scripture says, furthermore: *To bring back his soul from the pit, that he may be enlightened with the light of the living* (Job. 33:30), and other things of this tenor.

On the other hand, the Scriptures assert, in reference to the punishment of the wicked: [48] *And the strong shall be as tow, and his work as a spark; and they shall both burn together, and none shall quench them* (Isa. 1:31); and also: *Ye conceive chaff, ye shall bring forth stubble; your breath is a fire that shall devour you* (Isa. 33:11); and again: *Yea, fire shall devour thine adver-*

48. "of the wicked"—added by Ibn Tibbon.

saries (Isa. 26:11); and furthermore: *For a hearth is ordered of old; yea, for the king it is prepared, deep and large; the pile thereof is fire, etc.* (Isa. 30:33). They say also: *For the company of the godless shall be desolate, and fire shall consume the tents of bribery* (Job 15:34); and *Surely their substance is cut off, and their abundance the fire hath consumed* (Job 22:20); and *All darkness is laid up for his treasures; a fire not blown by man shall consume him* (Job 20:26); and *Upon the wicked He will cause to rain coals; fire and brimstone* (Ps. 11:6); as well as *Let burning coals fall upon them; let them be cast into the fire* (Ps. 140:11); and the like.

If someone were now to demand that we picture to him how a body and soul can subsist without the regular ingestion of food and drink,[49] we might present to him the example of *Moses, our teacher, peace be upon him,* whom God, blessed be His name, kept alive three times for forty days and forty nights without food, as Scripture puts it: *And he was there with the Lord forty days and forty nights; he did neither eat bread, nor drink water* (Exod. 34:28). He must, therefore, have been sustained solely by the light which God had [specially] created and with which He covered his face, as is stated by Scripture: *And Moses knew not that the skin of his face sent forth beams* (Exod. 34:29).

God's purpose herein was to present to us an indication and a rationally comprehensible means <268> of deducing that the righteous will subsist in the hereafter on light and not on ordinary nourishment. It was in accordance with this thought that God said to Moses: *Before all thy people will I do marvels, such as have not been wrought in all the earth, nor in any nation* (Exod. 34:10). This statement, again, is of the same tenor as Scripture's declaration to the righteous: *And whereof from of old men have not heard, nor perceived by the ear, neither hath the eye seen a God beside Thee, who worketh for him that waiteth for Him* (Isa. 64:3).

As for the manner of the resurrection of those who are to be punished by being left to burn perpetually in fire, we have not

49. "and drink"—added by Ibn Tibbon and M.

found anyone in the past who met with an experience of such a nature that we might use him as an example. But it is precisely because we do not find any analogue thereto that Scripture emphasizes it and declares explicitly concerning the godless: *For their worm shall not die, neither shall their fire be quenched* (Isa. 66:24).

This last statement carries the necessary implication that their spirits will be preserved within their bodies by means of a fine substance external to the heat that will cause them the pain which will thus constitute the punishment that they will have to endure. Similarly it stands to reason that the spirits of the others—I mean of those who are to be rewarded—will also be preserved within their bodies by means of a fine substance other than the element in which they will have their being, so that the light which reaches them may be a source of everlasting pleasure.

However, the urgency of assuming the existence of a fine preservative substance is greater in the case of those who are to be punished than in that of those who are to be rewarded. Seest thou not that, when kings make up their minds to inflict punishment on a person for a long period of time, they obligate themselves to provide him with food and drink lest he perish before their punishment has been completely carried out upon him, the reason being that their punitive acts are intended by them to fall within the natural capacity for enduring pain? As for the Creator, magnified be His Majesty, however, whose acts are above nature, He can sustain and preserve without food.

Now the reward of the hereafter has been called *Garden of Eden* only because there does not exist in this world anything more magnificent than this garden in which God caused *Adam,* peace be upon him, to dwell. The future punishment, again, has been called *Gehinnom* because the latter has been denominated by Scripture as <269> *Tophta,* which is the name of a place in the valley facing the Temple which is referred to as *Topheth and the valley of the son of Hinnom* (Jer. 7:32), and also as *Valley of Hinnom* in the book of *Joshua* (Josh. 15:8).

Thus the garden of *Adam* came to serve as a byword for excellence, as is illustrated in the statement: *The land is as the garden of Eden before them* (Joel 2: 3). The place called *Topheth,* on the other hand, constitutes an example of baseness, as has been said in Scripture: *And the houses of Jerusalem, and the houses of the kings of Judah, which are defiled, shall be as the place of Topheth* (Jer. 19:13).

CHAPTER VI

Inasmuch as I have now made clear the character of the two types of retribution, let me answer the third question; namely, that of the locale in which the requital of these individuals who are to be rewarded or punished is to take place. For since they are human beings composed of bodies and souls, they must needs have a place upon which they are established and surroundings encompassing them, which the Creator, magnified and exalted be He, would consequently have to create and cause them to dwell in. This hypothesis is the necessary inference from the concept of creation. Nevertheless the existence of such a locale is expressly mentioned by the Scriptures. Nay, more, it is called by them "heaven" and "earth" in order to render it accessible to our understanding, since we can see only a heaven and an earth. This is illustrated by the statement of Scripture: *For as the new heavens and the new earth, which I will make, shall remain before Me, etc.* (Isa. 66:22).

Pursuing this subject more thoroughly, I ask [myself]: "What was the reason that motivated [divine] Wisdom in creating a *new heaven and a new earth?* Could not God compensate His creatures in this place that is known to us?" I must, therefore, explain that the [latter course would be impossible] because this earth of ours is equipped only to provide the necessities of alimentation first and foremost. That is why it contains grain fields and orchards, and rivers and streams [50] for the watering of trees and plants, and mountains and valleys for rains and torrents, and steppes in which there are pastures for the beasts, and waterless regions in which there are roads for pedestrians. All these advantages are needed

50. "streams"—Ibn Tibbon.

by us <270> in our present abode because of our requirement of nourishment and material possessions. In the world to come, however, in which nourishment and material possessions have no place, there would be no purpose to the existence of fields or plants or rivers or mountains or valleys or any of the things mentioned previously or aught that resembles them. All that the servants of God will stand in need of at that time will be a center and an environment which will be created for them by God as it will please Him.

Now the interpretation of God's statement: *For as the new heavens,* quoted above, is unlike that of His remark: *For, behold, I create new heavens and a new earth* (Isa. 65:17). For the latter refers to the time of the *salvation* of God's people, the conditions prevailing during which would make it seem as though God had created the world for them anew. Needless to say, this metaphoric construction is to be applied to the statement following this one; namely: *For, behold, I create Jerusalem a rejoicing, and her people a joy* [51] (Isa. 65:18). It could not have been meant hereby that God was going to renew the creation of Jerusalem, but rather that He would renew His people's complete rejoicing. This is evident from the conclusion of the remark: *a rejoicing, and her people a joy;* that is to say, as though He had created them to be creatures of joy.

As for God's statement: *For as the new heavens* (Isa. 66:22), since it applies to the world to come, it must literally refer to the place and the environment that God is destined to create for His servants upon the annihilation of our present center and surroundings, as has been explained elsewhere: *Of old Thou didst lay the foundation of the earth; and the heavens are the work of Thy hands. They shall perish, but Thou shalt endure; . . . but Thou art the selfsame, and Thy years shall have no end. The children of Thy servants shall dwell securely* [52] (Ps. 102:26–29).

This remark *shall dwell securely* after the annihilation of heaven and earth presupposes necessarily the creation of a second place

51. This quotation follows the reading of Ibn Tibbon.
52. This quotation follows the reading of Ibn Tibbon.

in which they will dwell. [The necessity of such a place is also evident] from the fact that the air, which lies between the extremities [of heaven and earth], extracts from our bodies [elements] which have to be replaced by means of nourishment.[53] Since human beings will, in the world to come, not be nourished [by ordinary food], it follows, of necessity, that the atmosphere must be of a different nature from that [which exists] here [on earth], so that they will not require such nourishment. And if the two extremities [that is, the heaven and earth of the world to come] be different from those [of the present world], it would be quite proper <271> for the atmosphere between them to be other than the present one and of a different nature from this air [of ours].

As for the nature of the time [that will obtain in the hereafter], that constitutes the answer to the fourth question. Apropos of that subject, let us say that time will here be composed entirely of light uninterrupted by darkness. I mean there will be no alternation of night and day following each other successively. For the reason that motivated [divine] Wisdom, when it caused men to dwell on earth, in making the distinction between night and day, which is the result of the peregrination of the sun and its movement, was merely in order that they might employ the daytime in working for their livelihood and other occupations and spend the night in relaxation, rest, cohabitation, the practice of solitude, and similar pastimes. Since, however, in the world to come none of these things have any place, the divisions of night and day can very well be dispensed with.

The same applies to the division of time into months and years, the only reason for which, on earth, is the need for making computations, for fixing wages, and for figuring the period of growth of what grows on the earth. The only kind of time division that will have pertinence in the hereafter will be that which may serve as an indication of the periods when divine service is due,[54] as I shall explain later.[55]

53. Cf. above, p. 279.
54. Cf. Guttmann, p. 249 and n. 1.
55. Cf. below, p. 353.

CHAPTER VII

As for the fifth and the sixth [questions]: namely, those concerning the necessary assumption of the perpetuity of the reward in the hereafter of the righteous and of the punishment of the sinful, I shall now discourse about this matter from the standpoint of reason. I say, then, that inasmuch as God made it incumbent upon man to serve Him, it was necessary that He arouse his desire therefor by means of the best of stimulants. For if the stimulant used were weak and the individual did not render God the service due Him, it might be said that, if a stronger incentive had been employed, he would have served God. Where, however, the stimulant employed is unlimited, there is no longer any excuse left.

To explain this in greater detail, let it be assumed that the duration of the reward of the righteous was set at one thousand years. It could possibly be said [in that event] that certain people would have no desire for that reward on account of its diminutive measure. A similar pretext might be offered in the case of two thousand or three thousand years. In fact, for whatever is limited in extent, reason could find another measurement <272> exceeding it. If, however, their reward were to be made unlimited and unending and their well-being would never cease, there would be no excuse left that anyone could give.

Now someone might perhaps remark, "I consider such a policy quite proper in the case of the reward of the righteous, since that consists of well-being and bliss and the bestowal of favors [which are compatible with the nature of God]. However, when it comes to punishment and condemnation to perpetual hell-fire, I see therein a mercilessness and cruelty which do not tally with God's nature."

In reply thereto I say, with equal cogency, that, just as it is necessary for God to use the strongest stimulant to arouse in men the desire to do good, so must He employ the strongest deterrent to keep them from doing evil. For if the deterrent used by Him were to consist of the threat of torments lasting a hundred or two hundred years, and men would not be distrained thereby from sinning, it might be said by someone that, if God had made it last a thousand years, they would have been frightened by it. Similarly, if the punishment were to be fixed for a period of two thousand years, one might say that if God had made it last a myriad, men would have been terrified thereby.

That is why God made the torment of the hereafter limitless, employing the strongest possible deterrent, that leaves no loophole for anyone. And once He has thus employed the most forcible means of intimidation and they still do not heed the warning, it would not be proper for Him to go back on His threats against them and belie His own word. On the contrary, in order to prove the truth of His word and His statement, it is necessary for Him to subject them to perpetual torment, for which they have only themselves to blame [56] on account of their rebellion against God and their denial of Him.

This threat is, on the other hand, an act of kindness on the part of God, since His aim in warning [57] them against everlasting punishment is to put them in the proper state of mind for serving Him. This matter resembles others which God, in His wisdom, has created in this world [for man's benefit], but which are turned into evil through man's own fault. Thus, for example, if a person goes out at night and falls into a well, or eats food at the wrong time, or uses as medicine something that is harmful, or the like [he has only himself to blame for it].

Next let me assert that Scripture, too, confirms the view [that the retribution in the hereafter] is everlasting. This is evident, first of all, from its statement: *Some to everlasting life, and some to reproaches and everlasting abhorrence* (Dan. 12:2). It says, furthermore: <273> *In Thy right hand is bliss for evermore* (Ps. 16:11); and also: *They shall never see the light* (Ps. 49:20). Moreover, its declaration: *But Thou art the selfsame, and Thy years shall have no end* (Ps. 102:28), is followed immediately by

56. "to blame"—Ibn Tibbon.
57. "warning"—added by Ibn Tibbon.

the statement: *The children of Thy servants shall dwell securely, and their seed shall be established before Thee* (Ps. 102:29). By means of this statement Scripture affirms that, just as the existence of God, magnified and exalted be He, is eternal, without end, so will the righteous exist eternally and without end.

At this point one might raise an objection, saying: "If it is conceivable that His creatures should, together with God, live eternally in the future, why is it not equally allowable that they shall have been in existence together with Him since eternity in the past?" Let me, therefore, explain the difference between the two theories and say that it is impossible that any creature could have been in existence since eternity together with its creator, because the author of anything must, by logical necessity, have preceded this work of his. Once, however, this precedence on the part of the author has taken place and the thing has been produced, then, just as we consider it logically possible for its creator to maintain it for any one day, we must believe him to be capable of maintaining it another day. If, therefore, the author assured his handiwork that he would do this for it perpetually day after day and time after time, the possibility of eternal existence in the future on the part of things created would not only not be denied but even be considered admissible by reason.

But suppose someone were to ask now: "What, in that case, would be the difference between the Creator and His creation?" Our reply hereto is that such a question does not deserve an answer. How, indeed, can one compare a being composed of a soul and a body, dependent on time and place, subject to the experience of pleasure, to commandments and prohibitions, standing in need of the means of subsistence, to One who is exalted above all such things and whatever resembles them? Nay, those who are to be rewarded with eternal life stand in the same relationship to God as he whose eye and soul look forward to whatever He would create for him, as has been expressly stated by Scripture: *And their seed shall be established before Thee* (*ibid.*).

CHAPTER VIII

In answer, again, to the seventh question, namely, whether the reward of those to be rewarded and the punishment of those to be punished will be equal in duration, I say that, just as the reward of a thousand good deeds will be unending, <274> so, too, will the reward of one good deed be infinite. Similarly, just as the punishment of a thousand evil acts will be unending, so, too, will the punishment of a single wicked deed go on forever.

However, even though the reward and the punishment, whether they apply to one or to a thousand acts, will be everlasting, their extent will vary according to the act. Thus, for example, the nature of a person's reward will be dependent upon whether he presents one or ten or one hundred or one thousand good deeds, except that it will be eternal in duration. For the sake of illustration, we see in this world of ours people whose happiness consists solely in being at rest; and others who, in addition thereto, enjoy eating and drinking; and still others, who, besides that, are well sheltered; and others, again, who, together therewith, put on resplendent clothes; and, finally, people who, in addition to all the aforementioned, occupy high positions of honor.

Similarly will it be in the world to come. There will be people there whose bliss has been described in such terms as *My flesh also dwelleth in safety* (Ps. 16:9). There will be other people concerning whom it has been said: *They take refuge in the shadow of Thy wings* (Ps. 36:8); and still other persons who will be *Abundantly satisfied with the fatness of Thy house* (Ps. 36:9); and others to whom the verse *And I will clothe thee with robes* will apply (Zech. 3:4). Finally, there will be those who will be in the category of him to whom it was said: *Then I will give thee free access among these that stand by* (Ps. 3:7). The allusion in this last sentence is to the angels, of whom it has been said: *Above Him stood the seraphim* (Isa. 6:2).

Likewise will the extent of a person's punishment vary according to whether he presents one or ten or a hundred or a thousand evil deeds, except that, whatever the intensity of the punishment may be, it will be everlasting. As an analogy drawn from the experience of this world of ours, we might cite the case of people the extent of whose torment is comprised in their being confined to a prison; and others who, in addition thereto, drag their fetters; and still others who are bound besides; and others, again, who, on top of that, are shaken up; and, finally, those who, in addition to being subjected to all the aforementioned, are beaten so that it hurts.

Thus, too, will it be in the world to come. There will be people there whose torment has been described in such terms as *And they shall be gathered together, as prisoners are gathered in the dungeon, and shall be shut up in the prison* (Isa. 24:22). There will also be other people of whom it has been said: *His own iniquities shall ensnare* <275> *the wicked, and he shall be holden with the cords of his sin* (Prov. 5:22); and others of whom it has been said: *And if they be bound in fetters, and be holden in cords of affliction* (Job 36:8); and still others [to whom may be applied the verse]: *A sweeping storm; it shall whirl upon the head of the wicked* (Jer. 30:23).

As for the eighth question, namely, whether there will be any difference of gradation among the righteous and similarly among the wicked, the general answer thereto has already been given in the preceding statement. Nevertheless I deem it proper now to single out seven subdivisions embraced under the heading of the varieties of virtuous men, and I say that the existence of differences of degree in the reward of the righteous is a conclusion forced upon us first of all by reason. Furthermore, we also find support for it in the Scriptures, which mention seven different gradations.

The first gradation is that of those who will be endowed with a radiance equal to the light of the sun at sunrise. Of them Scripture says: *But unto you that fear My name shall the sun of righteousness arise* (Mal. 3:20). Some, again, will, in addition thereto, derive pleasure from the warmth of its rays, as Scripture says right there: *With healing in its wings (ibid.)*. For some, furthermore, this light will be confirmed like something implanted in them, as has been expressed by Scripture in the sentence: *Light is sown for the righteous* (Ps. 97:11).

For some, again, the light will be increased, as Scripture puts it: *The light of the righteous rejoiceth* (Prov. 13:9). The light of some, moreover, will have the clarity of that of the bodies of the heavenly spheres, as it has been said of them: *And they that are wise shall shine as the brightness of the firmament* (Dan. 12:3). The light of others, again, will be like that of the stars, with the exception of that of the sun, as Scripture says in the same place: *And they that turn the many to righteousness as the stars forever and ever* (*ibid.*). Finally, there will be those whose light will be like that of the body of the sun itself, as Scripture says: *But they that love Him be as the sun when he goeth forth in his might* (Judg. 5:31).

This difference of gradations is confirmed also by what we know about the face of *Moses, our teacher, peace be upon him,* which is supposed to have been full of radiance, whereas that of Joshua was less resplendent. Thus Scripture remarks: *And thou shalt put <276> of thy splendor*[58] *upon him* (Num. 27:20), not saying simply: *thy splendor* nor *all thy splendor*. The faces of the seventy elders, again, were even less resplendent than those of these two, for Scripture says: *And He took of the spirit that was upon him, and put it upon the seventy elders* (Num. 11:25); whereas when God stated as the reason for Moses' putting some of his *splendor* on Joshua: *That all the congregation of the children of Israel may hearken* (Num. 27:20), He included the seventy elders in the totality of the people.[59]

A proof that among those to be punished in the hereafter, too, there will prevail a difference of degrees is furnished by the fact that we find applied to them in Scripture seven degrees of the incendiary activity of fire. Some of them will have their faces set aflame by fire so that they become red. Of such individuals does Scripture say: *Their faces shall be faces of flame* (Isa. 13:8). The faces of others, again, will become black like the bottom of pots.

58. "splendor"—the usual translation is "honor."
59. Cf. Lev. Rab., chap. xxx, par. 2, as a parallel to this view.

Of persons like these Scripture says: *All faces have gathered black-ness* (Joel 2:6).

Some of them will be as affected by it as though they were roasted and stewed. Of them does Scripture say: *For, behold, the day cometh, it burneth as a furnace* (Mal. 3:19). Some, again, will be affected by it as though they were consumed by the fire. Concerning them Scripture says: *A fire not blown by man shall consume him* (Job 20:26). On some of them its effect will be like that of wood which is consumed by fire. About them does Scripture say: *The pile thereof is fire and much wood* (Isa. 30:33).

On others, again, the effect will be of the same nature as when fire consumes earth and stones. To such persons applies the statement of Scripture: *And it devoureth the earth with her produce, and setteth ablaze the foundations of the mountains* (Deut. 32:22). Finally, there will be those who will be affected by it as by a fire whose destructive fury reaches down to the depths of the earth or as if they were struck by lightning. Concerning them Scripture expresses itself as follows: *For it is a fire that consumeth unto destruction* (Job 31:12).

[This theory that there will be gradations in the punishments to be borne in the hereafter is] also [corroborated] by what we know about the misfortunes that were visited upon the Egyptians. Although they were of an all-embracing character, yet each sinner was struck by them in accordance with his desert. This is borne out by the statement of Scripture: *He weighs* [60] (*yĕphalles*) *a path for His anger* (Ps. 78:50). The expression *yĕphalles* is to be interpreted, "He weighs it as with a balance," as in the sentence: *A just balance* (*peles*) *and scales are the Lord's* (Prov. 16:11).

CHAPTER IX

In answer to the ninth question, namely, who it is that deserves this perpetual torment, let me say that it is the nonbelievers <277> and the polytheists and the impenitent perpetrators of grave sins. So far as the nonbelievers and the polytheists are con-

60. "weighs"—the usual translation is "leveled."

cerned, their fate has been clearly described in the declaration of Scripture: *And they shall go forth, and look upon the carcasses of the men that have rebelled against Me; for their worm shall not die* (Isa. 66:24).

As for the unregenerate perpetrators of grave sins, they are the group for whom *extirpation or death at the hand of the court* has been prescribed. The consequence of their [61] being cut off from this world is to be cut off also from among the righteous in the world to come by reason of their failure to repent. Should it happen, however, that one belonging to this category was not cut off before his time but was permitted, by way of reprieve, to complete his life even though he had never repented, then his punishment in the hereafter would be all the more severe and his being cut off from among the righteous all the more compulsory by reason of the fact that, although he had been granted a reprieve, he did not repent.

Now all sins that do not belong to the categories previously described by us are excluded therefrom and classified as lesser transgressions that are pardonable. Should someone ask, however, on what ground they are pardoned, seeing that no repentance of them has taken place, we would answer: "Is it not our basic assumption that these individuals are charged solely with lesser transgressions? That in itself is proof that they have guarded against sins of a grave character. Now how could they have kept aloof from them except by doing the opposite: namely, instead of denying God's existence, believing in Him; instead of going astray, being led aright; instead of committing murder and theft and adultery, doing what is right and just and fair? Now when a person follows such a course and most of his actions are good, retribution for these relatively minor misdeeds is exacted from him in this world, so that he departs from it cleared of all blemish, as I have explained in the fifth treatise." [62]

In regard to the tenth question, namely, whether those to be requited in the hereafter will meet each other, let me say, on the

---

61. "their"—Ibn Tibbon.
62. Cf. pp. 210 ff.

basis of my studies and findings, that, so far as the righteous and the wicked are concerned, they will only look at one another with their eyes. Thus Scripture says concerning the righteous: *And they shall go forth, and look upon the carcasses of the men that have rebelled against me* [63] (*ibid.*). Whenever, then, they regard their sufferings, they will say: "Praised be He who saved us from this torment!" and they will rejoice and be glad over their own condition.

Likewise Scripture remarks concerning the wicked: <278> *The sinners in Zion are afraid; trembling hath seized the ungodly: Who among us shall dwell with the devouring fire? Who among us shall dwell with everlasting burnings?* (Isa. 33:14). In amazement they will watch the righteous abide in the burning fire without being in the least hurt by it, and they will sigh regretfully over the reward which they forfeited.

Further [bearing out this view] is the analogy given elsewhere in Scripture of people who are invited to a banquet whilst others are brought there merely in order to be tormented, with the result that the latter, when they see the former eat, give vent to sighing. That is the import of the statement: *Behold, My servants shall eat, but ye shall be hungry; behold, My servants shall drink, but ye shall be thirsty; behold, My servants shall rejoice, but ye shall be ashamed; behold, My servants shall sing for joy of heart, but ye shall cry for sorrow of heart, and shall wail for vexation of spirit* (Isa. 65:13, 14).

So far as the righteous among themselves are concerned, on the other hand, those whose ranks are close to one another will meet, whereas those who are distant from each other in station will not. It would seem to me, however, that in the case of those who are destined for punishment there will be no meeting on the part of those who are of similar rank on account of the separation produced by their sufferings and their preoccupation with themselves.

63. This quotation is based on the reading of Ibn Tibbon.

CHAPTER X

In reply, again, to the question [64] as to whether in the hereafter men will still be charged with the obligation of rendering service to their Master, I would say: "By all means," since sound reason would not permit itself to be completely divested of commandment and prohibition. If anything like that were feasible in the world to come, it would have been so in this world also. Hence men will be obliged [in the world to come to carry out such duties as] acknowledging the sovereignty of God, not to make insulting remarks about Him or ascribe to Him unworthy attributes, and other such obligations of a purely rational nature, which are therefore inescapable.

In addition to these, the Scriptures speak of another type of service prescribed by revelation, such as the establishment in their land of a specific place whither they would be required to travel at every appointed season; this will occupy the place that the Sabbath and the new moon have with us at present, and enable them to serve God there in whatever manner He may prescribe for them so that they may not remain without the means of worshiping Him. This thought has been expressed by Scripture in the statement: <279> *And it shall come to pass, that from one new moon to another, and from one sabbath to another, shall all flesh come to worship before Me* (Isa. 66: 23).

Having fulfilled this obligation, they will then go forth in order to look at those who are being punished. For when Scripture states in the verse immediately following: *And they shall go forth, and look upon the carcasses of the men* [65] (Isa. 66: 24), that is necessary because of the previous remark: *All flesh shall come;* [that is, from their regular abode to the place specially appointed for worship]. This theory that the righteous will no more be exempt from divine service in the world to come than they were in this world is also supported by rabbinic tradition, which asserts:

64. The Arabic text erroneously adds the word "last."
65. This quotation follows the reading of Ibn Tibbon.

The disciples of the wise have no rest either in this world or in the world to come (Běr. 64a).

As for those who will be punished [in the hereafter], they will not be charged with the duty of divine service on account of the suffering to which they will be subjected, and also because such service might bring about their transfer from their state—I mean that of perpetual torment, of which we have spoken previously.[66]

The reply, finally, to the last two questions, one of which was: "What would be the reward of men for their obedience to God in the hereafter?" while the other [asked]: "And what would be their fate if they disobeyed?" I have already given at the end of the seventh treatise.[67] I stated there that God would not have assured them eternal reward unless He knew that they would choose to obey Him and not anything else, and that, in return for this choice on their part, their abundant happiness would be still further increased by Him, as we have explained. The elimination, then, of these last two questions that have already been dealt with, as well as of the first, which was also expounded previously,[68] left only the ten remaining ones [which were discussed in this treatise].

CHAPTER XI

As an appendix to this exposition, I deem it proper to ask: "But what, specifically, will be the reward in the hereafter for the fulfillment of every tradition and precept and the effort made therein? Similarly, what, specifically, will be the punishment for the neglect of these precepts and traditions and the lack of effort to fulfill them?" This has not been defined by God in this world of ours for several reasons that motivated [divine] Wisdom.

One of these is that since the operation of the principle of reward and punishment in general is not directly observed by us but is

66. Cf. above, pp. 344 ff.
67. Cf. above, p. 289. The faulty reading "eighth" has been corrected to "seventh" by Landauer.
68. Cf. above, n. 45.

recognized only by approximation and inference, how can we expect to obtain a knowledge of its more hidden and more subtle details? Another reason [for not specifying the details] <280> was that it would have required too lengthy a discussion, too extensive a statement, and have imposed too great a burden.

A further [object in omitting the definition of the detailed rewards] was to prevent our singling out from among the total certain specific rites of divine service, seeing that the remuneration of each would have been defined for us by Him.[69] Then, again, since our minds occupy themselves chiefly with events that are near at hand—I am referring to the matter of the *redemption* —the Scriptures dwell upon this subject at greater length and expatiate upon it.

We hope, however, that at the time of the *redemption* there will be vouchsafed to us a full itemization of the reward for every act of divine service and a specification of the various types of punishment corresponding to each individual; for the community of Israel will then be endowed with the gift of prophetic revelation and [men's] minds will be free to dedicate themselves to the quest of wisdom and their characters [70] will have been sufficiently refined to be susceptible to instruction, inasmuch as our people will then be prepared,[71] nay ready, to pass over to the world to come.

I say, therefore, that this is precisely the reason why Scripture says that the power of prophecy will extend to all. It says, namely: *And it shall come to pass afterward, that I will pour out My spirit upon all flesh; and your sons and your daughters shall prophesy* (Joel 3: 1). Now they will, of course, prophesy about what will then lie in the future, and the futurities of that time will consist of the reward and the punishment in the hereafter.

In giving them this information, God will furnish them miracles and marvels in support thereof, as Scripture says: *And I will show wonders in the heavens and in the earth, blood, and fire, and*

69. Cf. Mišnah 'Abhoth 2: 1.
70. "characters"—Ibn Tibbon and M.
71. "prepared"—literally "near."

pillars of smoke (Joel 3: 3). All these things, so it is further stated there, are to transpire prior to the day of the resurrection. Scripture says, namely: *The sun shall be turned into darkness, and the moon into blood, before the great and terrible day of the Lord come* (Joel 3: 4).

He, then, that will himself understand these matters will belong to the company of the *wise* (Dan. 12: 3). He, again, who will fit men to serve their Master and teach them what they must know in order to come nigh unto Him, will be classified among those *that turn the many to righteousness* (*ibid.*). This prospect should serve as an incentive to every man of learning to invoke the assistance of Providence in instructing [his] fellowmen and guiding them aright.

The ninth treatise of the Book of Beliefs has hereby been completed.

TREATISE X

<281> CONCERNING HOW IT IS MOST PROPER FOR MAN TO CONDUCT HIMSELF IN THIS WORLD

EXORDIUM

THE principle which forms the subject of this treatise is a matter that many men have attempted to fathom but of which only a few have reached a satisfactory view. Let me, therefore, state by way of introduction, that, inasmuch as the Creator of the universe, exalted and magnified be He, is essentially one, it follows by logical necessity that His creatures be composed of many elements, as I have made clear in the foregoing.[1]

At this point, now, I would say that the thing that generally gives the appearance of constituting a unity, whatever sort of unit it be, is singular only in number. Upon careful consideration, however, it is found to be of a multiple nature. To reduce this generalization to simpler terms, when the substances of all beings are analyzed, they are found to be endowed with the attributes of heat and cold and moisture and dryness.[2] When the substance of the tree is examined, it is found to include, in addition to the aforementioned, branches and leaves and fruits, and all that is connected therewith. When the human body, again, is examined, it is found to be composed, besides the elements listed above, of flesh and bones and sinews and arteries and muscles and all that goes with them. This is a matter about which no doubt can be entertained and the reality of which is not to be denied.

All these phenomena are in accord with the laws of creation: namely, that the Creator, exalted and magnified be He, be one and His works manifold. That is also borne out by such statements of

1. Cf. pp. 96 ff.
2. Cf. the first treatise, p. 66.

the Scriptures as *How manifold are Thy works, O Lord! In wisdom hast Thou made them all* (Ps. 104:24). Even heaven is made up of various parts, dimensions, forms, colors, and movements without number.[3] That is what makes it heaven, as is stated in Scripture: *Who maketh the Bear, Orion, and the Pleiades, and the chambers of the south* (Job 9:9).

CHAPTER I

Having made this preliminary observation, I say now that the same thing applies to the tendencies exhibited by man. He evinces a liking for many things and a dislike for others. This is borne out by such statements of Scripture as <282> *There are many devices in a man's heart; but the counsel of the Lord, that shall stand* (Prov. 19:21).

Now just as the material objects do not consist of just one of the four elements [of which they are said to be composed], and the body of the trees cannot exist with only one of the parts mentioned by us, and man cannot live if he has bone or flesh alone—in fact, even the heavens are not illuminated by just one star—so, too, man's conduct in the course of his lifetime cannot logically be based on just a single trait. But just as in each instance the final product is the result of a combination of ingredients in larger or smaller proportions, so too, is man's behavior the resultant of a combination of his likes and dislikes in varying proportions.

Man acts as though he were a judge to whom the disposal of the different tendencies is submitted for decision, as Scripture says: *Well is it with the man that dealeth graciously and lendeth, that ordereth his affairs rightfully* (Ps. 112:5). Or his position might be compared to that of one who would weigh these impulses with a balance and give to each its due measure, as Scripture also puts it: *Balance [4] the path of thy feet* (Prov. 4:26). When, then, a person behaves in this manner, his affairs will be properly adjusted and well regulated.

3. Cf. p. 43.
4. "Balance"—the usual translation is "Make plain."

What impelled me to put this theme at the beginning of the present treatise is the fact that I have seen people who think—and with them it is a firm conviction—that it is obligatory for human beings to order their entire existence upon the exploitation of one trait, lavishing their love on one thing above all others and their hatred on a certain thing above the rest. Now I investigated this view and I found it to be extremely erroneous for sundry reasons.

One of these is that if the [exclusive] love for one thing and its preference [above all others] had been the most salutary thing for man, the Creator would not have implanted in his character the love for these other things. Also if that were so, God could have created man out of one element and of one piece, and He would have done <283> likewise for [5] the other creatures so that they would have been similarly constituted. Seest thou not how individual functions cannot very well be executed by the use of a single medium? Still less is this possible in human conduct in general.

Another argument [that might be advanced against the exclusive cultivation of one trait] is that, if an architect were to build a house of stones or teakwood or mats or pegs alone, it would not be as well constructed as if he had built it of all these materials put together. The same might be asserted with regard to cooking, food, drink, dress, service, and other matters. Must not the person who notes how all these items which exist for the purpose of serving man's needs and well-being are not composed of just one ingredient open his eyes and realize how much less that would be possible in the case of the inclinations of his soul and its characteristics?

CHAPTER II

Now it is also necessary for me to explain that the evil resulting from such a one-sided choice is not trivial but quite serious, as I shall illustrate. I say, then, that there are people who give them-

5. "done likewise for"—literally "joined with him." Through a typographical error what should be one word became two in Landauer's edition of the Arabic text.

selves up to long mountain trips, which leads to their becoming insane. Others indulge in excessive eating and drinking, which causes them to contract hemorrhoids.[6] Others, again, lavish all their energies on the gathering of wealth, only to accumulate it for other men. Furthermore, there are those who dedicate themselves entirely to satisfying their thirst for revenge, with the consequence that their vindictiveness reacts against themselves. I might also cite other such instances, as I shall explain in the middle of this treatise with the help of God.

Let me, however, state here, prior to that discussion, that it is for the above-mentioned reasons that man stands in constant need of a wisdom that would regulate his conduct and behavior, as Scripture says: *When thou walkest, it shall lead thee* (Prov. 6:22). Principally that consists, in this particular instance, in his exercising control over his impulses and having complete mastery over his likes and dislikes, for each has its distinctive role in which it must be made to function. Once, then, he recognizes the role belonging to a given impulse, he must give it full opportunity to discharge its function in the required measure. On the other hand, if he sees an instance in which the said impulse should be checked, he must restrain it until the ground for such restraint no longer exists for him. All this is to be done with due deliberation and with the power to release or hold, at will, as Scripture has said: <284> *He that is slow to anger is better than the mighty; and he that ruleth his spirit than he that taketh a city* (Prov. 16:22).

I have already stated previously that the soul has three faculties —the appetitive, the impulsive, and the cognitive.[7] As for the appetitive faculty, it is that whereby a human being entertains the desire for food and drink and sexual intercourse [8] and for seeing beautiful sights and smelling fragrant odors and for wearing garments that are soft to the touch. The impulsive faculty is that which renders a person courageous and bold, and endows him with zeal for leadership and championing the common weal, and makes

6. "hemorrhoids"—Ibn Tibbon.
7. Cf. pp. 243 ff.
8. "sexual intercourse"—Ibn Tibbon.

him vindictive and vainglorious, and other such things. As for the cognitive faculty, again, it exercises judgment over the two other faculties. When any one of them or [9] of their subdivisions is aroused, the cognitive faculty takes it under consideration and investigates it. If it notes that it is sound from beginning to end, it points this fact out, not to speak of the case where the consequences are desirable. Should it, however, observe in any aspect thereof something deleterious, it would advise that one desist therefrom.

Any person, then, who follows this course of giving his cognitive faculty dominion over his appetites and impulses, is disciplined *by the discipline of the wise,* as Scripture says: *The fear of the Lord is the discipline* [10] *of wisdom* (Prov. 15:33). Any man, on the other hand, who permits his appetites and impulses to dominate his faculty of cognition, is undisciplined. And if someone wrongly calls such conduct discipline, it is *the discipline of the foolish,* as Scripture says: *But the foolish despise . . . discipline* (Prov. 1:7), and also: *Or as one in fetters to the discipline* [11] *of the fool* (Prov. 7:22).

CHAPTER III

Having demonstrated, then, in this introductory statement how logical necessity leads to the assumption of the existence of an All-Wise Being who arranged for us the order of these our likes and dislikes and indicated to us the manner of our procedure with them, let me say that the sage Solomon, the son of David, may peace be upon them both, has fathomed this subject for the purpose of enabling us to attain what is best. He says, namely: *I have seen all the works that are done under the sun; and, behold, all is vanity and a striving after wind* (Eccles. 1:14).

Now he does not refer, when he makes the remark: *All is vanity and a striving after wind,*[12] to the union and combination

9. "or"—added by Ibn Tibbon.
10. "discipline"—the usual translation is "instruction."
11. "discipline—the usual translation is "correction."
12. "when . . . wind"—added by Ibn Tibbon.

of all works, for it was the Creator, <285> exalted and magnified be He, who established them and set them up, and it is not fitting for a sage like Solomon to say of what the Creator, exalted and magnified be He, has established: *It is all vanity*. What he meant to say was, rather, that any act that a human being undertakes to carry out in isolation—that is to say, every one of the acts of man that receive exclusive attention—is as futile for him as associating with the wind.

With reference to this sort of one-sided procedure, he says also: *That which is crooked cannot be made straight; and that which is wanting [cannot be numbered]* (Eccles. 1: 15). That is to say any act practised exclusively constitutes a distortion from what is straight and is lacking in completeness, while in their combination [with the full range of pious works, single acts] do not constitute a *deficiency* but rather completion and perfection.

The correctness of the foregoing interpretation is confirmed by the fact that the author presents three classes of objects of mundane ambition, each of which he decides is *hebhel*, the meaning of which is "vanity." This [rendering of the word] is borne out by such statements of Scripture as *They lead you unto vanity (mahbilim)* (Jer. 23: 16); that is: "They deceive you with vain hopes"; and *Trust not in oppression, and put not vain hope ('al tehbalu) in robbery* (Ps. 62: 11).

The first of these [strivings that Solomon considers futile] is the exclusive devotion to wisdom to the neglect of all other objects of [human] desire. He says, namely, in reference thereto: *And I applied my heart to know wisdom, and to know madness and folly— I perceived that this also was a striving after wind* (Eccles. 1: 17). As his reason for regarding it thus he gives the fact that as a person's knowledge increases, there is also an increase for him of sorrow. That is due to the circumstance that with the increase of his knowledge there are revealed to him the flaws in things concerning which he was fully at ease before they became evident to him. That is the import of his remark: *For in much wisdom is much vexation; and he that increaseth knowledge increaseth sorrow* (Eccles. 1: 18).

He next repeats [this observation] with reference to the exclusive cultivation of mirth and gaiety, saying that if a person gave all his attention and devotion to them alone, they, too, would prove a disappointment to him. Thus he says: *I said in my heart: "Come now, I will try thee with mirth, and enjoy pleasure"; and, behold, this also was vanity* (Eccles. 2:1). As his reason for this conclusion he gives the fact that a person experiences, when he laughs and <286> jests, a sense of degradation and debasement putting him on a level with the behavior of the beasts. That is the import of his declaration: *I said of laughter: "It is mad"; and of mirth: "What doth it accomplish?"* (Eccles. 2:2).

After this he makes the same remark for the third time about the upbuilding of the material world and he informs us that the preoccupation therewith, too, is vanity. He does this in his statement: *I made me great works; I builded me houses; I planted me vineyards; I made me gardens and parks* [13] (Eccles. 2:4) and all the other things that he relates about his doings until the end of the passage in question. The reason he gives as his objection to all this sort of activity is that he has to leave whatever he has achieved to those that will come after him and that, therefore, his labor will have been wasted. Thus he says: *And I hated all my labour wherein I laboured under the sun, seeing that I must leave it unto the man that shall be after me* (Eccles. 2:18).

Having, then, enumerated these three types, he desists from mentioning other worldly strivings [14] lest he be diverted thereby from his central theme. Yet in the very midst of his discussion of these types he hints at the need for the proper balancing of these three strivings. This is to be effected by devoting some attention to the cultivation of wisdom and to indulgence in pleasure without neglecting to inquire into what is best for man. Thus he says: *I searched in my heart how to pamper my flesh with wine, and my heart conducting itself with wisdom, [how yet to lay hold on folly, till I might see which it was best for the sons of men that they should do]* (Eccles. 2:3).

13. This quotation follows the reading of Ibn Tibbon.
14. "strivings"—Ibn Tibbon.

CHAPTER IV

Now the thought occurred to me, may God guide thee aright, to collect [here] thirteen principal types of the [human] strivings [14] that we are discussing, noting what I know to be the motives impelling people to occupy themselves exclusively all their life long with one in preference to all others. Next I shall present an exposition of men's omissions and failures in that very matter, making definite mention in each instance of the role assigned by nature to the various impulses in the fulfillment of which they might most appropriately be used. Aye, if I were to collect all that I remember of what the devotees of these thirteen [classes of human aspirations] neglected and give the collection a name, it would constitute [14a] a complete book of asceticism.

Let me, however, first enumerate them <287> and say that there are thirteen principal pursuits [to which men dedicate themselves]; namely, abstinence, eating and drinking, sexual intercourse, eroticism, the accumulation of money, [the begetting of] children, the [material] development of the land, longevity, dominion, the nursing of revenge, [the acquisition of] wisdom, worship, and rest. Each of these will be subjected by me to rational analysis. I shall furthermore note their desirable aspects, set down what should be avoided thereof, and assign to each its appropriate place.

On Abstinence

I say that there are first of all people who entertain the opinion that man should lead a life of asceticism in this world, wander off into the mountains, and give himself up to weeping, melancholy, and mourning over this earthly existence. "What compels us to adopt this view," they say, "is the fact that this world is only a transient abode, whose denizens are in constant flux, never permanent." No matter how happy or serene a person may be in it, his fortune changes quickly, with the result that his gladness turns to sorrow, his glory into humiliation, and his well-being into misery. It is

14a. "constitute"—Ibn Tibbon.

just as Scripture says: *He lieth down rich, but there shall be nought to gather; he openeth his eyes, and his wealth is not. Terrors overtake him like waters; [a tempest stealeth him away in the night.] The east wind carrieth him away, and he departeth* (Job 27: 19–21).

The person who strives zealously to become wise in it is overwhelmed by his folly. He that makes an effort to purify himself succumbs to his impurity. If he tries to keep well, his temperament makes him sick; and if he aims to be sensible, his tongue causes him to trip. It is as Scripture puts it: *Though I be righteous, mine own mouth shall condemn me; though I be innocent, He shall prove me perverse* (Job 9: 20).

Moreover, no one knows in this world what illness, adversity, bereavement, worry, loss, or other misfortune may befall him, as Scripture says: *Boast not thyself of tomorrow; for thou knowest not what a day may bring forth* (Prov. 27: 1). The consequence is that the more a person slakes his thirst therewith, the more intense does his thirst become; and the more tenaciously he clings to it, the more certainly are the handles in his hand and the things he relies on severed. It is just as Scripture says: *Whose confidence is gossamer, and whose trust is a spider's web. He shall lean upon his house, but it shall not stand <288> he shall hold fast thereby, but it shall not endure* (Job. 8: 14, 15).

Man's situation in this world is nought but disappointment and illusion and lies, as Scripture says: *Yet is their pride but travail and vanity* (Ps. 90: 10). Many proud giants have been beaten down and brought low by it, as Scripture says: *The stout-hearted are bereft of sense, they sleep their sleep* (Ps. 76: 6). Many of the mighty have been humbled and brought into disrepute by it. *To pollute the pride of all glory, to bring into contempt all the honourable of the earth* (Isa. 23: 9). Many a one who had expected good from it found it exchanged for evil, and, opening his eyes to look upon its light, beheld it grow dark in his sight, as Scripture says: *Yet, when I looked for good, there came evil; and when I waited for light, there came darkness* (Job 30: 26).

It is as though the world had cast all its heat upon the race of man and hurled its passion upon his weakness, as Scripture expresses it: *Thy wrath lieth hard upon me* (Ps. 88:8). And what about man's iniquities and sins, and the accounting and the punishment? And what about the distance that mundane life sets up between him and his Master so that the latter becomes toward him like one who is ready to tear him to pieces in His wrath, as Scripture says: *And if it exalt itself, Thou huntest me as a lion; and again Thou showest Thyself marvelous upon me?* (Job 10: 16.) And there is also the statement of Scripture *Behold, the day of the Lord cometh, cruel, and full of wrath and fierce anger* (Isa. 13:9).

They say, therefore, that an intelligent person ought to reject this world, so as not to engage in building or planting, not to marry or beget offspring or dwell among those who choose such activities, lest they influence him and some of their traits infiltrate into him. Rather should he seek the solitude of the mountains, subsisting for his food on whatever plants he may find until he dies in sorrow and sadness.

Now I considered carefully their allegations and found them to be for the most part correct, except that they go to impossible extremes in abandoning the amenities of civilized existence. For they leave out of consideration the essentials of sustenance, clothing, and shelter. Nay they fail to think of their very lives, <289> for by renouncing marriage they cause the process of procreation to be interrupted. But if this were proper, all men would have followed such a course, and if they were to do so, then the human species would die out and with it there would be an end to science and law and [the possibility of] resurrection and [a new] heaven and earth. And what about the danger that would, under such conditions, be presented to human life by wild beasts and lions and snakes and heat and cold and mishaps of every variety? And what about the coarsening of man's nature and the froth and the mental derangement and insanity resulting solely from the lack of good food and cold water? Furthermore, there comes about a deterioration of the blood and an excitation of the black gall compelling these hermits to resort to medical treatment by the inhabitants of the settled communities, which is sometimes effective and sometimes not.

Again, these solitary individuals are apt to become so shy of human beings as to imagine that the latter are going to kill them. Also they sometimes conceive such a hatred for other men, because they look upon them as evil-doers and sinners, that they have no compunctions about shedding [15] their blood. At times, too, they contract the characteristics of beasts, so that they cease completely to behave like human beings. Thus, for example, Scripture tells us: *The daughter of my people is become cruel, like the ostriches in the wilderness* (Lam. 4: 3); and also: *In the clefts of the valleys must they dwell, in the holes of the earth and of the rocks. Among the bushes they bray; under the nettles they are gathered together* (Job 30: 6, 7). Thus they do complete injury to themselves.

Now the trait of abstinence on the part of man in regard to this world is commendable only if employed in its place. That is to say, if forbidden food or sexual intercourse or wealth present themselves to him, he should make full use of this trait so that it will restrain him from these things, as Scripture says: *For what hath a man of all his labour, and the striving of his heart, wherein he laboureth under the sun* (Eccles. 2: 22).

CHAPTER V

ON EATING AND DRINKING

Certain men, again, are of the opinion that the thing with which a human being should occupy himself is eating and drinking. They assert, namely, that the subsistence of body and soul is dependent on nourishment. Furthermore, nourishment <290> affords man extraordinary pleasure, besides being the cause of the growth of bodies and their physical development and the production of off-spring. We note, for example, that when a person fasts for a day, his hearing and sight and power of reflection and memory and thinking faculty become impaired, and when he takes nourish-ment, these faculties return to their original condition. It may even happen sometimes that, as a result of being hungry, a human being deny his Lord or be unaware of what he says in his prayer to Him.[16]

15. "shedding"—Ibn Tibbon.
16. "to Him"—added by Ibn Tibbon and M.

Thou seest, furthermore, that all human settlements are established on the sites of rivers in order to make possible the sowing and watering [of the soil for the production of food]. Thereby, too, are defrayed the taxes imposed by the kings and the contributions for the maintenance of the army. Food is the byword for all that is good, for everybody uses the expression: "This is my bread." Thou findest also that the Scriptures hold it out as an incentive to the righteous, saying: *And ye shall serve the Lord your God, and He will bless thy bread, and thy water* (Exod. 23:25); and thus also: *And the land shall yield her fruit, and ye shall eat until ye have enough* (Lev. 25:19). Numerous other such examples could be cited. Again, there would be no rejoicing at the conclusion of nuptials or at a betrothal or a circumcision or a confinement or a festival without food, and the same applies to social intercourse and friendly commerce among people and their friends.

As for wine,[17] they say, it is beautiful in color, goodly in fragrance, and pleasant of taste. It renders him that is sad joyful, the miserly generous, the cowardly brave. Scripture pays tribute to these sundry virtues [of wine] when it says: *And wine that maketh glad the heart of man, making the face brighter than oil, and bread that stayeth man's heart* (Ps. 104:15).

Now I studied this theory of theirs carefully and I found it to be, for the most part, far fetched. Also they regard only the good consequences of addiction to eating and drinking and overlook the ill effects. That is to say, they fail to realize that overeating produces indigestion and heaviness of the limbs and a filling up of the head and the eyes. [An excess of food] also [generates] faintness and dulls the mind and changes man's disposition, inclining him to greediness and voraciousness, so that he does not realize when he is sated.

The result is that he comes to resemble the dogs in his behavior, of whom Scripture remarks: *Yea, the dogs are greedy, they know not when they have enough* (Isa. 56:11). Nay, more, he becomes like the fire, which <291> devours whatever is thrown into it

17. "wine"—Ibn Tibbon.

without feeling it, in accordance with the statement of Scripture: *The people also are become like what is consumed by* [18] *fire* (Isa. 9:18). In fact, he assumes the characteristics of death, which draws all creatures unto itself and is never satisfied, as Scripture says: *He who enlargeth his desire as the netherworld, and is as death, and cannot be satisfied* (Hab. 2:5).

[We might even go] further [and say that] he becomes like the four causes of annihilation put together: namely, fire, water, death, and barrenness, of which Scripture says: *The horseleech hath two daughters: "Give, give." There are three things that are never satisfied, yea, four that say not: "Enough": the grave; and the barren womb; the earth that is not satisfied with water; and the fire that saith not: "Enough."* (Prov. 30:15, 16).

The consequence is that he begrudges anybody's eating of a loaf of his bread though he be a rich man, and if he gives it to him, he does it with complete indifference. It is just as Scripture puts it: *For as one that hath reckoned within himself, so is he: "Eat and drink," saith he to thee; but his heart is not with thee* (Prov. 23:7).

Now once such traits make themselves apparent in a person, kings and the elite of men and people of intelligence avoid him and refuse to sit in his company, because he is in a hurry when he eats, and whenever he sees an ample portion, he pounces on it. He is the first to stretch forth and the last to remove his hand, his eyes being turned to the food being brought in that his heart longs for. In reference to such conduct does Scripture say: *When thou sittest to eat with a ruler, consider well him that is before thee; and put a knife to thy throat, if thou be a man given to appetite* (Prov. 23:1, 2).

Aye, [this gourmand] is constantly intent on studying how he may purge himself so that he may be in a position to continue to eat the things he lusts for. He acts as though he were a funnel [19] which is poured into from above and which emits from below. It is such a one that is alluded to in the statement of Scripture: *For all tables*

18. "like what is consumed by"—the usual translation is "as the fuel of."
19. "funnel"—Ibn Tibbon.

are full of filthy vomit, and no place is clean (Isa. 28:8). Or else he vomits up, because of overeating, the food that his stomach cannot hold,[20] as Scripture puts it: *The morsel which thou hast eaten shalt thou vomit up, and lose thy sweet words* (Prov. 23:8).

And what about the coarsening effect that gluttony has on man's mind, <292> causing him to abandon his religion and to forget his Lord, as Scripture observes: *When they were fed, they became full, they were filled, and their heart was exalted; therefore have they forgotten Me?* (Hos. 13:6.)

They forget also that wine, when it is drunk raw,[21] has the effect of making the brain dry, and when it is drunk mixed, that of rendering it moist. It also constrains the mind and does injury to the intellect, as Scripture says: *Wine is a mocker, strong drink is riotous; and whosoever reeleth thereby is not wise* (Prov. 20:1). Furthermore, excessive drinking produces a softening of the nerves, tremors, agitation of the blood, chronic fevers, progressive weakness of the stomach, and feebleness of the liver, besides causing intense pains, as Scripture says: *Who crieth: "Woe"? who: "Alas"? . . . They that tarry long at the wine* (Prov. 23:29, 30).

Furthermore, what about the sins committed and the crimes perpetrated, and the abominations, and the sanction of what is ugly and the approval of what is forbidden that gradually insinuate themselves into the body of a person [22] solely as a result of his drinking wine, as Scripture says: *At the last it biteth like a serpent, and stingeth like a basilisk. Thine eyes shall behold strange things, and thy heart shall utter confused things?* (Prov. 23:32, 33.) And what about the murder of human beings and the commission of capital crimes and the flogging and beating and imprisonment and chaining and sundry punishments that are caused only by the drinking of wine? And what about the various types of deception and cunning and destruction that are brought about by it and it alone?

Moreover, the person who lavishes all his energies on obtaining

20. "because of overeating . . . hold"—added by Ibn Tibbon and M.
21. "raw"—Ibn Tibbon, i.e., "unmixed."
22. "and the abominations . . . person"—added by Ibn Tibbon and M.

food and drink will, if he cannot get them legally, seek to secure them wherever they are to be gotten, as Scripture says: *For they eat the bread of wickedness, and drink the wine of violence* (Prov. 4:17).

Hence it befits man to secure thereof only what he requires for his subsistence, namely, enough for the sustenance of his body, as Scripture says: *The righteous eateth to the satisfying of his desire; but the belly of the wicked shall want* (Prov. 13:25). So long as he recognizes this need with his reason, he could give free rein to his appetite for food and drink.[23] Once, however, he has attained what he needs for his subsistence, he should restrain it.

CHAPTER VI

SEXUAL INTERCOURSE

Some people are of the opinion that sexual intercourse should be preferred above all mundane <293> goods. They assert, namely, that it yields the most remarkable of all pleasures, since for all the others there are substitutes, whereas this pleasure has nothing that can take its place. It also increases the soul's gladness and gaiety and makes the body feel lighter, not to speak of the head and the brain.

Furthermore, it allays a person's anger, and drives out gloomy thoughts from his mind, and serves as an antidote against melancholy. The greatest value it possesses, however, is that it is the cause of the coming into being of the rational creature endowed with intelligence [called] "man." And what about the fact that it is the basis of men's sociability and of friendly relations which come about through it alone?

If sexual intercourse had been something inherently reprehensible, God, blessed and exalted be He, would have restrained His prophets and messengers, peace be upon them, from it. [But He did not do so.] Seest thou not how one of them said: *Give me my*

23. "and drink"—added by Ibn Tibbon and M.

wife (Gen. 29: 21) without any feeling of shame, and how another said without blushing:[24] *And I went unto the prophetess* (Isa. 8: 3)?

Now I examined this thesis of theirs and I found that it commits the error of being one-sided. That is due to the fact that they have overlooked the deleterious results and the reprehensible aspects of [too much addiction to] sexual intercourse. Among these may be listed the injury it does to the eyes, the loss of appetite, and the falling off of physical energy. Often, too, it is responsible for the prevalence of hectic fever and pains of the groin and of the soft parts of the womb.

Furthermore it makes the body flabby, wears it out quickly, and hastens senility. It is with reference to these facts that Scripture says: *Give not thy strength unto women, nor thy ways to that which destroyeth kings* (Prov. 31: 3). And what about the distraction of hearts and the confusion of the mind and the optic illusions which accompany it, as Scripture says: *Harlotry, wine, and new wine take away the heart?* (Hos. 4: 11.)

Moreover, he who gives vent to this impulse and enkindles its fire is unable to extinguish it except when his desire is completely satisfied, as Scripture puts it: *They are all adulterers, as an oven heated by the baker* (Hos. 7: 4). And what about the filth and defilement resulting from it, which, if a person has any sensitiveness and <294> delicacy of feeling, will cause his very clothes to declare him filthy, even though he clean himself scrupulously? Indeed it is just as Scripture has said: *If I wash myself with snow water, and make my hands never so clean; yet wilt Thou plunge me in the ditch, and mine own clothes shall abhor me* (Job 9: 30, 31).

Furthermore, what about the shame and the disgrace and the degradation and the unsavory memory left as a result of it for the future, as Scripture has so truly observed: *He that committeth adultery with a woman, lacketh understanding. . . . Wounds and dishonor shall he get, and his reproach shall not be wiped away?* (Prov. 6: 32, 33.) And what about [the effect that addiction to

24. "blushing"—Ibn Tibbon.

the gratification of the sex urge has in making the subject] believe all men to be blind and deaf to his doings, so that he will do what is unseemly in public and think that men are not cognizant thereof, as is illustrated in the remark of Scripture: *Thine adulteries, and thy neighings, the lewdness of thy harlotry, on the hills in the field have I seen thy detestable acts?* (Jer. 13:27.)

Again, what about the fact that [by delivering himself up to this urge] a person would make his home a place [25] of refuge for every adulterer, highwayman, and debauchee without its master's perceiving it, as Scripture says: *And when I had fed them to the full, they committed adultery, and assembled themselves in troops at the harlot's houses?* (Jer. 5:7.) Thus he may bring it about that neither he nor his children have any clearly legitimate offspring, just as he has been responsible for such an eventuality in the case of others. In this way the punishment would exactly fit the crime. Similarly, too, does Scripture remark: *If my heart have been enticed unto a woman, and I have lain in wait at my neighbor's door; then let my wife grind unto another, and let others bow down upon her, for that were a heinous crime; yea, it were an iniquity to be punished by the judges* (Job 31:9-11).

It is proper for man to satisfy this appetite only in order to produce offspring, as Scripture also says: *And you, be ye fruitful, and multiply; swarm in the earth, and multiply therein* (Gen. 9:7). Hence he should give this impulse free rein when in the estimation of reason it seems necessary, and check it when that need has been fulfilled.

CHAPTER VII

EROTICISM

Even though it is repulsive [26] to mention this subject, it is no more so than to discuss the theories of the nonbelievers. Just, therefore,

25. "his home a place"—Ibn Tibbon and M.
26. Saadia seems to have in mind pederasty, which was prevalent among the ancient Greeks as well as the medieval Arabs. Cf. Guttmann, p. 270 and n. 1.

as we reported these latter for the purpose of refuting them and thereby rendering the minds of men immune against the doubts they might arouse, <295> so, too, shall we make an exposition of this subject in order to refute it and thus protect men's minds against confusion. There are, namely, people who entertain the view that human conduct is best regulated by being geared to some dominant love. This, they believe, has the effect of giving subtlety to the spirit and of refining the temperament to the point where the soul becomes something gossamerlike because of its refinement.

The process [they aver] is one of an extremely delicate character, attributable to the influence of nature. A substance, originating in the look of the eye, is poured into the heart. A desire is thereupon aroused which is further strengthened and intensified by the addition of other elements until it is firmly established.

They go even further in this matter, attributing the workings of this dominant passion to the influence of the stars. Thus they assert that, if two human beings were born in the ascendant of two stars facing each other, in full or in part,[27] and both stand under the influence of one zodiacal sign, they will inevitably love and attract one another.[28]

In fact, they carry their theory still further, attributing the consuming passion to the work of the Creator, magnified and exalted be He. They maintain, namely, that God has created the spirits of His creatures in the form of round spheres, which were thereupon divided by Him into halves, each half being put into a different person. Therefore does it come about that, when a soul finds the part complementing it, it becomes irresistibly drawn to it.[29] From this point they proceed further yet, making a duty of man's surrendering himself to his passion. They assert, namely, that this is only a means of testing the servants of God, so that by being taught submissiveness to love, they might learn how to humble themselves before their Master and serve Him.

27. "in full or in part"—literally "as triangle or hexagon."

28. Cf. Malter, p. 251, and Ventura, p. 281, for this rendering.

29. This is the myth of the origin of Eros related in Plato's Symposion. Cf. Guttmann, p. 270, n. 4.

Now the advocates of all that has been mentioned above are really thoughtless and without intelligence. I, therefore, deem it proper in this chapter, first of all, effectively to refute the spurious doctrines propounded by them. After that, I shall demonstrate the very opposite [30] of the theories to which they cling to be true.

I say, then, that so far as the thing they ascribe to our Lord, magnified and exalted be He, is concerned, it is inconceivable that He should use as a means of trial something that has been prohibited by Him. Indeed, it is as Scripture has said: *God imputeth not* [31] *unseemliness* (Job 24:12), and also: *For Thou art not a God that hath pleasure in wickedness; evil shall not sojourn with Thee* (Ps. 5:5). As for the doctrine of the division of the spheres to which they cling so tenaciously, since we have already refuted that in our refutation of the theory of uncreated spiritual <296> beings,[32] making it clear that the soul of every human being is created simultaneously with the perfection of his form,[33] this theory has become completely null and void.

As for their allegation in regard to the influence of the stars and the tallying of the two parts of the love-match, as well as of the constellations, if it were really as they say, it could never happen that Zeid should love Amr without Amr's reciprocation, seeing that they are both equal. We do not, however, find the matter to be so.

As for their assertion, again, that this emotion originates from a look, after which desire is generated in the heart, I say that it was precisely on that account that our Lord, exalted and magnified be He, commanded us to devote both our eyes and our hearts to His service, as Scripture says: *My son, give me thy heart, and let thine eyes observe my ways* (Prov. 23:26). He also forbade us to employ them in rebellion against him, when He said: *And go not about after your own heart and your own eyes, after which ye use to go astray* (Num. 15:39).

This latter warning was issued against the consolidation of this

30. "opposite"—Ibn Tibbon, by the emendation of just one letter.
31. "imputeth not"—the usual translation is "imputeth it not for."
32. Cf. pp. 50 ff.
33. Cf. p. 235.

state in the heart to the point where it would hold the subject in its grip and have such dominance over him that he would cut down on his eating and drinking and all other functions basic to his well-being. The consequence [of such a course] would be that his flesh would waste away and his body fall off and maladies would make their inroads on him in all their severity. And what about the inflammation and the fainting and the heart throbs and the worry and the excitement and the agitation, of which Scripture says: *For they have made ready their heart like an oven, while they lie in wait?* (Hos. 7:6.)

These effects are sometimes carried to the brain, weakening the faculties of imagination, reflection, and memory, and sometimes even destroying the powers of sensation and motion. It may also happen that, upon catching sight of his beloved, the lover should swoon away and fall into a dead faint, his spirit leaving his body for twenty-four hours,[34] so that he would be thought dead and be carried out and buried.[35] Again it is possible that upon seeing his beloved or hearing him mentioned, the lover might emit a rattle and really die, thus proving the truth of the parable coined by the proverbist: *For she hath cast down many wounded; yea, a mighty host are all her slain* (Prov. 7:26).

How now can a person allow himself and his reason to be taken prisoner [by his passion] to the point where he will not know that he has a Master, nor any strength, nor <297> this world nor the next, outside of that passion, as Scripture has put it: *But they that are godless in heart lay up anger; they cry not for help when He bindeth them?* (Job 36:13.) And what about the slavish submissiveness to the object of one's passion and to his retinue, and the sitting at the gates and waiting upon him everywhere, as Scripture expresses it: *Lift up thine eyes unto the high hills, and see: Where hast thou not been lain with? By the ways hast thou sat for them?* (Jer. 3:2.) And what about the vigils at night and the rising at dawn and the secrecy practiced so as not to be surprised in the

34. "his body . . . hours"—added by Ibn Tibbon and M.
35. "so . . . buried"—added by Ibn Tibbon and M.

act, and the deaths one dies whenever one is discovered in one's shame?

It is just as Scripture has expressed it: *The eye also of the adulterer waiteth for the twilight, saying: "No eye shall see me"; and he putteth a covering on his face* (Job 24: 15). And what about the murder of the lover or the beloved or of one of their retinue or of both them and those attached to them and of a great many human beings together with them that often results from being madly in love, as Scripture says: *Because they are adulteresses, and blood is in their hands?* (Ezek. 23: 45.)

Again, if he should one day be successful in attaining the object of his quest and realize in adequate measure that for which his soul has made such strenuous efforts, he might be filled with remorse and hate what he had loved to an even greater degree than he had loved it, as Scripture remarks: *And Amnon hated her with exceeding great hatred; for the hatred wherewith he hated her was greater than the love wherewith he had loved her* (II Sam. 13: 15).

It should, therefore, be clear to a person that he has sold his soul and his religion and all his senses, as well as his reason, once this arrow has been released that cannot be taken back by him any more, as has also been expressed by Scripture in its remark: *Till an arrow strike through his liver; as a bird hasteneth to the snare* (Prov. 7: 23). This emotional state, therefore, has its appropriate place only in the relationship between husband and wife. They should be affectionate to each other for the sake of the maintenance of the world, as Scripture says: *A lovely hind and a graceful doe, let her breasts satisfy thee at all times; with her love be thou ravished always* (Prov. 5: 19). A husband should give vent to his desire for his wife in accordance with the dictates of reason and religion and to the extent required in order to bind them closely together but restrain it vigorously and forcefully beyond that point.

<298>

CHAPTER VIII

ON THE ACCUMULATION OF MONEY

Others, again, are of the opinion that the best course for man to follow in his conduct in this world is to devote himself to the accumulation of money. They were deluded into adopting this view by a number of considerations. Among these was the allegation made by them that food and drink and sexual intercourse, which are the basis of physical existence, are made possible by it and it alone. Similarly commerce and marriage and all transactions among men are executed by means of it.

Even the investiture of kings with their duties of government and the homage paid to them requires money. Armies are collected and fortresses conquered because of the monetary advantages they afford. Mines and concealed treasures are dug up for the purpose of extracting the wealth they contain. And whither do men repair and where do they meet and visit if not at the gates of those who are financially successful? And who else can be liberal and charitable and philanthropic, and who else is the recipient of greetings and thanks except such persons?

It is just as Scripture says: *Many will entreat the favour of the liberal man; and every man is a friend to him that giveth gifts* (Prov. 19:6). It was with money that God favored His nation in return for obedience, as Scripture says: *And thou shalt lend unto many nations, but thou shalt not borrow* (Deut. 28:12). It says likewise: *And thou shalt lend unto many nations, but thou shalt not borrow; and thou shalt rule over many nations* [36] (Deut. 15:6); and this *rule* is, of course, exercised by means of money, as Scripture says: *The rich ruleth over the poor* (Prov. 22:7).

Now I studied their theory carefully and I came to the conclusion that all was well with the acquisition of money so long as it comes to a person spontaneously and with ease. However, once

36. This quotation is based on the reading of Ibn Tibbon.

one undertakes its quest in earnest, one realizes that it entails efforts of thought and exertion of the mind and staying awake at nights and hardship by day, so that, even when one has attained what one desires thereof, one is often unable to sleep properly. As Scripture says: *Sweet is the sleep of a labouring man, whether he eat little or much; but the satiety of the rich will not suffer him to sleep* (Eccles. 5:11).

On the other hand, when a person makes it the object of his striving and devotes himself to it with mad ambition and avidity, as I have mentioned that some do in the matter of food and drink,[37] then the love of money becomes for him like a consuming fire, like a wilderness, like death or barrenness <299> that are never sated. Nay it even exceeds the latter in its effects upon him, as Scripture says, with particular reference to this madness: *The nether-world and Destruction are never satiated; so the eyes of man are never satiated* (Prov. 27:20).

And what about the quarrels and contentions and animosities and the fighting which is similar to what lions and lionesses do, until they have gathered their prey, according to the metaphor used by Scripture: *The lion did tear in pieces enough for his whelps, and strangled for his lionesses?* (Nah. 2:13.) And how can one bear to hear the cries of orphans and widows and the poor and the oppressed to whom he who is [completely] intent on the accumulation of money pays no attention, as Scripture says: *And behold the tears of such as were oppressed, and they had no comforter?* (Eccles. 4:1.)

Furthermore, what about the unlawful seizure of other people's wealth and sustenance, and the loss of honor and the disappearance of trust and the removal of all reticence, which are occasioned solely by [the eagerness] to accumulate money, as Scripture says: *Then is the iniquity of Ephraim uncovered, and the wickedness of Samariah, for they commit falsehood; and the thief entereth in, and the troop of robbers maketh a raid without?* (Hos. 7:1.) And what about the broken promises and the false oaths taken because of it, with the result that truthfulness becomes completely non-

37. Cf. p. 369.

existent, as Scripture puts it: *Faithfulness is perished, and is cut off from their mouth?* (Jer. 7:28.)

Moreover, if all goes well and runs smoothly for him [who is engaged in the accumulation of money], he is apt to put his entire trust on it and forget to make mention of his Master and deny his Provider, as has, indeed, been expressed by Scripture: *And thy silver and thy gold is multiplied, and all that thou hast is multiplied, then thy heart be lifted up, and thou forget the Lord thy God* (Deut. 8:13, 14).

Often, again, this money [that a person is so eager to acquire] may be the cause of his being killed or ruined, either by robbers or by the government or the like, so that he and his children remain bereft of everything. This, too, has been remarked by Scripture, which says: *Riches kept by the owner thereof to his hurt* (Eccles. 5:12); *As he came forth of his mother's womb, naked shall he go back as he came. . . . And this also is a grievous evil, that in all points as he came, so shall he go* (Eccles. 5:14, 15).

On the other hand, if his wealth should be left to his child when the father dies, the weight of this ill-gotten wealth would be carried by the father into the grave [38] and the guilt thereof would be borne by him, as Scripture says: <300> *As for his father, because he cruelly oppressed, committed robbery on his brother . . . behold, he dieth for his iniquity* (Ezek. 18:18). This wealth, however, that he bequeathes to his son is unlucky. The blessing of God does not rest on it, as Scripture says: *An estate may be gotten hastily at the beginning; but the end thereof shall not be blessed* (Prov. 20:21).

The only reason why man has been endowed with the love of money is in order that he might take good care of that which God has so graciously bestowed upon him and not squander it, not for any other purpose, as Scripture says: *The blessing of the Lord, it maketh rich, and toil addeth nothing thereto* (Prov. 10:22).

38. "into the grave"—added by Ibn Tibbon.

CHAPTER IX

CHILDREN

Others, again, are of the opinion that [men] ought to dedicate themselves earnestly to the begetting of children. This, they say, affords serenity to the soul and solace to the eye and produces joy and gladness. Furthermore, if there were no children, mankind could not exist and the world would not perpetuate itself. Children serve, moreover, as provision against old age and remember a person for good after his demise. And to whom else but to them are mercy and compassion shown? And from whom, if not from them, does one obtain affection and honor?

Is it not sufficient to point out that every distinguished prophet implored God for them? Thus thou seest Abraham saying: *Behold, to me thou hast given no seed* (Gen. 15:3). Again, the Torah says: *And Isaac entreated the Lord for his wife, because she was barren* (Gen. 25:21); while Rachel said: *Give me children, or else I die* (Gen. 30:1). Also, by teaching his children the Torah of God and His religion and wisdom, the father might earn reward through them, as Scripture observes: *The father to the children shall make known Thy truth* (Isa. 38:19).

Now I considered this allegation on their part carefully and I noted that it was correct so far as those children are concerned whom the Creator grants to His servant in accordance with His wish. The mistake of the advocates of this theory lies in their requirement that one pay attention to this matter alone, to the exclusion of everything else. I say, however: Of what benefit are children to a person if he is unable to provide for their sustenance, covering, or shelter? And what is the good of raising them if it will not be productive of wisdom and knowledge on their part? And of what use are the pity and sympathy lavished upon them in the absence of these factors unless it be to add to the heartache of the <301> parents? As for their affection and the honor they might confer, how can these things be expected from them if the preliminaries are lacking?

Furthermore, what about the pains of pregnancy and the pangs of childbirth and the birth itself and the confinement and all the attendant ailments to which Scripture refers in its statement: *In pain thou shalt bring forth children?* (Gen. 3: 16.) Besides, it is also apt to happen that a mother die at the time when she gives birth, with the result that the joy is turned into sorrow. Thus, for example, Scripture tells us: *And it came to pass, as her soul was in departing—for she died—that she called his name Ben-oni (son of my sorrow)?* (Gen. 35: 18.)

Furthermore, what about the exertions made by the father and the hardships endured by him and the perils braved by him solely for the purpose of providing bread for his family and his young, as Scripture says: *Her young ones also suck up blood; and where the slain are, there is she?* (Job 39: 30.) And what about the trouble of raising them, and the care in the event of illness, and the preparation of medicines, and the supervision of the barley water or the oxymel—all of which are mostly occasioned by them only? And it is, of course, unnecessary to speak of those cases in which the matter ends in death and bereavement, for then there is real wailing and woe, as Scripture says: *Yea, though they bring up their children, yet will I bereave them, that there be not a man left; yea, woe also to them when I depart from them* (Hos. 9: 12).

Should the children live, on the other hand, the fear of what they might do, if they happen to be males, keeps the parents from closing their eyes at night, as Scripture says: *A son that dealeth shamefully and reproachfully will despoil his father, and chase away his mother* (Prov. 19: 26). The dread, again, of what might happen to the females inflames the parents' eyes, as Ben Sira says: *A daughter is to her father a false treasure. Because of his anxiety for her he does not sleep at night* (Sanh. 100b, quoting Ben Sira 42: 9). But, in general, if they are disobedient,[39] the expectations of joy from them are cut off, all the more so if they are malefactors. Of such children does Scripture say: *There is a generation that curse their father, and do not bless their mother* (Prov. 30: 11).

The sole reason why the love of children has been implanted in

39. "disobedient"—Ibn Tibbon and M.

the hearts of men is in order that they might hold on to those with whom their Lord has favored them and not lose patience with them, as Scripture says: *Lo, children are a heritage of the Lord; the fruit of the womb is a reward* (Ps. 127: 3).

CHAPTER X

HABITATION [OF THE WORLD]

Others, again, are of the opinion that <302> the worthiest occupation of man is the habitation of the world. They declare, namely, that, so far as the construction of houses is concerned, that is a necessity, since, without them, man would have no place that would afford him shelter from the heat and the cold and where those who are attached to him could assemble. His cultivation of the fields, again, is necessary for the production of food which is indispensable for his existence. Altogether [such improvements] are for man sources of joy and satisfaction and mirth and gladness, as Scripture says: *But the profit of a land every way is a king that maketh himself servant to the field* (Eccles. 5: 8). Moreover, it is on [such] cultivation of the soil and constructions that kings and ministers pride themselves, as Scripture says: *With kings and counsellors of the earth, who built up waste places for themselves* (Job 3: 14). Furthermore, it is such things that were promised as reward to the believers: *And houses full of all good things, which thou didst not fill* (Deut. 6: 11).

Now I examined this opinion of theirs and I found that they had committed the error of going to extremes in requiring that one give up all else and occupy himself exclusively with this activity. For how can any of the above-mentioned developments be carried out unless it be by means of wisdom and deliberation and a knowledge of engineering and planning? For unless he who engages in them possesses a broad knowledge of these subjects, he could not achieve aught of that which he aims for. Again, if a person burdens himself with such tasks of construction, he lets himself in for exertion and hardship and worry and anxiety and the expenditure of all of his own, as well as of other people's money because of his eagerness to finish what he has begun. Thus Scripture says: *Woe unto him that buildeth his house by unrighteousness, and his chambers by injustice; that useth his neighbour's service without wages* (Jer. 22:13).

On the other hand, if he should finish what he has planned to do, and then should note the least little thing that does not please him or that does not seem good enough to him, what he has done would be worth nothing to him and all his exertion and his hard work would be wasted. It would be just like the case mentioned by Scripture, namely: *And Hiram came out from Tyre to see the cities which Solomon had given him; and they pleased him not* (I Kings 9:12).

Besides, what about the perpetual anxieties and the constant heartaches that accompany such activities? And what about the envy of human beings and the wrath of rulers that they engender and the misfortunes into which they hurl a person? <303> Is it not just as Scripture says: *Ye have built houses of hewn stone, but ye shall not dwell in them. Ye have planted pleasant vineyards, but ye shall not drink the wine thereof* (Amos 5:11).

If, again, the developments consist of the cultivation of fields, then the plants that are in them grow not according to the desire of the person that planted them but according to the will of his Lord. The former is, therefore, constantly worried about them. And if the cultivator uproots them and plants others in their place,[40] he is doubly worried and his anxiety is all the greater in the event of a restraint of rain.[41] The same holds true also in the case of drought and intense heat [42] and mildew [43] and locusts and torrential floods, as is indeed stated in Scripture: *If there be in the land famine, if there be pestilence, if there be blasting or mildew, locust or caterpillar, if their enemy besiege them* (I Kings 8:37). And what about the oppressive taxes imposed by rulers and the violence exercised

40. "plants others in their place"—Ibn Tibbon.
41. "and his anxiety . . . rain"—Ibn Tibbon.
42. "intense heat"—Cf. Dozy.
43. "mildew"—as in Deut. 28:22.

by their underlings, which bring it about that the entire produce of the fields is diverted to them and that nothing thereof ever reaches its owner? Thus has it been described by Scripture in the statement: *When goods increase, they are increased that eat them; and what advantage is there to the owner thereof, saving the beholding of them with his eyes?* (Eccles. 5: 10.)

Again, if what he has sown should happen to grow and its produce be garnered from the field, his aim and inmost thought is to wait until prices are high and hard times come, so that he may take away [44] everything from the needy and the poor, as Scripture says: *That we may buy the poor for silver, and the needy for a pair of shoes, and sell the refuse of the corn* (Amos 8: 6).

The only purpose for which the inclination to engage in [such activities of] improvement has been implanted in man is that he may thereby serve his needs as far as they go, as Scripture says: *And there he maketh the hungry to dwell, and they establish a city of habitation; and sow fields, and plant vineyards, which yield fruits of increase* (Ps. 107: 36, 37).

CHAPTER XI

LONGEVITY

Others, again, entertain the view that the highest aim of man's endeavor in this world should be to concern himself with increasing the length of his life span. They declare, namely, that by means of long life a person can realize all his wishes in spiritual, as well as in material matters. Should he neglect this, however, what can he attain that is of any value? It is for this reason that the Scriptures present long life as an incentive to virtuous conduct, saying: *That thy days be long upon the land* (Exod. 20: 12); <304> [and] *That ye may live many days* (Jer. 35: 7).

Now the means whereby life [is extended], in the opinion of the advocates of this doctrine, are regularity in eating and drinking, moderation in sexual intercourse, the endeavor to be cheerful, and

44. "take away"—Ibn Tibbon.

the avoidance of involvement in terrifying or dangerous undertakings of either religious or mundane character. By my faith,
however, while these conditions may contribute to the welfare of
the body, they are not the means for prolonging life. For we find
that there are many people who, although they fulfill these conditions, are short-lived, whereas others, who do the opposite, enjoy
longevity. Furthermore, we note that bodies of strong constitution
break down quickly, whereas others of weak constitution are long-
lived. If what the proponents of the above-mentioned theory assert
were really so, then kings should live longer than other men, since
they are able to commandeer all foods, medicaments, and enjoy-
ments of life, and everything else that has been described above.

Besides, let me mention what the advocates of this doctrine have
overlooked on this subject: namely, that the longer a person lives,
the greater are his cares and worries and troubles. It is as Scripture
puts it: *The troubles of my heart are enlarged; O bring Thou me
out of my distresses* (Ps. 25: 17). Also the toll of his iniquities and
sins increases and the computation and summation thereof becomes longer, and it is as though they were renewed every day, as
Scripture remarks: *But they arose early to corrupt all their doings* (Zeph. 3:7).

So long as man is still in the stage of childhood, he is ignorant,
knowing nothing, as Scripture says: *Foolishness is bound up in the
heart of a child* (Prov. 22: 15). When he reaches the age of boy-
hood, he gets into mischief, as Scripture observes: *But a lad* [45]
left to himself causeth shame to his mother (Prov. 29: 15). Then,
when he grows up into young manhood, he takes upon himself
exertion, toil, and hard work, as Scripture says: *The hunger of
the labouring man laboureth for him; for his mouth compelleth
him* (Prov. 16:26).

Finally, when he attains old age, all his desires cease and he lives
only by compulsion, as Scripture says: *Before the evil days come,*
<305> *and the years draw nigh, when thou shalt say: "I have
no pleasure in them"* (Eccles. 12: 1). The consequence is that his
luster, color, beauty, senses, and faculties diminish, and he be-

45. "lad"—the usual translation is "child."

comes like a cloud from which the rain has been extracted and the dry mist of which alone is left, which is thoroughly useless, as Scripture states: *Before the sun, and the light, and the moon, and the stars, are darkened; and the clouds return after the rain* (Eccles. 12:2); and the rest of this passage until the end.

The righteous servant of God, therefore, loves the life of this world merely because it serves as a stepladder by means of which he reaches and ascends to the next world, not for its own sake. Its love has been implanted in man solely in order that he might not kill himself when trouble befalls him, as Scripture says: *And surely your blood of your lives will I require; at the hand of every beast will I require it* (Gen. 9:5).

CHAPTER XII

ON DOMINION

Others, furthermore, are of the opinion that the highest object of human striving in this world ought to be eminence, majesty, and the occupation of a position of leadership. They assert, namely, that the soul has an inclination for elevation. Thou notest that it comes hard to it to be humble and submissive to another person and to do homage to him. Thou findest, furthermore, that the exercise of dominion gladdens and uplifts it and increases its cheerfulness and joyousness. Thus, too, does the right to issue commands and prohibitions afford it pleasure. Moreover, were it not for this aspiration toward leadership, there would have been no means of keeping the world in order or of looking after its welfare. It is thanks to its authority that kings are able to conduct wars and take charge of their countries' defense, that judges can judge among law-abiding men and the overseers correct the incorrigible among them. Of it consisted also the blessings that the righteous invoked upon each other, as Scripture says: *Let peoples serve thee, and nations bow down to thee. Be lord over thy brethren, and let thy mother's sons bow down to thee* (Gen. 27:29).

Now as far as their allegation about the regulation of the affairs of the world by the maintenance of a system of defense and by the exercise of justice and correction is concerned, it is not to be refuted. In fact, that happens to be our own thesis and the point we endeavor to make. However, they make use of the justification of the exercise of authority for bolstering their theory [of glorifying the wielding of power for its own sake]. For the orderly control of the world can be effected only by the application of wisdom [in government]. They, however, lower the importance of wisdom by making the love of dominion in and by itself [the goal of human striving].

<306> I feel compelled, furthermore, to note down some of the injurious consequences of haughtiness and the love of dominion which they overlook. One of these is that when a person becomes haughty and conceited about his importance, he oversteps the bounds of his rank, and lords it over his fellowmen both near and far, and regards himself as unique among men, and looks down upon the opinion of everyone else, and stubbornly persists in his own view, contesting every other theory. As Scripture says: *He that separateth himself seeketh his own desire, and snarleth against all sound wisdom* (Prov. 18:1). Moreover, he rejects what the elders have learned by experience and excludes what practice has taught them to be right, and does not accept their advice and recommendation. He behaves rather as Scripture says: *The way of a fool is straight in his own eyes; but he that is wise hearkeneth unto counsel* (Prov. 12:15).

The result is that he makes a failure of his worldly affairs, and whatever success he may reap therein he attributes to his own cunning and power and management and judgment. All this is borne out by the statement of Scripture: *I will punish the fruit of the arrogant heart of the king of Assyria, and the glory of his haughty looks. For he hath said: By the strength of my hand I have done it, and by my wisdom for I am prudent; in that I have removed the bounds of the peoples, and have robbed their treasures, and have brought down as one mighty the inhabitants* (Isa. 10:12, 13).

From that point he would proceed to dispute with craftsmen about their craft, with the result that they would regard him as ignorant and make light of him. He would also contend with scientists about their scientific work, endeavoring to refute them. But there is more hope for the ignoramus who keeps quiet [46] than there is for him. *Seest thou a man wise in his own eyes? There is more hope of a fool than of him* (Prov. 26:12).

Thence he might go on to argue [47] with kings and ministers, being displeased with their opinion and disapproving of their directives. Of such a one does Scripture say: *The sluggard is wiser in his own eyes than seven men that give wise answer* (Prov. 26:16). Finally he reaches the point where he would find fault with the wisdom of the Creator and His knowledge so as to reject much of it and regard it with contempt, as Scripture says: *And they say: "How doth God know? And is there knowledge in the Most High?"* (Ps. 73:11).

Such an attitude would cause him to fall into every conceivable kind of danger, because of his confidence that his cleverness would extricate him therefrom, but that is precisely what caused him to stumble. It is just as Scripture says: *He frustrateth the devices of the crafty, so that their hands can perform nothing <307> substantial. He taketh the wise in their own craftiness, etc.* (Job 5:12, 13).

Again, once a person is successful in attaining dominion and sovereignty, individuals who are envious of him make their appearance from the air, as it were, and his enemies become numerous, although he has done them no wrong, as Scripture says: *Without my fault, they run and prepare themselves; awake Thou to help me, and behold* (Ps. 59:5). In fact, as soon as it seems to them that he is about to attain to leadership, they become eager to slay him, like those who said: *Come now therefore, and let us slay him, and cast him* (Gen. 37:20). He therefore never eats any food except that which is sealed and never drinks any beverage except that which has been watched, and he feels as though he were in the

46. "keeps quiet"—Ibn Tibbon.
47. "argue"—a Hebraism.

position of one that is seated underneath the edge of a sword or whose life hangs by a hair, as Scripture puts it: *There is but a step between me and death* (I Sam. 20: 3).

Finally his entourage might divert him from following the strict line of justice and lead him into all sorts of suspicions [48] and doubts, with the result that he would incur the intense dislike of men and be called heavily to account by his Lord, as is also stated in Scripture: *And give ear, O house of the king, for unto you pertaineth the judgment; for ye have been a snare on Mizpah, and a net spread upon Tabor* (Hos. 5: 1).

The only reason, then, that the Creator implanted in the soul of men the love of high position and eminence was that it might thereby be induced to long for the reward of the world to come, as Scripture says: *He withdraweth not His eyes from the righteous; but with kings upon the throne he setteth them for ever, and they are exalted* (Job 36: 7).

CHAPTER XIII

THE SATISFACTION OF THE THIRST FOR REVENGE

Others maintain, again, that the best thing for man to strive for in this world is to take revenge on his enemies. They assert, namely, that the satisfaction of the thirst for revenge removes from the soul the worry with which it is laden and relieves it of the sorrow in which it is wrapped. It affords it the pleasure of seeing the discomfiture of its enemy, assuages the vehemence of its wrath, puts an end to excessive brooding, and prevents a second enemy from daring to do what the first was bold enough to attempt. Seest thou not that the best that was promised to the believers was: *Behold, all they that were incensed against thee shall be ashamed and confounded; they that strove with thee shall be as nothing, and shall perish. Thou shalt seek them, and shalt not find them, even them that contended with thee?* (Isa. 41: 11, 12.)

Now I considered all that they have mentioned and found that

48. "suspicions"—Ibn Tibbon.

they were laboring <308> under an illusion. For the effects upon the soul that they describe [as having been due to the exercise of vengeance] were entirely the result of action that took place spontaneously without any assistance on its part. Where, however, the soul has to meditate about the measures to be taken against the enemy, it falls into a sea of gloom and constantly thinks up new schemes, as Scripture expresses it: *Who devise evil things in their heart; every day do they stir up wars* (Ps. 140: 3).

Furthermore, the man [who is consumed by the desire for revenge] gets into the frame of mind of refusing to accept intercession or entertaining any feeling of compassion or pity or listening to any plea [for clemency], as Scripture says: *The soul of the wicked desireth evil; his neighbour findeth no favour in his eyes* (Prov. 21: 10). He is ready also to lavish his entire wealth and fortune [49] on the nursing of that revenge, as Scripture says: *Behold, I will stir up the Medes against them, who shall not regard silver, and as for gold, they shall not delight in it* (Isa. 13: 17).

Moreover, even though he is unable to succeed in killing that enemy except by killing a thousand friends or killing himself, he does not shrink back from taking that step, as Scripture says: *Let me die with the Philistines* (Judg. 16: 30). Nay he is not even deterred by the necessity of having to forsake his Master and His service in order to realize his ambition, as Scripture expresses it: *O God, the proud are risen up against me, and the company of violent men have sought after my soul, and have not set Thee before them* (Ps. 86: 14).

However, after having taken all these risks for the sake of getting satisfaction, it is still possible that he may not attain his objective, as Scripture says: *To break through unto the king of Edom; but they could not* (II Kings 3: 26). And, again, it may happen that fortune turn against him and he himself perish, as Scripture remarks: *Whoso diggeth a pit shall fall therein; and he that rolleth a stone, it shall return upon him* (Prov. 26: 27).

Should he, on the other hand, remain safe and attain the object of his quest, he will still have incurred the severe punishment of

49. "fortune"—Ibn Tibbon.

God from which no one can save him except the forgiveness of him whom he has wronged, as Scripture says: *A man that is laden with the blood of any person shall hasten his steps unto the pit; none will support him* (Prov. 28: 17).

How, furthermore, [can a person who is thus consumed by the thirst for vengeance] cherish the hope that he may succeed in resisting either the decrees of fate, if the doctrine of the fatalists be accepted, or the influence of the stars, if the theory of the astrologers be followed, or <309> maintain the vain hope to resist the decision of the Creator of the heavens and the earth,[50] if the view of the professors of the truth [51] be adopted? [Are they not foolish] to think themselves beyond God's control, as Scripture expresses it: *They encourage one another in an evil matter; they converse of laying snares secretly; they ask, who would see them?* (Ps. 64: 6.)

Moreover, what about the hatred on the part of human beings and the enmity of fellow creatures [that the vindictive invite], and the envy of their well-being and the gloating over their misfortune that they engender in the formers' hearts, as Scripture says: *So they make their own tongue a stumbling unto themselves; all that see them shake the head?* (Ps. 64: 9.) The consequence is that nobody sympathizes with them in their sorrow and none is pained over their misery but everybody [52] rejoices over their downfall, as Scripture says: *There is no assuaging of thy hurt, thy wound is grievous; all that hear the report of thee clap the hands over thee; for upon whom hath not thy wickedness passed continually?* (Nah. 3: 19.)

Often, again, this general enmity might in the end redound to the hurt of him who seeks revenge, as Scripture says: *And the cruel hatred wherewith they hate me* (Ps. 25: 19), and also: *Show no mercy to any iniquitous traitors. Selah* (Ps. 59: 6).

The only reason, then, that the desire to take revenge has been implanted in the soul of man is in order that God's justice might be carried out against the evildoers in the lands and that the welfare

---

50. "earth"—Ibn Tibbon.
51. "truth"—Ibn Tibbon, correctly.
52. "everybody"—Ibn Tibbon, correctly.

of mankind might be served, as Scripture says: *Morning by morning will I destroy all the wicked of the land; to cut off all the workers of iniquity from the city of the Lord* (Ps. 101:8).

CHAPTER XIV

ON KNOWLEDGE

Among the scholars there are some who maintain that there exists nothing with which an individual ought to occupy himself in this world except the quest of scientific knowledge. They assert, namely, that thereby one attains an acquaintance with the elements of nature, as well as with the various mixtures to be found on earth, and also an extensive knowledge of the stars of heaven and the celestial spheres.

This sort of knowledge affords pleasure to the soul, as Scripture says: *For wisdom shall enter into thy heart, and knowledge shall be pleasant unto thy soul* (Prov. 2:10). It also heals the soul of ignorance, as Scripture says: *It shall be health to thy navel* (Prov. 3:8). <310> Aye, it is as nourishing to it as food, as Scripture says: *And drink* [53] *to thy bones (ibid.).* It furthermore adorns the soul like pearls and jewels worn by kings, as Scripture says: *For they shall be a chaplet of grace unto thy head, and chains about thy neck* (Prov. 1:9). He who does not strive for such knowledge and has no understanding for it might almost be said not to belong to the human race and not to be worthy of such a privilege, as Scripture says: *Because they give no heed to the works of the Lord, nor to the operation of His hands* (Ps. 28:5).

Now I found all that they ascribed to scientific knowledge to be true and correct. Nevertheless there is this mistake that their thesis harbors; namely, the assertion on their part that one should occupy himself with it alone to the exclusion of everything else. For if, while engaged in acquiring knowledge, a person failed to concern himself about his sustenance, shelter, and clothing, his knowledge would be nullified, since his existence depends on these things.

53. "drink"—the usual translation is "marrow."

On the other hand, if he were to impose himself on other people for the securing of these necessities of his livelihood, he would be rejected, no longer relied upon,[54] and his advice would not be accepted any more, as Scripture also says: *Nevertheless the poor man's wisdom is despised, and his words are not heard* (Eccles. 9: 16).

Again, if he [who dedicates himself to the cultivation of knowledge] were to content himself with coarse, lean fare and try to get along on it,[55] his nature would become coarse, his mind dull,[56] and the clarity and delicacy of his knowledge would be impaired. For, as Scripture says: *A word fitly spoken is like apples of gold in settings of silver* (Prov, 25: 11). Seest thou not that the children of Israel were nourished in the wilderness by our Lord by only the finest food—I mean the manna—in order that they might learn divine wisdom, as Scripture says: *And the people shall go out and gather a day's portion every day, that I may prove them, whether they will walk in My law, or not?* (Exod. 16: 4.) Consider also the fact that, even though the children of Levi were entitled to only one-thirteenth part of the produce of the fields, since they constituted only one out of thirteen tribes, they were allotted by God a whole tenth so that their food might be fine.

Furthermore, if all men had agreed to abide by the principle advocated by these [one-sided lovers of knowledge], then the [cultivation of] knowledge would have come to an end because of the discontinuance of the propagation of the human race resulting from the neglect of marriage. Again, exclusive preoccupation with physical science would constitute an. abandonment of the cultivation of the science of religion and religious law, whereas the only reason why the love <311> of the former has been implanted in man is in order that it might support the latter, both together making an excellent combination, as Scripture says: *That I might make thee know the certainty of the words of truth, that thou mightest bring back words of truth to them that send thee* (Prov. 22: 21).

54. "relied upon"—Ibn Tibbon.
55. "coarse, lean . . . on it"—Ibn Tibbon.
56. "his mind dull"—literally "will throw up foam."

CHAPTER XV

WORSHIP

There exist many people who assert that the highest endeavor of the servant of God in this world ought to be to dedicate himself exclusively to the service of his Lord. That is to say, he should fast by day and arise at night in order to praise and glorify God, abandoning all mundane cares, in the belief that God will provide his sustenance, medicaments, and all his other needs. We also find that such service of God is productive of great pleasure, as Scripture says: *For it is pleasant, and praise is comely* (Ps. 147:1). It produces, moreover, joy and gladness, as Scripture says: *Serve the Lord with gladness* (Ps. 100:2). Furthermore, it is treasured up with the Creator of the universe for the time of reward, as Scripture says: *And I will spare them, as a man spareth his own son that serveth him* (Mal. 3:17).

All these, too, may God have mercy on thee, are right in whatever laudatory assertion they make with reference to the service of our Creator. In fact, all the epithets that might be ascribed to it cannot praise it sufficiently, as Scripture also remarks: *Great is the Lord, and highly to be praised; and His greatness is unsearchable* (Ps. 145:3).

Nevertheless, the objection must be raised against this view because of the exclusive devotion to this one [activity which it advocates] and the remark of its proponents that one should not engage in any other. For if a person were not to concern himself about his food, his body could not exist. Again, if he were not to concern himself with the begetting of offspring, divine worship would cease altogether, for if all the members of a particular generation were to agree upon such a course and then die, divine worship would die together with them. In reality, however, the duty of serving God is supposed to be carried out by parents and their children and their children's children, as Scripture says: *That thou mightest fear the Lord thy God, to keep all His statutes and His commandments, which I command thee, thou, and thy son, and thy son's son, all the days of thy life* (Deut. 6:2).

Furthermore, let me reveal [57] what has eluded the advocates of this view; namely, that the service of God consists in [the fulfillment of] all the rational <312> as well as the revealed precepts of the Torah, as Scripture states: *And now, Israel, what doth the Lord thy God require of thee, but to fear the Lord thy God, . . . to keep the commandments of the Lord* (Deut. 10: 12, 13). Which, then, of the laws of measures, weights, and balances, such as those contained in such injunctions of Scripture as *Just balances, just weights* (Lev. 19: 36), is the hermit saint able to fulfill? Which one, again, of the injunctions to judge justly and fairly, referred to in the exhortation of Scripture: *Thou shalt not wrest judgment; thou shalt not respect persons* (Deut. 16: 19), does he have the occasion to carry out?

What chance, moreover, does he have to comply with the rules of what is permitted and forbidden in such matters as the eating of meat and the like, in regard to which Scripture states: *These are the living things which ye may eat?* (Lev. 11: 2.) What opportunity does he have to abide by the laws of uncleanliness and cleanliness referred to by Scripture in such statements as: *To make a difference between the unclean and the clean* (Lev. 11: 47), and again: *To teach when it is unclean and when it is clean?* (Lev. 14: 57.)

Similar questions might be asked with reference to the agricultural laws, the tithes, vows, alms, and the like. If thou wert to say, however, "But why not let this person study so that he might instruct others how to comply with the law?" our answer would be that in that case it would be they and not he that would be serving God, since the service of God would be performed by them and not by him.

So far as their assertion that a person must rely upon the Creator in the matter of the welfare of the body and the provision of food is concerned, what they say is correct. They have left out only one consideration; namely, that God has established for the attainment of everything a special means and manner by which it is to be sought. If they had, indeed, been right in their assumption that

57. "reveal"—Ibn Tibbon and M.

reliance on God is to be universally applied, they should also have exercised it in the realm of worship, so that they would depend on Him to cause them to attain the reward of the hereafter without worshiping Him. Therefore, just as this is inconceivable because worship has been established by God as a means for the attainment of the reward of the hereafter, so, too, is it impossible to dispense with the effort to earn a livelihood and marriage and other occupations that have been designed by God as means conducive to the welfare of mankind. To be sure, there are occasions on which God provides some of these things by way of a miracle, without <313> the mediation of man. He does not, however, make it a regular practice to change the law of nature that has been fixed by Him.

CHAPTER XVI

ON THE THEORY OF THOSE WHO MAINTAIN THAT REST IS THE HIGHEST GOAL OF [HUMAN] CONDUCT

Certain people affirm that rest is the means of the recovery of the soul itself, besides making a person's nourishment effective and contributing to the body's growth and the strengthening of the senses. Whenever, indeed, a human being does fatiguing work, he longs for rest, which becomes the object of his striving. Seest thou not that kings are, of all men, those that rest the most? Were not rest, therefore, the greatest of all goods, they would not have chosen it for themselves. And what about the relaxation of the mind which it makes possible through the abandonment of all excitement and frivolity and care and worry? It suffices thee to note that rest has been used as a simile for [describing the effect of] the choice of the true religion. Scripture says, namely: [*Stand ye in the ways and see, and ask for the old paths, where is the good way, and walk therein,*] *and ye shall find rest for your souls* (Jer. 6: 16). Furthermore, rest has been prescribed on sabbaths and holidays.

Now I examined the view of the proponents of this theory and I found that they were the most senseless of all men. In fact, they do not know what they are speaking about. For rest is appropriate for man only after great exertion and the disposal of his needs and the preparation of the means of his livelihood. Then he can [afford to] rest and relax. As Scripture expresses it: *Prepare thy work without, and make it fit for thyself in the field; and afterwards build thy house* (Prov. 24:27). However, rest in and by itself, without any of these presuppositions, is rest in name only, resulting in laziness. Now do not ask what the consequences of long-continued laziness are. For when a person is negligent and lazy for a certain length of time, poverty befalls and overwhelms him, so that he feels the want of most of the things necessary for his well-being, as Scripture says: *"Yet a little sleep, a little slumber, a little folding of the hands to sleep"—so shall thy poverty come as a runner, and thy want as an armed man* (Prov. 6:10, 11).

Now when a person is lazy and consequently makes no provision for his sustenance, clothing, and shelter, the result is that he spends the live-long day in sighing, to the point where his appetites and the claims of his body literally kill him, as Scripture says: *The desire of the slothful killeth him, for his hands refuse to labour* (Prov. 21:25). The consequence is that <314> he becomes remiss in prayer and fasting and refuses to stand up or move in order to fulfill his religious duties or perform any useful task. That is why the *lazy* individual has been presented as the antithesis of the *righteous*, because the concept of *laziness* might also be applied to *wickedness*. Scripture, therefore, says: *There is that coveteth greedily all the day long; but the righteous giveth and spareth not* (Prov. 21:26).

Furthermore, what about the softening and the heaviness and the swelling of the body, and the growth of tumors, and the development of piles, and gout, and sciatica, and varicose veins,[58] and the tumid Barbadoes leg,[59] and many other afflictions which are the result purely of idleness? Nay, even persons whose wants are completely satisfied must not be indolent and go idle, as Scripture states [about the woman of valor that] *She looketh well to*

58. "varicose veins"—Cf. Dozy, I, p. 459, *daliah*.
59. "tumid Barbadoes leg"—Lane-Poole. p. 2474, *fil*.

the ways of her household, and eateth not the bread of idleness (Prov. 31:27).

The only reason we find the soul inclining [60] toward rest is that its Creator has implanted this [inclination] in the soul as a premonition of the quiet and the tranquility that will prevail in the world to come, and as an incentive therefor. This is borne out by the statement of Scripture: *And the work of righteousness shall be peace; and the effect of righteousness quietness and confidence for ever. And my people shall abide in a peaceable habitation, and in secure dwellings and in quiet resting-places* (Isa. 32:17, 18).

CHAPTER XVII

It has, then, become clear to any reader of this book, as a result of my exposition and elucidation, that whoever believes in the preoccupation with any of the thirteen types [of human endeavor] that have been enumerated is mistaken in his view, not right in it, by reason of the fact that he demands exclusive devotion to the said activity, rejecting the association of any other with it. The consequence is that he deviates from the road leading to his goal and that he fails to attain the object of his desire, as I have previously demonstrated in my comment on the statement of Solomon to the effect that whatever is *one-sided* [61] is *wanting* [62] (Eccles. 1:15). The only proper type of conduct consists of the combination of all these classes of activities.

On the other hand, however, it is not right to select [equal] parts from each of the above-mentioned thirteen categories; one should rather take from each type of activity the suitable proportion, as dictated by science and religious law. The extract yielded, then, by the combination of the fragments of <315> the aforementioned thirteen objects of human endeavor is that the intelligent person should secure food and drink and indulge in cohabitation to the

60. "inclining"—Ibn Tibbon.
61. "one-sided"—the usual translation is "crooked."
62. Cf. above, p. 362.

extent necessary to sustain his body and raise a posterity for himself. Whenever, then, he has the opportunity to do so legitimately, he may give vent to his appetite and permit it to realize its desire. Should it, however, wish [63] to exceed its bounds or seek to secure what is not permissible, he must withdraw it and check it. In the event, however, that it refuses to be held in check by him as he wishes, he must release against it the trait of abstinence to the point of refraining from the activity in question altogether.

Furthermore, a person should take as much care as is desirable of such wealth and children as he has been granted by God. He should also cultivate as large a proportion of the land as may be required to satisfy his needs. Should he, however, come close to being overpowered by greediness so as to do what is either forbidden or reprehensible, then he ought to employ the faculty of abstinence until he desists from such an activity.

Furthermore, the life of this world should be beloved by him only on account of the world to come because of its being the vestibule of the latter, not for its own sake. Nor should he manifest any eagerness for dominion or vengeance. Should these, however, come about of their own accord, then he ought to make use of them in executing the punitive laws prescribed by religion and in being kind toward fellowmen. Under no conditions, however, should laziness be adopted by him as a mode of behavior. Finally, whatever leisure time a person has left after providing for his sustenance should be devoted by him to worship and the cultivation of science.

When, then, he effects a harmonious blend of all these activities in accordance with our suggestion, he will find approval in both worlds, as Scripture also remarks: *Above all that thou guardest keep thy heart; for out of it are the issues of life* (Prov. 4:23). The pattern of his activities in their harmony, then, comes to resemble the composition of bodies out of the four elements of nature, or every material substance consisting of links that are joined together.[64] Or else they might be compared to medicines, which are usually made up of many ingredients, three drachmas' weight be-

63. "wish"—Ibn Tibbon.
64. Cf. above, pp. 357 ff.

ing taken of one item, and a drachma's weight of another, and four daniks [65] of another, and half a drachma of still another, <316> and two daniks of another, and of another a danik and a half, and of still another a danik, and half a danik of the last. It would not be proper, however, to take equal proportions of each.

CHAPTER XVIII

Now I deem it fitting, at the conclusion of this treatise, to offer an exposition of the [effect of the] blending of the various sensations in order that these may serve as an additional illustration and example of the point we have made previously about the [necessity of properly] blending the impulses of man's character. I say, then: It is well known that there are five types of sensations; namely, those of taste and sight and hearing and smell and touch. Now I shall leave alone two of these: in the first place, that of touch, because it gives pleasure in only one way: namely, by contact with what is soft. Next there is that of taste, which we shall not discuss, because its combinations are quite familiar. Thus, for instance, the dish called *faludaj* is a concoction of starch, sugar, honey, and saffron, and other ingredients. The same applies to all the varieties of foods and cooked dishes.

I shall, therefore, direct my discourse to the three other classes of sensations and say that a simple color, such as pure white or red or yellow or black, generally has the effect of weakening the sense organ when one looks at it. Thus, for instance, the sight is blinded by snow, and redness is harmful to the eye, and blackness weakens the eyeball,[66] and so forth. Furthermore, these colors have [in isolation] no cheering effect and do not produce much of a pleasant sensation. When, however, they are merged, they evoke all kinds of pleasant feelings and rouse many of the faculties of the soul to activity.

Thus [for example] I might say that when the color red is mixed with yellow, it stimulates the yellow gall and the traits of the

65. A danik is one sixth of a drachma, the larger coin. Cf. Lane-Poole, p. 920.
66. "eye-ball" or "power of vision"—Ibn Tibbon and M.

soul originating in it, causing [physical] strength to manifest itself. Again, when the color yellow is mingled with black, it acts as a stimulant, causing the production of phlegm, so that the soul's faculty of humility comes to the fore. A combination of black, red, yellow, and white reacts on the black gall and brings to the fore the soul's cowardice and sadness. Similarly, when the proportions in the mixture of these colors are increased or decreased, <317> corresponding effects are produced in the stimulation of the faculties of the soul.

The same applies to the single sound or musical intonation [67] or melody.[68] They arouse [in their simple state] only one of the impulses of the soul, and often their reaction upon the latter is injurious. When, however, they are blended together, they produce a harmonious effect on the emerging traits and faculties of the soul that make their appearance. Now it is necessary for thee to know what sort of impression they make individually because this, in turn, determines the effect they produce in combination.

Let me, therefore, say at this point that there are altogether eight distinct [rhythmic] modes,[69] each of which consists of measures derived from the beating.[70] The measure of the first of these modes is composed of three consecutive beats[71] and one quiescent[72] [beat].

The second, again, [is made up of] three consecutive beats[71] and one quiescent and one audible[73] [beat]. Both these modes stimulate the force of the blood and arouse the impulse to rule and dominate.

The measure of the third [mode] is composed of two consecutive beats, not separated by the time of a beat,[74] followed by a

67. Cf. Henry George Farmer, *Sa'adyah Gaon on the Influence of Music* (London, 1943), p. 32.

68. "melody"—the Arabic text reads "melodies," which should, however, be emended as Farmer (*ibid.*) suggests.

69. Cf. *idem*, p. 31, literally "melodies."

70. "beating," literally "intoning." Cf. *idem*, pp. 30 ff.

71. "beats," literally "notes." Cf. *idem*, pp. 30 and 78 ff.

72. "quiescent"—cf. *idem*, p. 78 for the meaning.

73. "audible"—cf. *ibid.* for the meaning.

74. "beat." Cf. above, n. 71.

solitary [75] beat. Between the downward and upward strokes [of the plectrum [76] and the upward] [77] and downward stroke, moreover, is the time of a beat.[78] This one mode reacts on the yellow gall and thus arouses man's courage and boldness and the like.

The measure of the fourth [mode] consists of three consecutive beats [79] which are not separated from each other by the time of a beat,[79] although there is such an interval between each three beats.[79] This mode alone stimulates the production of phlegm and brings to the fore the soul's potentiality for baseness, submissiveness, cowardice, and the like.

The measure of the fifth [mode] is made up of a solitary beat,[80] followed by two consecutive [81] [beats] which are not separated by the interval of a beat.[82] Also between [the downward and upward stroke of the plectrum and] the upward and downward stroke [83] is the time of a beat.[84]

The measure of the sixth [mode] consists of three audible beats.[85]

The measure of the seventh is composed of two consecutive beats [86] that are not separated by the interval of a beat.[87] Between each two of these beats,[88] however, is the time of a beat.[89]

The measure of the eighth, finally, is composed of two consecu-

75. "solitary," so according to Farmer, *op. cit.*, p. 35, on the basis of the parallel of al-Kindi. Landauer's text and the two Hebrew versions read "quiescent."

76. Cf. *idem*, p. 82.

77. Cf. *idem*, p. 31.

78. Cf. above, n. 71.

79. Cf. above, n. 71.

80. "beat." Cf. above, n. 71.

81. "consecutive," so according to al-Kindi. Cf. Farmer, *op. cit.*, pp. 31 and 36. Our text reads "separate."

82. Cf. above, n. 71.

83. "downward . . . downward stroke." This is the correction suggested by Farmer, *op. cit.*, p. 36. The text reads: "upward and downward stroke." Cf. also above, n. 76.

84. Cf. n. 71.

85. Cf. above, n. 71.

86. Cf. above, n. 71.

87. Cf. above, n. 71.

88. Cf. above, n. 71.

89. Cf. above, n. 71.

tive beats [90] that are not separated from each other by the time of a beat.[91] However, between each two beats [92] is the time of two beats.[93] These last four modes all stimulate the black gall, bringing forth various dispositions of the soul, leading at one time to gladness and at another to sorrow.

Now it is the practice among rulers so to blend these different modes as to harmonize them, the purpose being that the impulses stimulated by hearing these modes may put their souls in the proper disposition for conducting the affairs of the government. It should prevent them from being unfair by evincing either excessive mercy or severity <318> or by showing undue courage or cowardice or either too much or too little cheerfulness and gaiety.

The same holds true also for the sensations of smell taken individually. Each particular odor produces its peculiar effect. When they are mixed, however, an effect is brought about by the blend that varies in accordance with the proportions of the ingredients used. Thus, for example, musk is hot and dry. Camphor is cold and delicate. Saffron is hot and dry. Sandalwood is cold and moist. Amber is moderately warm. Rose-water is cold and delicate. Now, when all these ingredients are mixed together with each other, their properties, too, are blended and they exercise beneficial effects upon men.

CHAPTER XIX

Since it has become clear, then, that the harmonious blending of the sensations is generally very beneficial to man, how much more must this apply to the balancing of the tendencies of his character and the objects of his striving! The net result of our investigation, therefore, is that a person should exert himself in his mundane affairs to the extent required for his well-being. He should eat and drink what is permissible in accordance with

90. Cf. above, n. 71.
91. Cf. above, n. 71.
92. Cf. above, n. 71.
93. Cf. above, n. 71.

his need. Beyond that point his attention should be turned to the acquisition of wisdom, to the service of God, and to the establishment of a reputation for goodness and probity.

To each of the aforementioned objects of human striving, as we have listed them, a person should devote himself at its appropriate time. Such a laudable choice represents the net result of the remark made by Solomon, the son of David, in three different places in his book.

One of these passages is: *There is nothing better for a man than that he should eat and drink, and make his soul enjoy what is good* [94] *for his labour. This also I saw, that it is from the hand of God* (Eccles. 2:24). When he says *that he should eat and drink,* he refers, of course, to the matter of sustenance. When, again, he speaks of *his labour,* he has in mind the exertions for a livelihood. By the expression *from the hand of God,* furthermore, he means "from what is permitted to him insofar as God grants it to him," not from what he might take by violence. Finally, the statement *and make his soul enjoy what is good* alludes to seven different things which are described by him in his book as being good (ṭobh).[95]

The second passage is: *But also that every man should eat and drink, and enjoy what is good* [96] *for all his labour, is the gift of God* (Eccles. 3:13). Now this statement, too, embraces the matters of sustenance,[97] which is implied in the remark, *that he should eat and drink,* and the exertion for a livelihood, which is alluded to by the expression *for all his labour,* and that it must be from what is permitted for him, which must be inferred from the phrase <319> *the gift of God.* It also hints at the seven things [declared to be good] when it says: *and enjoy what is good.*

The third passage, finally, is: *Behold that which I have seen: it is good, yea it is comely for one to eat and to drink,* [and to enjoy what is good for all his labour, wherein he laboureth under

94. "what is good"—the usual translation is "pleasure."
95. Cf. below, p. 406.
96. "what is good"—the usual translation is "pleasure."
97. "the matters of sustenance"—Ibn Tibbon, omitting the number "7," which erroneously crept into the text.

the sun, all the days of his life which God hath given him] (Eccles. 5:17). This third passage contains references to all four of the matters that have been mentioned by us previously. To these, however, it adds *yea, it is comely*, whereby it points out that each of the tendencies of man's character, as well as of his desires, should be given vent to at the appropriate time—not at any other, as is explicitly [98] stated in this book: *He hath made everything comely* [99] *(yaphe) in its time* (Eccles. 3:11).

As for the meaning of the word *good* (ṭobhah), that is mentioned in this verse (Eccles. 5:17), it refers to three different types of wisdom, as explained by him in this book of his. He says, namely: *Wisdom is better (ṭobhah) than weapons of war* (Eccles. 9:18); *Wisdom is better (ṭobhah) than strength* (Eccles. 9:16); and *Wisdom is good (ṭobhah) with an inheritance* (Eccles. 7:11).

Each of these verses has its particular point of reference. Thus *Wisdom is good with an inheritance* refers specifically to the science of the elements of nature and the constitution of the world, because it concludes with the words: *Yea, a profit to them that see the sun* (Eccles. 7:11). *Wisdom is better than strength*, again, points specifically to the administrative functions of rulers and the government, for it is stated in the passage in which is found: *And there came a great king against it, and besieged it* (Eccles. 9:14). As for *Wisdom is better than weapons of war*, finally, that refers to divine worship and obedience of God, for it concludes with the remark: *But one sinner destroyeth much good* (Eccles. 9:18).

As for the explanation of the seven types of *good* (ṭobh) that we spoke of previously as having been referred to in this book [100] [of Solomon's], one of these is a good name and a reputation for virtuousness, concerning which he says: *A good name is better than precious oil.* (Eccles. 7:1). Another is to remember death, whenever anything happens, and not to forget about it. In regard to that he says: *It is better to go to the house of mourning than to go to the house of feasting* (Eccles. 7:2). Still another is

98. "explicitly"—Ibn Tibbon.
99. "comely"—the usual translation is "beautiful."
100. "book"—Ibn Tibbon.

indignation on behalf of God wherever that is possible and serves a useful purpose. In that connection he says: *Vexation is better than laughter* (Eccles. 7:3). Another of them, again, is the fore-seeing of the end of things, about which he says: *Better is the end of a thing than the beginning thereof* (Eccles. 7:8).

Among these is included also association with the learned and the righteous, with reference to which he says: *It is better to hear the rebuke of the wise* (Eccles. 7:5). Another of these things [that are good] is endurance, patience. Of this trait he says: *And the patient in spirit <320> is better than the proud in spirit* (Eccles. 7:8). Finally, there is included in this group the recognition on the part of the virtuous servant of God that he can never be com-pletely free from error, so that he might on that account be humble before his Master. With reference to this [Solomon] says: *It is good that thou shouldest take hold of the one; yea, also from the other withdraw not thy hand; for he that feareth God shall dis-charge himself of them all, etc.* (Eccles. 7:18). This is also what I had in mind.

It has thus been made clear that, upon subjecting the affairs of the world to analysis, the sage pointed out these eleven things, seven of which he labeled as *ṭobh* (*good* m.); three others of which he designated as *ṭobhah* (*good* f.); while one was called by him *yaphe* (*comely*), that is to say, the execution of every beloved or hateful [task] at its proper time and in the place that has been created for it, as we have explained. These eleven types of ac-tivity that we have listed above are, of course, to be engaged in after provision has been made for one's sustenance out of legiti-mate earnings, as we have explained.

Having now elucidated this subject by every possible means at my disposal, let me say that this entire book can serve a useful purpose only when it is coupled with sincerity of the heart and an earnest striving for its improvement, as Scripture says: *If thou set thy heart aright, and stretch out thy hands toward Him* (Job 11:13). Similarly the sage said: *With my whole heart have I sought Thee; O let me not err from thy commandments. Thy word have I laid up in my heart* (Ps. 119:10, 11). It therefore behooves the hearts [of men] to become refined and humble themselves to the name of our Lord, exalted and magnified be He, as Scripture says: *Because thy heart was tender, and thou didst humble thyself before the Lord, when thou heardest what I spoke against this place* (II Kings 22: 19). Seest thou not that, in such matters as things seen and heard and food and drink, much better results are achieved with the help of the concentration of the mind than without it?

The book is hereby completed, and praise be unto God.

APPENDIX

TREATISE VII

CONCERNING THE RESURRECTION OF THE DEAD, WHICH IS THE MOST GLORIOUS OF PROMISES MADE TO THE CHILDREN OF ISRAEL BY THE CREATOR FOR THE ERA OF SALVATION [1]

(CONSTITUTING THE VARIANT VERSION WHICH WAS THE BASIS OF THE HEBREW TRANSLATION OF TREATISE VII BY IBN TIBBON)

CHAPTER I

BLESSED and exalted be God, the God of Israel, who confirms His words and is truthful in His promises. Let me say now that I find that the masses of the children of Israel cherish the belief that the Creator, blessed and exalted be He, will bring the dead back to life at the time of the *redemption*. I find, furthermore, that they interpret literally every section of the Scriptures that appears to speak of the resurrection of the dead at the time of the *salvation,* citing, in support of their contention, traditions that embrace explanations of this doctrine. I find, however, that a minority of the nation do not acknowledge that this will transpire at the time of the *redemption.* They assert, namely, that the resurrection will take place at the time of the transition to the world to come. This assertion of theirs is based on rather doubtful and weak arguments, some of which I have heard expressed by them, and there are others which I can conceive of as having been advanced by them.

Now it is the duty of every righteous person to entertain in his mind, in the first place, approved ideas and to reject the opposite, as Scripture says: *The lips of the righteous know what is acceptable* (Prov. 10: 32). It is, furthermore, incumbent upon him to instruct the nation and facilitate for it the understanding of these matters and divert it from the words of the thoughtless, as Scripture also states: *The lips of the*

---

1. The Arabic text of this variant was published by Wilhelm Bacher in the *Festschrift zum achtzigsten Geburtstage Moritz Steinschneiders* (Leipzig, 1896), pp. 98–112.

righteous feed <99> [2] *many; but the foolish die for want of under-standing* (Prov. 10: 21). I therefore considered it necessary, in view of the fact that my aim is the truth—although I may not have attained it—to devote myself earnestly to the study of the subject of this book until it has become as clear in my mind as possible. Thereupon I shall note it down for our nation in order that it may serve it as a guide, helping it to serve our Lord and endure patiently what it has to suffer in *exile*.

I followed herein the course enjoined by God in recommending patience, when He said: *Strengthen ye the weak hands, and make firm the tottering knees. Say to them that are of a fearful heart: "Be strong, fear not"; [behold, your God will come with vengeance, with the recompense of God He will come and save you]* (Isa. 35: 3, 4). The translation of these verses is: "Strengthen the soft hands, and make firm the stumbling knees, and say to those that are foolish of heart: 'Be strong, fear not.' Behold your Lord will come with vengeance for you, with the best recompense for you will God come to save you."

Now when I investigated this matter in order to find out whether any valid objections could be raised against the belief on the part of Israel's masses in a resurrection of the dead at the time of the *redemption*, I noted that the sources that present themselves immediately to the mind as the possible bases from which such objections may be derived are, altogether, four in number, there being no fifth. I therefore considered every misgiving that I heard or could think of as being an argument against this belief and dedicated myself to its complete refutation, nullification, and demolition. This belief was then corroborated by means of evidence culled from the three sources from which the believers derive their proofs.

Now the four sources, which I examined for the purpose of seeing whether they contained any refutation of this belief, are those of nature, reason, Scripture, and tradition. I began with nature, because intrinsically it precedes the other sources, and said to myself: "Perhaps the idea of the resurrection of the dead ought to be rejected because of the impossibility of its being effected by nature. For it is not in accord with the ways of nature that, just as animals grow up and some wax old and die naturally, they should also come to life again naturally after having died."

2. Beginning of p. 99 of the Steinschneider Festschrift. Subsequent pages of the Arabic text will be similarly indicated.

But when I considered this hypothetical assumption, I found that it would be upheld only by the advocates of the doctrine of the eternity of the world [3] or by the dualists,[4] in whose opinion whatever happens comes about in accordance with the universally accepted and recognized laws of nature. However, so far as the monotheists are concerned, who believe that the Creator is capable of changing the ordinary laws of nature and of making them conform to His will at any time He pleases, they cannot possibly reject the doctrine of the resurrection of the dead on account of its being contrary to nature, since all of them avow that God has sent forth His messengers armed with supernatural miracles. And what is even more weighty than all this is their recognition that God had created the original elements out of nothing.[5]

<100> To elaborate on this subject—what I mean is that whoever denies the possibility of a *resurrection of the dead* at the time of the *salvation*, on the ground that such a thing cannot be effected by nature, will be compelled likewise to deny the miracle of the transformation of Moses' staff into a serpent (Exod. 4: 3 and 7: 10), and the changing of the water of the land of Egypt into blood (Exod. 7: 20), and the standing still and congealing of the water of the Red Sea (Exod. 14: 21), and the delaying of the great eastern movement which caused the sun to linger longer on the earth during Joshua's campaign (Josh. 10: 13), and all the other marvelous miracles that are mentioned by the Scriptures as having been performed by God by the hands of His prophets.

We might go even further and say that anyone who upholds such a view would have to make liars of all of God's messengers. Aye, he would be compelled to reject the doctrine of *creatio ex nihilo*, with the result that he would deny the existence of the Creator Himself and thus exclude himself from the community of the believers. Furthermore, as viewed from the standpoint of sound reasoning, the resurrection of the dead is easier to conceive of and more plausible than the doctrine of *creatio ex nihilo*.

It is, therefore, quite clear that whoever admits that the Creator produced everything that exists out of nothing and supported His prophets with marvelous miracles cannot reject the doctrine of the resurrection of the dead nor adhere to arguments from nature [to the contrary]. It goes without saying, of course, [that such a view would

3. Cf. pp. 75 ff.
4. Cf. pp. 59 ff.
5. Cf. pp. 38 ff.

be incompatible] with the acknowledgment that the son of the Shunammite was brought back to life by God in this world (II Kings 4: 35), a fact about which [6] no doubt is entertained by our nation.

But, to return to our investigation, I said to myself: "Perhaps this subject that I am attempting to analyze is one of those absurdities that cannot be ascribed to divine omnipotence, such as the bringing back of yesterday and causing the number five to be more than ten." What made me entertain such a thought was my assumption of the possibility of the decomposition, after the death of a living body, of its component parts into the four elements [7] from which they are derived, so that each part would rejoin its original element and be merged with it. Then portions of these elements might be combined and a second body be composed of them. These would then decompose again at the death of this body and return to their sources. Then they might be combined a third time and thus another body would be composed out of them, at the death of which they would disintegrate once more. How, then, could the first and the second and the third each be brought back to life in its complete form if the parts of each are conceived of as having entered into its successor at the time the latter was put together?

However, when I sifted this hypothesis and analyzed its premises, I found that the assumption on which it was based was incorrect. What I mean is that, if it were true that, after the elements of which a body consists disintegrate, each one rejoining its original source of heat or cold or moisture or dryness, and if there were no more raw materials in the original sources out of which to compose another body except for the decomposed portions of the first, then there would be only two possible ways of creating the second. Either the parts of which it would be constituted would be identical with those of the first or else an entirely new creation would have to take place. Either alternative, however, would eliminate the possibility of a reconstruction of the parts after their decomposition.

The fact is, however, that the original sources from which the elements are derived are countless numbers of times greater in bulk than the component parts of all composite bodies. For scientists know that the aerial space between the earth and the first part of the heaven has 1,089 times the volume of the entire earth, including its soil, mountains,

6. "a fact about which"—literally "just as about it."
7. Cf. pp. 66 ff. for the four natural qualities; i.e., dryness, humidity, heat, and cold; and the elements of earth, water, air, and fire.

seas, plants, and animals, because its measurements are thirty-three by thirty-three times [the earth's diameter].

Since, then, the mass of the source materials is so extensive, the Creator of the second body is able to derive the parts of which it is to be composed from portions of elements that have not been employed in [the creation <101> of] the first body. Similarly also would the third [body] be composed of parts that were not merged with the second, and thus, too, would the fourth be a combination of parts that were not mingled with the third because of the extensiveness of the realms of the elements and their sources.

[The Creator can, therefore, afford to] disregard the disintegrated portions of the first and second and third and all succeeding bodies in and by themselves, not using them in all subsequent combinations. Thus they would be ready for Him to reunite out of them the parts of every body and to restore the latter whenever it might please Him. That would be easy and simple also, since those to be resurrected from among the human beings who inhabited the earth during a total of five thousand years would constitute approximately fifty times its present human population,[8] whose entire bulk comprises only a fragment of the earth's mass.

Should someone ask, however, how someone who has been devoured by lions or other animals can be resurrected, seeing that he has been metamorphosed into other bodies, our reply would be that the maker of this assertion assumes that the bodies that are devoured lose their identity by assimilating with the bodies into which they have entered. We must, therefore, answer him on two points at the same time by citing to him a basic principle that we, the congregation of monotheists, profess and acknowledge; namely, that no body of any creature can in any way bring about the extinction of another body. Aye, even if the former were to burn the latter with fire, it could not cause it to be extinct forever, because no one is capable of so annihilating things as to render them nonexistent other than He that created them *ex nihilo* and brought them into being. So far as all creatures are concerned, however, they can only separate the parts of material bodies. Even when fire is enkindled in a certain body, its sole effect is to produce a resolution of its component parts into their original elements.

8. As Guttmann points out, Saadia arrives at this small figure because he has in mind the persons to be resurrected at the time of Israel's redemption, who will consist exclusively of Jews.

Thus the heat in it becomes part and parcel of the element of fire, and the moisture and cold rejoin their respective sources, while the earthy portion remains behind as ash cinders. In this wise none of the parts of the elements is annihilated.

Now the same effect that is produced by the fire which is visible to the eyes is produced by the fire within the animal upon that which is eaten. Thus, for example, when an animal eats an apple, its component parts are separated from each other. Then the air draws out of the body of the animal those parts of the apple which it usually absorbs. If it is unable, however, to absorb certain portions of the apple, it always draws something corresponding thereto out of the body of that animal, until only the earthy portion is left.

What holds true, now, for an eaten apple applies also to a human being who has been devoured. That is to say, the air draws out of the body of the animal that has devoured them the parts derived from three of the elements, leaving as a residue the earthy portion, which drops to the ground. There is no difference between the two cases except that the parts of the eaten apple that return to the air mingle with their original elements, whereas the parts of the body of the human being who has been devoured that have passed over to the air are preserved, not being merged with the original elements, so that they may be ready for the time of the resurrection and the revival of the dead, as we have stated previously.[9]

When, then, all these considerations were brought to my mind, all the misgivings I might have entertained on that score disappeared, and my conviction about this belief and my adherence thereto was confirmed, and I uttered praise unto the Omnipotent.

CHAPTER II

After that, I searched the second source of knowledge, namely, rational thought, for the purpose of inquiring whether <102> I might find some refutation of this belief [in the resurrection of the dead from that angle]. However, I discovered only three possible arguments [that might cast doubt upon its validity]. One of these is that the possibility of the resurrection of the dead constitutes a logical absurdity. But I have already pointed out that it is not so, as I have explained.[10]

9. Cf. the previous page.
10. Cf. above, p. 412.

The second is that God, who is able to bring the dead back to life, never promised that He would do it. I find, however, that He did make such a promise to His nation in many places of the *Bible*. These passages are, to be sure, susceptible of many different interpretations, so that they might be construed as referring to acts other than the resurrection of the dead. Nevertheless I see no necessity, from the standpoint of reason, for rejecting the literal sense of these passages in order to make room for a figurative interpretation.

I am making this last statement because of the fact that we, the congregation of Israelites, accept in its literal sense and its universally recognized meaning whatever is recorded in the books of God that have been transmitted to us. The only exceptions to this rule are those instances in which the generally recognized and usual rendering would lead to one of the four [following] results: either (*a*) the contradiction of the observation of the senses, such as [would be presented] by the Scriptural statement about *Eve: Because she was the mother of all living* (Gen. 3: 20); or (*b*) the contravention of reason, such as that which would be implied in the Scriptural remark: *For the Lord thy God is a devouring fire* (Deut. 4: 24); or (*c*) a conflict with some other Scriptural utterance, such as that which is occasioned by the statement of Scripture: *And try Me now herewith* (Mal. 3: 10), coming as it does after the injunction: *Ye shall not try the Lord your God* (Deut. 6: 16); or, finally, (*d*) a conflict with what has been transmitted by rabbinic tradition, such as we have in the Scriptural statement: *Forty stripes he may give him* (Deut. 25: 3), which clashes with the tradition according to which the penalty is thirty-nine stripes (Mak. 22b).

Now the method of interpretation to be adopted in these exceptional cases is to look for a rendering of the expressions [that are in doubt], which would be permissible in the usage of the Hebrew language and would make it possible for the contradictions to be reconciled. That such constructions can certainly be found is illustrated by the fact that the Scriptural remark: *Because she was the mother of all living*, lends itself to a suitable rendering if we take it in a restricted sense, saying that *Eve* was the mother of every living rational being descended from Adam.

Likewise we find for the statement of Scripture: *For the Lord thy God is a fire*, a good interpretation,[11] by way of metaphor or analogy, to the effect that God's punishment is like a consuming [12] fire that

11. "a good interpretation"—or "way out."
12. "consuming"—Ibn Tibbon.

burns up quickly, as Scripture says elsewhere: *For a fire is kindled in My nostril* (Deut. 32: 22).

As for the Scriptural statement: *And try Me now herewith,* following upon the injunction: *Ye shall not try the Lord,* we find the following distinction; namely, that there are two different modes of trying God. One of them is to try His omnipotence; [that is to say,] whether He is able or unable to do a certain thing. It is such testing of God that is prohibited. It was of such a sin that *they* were guilty of whom Scripture says: *And they tried God in their heart by asking food for their craving. Yea, they spoke against God; they said: "Can God prepare a table in the wilderness?"* (Ps. 78: 18, 19).

The other, again, consists of the test to which the servant of God subjects himself in order to find out whether or not he occupies a position of distinction and esteem with his Master, based on the previous acknowledgment of the fact that the particular act, [which is to serve as a criterion], lies within God's competence. Such a testing is permitted. Thus it is said of Gideon: *And Gideon said unto God: "If Thou wilt save Israel by my hand, as Thou hast spoken . . . let me make trial, I pray Thee, but this once with the fleece* (Judg. 6: 36, 39). In a similar vein does Scripture say: *And try Me now herewith* (Mal. 3: 10).

Finally, we find that so far as the Scriptural statement: *Forty stripes he may give him,* is concerned, it is really equivalent to the rabbinic tradition which records that the number of stripes administered was thirty-nine. We say, namely, that the equation is brought about by rounding out the thirty-nine and making them an even forty, just as the thirty-nine years of the people's wandering about in the wilderness were rounded out and referred to as forty in the statement of Scripture: *After the number of the days in which ye spied out the land,* <103> *even forty days, for every day a year, etc.* (Num. 14: 34.) Now the first year of their sojourn in the wilderness was already past at that time before that punishment had been decreed.

These are, then, the types of departures from the simple meaning that we and other persons of a speculative bent resort to when one of the four considerations described by us compels us to do so. However, when no such necessity brought about by one of the four causes mentioned by us for a nonliteral rendering of a Scriptural utterance or a tradition or a report exists, it is not necessary, nay not even permissible, to look for nonliteral interpretations and allegorical renderings of verses which contain a promise of the *resurrection of the dead* so as to deprive them of their literal meaning. On the contrary, they must be left as they are, since God, who uttered them, is omnipotent and at the same time the One who made the promise.

A third [possible argument against the doctrine of the resurrection of the dead that might be urged from the standpoint of reason] is that there might be certain conclusions deducible from such a premise that are unacceptable once they are brought to mind.[13] Since, however, the premises cannot be divorced from the conclusions and since the latter are untenable, it follows, of necessity, that the premise leading to them and implying [14] them is invalidated. I therefore inquired into the matter, but I did not discover a single deduction that I could not consider tenable, as I shall demonstrate in my description of each deduction and inference after the present discussion, when I shall also explain their tendency, correctness, and direction with the help of the Merciful.

CHAPTER III

Next I searched the third source, which consists of what is written in the Bible, wondering whether there was perhaps anything in it that might contradict the [doctrine of the] resurrection of the dead in this world. I did find [certain] passages throwing doubt [on this belief] that those who reject it might seize upon, and I therefore deemed it proper to mention them here and refute [the construction that the opponents of resurrection would put on] them.

One of these [passages] is the statement of Scripture: *So He remembered that they were but flesh; a wind that passeth away, and cometh not again* (Ps. 78: 39). Another is the statement: *As for man, [his days] are as grass. . . . For the wind passeth over it, and it is gone* (Ps. 103: 15, 16). There is also the statement: *As the cloud is consumed and vanisheth away, so he that goeth down to the grave shall come up no more. He shall return no more to his house, neither shall his place know him any more* (Job 7: 9, 10). Furthermore, there are such utterances of Scripture as: *If a man die, may he live again?* (Job 14: 14), and *So man lieth down and riseth not* (Job 14: 12), and others of the same tenor.

Now I made a serious study of all these passages and I found that not one of them definitely implied that God had stated that He would

---

13. Cf. Guttmann, p. 221, for the interpretation of this passage.
14. "implying"—reading of manuscript quoted by Bacher in his notes.

not bring the dead back to life. They are all merely characterizations of man's inability to rise [of his own accord] from the grave after his descent into it, or to shake off the dust from himself, or to return to his house or go back to his home. Pronouncements of this type that constitute the utterances of God's servants represent attempts on their part to win their Master's favor and requests of His mercy and compassion with them in view of their state of impotence.

Those, again, that constitute the word of God call attention to one of the reasons on account of which God has mercy and compassion on men; namely, the fact of their being in this weak state of impotence. The more the Scriptures dwell on this condition, emphasizing the dead man's inability to resurrect himself by his own efforts or to arise from his resting place, the greater becomes the esteem of the power of God as being able to resurrect mankind and bring about its return to life.

An illustration of how such a contrast contributes to the heightening of God's esteem is furnished by the remark of Scripture regarding the day of the assembly [15] at Mount Sinai: *For ask now of the days past, which were before thee, etc. . . . . whether there hath been any such thing as this great thing is, or hath been heard like it?* [16] (Deut. 4: 32). Similarly do the other amazing miracles and marvels that occurred in the past [enhance God's prestige]. And the same applies <104> to the miracles and marvels of the future.[17] Their occurrence, too, will be the cause of wonderment, as Scripture says: *Who hath heard such a thing? Who hath seen such things? etc.* (Isa. 66: 8).

Further Biblical utterances [that seem to support the opponents of the doctrine of resurrection] include such a statement on the part of Scripture as: *For to him that is joined to all the living there is hope, [for a living dog is better than a dead lion]. For the living know that they shall die; but the dead know not anything, [neither have they any more a reward; for the memory of them is forgotten]. As well their love, as their hatred, and their envy, is long ago perished; [neither have they any more portion for ever in anything that is done under the sun]* [18] (Eccles. 9: 4-6).

Now I looked into the meaning of these verses, which purport to

15. "assembly"—literally "standing."
16. This quotation follows the reading of Ibn Tibbon.
17. "of the future"—Ibn Tibbon.
18. This quotation is based on the reading of the Arabic text supplemented by that of Ibn Tibbon.

say, as I note, that whoever is connected with life possesses reassurance, and that a living dog is better off than a dead lion, the reason being that the living know that they shall die, but the dead know nothing, neither is there any gain left to them since their memory is forgotten, so that even their love and hatred and envy have completely perished, and no increase will ever be apportioned to them in anything that is done under the heavenly sphere. So I said to myself: "These [verses cast] grave doubts [upon the theory of the resurrection of the dead] which its opponents might possibly seize upon." However, when I regarded what preceded the passage in question, I found that the sage had prefaced it with the remark that these utterances did not represent his own point of view but were a recounting quotation by him of the speech of the foolish and of the insane thoughts entertained by them in their hearts.

This is borne out by what he says quite explicitly prior to these utterances; namely: *Yea also, the heart of the sons of men is full of evil, and madness is in their heart while they live, and after that they go to the dead* [19] (Eccles. 9: 3). The translation of this [verse] is to the effect that the hearts of the sons of man are full of evil and that there is insanity in their hearts while they are alive, as well as afterward when they are dead.

After this preliminary remark, he quotes the evil and insane thoughts that they harbor in their hearts, saying [on their behalf]: *For to him that is joined, etc. . . . For the living know, etc. . . . As well their love, etc.* This [quotation of a discredited point of view] is of the same order as the statement of the Torah: And Pharaoh said: *"Who is the Lord, that I should hearken unto His voice, etc.?"* (Exod. 5: 2), which was merely a quotation by God of the statement made by Pharaoh. Similarly the above-mentioned utterances on the part of the sage were a recounting by him of the remark of the foolish.

After the sage had designated the views in question as *evil* and *madness*, [it is clear that] whoever adheres to them is not deserving of basking in the light and the divine Presence of his Master, for God has stated explicitly that men of *evil and madness* could not abide with Him. Scripture says namely: *Evil shall not sojourn with Thee. Madmen* [20] *shall not stand in Thy sight* (Ps. 5: 5, 6). The [ultimate] fate, therefore, of [anyone who adheres to] this [false point of view] would be the same as that of him who was cut off, [that is to say, the same] as that of

19. This quotation follows the reading of Ibn Tibbon.
20. "Madmen"—the usual translation is "boasters."

Pharaoh, who is reported by Scripture as having asked: [21] *Who is the Lord* and the rest of that verse. We take refuge in God from such folly.

CHAPTER IV

Then I found that the text of Scripture is quite explicit in regard to our Master's promise to us of resurrection. An illustration hereof is furnished by its statement to the effect that, after reporting the words of the children of Israel: *"Behold our bones are dried up. Our hope is gone. We are clean cut off,"* the prophet said to them: *"Thus said God: 'Behold I shall open up your graves and I shall bring you up out of your graves, O My people, and bring you into the land of Israel, and put into you My spirit that ye may live, and I will cause you to dwell in your land, in order that ye may know that I am God' "* (Ezek. 37: 11–13); that is to say: "I have made you this promise and fulfilled it." [22]

This is the purport of the prophet's remark: *Then he said unto me: "Son of man, these bones are the whole house of Israel; behold, I will open your graves, etc."* [23] (Ezek. 37: 11, 12). The reason why the words *Behold, they say: Our bones are dried up, etc.* were put first is that God knew what sort of misgivings <105> would enter our minds and what afterthoughts we might entertain; namely, that we might say to ourselves: "How can the bones live again after having dried up, and the moisture return to them after having departed, and how can they be reunited with the soul after it has gone forth from them?"

God's statement, again: *And I will cause you to come up out of your graves, O My people* (Ezek. 37: 12) is to be interpreted as a promise to the children of Israel in particular. His statement: *And I will bring you into the land of Israel (ibid.),* moreover, serves as an assurance that this promise is to be carried out in this world, lest it be mistakenly thought that it was meant for the world to come.

His further statement: *And ye shall know that I am the Lord, when I have opened your graves, and caused you to come up out of your graves, O My people,* [24] (Ezek. 37: 13) which sounds like an unneces-

21. "cut off . . . having asked"—Ibn Tibbon.

22. Cf. a similar interpretation given by Rashi to this passage in Exodus 6: 2, based on Siphra on Lev. 22: 31.

23. This quotation is based on the reading of the Arabic text supplemented by that of Ibn Tibbon.

24. This quotation follows the reading of Ibn Tibbon.

sary repetition, serves to assure them that each one of them will, when he comes to life, know for certain that he is the person who has been alive and has died and that it is he himself who has come back to life again. Finally, the purpose of His statement: *And I will place you in your own land* (Ezek. 37: 14) is to assure us that the period of the *redemption* will be of long duration in this world.

I also found a statement by *Isaiah;* namely: *Thy dead shall live, My dead bodies shall arise—[awake and sing, ye that dwell in the dust— for Thy dew is as the dew of lights,*[25] *and to the earth shalt Thou cause the shades to fall*[26]] (Isa. 26: 19), which agrees with the ideas expressed in the passage quoted above and is a companion piece to it. It is, namely, interpreted as follows: "Thy dead will live and our corpses will arise when Thou wilt say: 'Awake and sing, O ye that dwell in the dust!' For Thy dew is the dew of lights, and thou wilt cause those that have perished to fall to the ground."

So far as [the utterance]: *Thy dead shall live* is concerned, it corresponds to the statement [in the book of Ezekiel]: *Out of your graves, O My people* (Ezek. 37: 12). [The declaration,] again: *My dead bodies shall arise,* tallies with the words: *And I will bring you up* (Ezek. 37: 12). As for the statement: *Awake and sing,* that resembles the verse: *And ye shall know that I am the Lord, when I have opened your graves* (Ezek. 37: 13), for he who will awake will relate, when he awakes, what he has seen in his sleep and will be aware of the fact that he is the person who has been asleep and has waked up.

As for [the sentence]: *For Thy dew is as the dew of lights,* it tallies with the statement made there: *Our bones are dried up, and our hope is lost; we are clean cut off*[27] (Ezek. 37: 11), for the resurrection constitutes a moistening and refreshment of the dry bones. As for [the word] *lights,* that is an allusion to the soul. His reason for putting it in the plural, instead of saying *light,* in the singular, is due to the many faculties possessed by the soul—sixteen faculties, to be exact—as I explained in connection with the account of the *creation* [of the world].[28] This,

25. "lights," as below, in the author's comment on this passage—The usual translation is "light."
26. "and to the earth shalt Thou cause the shades to fall"—the usual translation is "and the earth shall bring to life the shades."
27. This quotation follows the reading of Ibn Tibbon.
28. i.e., Saadia's commentary on the book of Genesis. Maimonides also speaks of this number of the faculties of the soul. Cf. Guttmann, p. 223, n. 2.

again, tallies with the statement made in the book of Ezekiel: *Our hope is lost* (Ezek. 37: 11).

I also found a statement by *Daniel* to reveal that *Many of them that sleep in the dust of the earth shall awake,* [*some to everlasting life, and some to reproaches and everlasting abhorrence*] (Dan. 12: 2). The interpretation of this verse is that many of those that sleep in the dust will awake, some to eternal life and some unto shame and everlasting tears. Now this declaration that was made by the angel to *Daniel* undoubtedly referred to this world. All the predictions pertaining to the future that were made by him are, namely, comprised in forty-seven verses.

The first of these deals with the government of the kings of Persia. I have reference to his statement: *And now I will declare unto thee the truth. Behold, there shall stand up yet three kings in Persia* (Dan. 11: 2). The reason one verse seemed enough to him was that the period treated was that of the end of their government. The next thirteen verses, again, are devoted to the government of the Greeks; that is to say, beginning with his remark: *And a mighty king shall stand up* (Dan. 11: 3) up to *But he that cometh against him shall do according to his own will* (Dan. 11: 16).

Then there are twenty verses pertaining to the rule of the Romans. That is from *But he that cometh against him shall do according to his own will* (*ibid.*) up to *And the king shall do according to his will; and he shall exalt himself, etc.* (Dan. 11: 36). After that come ten verses on the rule of the Arabs. <106> That is from his statement: *And the king shall do according to his will* (*ibid.*) up to *And at that time shall Michael stand, etc.* (Dan. 12: 1).

Next follow three verses dealing with the *redemption;* namely, *And at that time shall Michael stand up, etc.* (*ibid.*) and *And many of them that sleep in the dust of the earth shall awake,* etc. (Dan. 12: 2), and *And they that are wise shall shine, etc.* (Dan. 12: 3). The reason why these subjects are treated in summary fashion in the book of *Daniel* is that they have already been fully explained in the books of *Isaiah, Jeremiah, Ezekiel,* and others.

Now these forty-seven were revealed as a complete unit, relating one event after the other in strict chronological order. Hence, just as the kings of Persia and the Greek, Roman, and Arab rulers reigned in this world—not in the world to come—so, too, the prediction that *Many of them that sleep in the dust of the earth shall awake* (Dan. 12: 2) must apply to this world, not to the next.

When he says: *And many of them that sleep in the dust of the earth,* he means, of course, many of the majority. The expression must be thus construed because of the [qualifying] remark [that follows]: *of them that sleep in the dust of the earth,* which embraces all human beings. On account of that [broader term] he used the expression *and many* in order to single out the children of Israel. This expression is parallel to the statement [in the book of Ezekiel]: *Out of your graves, O My people* (Ezek. 37: 12), and to *Thy dead shall live* (Isa. 26: 19) [in the book of Isaiah].

Again, the word *dust* employed by him corresponds to *Our bones are dried up* (Ezek. 37: 11) [in the book of Ezekiel] and parallels *For Thy dew is as the dew of lights* (Isa. 26: 19) [in the book of Isaiah].

Furthermore, he says: *They shall awake,* which tallies with the remark: *Awake and sing* (Isa. 26: 19) and resembles *And ye shall know that I am the Lord, when I have opened your graves* (Ezek. 37: 13).

As for his statement: *Some to everlasting life, and some to reproaches,* he does not mean thereby a division of the resurrected, some being assigned to the Garden of Eden whilst others are destined for hellfire. He means, rather, that a division of those that lie in the graves will take place. Of them *many* will *awake*. These are the ones destined *for eternal life*. Others, on the other hand, will not awake. It is these that are fated *for everlasting abhorrence*.

CHAPTER V

Now when I found these verses and others like them, I pondered them well, asking [myself]: "Is it not possible that there might be some reason on account of which these verses might admit a figurative interpretation, so that they would not be construed as applying to the belief in the *resurrection of the dead* but be made to refer to the revival of the Jewish kingdom and the setting up of a sovereign Jewish government?" The logic of such a construction is indicated by the fact that the elevation of a person who is downtrodden from his lowly estate to a position of eminence is compared to raising someone from the dust. Thus Scripture says: *He raiseth up the poor out of the dust, etc.* (I Sam. 2: 8) and also: *Who raiseth up the poor out of the dust, etc.* (Ps. 113: 7). Furthermore God said to Baasa: *Forasmuch as I exalted thee out of the dust, and made thee prince, etc.* (I Kings 16: 2). Again, he who is in distress and trouble is likened unto the dead. Thus, for example, Scripture says: *Set apart among the dead, like the slain that lie in the grave, etc.* (Ps. 88: 6) and also: *I am forgotten as a dead man out of mind* (Ps. 31: 13). On the other hand, his rescue and release from such a state is likened unto revival. Thus Scripture says: *Thou, who hast made me to see many and sore troubles, wilt quicken me again, etc.*[29] (Ps. 71: 20) and also *Wilt Thou not quicken us again, that Thy people may rejoice in Thee?* (Ps. 85: 6).

Upon careful investigation, however, I came to realize that if it were necessary or allowable to interpret all these passages that deal with the *resurrection of the dead* in this figurative manner so that they would be stripped of their literal meaning without the requirement of a compelling reason, then, by the same token, it might be necessary or permissible to interpret all revealed [30] laws [of the Jewish religion] and historical accounts of antiquity and the miracles mentioned in Scripture by means of other types of allegory, so that none of them would retain their literal meaning but be given totally different significances.

< 107 > Let me give a few illustrations of what might happen as a result of the use of such a method. Let us take, for example, such revealed laws as the injunction: *There shall no leavened bread be eaten* (Exod. 13: 3). That might be interpreted figuratively as denoting: "There shall not be any harlotry among you." For harlotry has been compared to bread that has risen and cannot help clinging to the oven. Thus Scripture says: *And they are all adulterers, as an oven heated by the baker, who ceaseth to stir from the kneading of the trough until it be leavened* (Hos. 7: 4).

Again, the Biblical injunction: *Ye shall kindle no fire* (Exod. 35: 3) might be interpreted figuratively to mean: "Do not array armies for war." For armies have been compared by Scripture to fire, as, for example, in the statement: *For a fire is gone out of Heshbon, a flame from the city of Sihon* (Num. 21: 28).

Furthermore, the injunction: *Thou shalt not take the dam with the young* (Deut. 22: 6) might be interpreted allegorically to mean: "When

29. This quotation follows the reading of Ibn Tibbon.
30. "revealed"—these were discussed at length in the third treatise. Cf. pp. 143 ff.

you are victorious over your enemy, do not kill the old men and the old women together with the young." Such a construction could be supported by such statements of Scripture as: *Therefore shall a tumult arise among thy hosts, and all thy fortresses shall be spoiled, as Shalman spoiled Beth-arbel in the day of battle; the mother was dashed in pieces with her children* (Hos. 10: 14). The consequence [of the pursuit of such a procedure] would be that all revealed laws would be abolished.[31]

Among the accounts of earliest antiquity is that of the creation. Now it is quite possible to make the statement of Scripture relating thereto; namely, *In the beginning God created the heaven and the earth* (Gen. 1: 1), refer to the prosperity of a certain people. Thus Scripture says, with reference to the misfortune that attended the affairs of our nation: *I beheld the earth, and, lo, it was waste and void, etc.* (Jer. 4: 23), while, on the other hand, it says, in regard to the restoration of its prosperity: *For, behold, I create new heavens and a new earth* (Isa. 65: 17).

Similarly one might interpret the words: *Let the earth put forth grass* (Gen. 1: 11) figuratively to denote bodily health, on the basis of the statement of Scripture: *And your bones shall flourish like young grass* (Isa. 66: 14). In like manner the words *Fruit-tree bearing fruit* (Gen. 1: 11) might be made to signify: "The very great king," as it does in the statement of Scripture: *In the mountain of the height of Israel will I plant it; and it shall bring forth boughs, and bear fruit* (Ezek. 17: 23). Thus, too, the words: *Let there be lights* (Gen. 1: 14) might be made to refer to the Torah and prophets and wisdom, as they do in such statements of Scripture as *For the commandment is a lamp, and the Torah*[32] *is light* (Prov. 6: 23) and *Thy word is a lamp unto my feet* (Ps. 119: 105).

The result of the application of such a method of interpretation would be that there would not be an item left of the entire *story of the creation* [of the world] that would not have been divested of its literal meaning, which is the creation and origination of things.

The accounts of the extraordinary miracles also lend themselves to allegorical interpretation. Thus, for instance, the statement: *And the children of Israel went into the midst of the sea upon the dry ground, and the waters were a wall unto them on their right hand, and on their*

31. "all . . . would be abolished"—literally "no . . . would remain."
32. "Torah"—the usual translation is "teaching."

left [33] (Exod. 14: 22) might be construed as meaning that they had entered into the midst of the army of Pharaoh, which was standing to the right and to the left of them dry and desiccated. For troops have been likened unto bodies of water, as, for example, in Scripture's remark about Sennacherib: *Now therefore, behold, the Lord bringeth up upon them the waters of the River, mighty and many, even the king of Assyria* [34] (Isa. 8: 7). In fact, of Pharaoh himself Scripture says: *Before that Pharaoh smote Gaza. Thus saith the Lord: Behold, waters rise up out of the north, and shall become an overflowing stream, and they shall overflow the land and all that is therein, the city and them that dwell therein* (Jer. 47: 1, 2).

It is also possible to interpret figuratively the statement: *And the sun stood still, and the moon stayed* (Josh. 10: 13) as [signifying] the rise of the kingdom and its ascendancy, just as its disappearance and enfeeblement have been compared to the setting of the sun. Scripture says, namely: *And the sun shall go down upon the prophets, and the day shall be black over them* (Mic. 3: 6), and also: *Her spirit droopeth; her sun is gone down while it was yet day, she is ashamed and confounded* (Jer. 15: 9). On the other hand, in characterization of the prosperity of the kingdom, Scripture expresses itself in the following manner: *Moreover the light of the moon shall be as the light of the sun* (Isa. 30: 26).

The consequence [of the consistent use of this method] would be that there would not be a marvel or miracle left but would have been divested of its literal meaning and thus have become nullified.

<108> The evil [result] [35] of requiring or declaring permissible the figurative interpretation of the passages of Scripture that deal with *the resurrection of the dead* and making allegories of them, since they can be thus interpreted, is, then, to render necessary or permissible such a figurative interpretation also of the passages dealing with *creation of the world* and the miracles and all revealed *commandments,* which would thereby be transformed into allegories, since they can be thus construed. But if one adopts such an attitude, one automatically excludes oneself from the entire Jewish religion. On the other hand, if one refuses to do so, one thereby rejects the objections presented by such persons against *the resurrection of the dead.*

33. This quotation follows the reading of Ibn Tibbon.
34. This quotation follows the reading of Ibn Tibbon.
35. "evil result"—Ibn Tibbon.

CHAPTER VI

Next I scanned the Torah and I examined the *song* that God had set up as a witness for Himself against the children of Israel, as Scripture says: *That this song may be a witness for Me against the children of Israel* (Deut. 31: 19), and I found in it a mention of the resurrection of the dead at the beginning of the era of the *salvation*.

This [song] proceeds, namely, in chronological order. It describes first God's kindness to his people, saying: *Is He not thy father that hath begotten thee? Hath He not made thee, and established thee?* [36] (Deut. 32: 6) up to *And of the blood of the grape thou drankest foaming wine* (Deut. 32: 14). Next it speaks of their downfall and sin; that is, starting from *But Jeshurun waxed fat, and kicked* [37] (Deut. 32: 15) up to *Because of the provoking of His sons and His daughters* (Deut. 32: 19). Then it describes God's wrath against them and the descent of divine punishment upon them. That begins with the statement: *And He said: "I will hide My face from them, etc."* (Deut. 32: 20) and continues up to *I would make their memory cease from among men* (Deut. 32: 26).

Next it describes God's sympathy with them as they are assailed and attacked by the enemy. This is done in the statement: *Were it not that I dreaded the enemy's provocation, etc.* [38] (Deut. 32: 27). [It refers] also to the painful torment in store for the enemy, saying: *Is not this laid up in store with Me?* (Deut. 32: 34.) [It alludes] also to God's mercy on His people, as its weakness becomes great and its power diminishes, in its remark: *For the Lord will judge His people, etc.* (Deut. 32: 36) up to *Let him be your protection* (Deut. 32: 38). Next comes the promise of God's manifestation for the purpose of saving and redeeming the nation. This is expressed in the words: *See now that I, even I, am He* (Deut. 32: 39).

The verse quoted last contains a reply to four different types of heretics. The first are those who affirm that there is no Creator. The answer to them consists of the words *That I, even I, am He* (*ibid.*). The second group is made up of those who assert that there is a Creator, but that He had an associate in the work of creation. The answer to them is found in the words *And there is no god with Me* (*ibid.*).

36. This quotation follows the reading of Ibn Tibbon.
37. This quotation follows the reading of Ibn Tibbon.
38. This quotation follows the reading of Ibn Tibbon.

The third group is that of those who reject the doctrine of the resurrection. The answer to them is given in the words: *I kill, and I make alive* (*ibid.*). Since, however, God knew that there were people who might hold that by saying: *I kill, and I make alive,* He meant only that He lets one generation die and brings another to life after it, He added thereto the words: *I have wounded, and I heal* (*ibid.*) in order to give us the assurance that, just as he that is healed is the person that was previously wounded, so he that will be brought to life by God is the very one who has died previously. The fourth group, again, consists of those who deny that there will be a reckoning and a punishment in the hereafter. The answer to them is found in the words: *And there is none that can deliver out of My hand* (*ibid.*).

Then there are listed after this, in chronological order, the remaining details of the *salvation.* They are treated in the statements: *If I whet My glittering sword, etc.* (Deut. 32: 41): *I will make Mine arrows drunk with blood, etc.* (Deut. 32: 42); and *Sing aloud, O ye nations, of His people, etc.* (Deut. 32: 43). All this, of course, applies to this world, as I have explained.[39]

CHAPTER VII

Furthermore, I did not refrain from searching the fourth source, which consists of the writings of the prophets and the traditions of the sages, saying to myself that I might perhaps find in them an objection against the doctrine of *the resurrection of the dead,* since their utterances, *may their memories be blessed,* <109> are full of the mention of it and replete with descriptions of it. I therefore deem it proper to note down a few of their pronouncements as a reminder and sample thereof, because it would take too long to list them all on account of their extensiveness. Also many questions were asked of them on this subject by the rulers, to which each of the sages answered according to his own point of view. Furthermore, questions were asked by the common people of our nation. These, too, were answered by the sages in sundry ways.

Let me say, however, that in view of the fact that Scripture states: *Behold, I will send you Elijah the prophet* (Mal. 3: 23) and that it

39. i.e., above, p. 427, because of the fact that the poem dwells on events in chronological order.

says, furthermore: *Then shall we raise against him seven shepherds, and eight princes among men* (Mic. 5: 4), they were asked who those *seven shepherds* were, whereunto they replied: "We have it on tradition that they are *David, who will be in the center, Seth and Methuselah, who will be on his right, and Abraham, Isaac, Jacob, and Moses, who will be on his left*" [40] (Suk. 52b). They were also asked who the eight princes were, and replied: "We have it on the basis of tradition that they *are Jesse, Saul, Samuel, Amos, Zephaniah, Hezekiah, Elijah, and the Messiah*" (*ibid.*). Thus they have explicitly stated that these dead would be resurrected at the time of the *redemption*.

They have said, furthermore: "We have it on the basis of tradition that whoever will die during the years of the duration of the spoliation of the Jewish nation by God will not arise at *the resurrection of the dead*, because the procedure to be followed in connection therewith, according to their opinion, will be the same as that of the banquet preliminary to the wedding feast. Whoever participates in the former, participates also in the wedding feast, and whoever misses it, also misses the latter." This, in fact, is how they expressed themselves: *Said Rabbi Jonah: "Whoever will die during the seven years of Gog, will not be resurrected in the days of the Messiah. And take this as thy sign: 'He who eats at the prenuptial banquet eats also at the wedding feast'"* [41] (Pal. Talm. Šĕbh. 35c; Lev. Rab. beginning chap. xi).

They have said, besides, that whoever rejects the belief in the *resurrection of the dead* will not be resurrected in the days of the *Messiah*, even though the rest of his deeds were good (Sanh. 90a), because it is a principle of ordinary retaliatory justice that a person be denied the thing that he has rejected. This [principle] was illustrated in the case of the captain of Jehoram the son of Ahab. When he rejected the statement of Elisha and the good tidings he had brought to Israel of the plenty that would succeed the famine, he was informed by the prophet that he would not partake of this plenty. In fact, he would see it with his eyes, but not eat thereof (II Kings 7: 2). The actual wording of their remark is: *He denied the resurrection of the dead. Therefore he shall have no share in the resurrection of the dead, for all the dealings*

40. This quotation follows the reading of Ibn Tibbon. The Arabic text published by Bacher omits the name of Moses, whereas the Vilna edition of the Babylonian Talmud lists the name of Adam before Seth and omits Isaac.

41. For the variant readings of the different sources cf. the references listed by Bacher.

of the Holy One Blessed Be He are measure for measure. For it is said:
"Then the captain on whose hand the king leaned answered the man of
God, etc. . . . . And he said: 'Behold, thou shalt see it with thine eyes,' "
etc.[42] (II Kings 7: 2), (Sanh. 90a).

They also said that the dead would arise wearing their shrouds. That
is the purport of their statement: *The righteous are destined to rise*
clad in their garments (Kĕth. 111b). Now the restoration of their
clothes is not more difficult to conceive of by reason than the return of
their bodies and souls. When this idea became widespread among our
nation, certain people went to such extremes in their expenditures on
the shrouds of the dead that it produced great hardship. For he who
could not afford them would abandon his dead and flee. This condition
continued until Rabban Gamaliel instituted an ordinance for the nation
by leaving it as his will that he be wrapped in washed linen garments,
and all the people followed his example. Thus they said: <110> *At*
the beginning the expenditures made on behalf of the dead imposed
greater hardship on those who incurred them than his death, so that
they would leave him and flee, until Rabban Gamaliel came and set
the example of disregard of custom through himself, by having himself
brought out clad in starched linen garments, whereupon all the people
followed his example (Kĕth. 8b and M.Ḳ. 27b).

CHAPTER VIII

After making these investigations I began to follow up the derivatives of this belief and the inferences to be drawn from it, and I deem it
proper to make note of ten questions that occur to me in this connection.
These I shall answer from the standpoint of Scripture, reason, and
tradition.

The first question that one might ask is: "Who of our nation will
be included among those to be resurrected at the time of the salvation?"
In answer thereto I would say: "Every righteous person and penitent
of the Jewish nation. By God, only if a person dies without having
repented is he one of those who are destined to be punished."

This is also most proper from the standpoint of reason, since God
has in many verses promised every penitent that He would accept him.
These promises to every penitent follow also [43] as the necessary con-

42. This quotation from the Scriptures follows the reading of Ibn Tibbon.
43. "to every penitent follow also . . ."—Ibn Tibbon.

clusion from the statement made by our earliest teachers after listing various types of sin, which, they declared, were of four degrees. The first is *the transgression by a person of a positive commandment.* The next is *the transgression by him of a negative commandment.* Next come *infractions punishable by extirpation or death by the action of the court.* Then there is the category of *those by whom the name of heaven is profaned* (Tosephta Yoma 4: 6–8; Yoma 86a). After this they said: *Now one might suppose that his death would not atone for him. Therefore Scripture teaches, saying: "Behold, I will open your graves"* (Ezek. 37: 12; Měkh. Ex. 20: 7). Thus it has been conclusively proven that there will be resurrection for every penitent. I [44] will say, furthermore, that, in my opinion, those of our nation that die impenitent are few in number.

The second question is: "Will they die again after this [resurrection that is to take place during the era of the redemption]?" My answer hereunto is that they will not die but that they will be transported from the era of the Messiah to the delights of the next world. With reference thereto, our earliest teachers said: *The dead whom the Holy One Blessed Be He is destined to bring back to life will not return to their dust any more* (Sanh. 92a).

The third question is: "Will the earth be capacious enough to contain them?" I say, in reply thereto, that from the time our nation emerged among men two thousand, two hundred and two years ago there have been thirty-two generations, each of which comprised approximately 1,200,000 men and women. Now even if we were to assume that they are all equal and that they will all be resurrected, they would fill up only one one-hundred-and-fiftieth part of the earth, even if we were to allocate to each one more than two hundred cubits for his dwelling and his fields and his needs and his beasts and other such matters. For the total human population of all the generations would amount to approximately 1,200,000 by thirty-two, making a grand total of 38,400,000. Furthermore, if we were to cut off for them from the earth a strip of two hundred parasangs by two hundred parasangs, which constitutes one one-hundred-and-fiftieth part of the earth's area, and we were to compute it in cubits, assuming that every parasang is made up of three miles, and every mile consists of four thousand cubits, and every cubit measures two cubits and a half and a third of the standard, there would be an area of 288 cubits in width [by five hundred in

44. "for every penitent. I . . ."—Ibn Tibbon.

length] [45] for every person. What is there in this calculation about which scientists can be confused?

The fourth question is whether their families and relatives that would then be alive would recognize them. In answer hereto I would say that, inasmuch as the prophets and *shepherds* and *princes* [46] would have to be recognized by all other men, it follows that they would consequently have to recognize one another and that each person would become attached to his tribe, <111> as is explained in the geographic distribution of the tribes in the book of *Ezekiel* (Ezek. 48: 1 ff.).

The fifth question is: "What will be the condition, at the time he is resurrected, of him who died blind or deprived of his limbs or smitten with other afflictions or defects?" I say, in reply hereunto, that he will first be resurrected with that blemish still adhering to him so that his fellowmen may recognize him as being that particular person. After that, the Creator will cure him so that it may be a complete sign, as our earliest teachers have said: *They will rise from their graves with their blemish attached to them, and then be cured* (Sanh. 91b). It is for this very reason that the words *I kill, and I make alive* (Deut. 32: 39) are put before *I have wounded, and I heal* (*ibid.*). Scripture has also said: *Then the eyes of the blind shall be opened, and the ears of the deaf shall be unstopped. Then shall the lame man leap as a hart, and the tongue of the dumb shall sing* (Isa. 35: 6, 7).

The sixth question, again is: "Will the resurrected eat and drink and marry?" My reply hereto is: "Yes, just as the son of the *Zarephite* woman, whom the Creator brought back to life through *Elijah*, and the son of the *Shunammite* woman, whom He revived through *Elisha*, ate and drank and conceivably also married." [47]

The seventh question is: "How can these persons [who are destined to be resurrected at the time of the redemption] be transferred to the next world, in which there is no eating or drinking or cohabitation,[48] which they had to practice in this world in order to live?" I reply thereto: "They will do as *Moses, our teacher*, who, although he had

45. "in width by five-hundred in length"—so according to the emendation suggested by Solomon Gandz. Cf. above, the seventh treatise, n. 21.

46. Cf. Suk. 52b in interpretation of Mic. 5: 4.

47. Such a remark is made in the Talmud about the dead bones that had been brought back to life by Ezekiel. Cf. Sanh. 92b. Cf. also above, seventh treatise, n. 16.

48. Cf. Bĕr. 18a.

been accustomed to eating and drinking and cohabiting, nevertheless existed without these things three times for forty days and yet remained alive, as is written in the Torah." [49]

The eighth question is: "In view of the fact that those that will be resurrected at the time of the *salvation* will be left to their own choice, is it not possible that they might choose to disobey God so that they would not be resurrected in the world of retribution?" To this question I give the same answer as that which is given by our entire nation, the community of the believers, in regard to the behavior of the righteous in the next world. Since they have the power of choosing between obedience and disobedience, is it not possible that they might choose the latter? The reply is, however, that He that knows what will happen before it comes to pass would not have promised the righteous, who are destined to be in the next world, eternal reward except that He knew that they would choose to obey and not to disobey Him. Similarly I say that, inasmuch as He knows what will happen, He would not have promised the resurrection of the dead to the righteous of Israel unless He knew that at the time of the *Messiah* they would choose obedience to God and not disobedience to Him.

The ninth question is: "Will the resurrected receive reward for their obedience to God during the era of the *Messiah?*" I say: "Yes. Just as the righteous in this world are entitled to reward for their obedience to God, so will those living at the time of the *Messiah* be rewarded for their obedience to God, for it is inconceivable that such obedience should be unrewarded. And just as there is in store for the righteous a reward in addition to what their previous good deeds entitle them to, so will what they will do in the *days of the Messiah* net them an addition beyond that which their good deeds entitle them to."

The tenth question, finally, is: "What will be the status of those persons who are alive at the time when the *salvation* takes place, and, similarly, that of those who are born during the era of the *salvation?*" My answer thereto is that, inasmuch as Scripture has no express pronouncement on this subject and rabbinic tradition, too, carries no report thereon, opinion on the matter is divided into three groups. Some assert that they will not die at all. They base their belief on the statement of Scripture: *He will swallow up death forever* (Isa. 25: 8). Others affirm that they will die and come to life again in order that they

49. Cf. Deut. 9: 9, 18; 10: 10.

might be on the same plane as the other resurrected. Still others allege that they will live a long life and die and then not come to life again until [the era of] the next world.

Now my heart, may God guide thee aright, inclines me toward this third theory, because I find that the *resurrection of the dead* at the time of the *salvation* [50] was promised only to those who had been in *exile*. But I do not deem it proper to add anything of my own hereto, especially in view of the fact that the whole reason for the *resurrection of the dead* [at that time] is that they may not be excluded from this great *redemption*. However, he who witnesses it, either by being alive at the beginning or by being born [during the era of the redemption] will already have reached the goal.

Their lives, however, will be of long duration, in the neighborhood of 400 or 500 years, so that <112> a person who has died at the age of one hundred years during this epoch will be like one who has died at the age of twenty in our own, as Scripture says: *For the youngest shall die a hundred years old* (Isa. 65: 20). Furthermore, there will be no indulgence toward anyone a hundred years old who has sinned against men, since such a one will not be considered an old man by them. He will, therefore, rather be treated by them with contempt, as Scripture says: *And the sinner being a hundred years old shall be accursed* (*ibid.*). The life spans of human beings will be similar to those of great buildings and plants, as Scripture says: *They shall not build, and another inhabit, they shall not plant, and another eat; for as the days of a tree shall be the days of My people, etc.* (Isa. 65: 22).

CHAPTER IX

After duly considering the subjects that have been treated here, I became firmly convinced of their truth and I set them down in writing in order that they might serve as a source of confidence. I have, namely, arrived at the conclusion that the Jewish nation would be benefited by them for seven reasons: They will be helped, first of all, because the resurrection of the dead is a great miracle, one of the manifest miracles of God, the assurance of the occurrence of which corroborates the belief in God's omnipotence.

Secondly, there will be effected thereby a reunion of all the prophets.

50. "at the time of the salvation"—added by Ibn Tibbon.

Thou notest how eager we are today to see one of them, all the more so if it were possible to behold them all. Furthermore, all the righteous kings of Israel and all distinguished sages, to see even one of whom we are most anxious, will be reunited.

Again, the relatives of each person of whom he was bereaved and over whom he has mourned will be reunited with him, so that a son will see his father again, and a father his son, and a brother his brother, a sage his pupil, a friend his friend, and so for other types of relationships.

Moreover, many of the reports circulated about the phenomenon of death to which people adhere so tenaciously will then be cleared up. When, namely, men have come back to life again, they will describe for us what has befallen them or how they came to die and how they fared during their death and how they were resurrected.

Besides that, all the aforementioned generations of the children of Israel, totaling many myriads of human beings, will get together and will, as a community, enjoy splendor and glory and a position of esteem.

Finally, it will serve as a means of strengthening the belief in the world to come. For we would say that, just as this promise will be realized, so will all other promises pertaining to the world to come. We would, consequently, look forward to the latter as having been proven by experience, as Scripture says: *And it shall be said in that day: "Lo, this is our God, for whom we waited, that He might save us"* [51] (Isa. 25: 9).

What a wonderful promise that is, then, which combines all these advantages! It was these benefits, in fact, that compelled me to devote myself to the establishment of its verification and thereby to serve the Jewish nation and contribute to its well-being. It is my ardent wish that I might be among those who will witness it either in my own lifetime or by being resurrected as a reward for my contribution to the welfare of my people. And may God, who is truthful in His promise, be blessed, and may praise be His.

The seventh treatise is hereby completed.

51. This quotation follows the reading of Ibn Tibbon.

INDEX I

SUBJECTS AND NAMES

AARON, appointed to perform sacrifices, 168 f.; requited in this world, 211; lingered in servitude, 295

Abijah son of Jeroboam, rewarded in this world, 211

Abimelech, forbidden by God to touch Sarah, 197

Abraham, law of, different from that of Moses, 162; marriage of sisters forbidden in time of, 168; not ordered actually to sacrifice Isaac, 169; did not really lie about Sarah's relationship to him, 196; included among *the seven shepherds*, 276, 429; enslavement of descendants of, 299; age of, at time of departure from Haran, 299; journey to Palestine took thirty years, 299; name of *Children of Israel* applied to, 299; asked God for children, 381; what appeared to, was not a trinity, 108

Abrogation of the Law, 157 ff.; addition of the laws of Sabbath and Passover by Moses do not constitute, 162. *See also* Suspension, Torah

Absalom, sin of, 194

Abstention, by skeptics, 81; refuted, 81 ff.; of human beings, 86

Abstinence, 364 ff.; to be employed to restrain the appetites, 400

Accident, does not pertain to Creator, 111; cannot be source of wisdom, 237; cannot be bearer of other accidents, 237

Accidents, no bodies are without, 43; growth and diminution of animals, 43; heavens are not free from, 43; whatever did not precede, must be like them, 44; God is not subject to, 56, 111, 122, 129, 245; every material body is endowed with, 88; light and darkness are, 98; put together by Creator, 111

Act, every, must have an agent, 48; one and the same, cannot emanate from two authors, 60 ff.; no, without an agent, 69

Action, abstention of human beings equivalent to, 86; abstention of God not tantamount to, 86; of God, 127; God is never the recipient of, 129; of man consists of doing or desisting, 187; not interfered with by Creator, 188

Adam, men called *children of*, 100; daughters of, 168; in the Garden of Eden, 170, 340; driven out, 170; not created by angel, 232; all sons of, not included in promise of resurrection at time of *redemption*, 271; included among *the seven shepherds*, 276; garden of, a byword for excellence, 340; Eve was mother of all descendants of, 415

'Ădhonay, same as '*Ĕlohim*, 99. *See also* God

Adultery, punishment of, 225; considered reprehensible by reason but desired by nature, 325; severely punished, 326; prohibition of, not expressly mentioned to Adam, 327; grave sin, 351

Agent. *See* Act

Ahab, enticed that he might fall, 200; has no share in world to come, 335; Jehoram son of, 429

Ahaz, permitted to live so he might beget Hezekiah, 215

Ahitophel, has no share in world to come, 335

INDEX II

PASSAGES CITED

GENESIS

EXODUS

LEVITICUS

NUMBERS

DEUTERONOMY

JOSHUA

JUDGES

JEREMIAH

EZEKIEL

PSALMS

PROVERBS

JOB

LAMENTATIONS

ECCLESIASTES

ESTHER

DANIEL

GLOSSARY

Abstention (Ar. *wuḳuf*, Hebr. *'ămidhah*)
skepticism, abstaining from believing anything

Accident (Ar. *'arḍ*, Hebr. *miḳre*)
the changing conditions of all material things

Atom (Ar. *jiz' la yatajazza'*, Hebr. *heleḳ še'eno mithhalleḳ*)
an indivisible particle

Beat, Beating (Ar. *nagmah, tangim*, Hebr. *nĕ'imah*)
a rhythmic mode or note

Dualists (Ar. *aṣhab al-ithnayn*, Hebr. *ba'ale haššĕniyyim*)
the proponents of the doctrine of the existence in the world of two
opposing principles

End (Hebr. *ḳeṣ*)
the foreordained termination of Israel's exile

Eroticism (Ar. *'išḳ*, Hebr. *hešeḳ*)
passionate love lavished on human beings

Eternity, theory of (Ar. *dahr*, Hebr. *ḳadhmuth*)
the theory that the world has existed since eternity

Hyle (Ar. *hayula, ṭinah ḳadimah*, Hebr. *hiyuli, homer ḳadhmon*)
the original formless mass out of which the world is supposed to
have been formed

Leap, theory of the (Ar. *ṭafrah*, Hebr. *dillugh*)
the theory of leaping from particle to particle in order to explain
how a distance consisting of infinitely divisible parts can be traversed

Natural Qualities (Ar. *'aṭba'*, Hebr. *ṭĕbha'im*)
the qualities of heat, cold, moisture and dryness inhering in all
things material

Physiognomists (Ar. *ḳafah*)
individuals who are able to classify men by looking at the faces and
feet

Skeptics (Ar. *mutajahhilun*, Hebr. *mith'allĕmim*)
those who feign absolute ignorance, pretending that nothing can
be known

Sophists (Ar. *aṣhab al'unud*, Hebr. *ba'ale ha'iḳḳĕšuth*)
literally individuals who stubbornly refuse to acknowledge the truth,
making everything dependent on the opinions of men

Spheres, heavenly (Ar. *'aflak*, Hebr. *galgallim*)
 layers of concentric spheres containing the stars and planets of which
 heaven was believed to have been composed
Spiritual Beings, doctrine of (Ar. *ruḥaniyyat*, Hebr. *ruhaniyyim*)
 uncreated spiritual beings out of whom the world is supposed to
 have originated
Substance (Ar. *jawhar*, Hebr. *'eṣem*)
 the unchanging part of an organism
Substratum (Ar. *mawḍu'*, Hebr. *musam*)
 that which underlies all things, such as space is believed to be

NOTES ON THE SECOND PRINTING

Addenda

16, l.19	*after* aim of *add* the introduction of
16	*above* n. 25 *insert* 24a. I.e., the *futuwwah*. Cf. R. Dozy, *Supplement aux Dictionnaires Arabes*, II, 241.
336, l.25	*after* difference *add* of gradation

Corrigenda

9, l.18	*for* tend . . . else. *read* turn to the Master of Wisdom and not incline to anything outside of Him.
9, l.19	*for* Theirs will be *read* He will be for them
16, l.5	*for* affecting youthfulness *read* making pretense of belonging to the order of the knights [of the prophet Mohammed] [24a]
16, l.10	*for* Their [mere] ignorance . . . to *read* With their ignorance they will certainly not
33, l.11	*for* [his] investigations *read* the rational method
34, l.20	*for* he hurls . . . deliberation. *read* he ardently desires to render such acts permissible to himself, not realizing [the folly thereof].
47, l.29	*for* made it evident *read* affirmed, on the plane of reason,
139, l.3	*for* logic *read* rational intuition
139, l.7	*for* reason *read* rational intuition
139, l.10	*for* Reason *read* Rational intuition
139, l.15	*for* reason *read* rational intuition
139, l.18	*for* Reason *read* Rational intuition
140, l.10	*for* mundane *read* contemptible
141, l.12	*for* divine Wisdom *read* reason
141, l.21	*for* [divine] Wisdom *read* reason
141, l.30	*for* [divine] Wisdom *read* reason
142, l.4	*for* [divine] Wisdom . . . one *read* it is the part of reason, nay one

157, l.22   *for* Accordingly . . . principles *read* If, then, the traditions of our ancestors that have been transmitted in the above-mentioned principal forms are examined,

163, l.4   *for* Similar . . . arguments *read* He who advances this argument has to face also the objections raised against the previous arguments.

175, l.26   *for* But this . . . pain. *read* It is by reason—not by prophecy—that we believe that such compensation would take place, assuming that the existence of the excess of pain were demonstrable.

190, l.31   *for* objectionable . . . account, *read* objectionable. And if He made clear that a certain matter was objectionable in His sight, it was

228, l.24   *for* This type . . . mercy, *read* Although such cases are rare, this type of person is the recipient of God's mercy and

258, l.29   *for* lead us . . . virtue *read* put us on the road [60] to [eternal] bliss

290, l.26   *for* investigation and analysis [1] *read* of being adjusted and put in order [1]

290, n.1   *for* "analysis . . . M. *read* Cf. Georges Vajda, "Études sur Saadia" in *Revue des Études Juives,* n. s. IX (CIX), 75.

323, l.19   *for* the reality . . . proof. *read* at the beginning of this book [8] that the prophetic doctrines are implied in the arguments of reason.

323, n.3   *for* Cf. . . . 145 ff. *read* Cf. Vajda, p. 77.

336, n.43   *for* "difference" . . . original. *read* Cf. Vajda, p. 77.

392, l.10   *for* if the view . . . expresses it: *read* as the rancorous [51] believe, who imagine they are beyond God's control. Does not Scripture say:

392, n.51   *for* "truth" . . . correctly. *read* Ibn Tibbon's reading ḥ*ḵḵ* (truth) instead of ḥ*ḵd* (rancor) makes no sense. Cf. Vajda, p. 77.